Museum Philosophy for the Twenty-first Century

Museum Philosophy for the Twenty-first Century

Edited by
Hugh H. Genoways

A Division of
ROWMAN & LITTLEFIELD PUBLISHERS, INC.
Lanham • New York • Toronto • Oxford

Permission to reprint figure 7.1 is gratefully acknowledged. George Cruikshank, English (1792–1878), "All the World Going to See the Crystal Palace, London 1851," engraving 8-5/8″ × 10-3/4″. Gift of Nathan H. and Anna Creamer, Colorado Collection, CU Art Museum, University of Colorado at Boulder. From album 79.1427.G. Photo: Aaron Hoffman.

AltaMira Press

A division of Rowman & Littlefield Publishers, Inc.
A wholly owned subsidiary of The Rowman & Littlefield Publishing Group, Inc.
4501 Forbes Boulevard, Suite 200
Lanham, MD 20706
www.altamirapress.com

PO Box 317
Oxford
OX2 9RU, UK

British Library Cataloguing in Publication Information Available

Library of Congress Cataloguing-in-Publication Data

Museum philosophy for the twenty-first century / edited by Hugh H. Genoways.
   p. cm.
  Includes index.
  ISBN-13: 978-0-7591-0753-3 (cloth : alk. paper)
  ISBN-10: 0-7591-0753-X (cloth : alk. paper)
  ISBN-13: 978-0-7591-0754-0 (pbk. : alk. paper)
  ISBN-10: 0-7591-0754-8 (pbk. : alk. paper)
  1. Museums—Philosophy. 2. Museums—Historiography. 3. Museums—Management. 4. Museum techniques—Historiography. I. Genoways, Hugh H.
AM7.M8728 2006
069—dc22
                                   2005036427

Printed in the United States of America

♾ ™ The paper used in this publication meets the minimum requirements of American National Standard for Information Sciences—Permanence of Paper for Printed Library Materials, ANSI/NISO Z39.48–1992.

Contents

Introduction

The idea for *Museum Philosophy for the Twenty-first Century* arose in teaching a course in contemporary museum issues in our former Museum Studies Program at the University of Nebraska, Lincoln. Over time I assigned a variety of articles and books for student reading and discussion to help broaden their perspective of the larger museum world. Three of those assigned readings seemed to hit a special chord with the students and me—David Carr, "The Need for the Museum," *Museum News* (March/April 1999): 31–35, 56–57; Michael Kimmelman, "Museums in a Quandary: Where Are the Ideals?" *New York Times*, August 26, 2001; Timothy Luke, *Museum Politics: Power Plays at the Exhibition* (Minneapolis: University of Minnesota Press, 2002). The notes sounded by the students about these readings weren't always happy ones as they felt their perspectives being stretched and ideas being challenged. I was struck by the fact of how little of this type of literature is available about museums. I do believe that if museums are going to be successful in the twenty-first century we must broaden our perspectives and challenge the ideas that we have brought forward from the twentieth century. The contributors and I do not see this book as the final word on philosophy for museums in this century, but only as the starting point that we hope will lead to open and meaningful philosophical discussions that will guide museums into their uncertain future.

In planning this volume, I requested essays from contributors representing two major groups. One group of essays was requested from scholars who have written recent books about museums but who were trained and work in other disciplinary areas. I believe that some of the best scholarship being done today about museums is work being produced by individuals who I would place in this group. I hoped that this group would give a view of museum philosophy from "outside" the profession looking in. The plan was to pair these ideas on philosophy of museums with a second group of essays obtained from leaders working in the museum profession today. I tried to select representatives of the major museum-types in this group because of the diversity of approaches found among modern museums. This group, I hoped, would give a view of museum philosophy from "inside" the profession looking outward to the audience being served. As you probably have already guessed, the world is never so simple as to be divisible into an "outside/inside" distinction. The final group of contributors does include both scholars and current museum professionals, but it also includes people who have worked in museum situations and have taken academic positions, people who have gone from academia to museums, others who are in academic positions but do consulting work for museums and other nonprofit organizations, some who work for university museums, and finally there are those of us who teach in museum studies programs that really straddle both worlds. However, I feel that my initial goal has been fulfilled by bringing together writings from a diverse group of contributors who are highly knowledgeable about museums.

I asked contributors to this volume to respond to one specific question: "What underlying philosophy/mission should museums pursue in the first half of the twenty-first century?" As you will see in the following chapters, some authors responded directly to this question, whereas others rejected the question outright and others simply ignored it. This has resulted in a diversity of chapters, which have not always been easy to organize into meaningful groups. I finally chose to place the chapters into four groups—primarily philosophical or ethical in outlook, those that examined one or two specific institutions to illustrate their philosophy, chapters dealing with some major division of the museum community, and finally those that address outreach or engagement with the audience or community in which the museum is situated. I considered several other groupings of these chapters, including arranging them by the type of museums being addressed, but no arrangement seemed better than the one I have chosen. Although I did give serious consideration to ways to arrange the chapters, each chapter can easily stand on its own for reading and discussion.

Because this is a book about philosophy, I thought that it would be a good idea to begin with a chapter written by a philosopher. Hilde Hein has spent more than three decades teaching philosophy at Holy Cross College, Tufts University, and Boston University and has already authored two books on museums and has another in preparation. The next two chapters are by David Carr and Timothy Luke, authors who inspired my thinking about this book. You will find the ideas and style of the article by Carr to be challenging, but there are rewards at the end. Luke urges museums to not avoid controversy in their programs. Marilyn Phelan, a lawyer by training, challenges museums to reexamine their acquisitions policy, especially of material of questionable provenance and ownership. Sherene Suchy explores the importance of social capital and the social-emotional experience as an underlying philosophy for museums in the twenty-first century. The final two authors of this group both basically rejected my central question for this book, and Jean-Paul Martinon goes so far as to question whether or not museums have a future. Donald Preziosi urges museums to seek a future that is beyond their present and expresses a concern over the widening split between those "inside" and "outside" the museum profession.

The second grouping of chapters includes four dealing with one or a few specific museums. The chapter by Michael Mares leads this section with a discussion of the impact governance can have on university museums by contrasting recent events at the Sam Noble Oklahoma Museum of Natural History and the University of Nebraska State Museum. Charles Dailey explores his teaching philosophy based on his experiences in the Museum Studies Department at the Institute of American Indian Arts in Santa Fe. Lesley Lewis and Jennifer Martin look to the future of science centers through the lens of developments at the Ontario Science Centre. Douglas Sharon gives a similar presentation for anthropology museums based on recent developments at the P. A. Hearst Museum of Anthropology at the University of California, Berkeley. I believe that you will find the philosophical perspective of these chapters is quite broad even though they focus on specific institutions.

The third group of chapters is the largest and most diverse, having eight chapters dealing with a broad range of areas in the museum field. The first two chapters deal with issues of inclusiveness in museum presentations and exhibitions. Jennifer Eichstedt explores the challenges and opportunities for presentations dealing with slavery in plantation museums in the southern United States. Helen Coxall discusses her extensive experience in developing inclusive practices for museums in Europe and Australia. In an excellent chapter dealing with the history and challenges for African American museums, Christy Coleman finds direction for the future of these museums. Franklin Robinson and Didier Maleuvre map some potential futures for art museums based on the philosophical perspectives presented in their two chapters. Terry L. Maple and Suma Mallavarapu represent institutions holding living collections as they look to the future of zoological parks. Patrick Boylan brings his vast international perspective to bear on the massive changes occurring in the governance and management of museums in Europe and speculates on their uncertain future. Finally, as the title of my chapter implies, I speak to museum workers about three issues that need to be addressed by them in the future—the role of collections in museums, professional ethics, and the professionalization of individuals working for museums.

The final set of chapters deals with museums as sites for community education and outreach. Eilean Hooper-Greenhill discusses the power of museums as pedagogic sites. Jeffrey Patchen makes a case for a more purposeful and substantive inclusion of children and their families into the mission, vision, core values, and strategic and operating plans implemented by museums now and in the future. Because museums today face a crisis of attendance due to competition for leisure time, Scott Paris looks at ways museums can be more competitive for visitors in the future. The last chapter of the book by Robert R. Archibald discusses the value of museums becoming embedded in their communities so that they become seen as a site for important debates about our common future and where choices and agendas for our future are decided.

Following the chapters is a section containing biographical sketches of each of the authors. It is my hope that these sketches will aid the reader in gaining perspective on the included chapters. I hope that readers will all agree that this is a distinguished and diverse group of scholars and museum professionals.

In addition to attempting to include authors with diverse interests and backgrounds in museology, I have tried to give our reader an international perspective on museum philosophy. In addition to the United States, contributors are from Australia, Canada, and England. If readers are not familiar with theoretical museological writing from outside of the United States, they may be surprised and challenged by what they read here. It is my sincere hope that we are able to do this for all readers at some point in this book. To reiterate what I stated at the beginning of this essay, it is the hope of contributors to this volume that it serve as a starting point for discussions that result in a clearer picture of how museums can reach a successful future. It is my belief that museologists have not engaged in enough of these discussions. We tend to be "hands on" people who are committed to fulfilling our day-to-day duties. We take little time to ask and discuss the "why," "who," "where," "what," and "why again" questions. I believe that, if museums are going to meet the challenges of the twenty-first century, museum workers must become more scholarly and engage in discussing and writing about these issues.

On a personal note, I would like to thank Susan Walters and Mitch Allen of AltaMira Press who have encouraged and supported this project from its inception. To the contributors to this volume, you have exceeded my expectations at every point of this project. I have sincerely appreciated your time and support in making this book a reality.

The contributors and I hope that you will both enjoy and be challenged by *Museum Philosophy for the Twenty-first Century.*

1

Assuming Responsibility: Lessons from Aesthetics

Hilde Hein

Like its sister-science—pure knowledge—aesthetic enjoyment was at one time idealized as free from the cares of the everyday world. In their loftiest form, both beauty and wisdom were prized for their own sake and contemplated without regard for the practical consequences they might yield. Troublesome concerns such as those were for less exalted minds than the inheritors of the great tradition of Plato and Aristotle, for whom theory outclasses praxis and thinking outranks doing. The life of the mind, unconstrained by vulgar need and the struggle for survival, was the crowning glory of human activity: This thesis, albeit drastically modified, still resonates in our educational system and is deeply embedded in our social hierarchy.

Museums, though born centuries after the golden age of Greece, derive from this classical heritage. They bake no bread—except from time to time as part of a special exhibition. They are centers of study and research, but assign no homework, and nobody flunks an exam there. They gratify certain spiritual interests, but impose neither duties nor penance. Sometimes they inspire awe, but no one prays in them. They promote social and civic values, but have no powers of enforcement. Truly, their presence has been gratuitous and wondrously unencumbering. We cannot forget that idealized perception of their detachment even as we live in today's goal-centered era preoccupied with the "needs" of the public and the museum's mission to "serve" it.

Fascination with things whose value is intrinsic, with anything that is an "end in itself," seems archaic in today's world where nearly all art, all science, all activity is engaged or harnessed to some purpose. Even those few

1

instances of activity that purport to be strictly autonomous, the pursuit of "pure" research or the creation of "fine" art, are quickly deconstructed to reveal some implicit agenda that the author knowingly or unconsciously intended. Play is no longer just playful; leisure is merely restorative. And no object is identifiable apart from an environment of gestural function or use. The work of art morphs into the "art event," and the research project is revealed to be part of a social or political strategy. Things dissolve into meanings, whose stability is of the moment.

We cannot help being children of our time and place, and so we carry the burdens of our culture with us. The questions we pose, the manner in which we formulate them, and the answers we are willing to accept all arise out of a discourse of practice whose unexamined ends justify our means. Our busyness must be good for something. Contemplation as sheer pleasure, indulged in for its own satisfaction, now seems an incomprehensible pastime; it cannot then be an end either for individuals or institutions.

Thus museums, torn from their idle roots, have become part of the learning industry. Note the ".edu" at the end of your e-mail address. What they purvey is designated "informal" only because they do not grant degrees and, as yet, there is no verifiable measure of achievement, but we should not underestimate their serious purposiveness. The vagueness of their mission is an obstacle from some perspectives, but there are concrete compensations. A primary asset is the polysemic character of objects; they lend themselves to a multitude of interpretations, and museums thrive on the variety of contexts they can support. Unbound by the rigid structure of the schoolroom, museums can weave together the stories of different peoples, generations, and ideological persuasions—all told in a medley of material languages. As they strive consciously and conscientiously to be pluralistic, museums are adapting the means at their disposal to novel learning theories and unconventional educational goals that are less directive and more permissive than those that prevail in traditional institutions of formal learning. Thus they aim to complement, rather than compete with, the work of these institutions. In many instances, museums now collaborate with individual teachers and entire school systems to broaden and improve the quality of education at all levels.

Museums have also assimilated the methods of other industries. They have developed ingenious ways of communicating noncognitive attitudes, cultural habits, and even abstract ideas through the use of media technologies, nonlinear aesthetic and architectural devices, and theatrical and design elements. I have in mind evocative features like the darkly narrowing passages of the Holocaust Museum, eerie walk-through rain forest exhibits full of mist and screeching, period-conforming utensils and costumes that visitors can try while viewing history exhibitions or genre paintings. These address their audiences experientially in non-information-dispensing ways with direct impact. So successfully have museums mastered the techniques of influencing visitors' experience kinaesthetically, empathically, affectively, that they now vie with commercial entertainment centers whose object (apart from financial profit) is no more than to produce thrills and chills. But this is an achievement with mixed consequences. Setting aside complaints that museums are pandering to the lowest common denominator—I have no objection to people having fun in museums, as elsewhere—there are more fundamental concerns. In relying on "simulation and simulacra," however moving, museums are displacing the very thing that previously distinguished them, namely their presentation of "the real thing." Experience is real, but it is not a thing.

Granted that contention over their entitlement to claim ownership of reality is what evoked the pluralistic rebellion in the first place, it nevertheless is the presence of those material realia and their associated "truths" that differentiates a museum from an amusement park. The classical museum collected, preserved, and presented *things,* rightly or wrongly deciphered. Focusing instead on the conditions of encodement and multiplicity of interpretation, the new museum abandons itself and its guests to spectacle and fantasy. There is no doubt that an experience of fear and trembling (shock and awe?) can be generated by various means, perhaps more successfully even with today's virtual procedures than with a dust encrusted, history-laden bit of matter whose story must be read off a wall panel. Who now thinks of skulls as a terrifying *memento mori*? Yet there they are, depicted in many a Renaissance portrait, grimly leveling reminders to sitter and viewer alike of the vanity of earthly existence and the humbling certainty of death. What will it take to similarly shake up our own violence-sated generation?

The issue here is not the reality of the experience induced—you really do touch, smell, blink at, or hear something that the museum has put in front of you. Maybe it makes you weep or feel dizzy. You have an experience, a real one. But what is the purported association of that experience with whatever the museum or any other interpreter designates as its meaning or message? This is where the truth claim abides; and it is irrelevant to the commercial amusement center, whose interest stops short of what you may come to think or believe as a result of your experience. Museums identify themselves with the education world and not with the entertainment world because of that ephemeral relation to truth and reality. What matters is not the intensity of the experience, but where it takes you. Without that connection, children's museums would be only elaborate playgrounds; science centers would be clever circuses.

What, then, is it that the museum teaches? We cannot evade the question by calling it a "learning center," thereby denying the museum's responsibility for what visitors might learn. It is, after all, the museum that sets the parameters. Why this object instead of another one? Why this particular sequence of experiential stimuli? Where does the museum end and the free fall of the world begin? Their ambition notwithstanding, museums can neither re-create nor reproduce the world, but they can help us perceive it with renewed wonder.

Audiences are accustomed to the museum's voice of authority, whether or not they agree with it or are prepared to accept its message. They are free to dispute it, although most visitors are not trained to do so. While not bound to obey, many visitors are bewildered by the absence of authority. That expectation is significant. It conveys a readiness on the part of visitors to be "impressed" (if not illuminated) and not simply by the sheer having of an experience (as in an amusement center). Recall that most people go to museums voluntarily. They could get shocked, be thrilled, taste a new flavor, or be repulsed somewhere else. They choose to go to the museum well aware that it is a museum (even though their primary motive might be to spend a pleasant afternoon with a friend). It is conceivable that they will learn something there. Perhaps something a visitor encounters will intrigue her or him to go and learn more elsewhere—to the library, or to sign up for a class. This sort of stimulation cannot be preprogrammed or condensed into a lesson plan, but it is—and should be—very much a part of the museum's raison d'être. The museum works as a conduit back to the world, a route of inspiration that many distinguished individuals now cite gratefully as a primary formative influence. Ideally the museum is not an end, but a beginning. More correctly, it is a part of a process.

This observation brings me to the point from which I initially departed and to which I return with some trepidation. It was that some things are worth doing for themselves alone, apart from whatever consequences may flow from them. Aristotle held that philosophy, the noblest pursuit, begins with wonder. The twentieth-century philosopher Ludwig Wittgenstein wrote, less grandiosely, that philosophy is "puzzle solving"—but even puzzles may be approached for the joy of it. The satisfaction of knowing and exercising the capacity to know is related to doing, but not subservient to it. Learning fulfills desire as much as need, and generates its own desires. Museums are both the source and product of such desires; they grow out of someone's sense of wonder and help restore our own. Stopping to wonder, we are moved to question—and so to wonder and ask anew.

Habit and indoctrination lead us to demand justification. Should indiscriminate wonder and aimless pleasure be encouraged? Why indeed at public expense? Ought we not to insist that museums have some utility—the preservation of cultures? Recreative rehabilitation? Teaching to think "outside the box"? Mental exercise and emotional expansion? Dispensing information? Showing things in a new light? Certainly all of these do occur from time to time in museums, but they are hardly to be counted upon. Sometimes people just go for lunch. Is it an insult to the people whose labor, time, and energy maintains the museum to leave blank what it is "good for"? I think not. However, I want to differentiate between the museum's intrinsic value and the success or failure of its various enterprises. A caveat is necessary here: my evaluative language is not referenced to the merit of particular institutions. World-class or garage-scale is not the point. There are great museums and mediocre ones, so reputed in light of the quality, quantity, and disposition of their content. The present discussion is not a critique of specific instances, but relates to a concept, *the museum*, which has evolved over time and whose embodiments are many and various.

To believe in the worth of the concept, we are not obliged to esteem every one of its embodiments. I have recently learned of plans to open a snowboarding museum that will celebrate the sport's history and champions. I am not especially interested in snowboarding and am not likely to be inspired by a visit to this new museum. At one time or another quite a few museums have left me disappointed or unimpressed. But neither must I enjoy every book in the library or relish every concert I attend to endorse the existence of those institutions. Other people can appreciate them, and someone other than me may discover a latent passion or find a true calling as a result of that experience. We do not all dance to the same tune.

It is not necessary that all museums gratify the same interests. Even second-rate museums have their place in the world, as does bad art. They give us instances for comparison and sharpen our sensibility. There is a pleasure in assessing them that is unlike the reverential bow to the masterpiece. Indulgence in disapproval also has its comforts, and trying to figure out what is wrong or why something fails to work is every bit as rewarding as, and sometimes more illuminating than, affirming the good and successful. Museums offer a safe environment in which downsides and other sides of things can be explored and exposed without devastating consequences. With few exceptions, inferior museums are relatively harmless and may be left to collapse of their own weight.

There is a difference, moreover, between a bad museum—one that falls short as a museum—and a museum that displays negative things. Bad art, quack science, or the prevalence of prejudice, for example, can be well or badly exhibited. They have been provocatively featured by first-rate museums. Inferior museums take refuge in the plurality of judgment by disguising or denying their own. Declaring themselves neutral and noncoercive, they pretend to be nonjudgmental; yet they are distraught if visitors "misuse" exhibits or draw "wrong" conclusions from them. In fact, the visitor's freedom to "make meaning" is neither absolute nor unlimited. If you were to exit a "Holocaust" museum endorsing eugenic selection, the curators would rightly be dismayed, for it was not their intention to be impartial. Museums that rely on evoking experience have some expectation of what the visitor's experience will be and mean it to reinforce a construction foreseen by the museum. Often, as in science center exhibits, the anticipated discovery is of some common physical or physiological phenomenon—for example, color complementarity, optical illusion, or the Doppler effect. By isolating and attending to their own experience, visitors unfamiliar with the phenomenon come to consider it more generally, perhaps to study it in depth. That is the point of the exhibit; the induced experience is a means to creating a broadly anticipated effect and drawing attention to it. Should the visitor have an unexpected experience or fail to have the expected one, this situation would itself be a basis for further inquiry. It is disingenuous on the museum's part to claim "hands off" neutrality; indeed that would be irresponsible. Although the museum has no vested interest in the visitor's judgment, it does have an obligation to ensure that the visitor's experience not be fraudulent. That is its commitment to "the real thing." The museum's integrity and chief claim to authority lies in its warrant that visitors can trust *their own* judgment. The museum is not a magic show. Whether object or experience, whatever the museum presents must be genuine; the stimulus must not be fraudulently contrived. It must be what it purports to be, but the effect on visitors cannot be guaranteed.

No explicit lesson follows with necessity from what visitors undergo in the museum, although certain impressions and insights are normal. Even where they display "masterpieces" or illustrate "established fact," museums should not retail foregone conclusions as absolute. Inevitably they present something, and they must do the appropriate research to establish the provenance, authenticity, truth, or reliability of what they present. But they cannot control all possible reactions to it. Lately, in the face of pluralist and postmodern challenges, a crisis of self-doubt has overtaken many museums, and they have backed away from making univocal declarations. Although such self-restraint may be laudable in principle, it can lead to a bland superficiality, a misguided attempt to cover all bases—if not to disingenuous posing. Very likely, all bases will never be covered. Moreover, the much-heralded recontextualization that museums impose on everything they display adds a dimension that necessarily distorts its content. By definition, museums are full of "museum objects"; their visitors are inevitably a "museum audience," and their confluence produces "museum experiences," which cannot precisely replicate what takes place anywhere else. Nevertheless, they can generate reflection on real events and encounters, and that is the museum's gratuitous mission.

I come back once more to Aristotle's dictum, somewhat recast: museums begin with a sense of wonder, and that is sufficient justification. We describe them as repositories for things of great value—because they are lovely or significant historically or scientifically. But this matters only in light of the interest we profess, and what we find interesting varies from time to time and place to place. Not everyone agrees even that interesting things should be preserved. Think of Navajo or Tibetan sand paintings, which are erased instantly upon completion. They are all the more precious for their evanescence. The premium assigned to longevity happens to be an element of our Western museal culture, which is rapidly spreading to other parts of the world, but it has no inherent connection with the sense of wonder.

Let me now draw on a less ancient lesson from aesthetics, one less static and more adapted than Aristotle's to the drama of modern uncertainty. John Dewey celebrates art as *experience*, which enhances the *power to experience* the common world in its fullness. While art, says Dewey, accomplishes that end through the expressive conjunction of matter and form, museums, too, have many resources for the promotion of that objective. Museums, like art, transform matter into energy, funneling embedded ideas through a variety of media and technologies to be variously savored by their users. Dewey distinguishes between types or phases of experience. Much of our experience, he says, takes place almost unnoticed (like breathing) and is instrumental to other ends. Some experience (like playing games) is engaged in for its own sake and is "final," but our most developed experience is *consummatory*. It absorbs the instrumental and final phases, merging them in the immediacy of a felt present. Consummatory experience unites subject and environment, reconfiguring and expanding a whole that "carries with it its own individualizing quality and self-sufficiency."[1] This he designates *an experience*: it involves pattern and structure, composed and undergone by a sentient, feeling agent, who takes it in attentively as a whole, is enlarged by it, and empowered to expand the experience of others. Dewey thus endorses not experience as such, but the self-perpetuating maturation of the capacity for productive experiential growth. Here Dewey abandons Aristotle's sharp distinction between means and ends and between practice and contemplation. No end is ultimately final, he says; for each is a means that opens to further change and discovery. Each discovery affects the discoverer, transforming that person's judgment and purposes and so the world in which he or she interacts. So understood, experience is a process, not a terminus. Ideally it is reflexive; guided by its goal, it looks back upon its course with newly illuminated foresight. Neither active nor passive exclusively, it leads the agent onward, linking past to future, into a world of new possibilities.

Dewey exceeds Aristotle in his belief in historic growth and the need to reinterpret old truths and institutions in light of new practice and utility. In that vein he also believed in a more robust form of experimentalism and in more inclusive social democracy. Following that reasoning, he would approve the museum's current self-assessment in the context of ever-changing social values. He would insist, moreover, on a higher level of activism than Aristotle advocated; for growth is not just fulfillment, but rather a creative transformation. An experience, Dewey says, is not achieved by mere receptivity, nor is it a minimal recognition. It entails an effortful re-creation of its parts that is holistic and dynamic, merging past into future. The agent integrates mind with matter and fuses memory with feeling and purpose. Overemphasis on activity as an end, however, leads to impulsive incoherence often misidentified as freedom.

There is a lesson for museums in Dewey's philosophy of experience. If museums are to foster experience that is meaningful, they must balance objective environmental conditions with unknown possible consequences. They must guide visitors purposively into a world of expanding subject matter. Aimlessly presenting a succession of excitations without a form that sustains them throughout fails to lead to growth, yielding ultimate incoherency and arrest. At the same time, enforcing the necessity of doing one thing as a coerced antecedent to the occurrence of another is equally stifling. Dewey suggests that an end is not simply a last and closing term, but is a phase of a continuing process composed of prior ends of which it becomes a productive part. Museums can use their resources creatively, conferring upon them through their interactions qualities previously unrealized or unrecognized. And through such material engagements new orders of experiential consequences are generated.

I believe that museums can learn from both Aristotle and Dewey. Dewey's emphasis on education and change is timely. He rightly rejects the gulf that Aristotle places between consummatory enjoyment and the effort of its achievement, affirming that ends are constituted and valorized by their means—not just their product: They are in and of it. But Aristotle correctly places sheer wonder at the beginning as well as the end of the exploratory project. We are motivated as much by our pleasure and delight as by conflict and the need to solve problems. Certainly the grain of sand is a consequential prod to the oyster's labor, but we are also inspired to climb mountains "because they are there" and not only as obstacles to the valley beyond. Learning is not valued simply as conducive to knowledge, but often as an intrinsically satisfying enterprise that may or may not have other outcomes.

Museums owe their existence to, as well as being both a source and instrument of, open-ended seeking. They do not address a defined audience, as schools do, but issue an invitation to a broad public to come and enjoy. However topical the exhibitions they mount, they do not reward the accomplishment of specific tasks, and visitors can take from them more or less what they choose. The initiating conditions they propose are necessarily general and cannot be controlled for individual reference, so they have the potential to bring forth imaginative responses. Aristotle spoke for a stratified society in which only a tiny portion of the population could aspire to the conventional good life he advocated. Dewey, more democratic in outlook and resistant to the uniformity of a "block" universe, reflects a partiality toward *criticism* seasoned by experience and tempered through interaction. I suspect he believed there would be agreement in the end—if there is one—where reason prevails. I do not share that faith. I believe we can and must live with difference. Museums can show us how that is done and how to enjoy it. There need be no pretense of universality or uniformity. Beginning somewhat arbitrarily with existing collections, donations, acquisitions, constructions, and the preoccupations of the moment, museums are able to make sense of alternative modes of coherence. Some will be curatorially conceived, others will be evoked dialogically or oppositionally, and some will be the effulgence of solitary genius. They are not at war! Synoptically viewed, they release new understanding and increased gratification. Aesthetically appreciated they irradiate one another. No museum is obligated to cover the world, but in being true to its own vision each museum has a share in the world's renewal.

NOTE

1. John Dewey, *Art as Experience* (New York: Minton, Balch & Company, 1934); *Experience and Nature* (Chicago: Open Court, 1925).

2

Mind as Verb

David Carr

The world as it happens and as it is experienced is fluid; the world as it is known in evidence and description is captive. All learning is grounded in the captivity of evidence and the fluidity of experience. We learn through our systematic gathering and observing of evidence, through drawing and combining insights, and through our opening of interpretive possibilities by departing from the evidence through imagination. A learner's task and a museum's task are identical: to open the world that flows beyond the museum's captivity—and the mind's own captivity—in the continuously unfolding situations of experience.

Because the living, fluid world can be known only in an unfinished and open state—a state of potential and promise and improvisation—our knowledge of the world in museums is incomplete and unfinished. When we work and think in museums, we dwell, like Emily Dickinson, in possibility. We perceive the moving energy in the captured thing, the aggregate energies of a whole collection of things, and the origin of those energies in the motives and behaviors of human experience, as well as we can understand them. We find the human dimensions of activity and inquiry, making and minding the evidence and its implications. We ask, *What intelligence has been at work here?* When we can see it as a seamless ensemble of telling evidence, a museum inspires invisible actions, connections, and reflections. Mind surrounds and constructs the meanings of objects.

Mind surrounds. Mind fabricates. Mind acts invisibly. Mind leads forward. When we stand still at the center of a museum, our minds are in motion—we are unfinished with ourselves but uncertain of our tasks. We do not carry our minds with us like briefcases or pails. John Dewey says mind is not something we have, but something we do—we attend, care, and feel. Mind leads us to see. Mind engages in "active looking after things that need to be tended; we mind our step, our course of action, emotionally as well as thoughtfully." Mind questions. For Dewey, the infinitive "to mind" is defined by intellect and notation. It signifies memory and purpose. "Volitional, practical, acting in a purposive way. Mind," he says in *Art as Experience*, "is primarily a verb."[1] (I think of mind as verb like the motion of a hand—indicating, holding, tracing, leaving traces, beckoning, pointing elsewhere.)

A collection stimulates resonance among its pieces. Neither objective nor passive, museum collections stir with energy, urgency, and intensity. These are the invisible, moving parts of artworks and artifacts, continuously generative, alive with what Gerard Manley Hopkins calls "the dearest freshness deep down things."[2]

Gathering, containing, and ordering evidence in a collection are processes that generate energy. An ensemble of objects resonates with energy. The collection, insofar as it offers classifications, juxtapositions, tensions, and definitions, also creates opportunities for comparisons, reflections, observations, and speculations; these are also sources of energy.

A museum implies the difference of energy and value inherent in the existence of the object. What we understand of the world must be different because this object or this knowledge is in it. A museum user carries this difference—this energy, mixed with the urgency and intensity of insight—beyond the museum. *Without this object, we would know less, we would see less far.*

An offering of knowledge means more than abundant information. In *The Social Life of Information*, John Seely Brown and Paul Duguid write that any presentation of knowledge entails a knower, is embedded in a purposeful context, and requires both understanding and commitment.[3] A museum's voice, transmitting knowledge to engage the understanding and attention of its users, must speak as if from knower to knower. This voice "returns attention to people, what they know, how they come to know it, and how they differ."[4]

Learners, like witnesses, take different experiences in; then they live out and express different experiences of the evidence. To be fresh, knowing transcends all expectations and surprises and leads us where we did not expect to be. When we see these differences in a museum, we see knowledge that is fresh and perhaps inspired, a personal synthesis and transformation of the evidence. A museum enables astonishment evoked by unsuspected possibility, without which we are incomplete.

In the museum, knowing is the work at hand. To matter in the experience of the user, knowing must be contextual and transparent, following from authentic questions. When a museum conceives of its work and value as knowledge-driven, it uses the names and ideas of those who know, from scholars to more mundane observers; it quotes their words directly, and implies the practices and applications such knowledge supports. A museum that envisions itself engaged in "circulating human knowledge"[5] can also understand itself to be what Jean Lave and Etienne Wenger call a "community of practice,"[6] or, in this case, a community of interpretation, a setting where "learning needs to be understood in relation to the development of human identity."[7]

Nothing without energy or story holds possibility for us. We encounter and grasp knowledge as part of something passionate and compelling, happening in our presence now. Holding evidence in place, a museum makes intricate variations and improvisations of thought possible. Observing, we come to infer what cannot be present—the situation the evidence implies. Through inferences and implications, the collection is more than itself, as a living human body is understood to be more than liquid and flesh, bone, and hair. The meaning of all evidence is charged, again, in the sense of Hopkins.[8] Meaning appears only as an expression of energy and change.

We think and feel the artifact having motion and power, a narrative, an origin. Walt Whitman sings "the body electric."[9] D. H. Lawrence writes, "As we live, we are transmitters of life./And when we fail to transmit life, life fails to flow through us."[10] As a museum transmits to us new knowledge of life, the body electric, it also transforms and transmits life through us. We are charged; we are changed by what we see and experience.

A great museum is specific and practical; a great museum is also abstract and theoretical. A comprehensive museum learns to communicate through smallness and intimacy or it fails; a small, constrained museum learns to communicate its place in the universe, or it too fails. Although knowledge is vast, knowing begins in small, personal, particular, temporal contexts. We construct knowledge by whatever idea, small or large, has been placed in the palm of the hand and sensed through the fingertips. The intimate idea generates the great concept.

The center of all thinking about evidence is context—the foreground and background of time, the breadth and depth of its relevance to our own leading questions and unfinished processes. Our interest in a museum lies in how context contributes to cognitive order and leads us toward understanding the logics and relationships of the lived world. Collections and contexts make critical, cognitive acts possible.

A museum creates the situation of difference. We do not hunger for different information; we hunger for different perspectives. Almost all change we experience as learning in a museum will be a change in our understanding of pattern, not its details or substances. A human system (comprising memory, attention, continuity, perception, and sensation) trains itself to recognize difference: this is new, there is unprecedented information here, and there are unusual observations to be made. To the attuned organism, the main theme of experience is giving mind to, or minding, differences.

Difference teaches. Gregory Bateson says that "the word 'idea,' in its most elementary sense, is synonymous with 'difference.'" From an "infinitude" of differences in any object (Bateson uses a piece of chalk as an example) "we select a very limited number which become information. In fact, what we mean by information . . . is a *difference which makes a difference*, and it is able to make a difference because the neural pathways along which it travels and is continually transformed are themselves provided with energy. The pathways are ready to be triggered. We may even say that the question is already implicit in them."[11] William Blake called these pathways "the doors of perception"[12]—a metaphor that implies the sensing organism as ready to "receive" (Bateson's word) differences. We observe the beautiful or interesting thing because "we are aware that the combination of differences" come to us in one way only, by processes of thought.[13] We are minds minding complexity.

Complexity does not diminish. A museum offers us ways to construct our awareness of complexity in our experiences. However difficult our learning, the excitement of complexity is the concept to be communicated, not difficulty. Complexity invites; complexity engages. No understanding that does not grasp implications and complexities will last long for us. Some simple thoughts deserve to die young.

We come to understand that multiple perspectives on single objects are possible. We come to understand that all complex knowledge harbors a more complex unknown within it. We want more and more. We are insatiable. We understand that the reduction or removal of any element of our gaze will diminish our possible knowledge of it; therefore, we will always want more evidence to be placed before us. As our lives become more complex, we learn to imagine ourselves living and acting fearlessly within them, because we have neither the choice nor the desire to do otherwise.

Intellectual experiences in a museum are sustained by collaboration and improvisation. Assume the mind is a collaborative, improvisational entity, remaking itself as needed, using all available materials at hand. How then shall we think of it, prepare for it, and meet its needs?

Our thoughts begin with invisible actions, our bare urges toward an idea or a fresh way of thinking. The challenge of finding structure and order requires us to reach for our memories. The great human themes are memorable within us, embedded in recollections of need and loss, and they are essential to thinking about human knowledge. When moved, we recover and rescue them and renew their immanence and power. We might say of a museum user, as Louise Rosenblatt says of reading and the reader, "An intense response to a work will have its roots in capacities and experiences already present in the personality and mind of the reader."[14] The museum is evocative; it evokes us.

Thinking in a museum, we adapt and transform our experience. We combine evidences to make something stronger than its pieces. We undertake our work in a museum—the discovery of what is already present in each of us—hoping to arrive at balance and integrity. Given the density of our lives and relationships, and the complexity of our capacities and experiences, this is not easy. And yet, no matter how much we know, or what we bring to it, a museum object can rock us, can rock our assumptions and expectations. We would be shallow to wish it otherwise: we go to a museum in order to be rocked. It is difficult work, this knowing and feeling and being rocked: it means projecting, hypothesizing, imagining oneself elsewhere. It means questioning.

We learn to ask; we learn to act. Our work is transformation.[15] For every learner the tasks are the same—expand self-awareness; reconsider habits, assumptions, and perspectives; question the premises of belief and behavior; strive for moments of critical reflection and extend them; and remain calm and unafraid of error.

No design for our experience in a museum will last long. We live and connect, often by luck. We work with chance. We think and become. In a museum we are like our ancestors more than we know—tool making, constructing, connecting; hunting, gathering; planning, designing shelters; trying out, tentatively whispering our crafted truths, barely leaving traces for someone to find later.

To know courage and fear, let people come to a museum.[16] A robust museum displays human energy and intensity, the lifelong tasks and objects of passion—caring, commitment, vitality, empathy; sensuality, adoration; engagement, risk, renewal, reflection; endurance, solace, respect, kindness; integrity, evolution. A faint character cannot tolerate these things, or easily summon the engagement and strength their presence requires.

In a museum, we are always at work on ourselves. When we think in the presence of problems and experiences that provoke and engage us, we complete parts of our unfinished selves and begin to discover new unfinished parts of ourselves. In this way, we might see that human experiences can themselves become inspired works of art, works of improvisation like laughter or tears. Our selves remain dynamically, unpredictably open, capable of change, renewal, and transformation, until we die. Our lives and strengths are proven in the presence of things we do not understand. A learner is always in motion toward possibilities never seen before, and toward things that have not yet happened. Improvisation in the construction of a future is the critical act in a learning life.

Our lifelong human task is to become more capable, and this requires us to work constantly at our edges, and to strive to see what we have not yet seen.

When we dare to behave and think as ourselves alone, we become original and renewable beings, and only then do we break from mindless pattern, imitation, and expectation, and only then can we have integrity. We go to a museum in order to see what unfolds within us when we are there: we are folded up, and we unfold before the object, becoming capable of saying something new about ourselves. Living at such edges constantly unfolds us. This unfolding, and the constantly new topography revealed as we unfold, is one promise of cultural institutions.

Our situation at the start of this century can be expressed in configurations of pervasive, essential tensions and imbalances. We live among multiple, divergent, conflicting, and often harshly different experiences. In a wounded civilization, violence is both political ethos and popular entertainment. Narrow political values and religious expressions are at times indistinguishable; politics, race, and faith separate and reduce us. Cynicism inures us, and critical thinking challenges us. Consequently, the possibilities of good thinking escape us. Education is reduced to its least constructive function—the test that classifies its taker. We gaze at the desert of public life with an absence of depth and trust, aware of the incapacity of inquiry, literature, art, and history to express useful lessons. Only critical thought, courage, and human relationships offer respite from our fears.

A museum is not about what it contains; it is about what it makes possible. It makes the user's future conversations, thoughts, and actions possible. It makes engagements with artifacts and documents that lie beyond the museum possible. It constructs narratives that help us to locate our memories, passions, and commitments. The museum illuminates irresistible new thoughts and stimulates revisions of former thoughts. The museum invites us to reconsider how we behave and what we craft in the worlds of lived experience. The gift of a museum for every user is an appreciation of complexity, a welcoming to the open door of the unknown, the possible, the possible-to-know, and the impossible-to-know. Every institution is a teacher.

To communicate its respect and integrity, the great museum understands and acts on three things. First, it sustains itself for use by the whole culture, inviting every possible user. Second, it recognizes that most dimensions of new thinking are hidden; they become visible only to the inspired user, and not immediately. Therefore, and third, the great museum inspires patience and courage. It gives the user attention and keeps the user in mind. It promises and begins a long conversation.

Knowing inspires and requires conversations. When museums go beyond information, by helping collaborations among those who know and those who wish to know, they must make a place where users can articulate their experiences, insights, and sensations. This idea, or some variation of it, engages a museum in the construction of a social world of learning.

Apprenticeship is a way of becoming stronger in the presence of the unknown. We need to see the evidence of another intelligence at work next to ours; we need to see our own thinking among other intelligences at work, in order to understand what we might independently become. We need to see enough to say, "This is a form of intelligence of which I too am capable."

We make a museum work when we stand in it, as hopeful people talking together in a small space and time. When we speak of our own experiences of knowing and feeling, our experiments of observation and reflection, we confirm and extend our connections to other lives and their experiences. In an insular world, we create the fabric of a museum by being and speaking with no other purpose than expressing and extending our integrity and observations, however tentatively, to others.

We need to go beyond the usual. From a wall in the Phoenix Art Museum, I copied these words of the painter Robert Henri.

> There are moments in our lives, there are moments in a day, when we seem to see beyond the usual. Such are the moments of our greatest happiness. Such are the moments of our greatest wisdom. If one could but recall his vision by some sort of sign. It was in this hope that the arts were invented. Sign-posts on the way to what may be. Sign-posts toward greater knowledge.

A museum holds evidence in the trust that a thoughtful person will think again in its presence, and will remember the past; that an unreflective person might pause to "see beyond the usual," and understand the difference of that moment.

There is not one of us who does not need the capability to imagine and construct a whole life. These words are from the final section of Azar Nafisi's memoir, *Reading Lolita in Tehran.*

> I have a recurring fantasy that one more article has been added to the Bill of Rights: the right to free access to imagination. I have come to believe that a genuine democracy cannot exist without the freedom to imagine and the right to use imaginative works without any restrictions. To have a whole life, one must have the possibility of publicly shaping and expressing private worlds, dreams, thoughts and desires, of constantly having a dialogue between public and private worlds. How else do we know that we have existed, felt, desired, hated, feared?[17]

We must work to imagine a museum in service to that nonexistent article assuring the right to imagine freely.

Consider a museum to be an agent, teacher, and advocate for the free imagination and the imagination of possible freedoms. Imagine a museum to nurture the whole life of a person, active and reflective, inquiring and remembering moments in a day when we seem to have seen beyond the usual. Imagine the museum as an experiment in human consciousness. Imagine a museum, guided by a passionate trust, to live up to the user and what the user carries—memory, interest, insight, energy, and an undiminishing capacity for change.

NOTES

1. John Dewey, "Art as Experience," in *The Later Works, 1925–1953*, vol. 10, ed. Jo Ann Boydston, 268 (Carbondale: Southern Illinois University Press, 1987).

2. Gerard Manley Hopkins, *Poems and Prose of Gerard Manley Hopkins*, ed. W. H. Gardner (New York: Penguin, 1953), 27. "It will flame out, like shining from shook foil."

3. John Seely Brown and Paul Duguid, *The Social Life of Information* (Cambridge, Mass.: Harvard Business School Press, 2000), 119–20.

4. Brown and Duguid, *The Social Life of Information*, 121.

5. Brown and Duguid, *The Social Life of Information*, 124.

6. Jean Lave and Etienne Wenger, *Situated Learning: Legitimate Peripheral Participation* (New York: Cambridge University Press, 1991), 94–99, passim.

7. Brown and Duguid, *The Social Life of Information*, 138.

8. Hopkins, *Poems and Prose of Gerard Manley Hopkins*, 27.

9. Walt Whitman, *Leaves of Grass* in *Walt Whitman: Complete Poetry and Collected Prose* (New York: Library of America, 1982), 250.

10. D. H. Lawrence, *The Collected Poems of D. H. Lawrence,* ed. Vivian de Sola Pinto and F. Warren Roberts, vol. 1 (New York: Viking, 1964), 449.

11. Gregory Bateson, *Steps to an Ecology of Mind* (New York: Ballantine, 1972), 453; italics in original. "Let me invite you to a psychological experience," Bateson writes, "if only to demonstrate the frailty of the human computer. First note that differences in texture are *different* (a) from differences in color. Now note that differences in size are *different* (b) from differences in shape. Similarly ratios are different (c) from subtractive differences. Now let me invite you . . . to define the differences between 'different (a),' 'different (b),' and 'different (c)' in the above paragraph. The computer in the human head boggles at the task." Bateson, *Steps to an Ecology of Mind*, 457–58; italics in original.

12. William Blake, *The Poetry and Prose of William Blake*, ed. David V. Erdman (New York: Doubleday, 1965), 39. "If the doors of perception were cleansed every thing would appear to man as it is, infinite." Blake, "The Marriage of Heaven and Hell," in *The Poetry and Prose of William Blake.*

13. Bateson, *Steps to an Ecology of Mind*, 465.

14. Louise Rosenblatt, *Literature as Exploration*, 5th ed. (New York: Modern Language Association, 1995), 41.

15. Jack Mezirow, *Learning as Transformation: Critical Perspectives on a Theory in Progress* (San Francisco: Jossey-Bass, 2000), 3–33, passim.

16. At the Phoenix Art Museum, a wall of quotations includes this from Robert Frost: "If you're looking for something to be brave about, consider the fine arts."

17. Azar Nafisi, *Reading Lolita in Tehran* (New York: Random House, 2003), 338–39.

3

The Museum: Where Civilizations Clash or Clash Civilizes?

Timothy W. Luke

It is difficult to determine which single underlying philosophy or mission the museum should pursue in the first half of the twenty-first century, mostly because there are so many essential missions and critical philosophies that require continuous attention at all important museums. Fortunately, the range of respondents in this collection will cover many of the other most pressing challenges, so this chapter reconsiders larger political shifts unfolding at the dawn of this century, which almost all major museums must confront. Whether it is world order, national identity, cultural crisis, technological revolution, or historic change, the museum must pursue open, inclusive, and even agonistic approaches to preserving the past, exploring the present, and testing the future. And, it must do this despite public outcries or local protests.

This mission is, of course, not easy. In too many ways, the plight of museums in the early twenty-first century reflects the deeper cultural drift that Jane Jacobs worries about in her recent *Dark Age Ahead*.[1] Because too many now believe stability equals a lack of controversy, survival requires corporate backing, science must be infotainment, public support is gone forever, and media punditry carries as much weight as learned professionalism, the higher educational missions of museums are being abridged. Vital cultural links between communities and families, collectives and individuals, and traditions and innovations have been, and still are, drawn at museums, but these once solid educational connections are being corroded.

As a house of the Muses, museums must continually renew their commitment to shelter and secure the virtues, wisdom, or arts that such sites are meant to represent. Without this institutional work, civilizations can be easily lost to nothing but violent clashes. Perhaps counterintuitively, it is, however, the ongoing clash of differing philosophies, perspectives, and people over museums and their work that actually can keep a culture engaged in the core renewal of its civilizational truths.[2]

Maintaining an unfettered devotion to open inquiry always has been difficult, because any society's tactics and strategies for collective order and individual freedom frequently are contradictory.[3] Local audiences may profess to be open-minded in the abstract, but particular museum shows often spark intense calls for harmful censorship. The cost of exhibitions forces museums to solicit private sector support; and, once again, specific displays can offend corporate management, or even lead to the loss of their financial backing. Moreover, unanticipated political issues over ordinary curatorial approaches can agitate the viewing public, community figures that provide exhibition materials, or the national media. Such clashes are often treated as embarrassments, failures, or even malpractice by the press. Yet, this rhetorical frame could not be more mistaken. These controversies can be, as John Stuart Mill's liberal credo holds, salutary opportunities for truth to confront error, either revealing the enduring strength of the truths so tested or unveiling the erroneous superstitions once accepted as commonsensical. The civilizing clash of curatorial vision, conceptual exploration, and community contact can bring out the best of museums as sites of civilizational preservation, renewal, and truthfulness.[4]

Samuel P. Huntington directs the Harvard Academy for International and Area Studies. As a former director of security planning at the National Security Council, a chaired professor at Harvard University, and a well-known, albeit not always highly regarded or well-respected, public intellectual, Huntington has meandered during his career back and forth between mainstream and maverick views. In the 1970s, he became somewhat infamous for fretting over the "distemper of democracy." During the 1990s, he reimagined the post–Cold War world as one in which the "clash of civilizations"[5] would reshape world order. Seeing global alignments between nations changing from those denominated by competing modern secular ideologies to ones delimited by culture and civilization, he outlined a vision for world order which strangely coincided with the prevailing views of many—both inside and outside of the United States. For those devoted to waging culture struggles, science wars, or religious debates in the United States, the culture crises discussed by Huntington as a clash of civilizations often have proven to be rich rhetorical resources for culture warriors over the past decade.

More recently, Huntington's newest work asks, "*Who are We?*"[6] and, once he raises this question against the backdrop of his clash of civilizations conundrum, the place of museums in the everyday life of the world's public cultural consciousness cannot be ignored. At least since the nineteenth century, museums—scientific, natural, historical, and cultural—have all served as central sites for answering bits of Huntington's question. From exhibitions of scientific discovery, natural phenomena, historical change, and cultural achievement many learn at museums who "we" are, how we "are" as we are, and whom the "who" in question gathers to answer such questions. Yet, most importantly, the best answers to such queries are those that bypass the pat acceptance of a clash of civilizations thesis and embrace the civilizing influence of clash itself as the path for asking, and answering, such foundational questions. William Blake's poetic project asserts, "Without Contraries There is No Progress." Some of the best museums express the truth of Blake's insight when they eschew the impulse to become seamless pure "white cubes" in which truth is already regarded as a closed black box with no holes, no doubts, and no contraries. Outstanding museums instead admit that truth cannot be imprisoned forever inside such closed, blackened boxes. Instead, museums exist, in part, to foster and fuel the civilizing qualities of conceptual and cultural clashes. Posing as a ready-made, white cube for truth to repose unchallenged is a dead end.

Huntington argues that everyone requires, and mostly already holds, "some sort of simplified map of reality, some theory, concept, model paradigm" simply in order "to think seriously about the world, and act effectively in it."[7] While he pitches his arguments to audiences in the fields of diplomacy, international politics, or foreign affairs, his ideologically charged vision of clashing civilizations rests upon establishing definite epistemic first-principles. "For in the back of our minds," Huntington believes, "are hidden assumptions, biases, and prejudices that determine how we perceive reality, what facts we look at, and how we judge their importance and merits."[8] Without saying so, and probably with little consciousness of where his claims lead, Huntington touches upon much of what museums do in any society to shape individual and collective subjectivity.

While they are not the only institution involved in these epistemic, engineering exercises, museums do provide explicit or implicit models so as to enable individuals and groups to become able to:

1. order and generalize about reality;
2. understand causal relationships among phenomena;
3. anticipate and, if we are lucky, predict future developments;
4. distinguish what is important from what is unimportant; and,
5. show us what paths we should take to achieve our goals.[9]

Of course, Huntington's muses lead him to see a clash between civilization and barbarism from the beginning of humanity's settled, civilized existence, and a never-ending clash of civilizations over perceived and real barbarisms ever since, as the source for unveiling these foundational, epistemic assets. Civilizations, then, in Huntington's analysis are enduring concrete totalities in which "the overall way of life of a people" and "a culture writ large" express imperative epistemic categories, ontological first principles, evaluative criteria, institutional strata, and personal identities.

Clearly, the activities of museums cannot be separated easily from Huntington's clash of civilizations arguments, because they are important sites where the overall way of life of a people is writ large as part of local, national, and global culture.[10] Huntington's even more polemical new book, *Who Are We? The Challenges to America's National Identity*, openly agonizes about how America possibly is losing its "core culture" and "identity" as a nation, as Americans allegedly face dangerous new threats from "deconstructive criticism," "Mexican immigration," and "globalization."[11] Amid such intense social, political, and cultural anxieties, it is no surprise that museums today are a crossroads for cultural conflict, dissent, and struggle. Yet, once again, this should not always be viewed as a negative development; instead, it can be quite positive.

If the muses of memory, meditation, and all of the arts themselves are under suspicion, in doubt, or at question at the dawn of the twenty-first century, then it is not surprising that the museum will be subjected to critical scrutiny as well.[12] Yet, the innate conservatism of many museum boards, curators, and directors leaves most of them too worried about such disputes and debates.[13] They might well be right in a world allegedly wracked by the clash of civilizations to be unwilling to admit any controversies into their museums. Still, they could also proceed far too cautiously. Rather than regarding museums as the traditional white cubes of stabilized purity, these institutions must serve as crucibles of conceptual, ethical, and aesthetic confrontation where uncertain truth and error are both examined to allow all to discern, or at least begin to define, the truth as they determine, or perhaps start to delimit, error.[14] Real learning comes to curious people witnessing the collision of contraries rather than enduring their enlightenment as the unwashed masses. There is less and less stabilized security in sanctified systems of standardized convention, even though many museum professionals often accept the task of creating or maintaining the appearances of such stabilized systems where they work. Far too many museum boards, curators, and patrons, then, see clash as always and everywhere a bad thing. At some points and in many times, however, there is much to be said for the rough and tumble of the free display and open debate of whatever concerns that confront many different publics. It is worth the risk to have them come into consideration at the museum.[15]

Museums—as valued sites for civilizing episodes of clashing contradictions, opposite opinions, and disturbing depictions—must be respected and, more importantly, protected. In far too many places, this moment in history is proving not to be the best of times to single out museums for service as special sites for cultural contestation.[16] For at least four decades in the United States, there have been high levels of worry, uncertainty, and doubt about the nation's cultural values. Plainly, the cultural wars of the 2000s only have escalated and broadened these splits. Nonetheless, it is because of this ongoing cultural war, and the passions, contradictions, and anxieties they foster, that museums must support programs of civilizing clashes.[17]

Museum exhibitions frequently are stitched together out of cultural scraps taken from much more specific discourses and practices, which have not always been fabricated with objective detachment or dispassionate consideration in mind. Objects placed in museum displays are taken out of their social contexts, and the viewing subjects are kept back from such conflicted realities as they view only objectified representations inside of some museum's exhibition. As Homi Bhabha notes, this is unavoidable as any society's positioning of acculturating strategies requires special sites to be effective.[18] Therefore, the enduring values that many museums claim to espouse might not provide a strong draw for building an audience, a donor list, or a public. These values express both power and knowledge. Knowledge's indirect systems of legislation operationalize themselves by nesting in museums, because they are key nodes of power, critical regimes of rules, and important spaces of subjectivity to underpin civilizing sensibilities.[19] Museums help to wright reality, and then organize the collective rites of this unstable reality's public reception into a form that can then be used to write out authoritative accounts of the past, present, and future in their displays.[20]

By civilizing clash in a world of clashing civilizations, museums should script their ongoing shows of force as projects that might fashion fresh patterns of subjectivity in which individuals and collectivities, without denigrating others, can affirm themselves culturally as political subjects with particular identities and peculiar values.[21] Knowledge and power will compound each other's effects at museums by providing special codes of guidance for recognizing as well as reaffirming the range of cultural discoveries to be found in museum exhibitions. Museums in the United States serve those who seek to know the latest about what learned authorities in American society sanction as being "the technical," "the natural," "the past," and "the culture." And each museum tries to present the most artful display of its artifacts and ideas to entertain and educate its visitors.[22] All of this transpires, at the same time, through materialized, ideological narratives, which convey normative codes of practice and value in peculiarly arranged displays with historical artifacts, corporate products, natural organisms, technological devices, or art works. While their rhetorical stance essentially is one of cool, detached objectivity, museums are unavoidably organized around engaged political principles.[23] Moving beyond the clash of civilizations to enable clash itself to civilize requires enough narrative complexity to allow for a vernacular positioning of professional exhibits. The acceptance of multiperspectival narratives also should point out inconclusive discourses, and facilitate do-it-yourself interpretations. Such open, inclusive, and controversial philosophies of museum practice would accept clash as civilizing rather than taking the easy way out by accentuating the clash of civilizations as a "new world order" project for all to adopt as tacit knowledge of how "the West" still bests "the rest."

Patrons and visitors therefore should not cavil before controversy at the museum. Without contraries there is no progress, no enlightenment, no truth testing. At times, the vision of truth ensconced in exhibits fails to meet the measure of public debate and critical controversy. At other times, the common sense of visitors and local audiences is shown a side of history, nature, science, or art that pushes received opinion out of the ruts cut by empty, settled certainties. In both instances, museums are doing some of their best work by unleashing the civilizing clash of community self-reflection, debate, and revitalization.

NOTES

1. Jane Jacobs, *Dark Age Ahead* (New York: Random House, 2004), 24.

2. Ivan Karp, Christine Mullen Kreamer, and Steven Lavine, eds. *Museums and Communities: The Politics of Public Culture* (Washington, D.C.: Smithsonian Institution Press, 1992).

3. Michel De Certeau, *The Practice of Everyday Life* (Berkeley: University of California Press, 1984).

4. Timothy W. Luke, "Arctic National Wildlife Refuge: Seasons of Life and Land, A Photographic Journey," *The Public Historian* 26 (Winter 2004): 193–201.

5. Samuel Huntington, *The Clash of Civilizations and the Remaking of World Order* (New York: Simon & Schuster, 1996).

6. Samuel Huntington, *Who Are We? The Challenges to America's National Identity* (New York: Simon & Schuster, 2004).

7. Huntington, *The Clash of Civilizations*, 29.

8. Huntington, *The Clash of Civilizations*, 30.

9. Huntington, *The Clash of Civilizations*, 30.

10. Timothy W. Luke, *Museum Politics: Power Plays at the Exhibition* (Minneapolis: University of Minnesota Press, 2002).

11. Huntington, *Who Are We?*, 17–27.

12. Jacobs, *Dark Age Ahead*.

13. Nathan Glazer, *We Are All Multiculturalists Now* (Cambridge, Mass.: Harvard University Press, 1997).

14. Jürgen Habermas, *The Philosophical Discourse of Modernity* (Cambridge, Mass.: MIT Press, 1987).

15. Stephen E. Weil, *Making Museums Matter* (Washington, D.C.: Smithsonian Institution Press, 2001).

16. Amy Henderson and Adrienne Lois Kaeppler, eds., *Exhibiting Dilemmas: Issues of Representation at the Smithsonian* (Washington, D.C.: Smithsonian Institution Press, 1997).

17. Luke, *Museum Politics*.

18. Homi K. Bhabha, *The Location of Culture* (New York: Routledge, 1994).

19. Michel Foucault, *Power/Knowledge: Selected Interviews & Other Writings* (New York: Pantheon, 1980).

20. Timothy W. Luke, *Shows of Force: Power, Politics, and Ideology in Art Exhibitions* (Durham, N.C.: Duke University Press, 1992).

21. Karp, Kreamer, and Lavine, *Museums and Communities*.

22. Ivan Karp and Steven Lavine, *Exhibiting Cultures: The Poetics and Politics of Museum Display* (Washington, D.C.: Smithsonian Institution Press, 1991).

23. Luke, *Shows of Force*.

4

Legal and Ethical Considerations in Museum Acquisitions

Marilyn Phelan

I was asked to provide the perspective of one who views museum philosophy from the "outside" of the profession looking in to answer a specific question: What underlying philosophy/mission should museums pursue in the first half of the twenty-first century? This was a challenge, but from my perspective, which includes many years of studying laws relating to museums, I must answer this question by focusing on the need for museum professionals to adopt a different philosophy regarding museum acquisitions from that which was prevalent in the twentieth century. Although most museums have developed codes of ethics with respect to accessioning and deaccessioning objects in their collections, I have observed that many museum officials tend to apply ethical considerations more readily to deaccessioning their collections than to their acquisition policies. Unfortunately this has led to many museums accessioning cultural treasures without exercising due diligence to review the history of such cultural properties.

In my many years of researching, complying with, and teaching laws relating to museums, I have attempted to relate such laws to ethical principles, particularly with respect to the interplay of legal axioms and ethical theorems regarding the collection and protection of cultural property. One cannot de-emphasize the importance of the law in preserving the archaeological record. We clearly are dependent on the law to protect our cultural heritage, but there are gaps in the law that ethical principles must fill. Countless countries have been stripped of their cultural property through thefts at archaeological sites. Nations, museums, and individuals have lost artworks and other

27

cultural property as a result of pillage during military conflicts. Works of art especially have been part of the spoils of war. In my opinion the greatest challenge to museum officials in the first half of the twenty-first century is how they will deal with the problem that much of this looted cultural property has found its way into museum collections. Indeed some museum officials have accepted and even condoned the pillage of the cultural heritage in the interest of enhancing their collections. As the law continues to evolve at both the national and international level, we hopefully can expect that we will acquire sufficient legal means during the twenty-first century to address and correct the past pillage of archaeological sites and other thefts of cultural property. In the process though, because legal principles are not yet sufficiently adequate to address these issues, ethical principles must provide for needed self-regulation.

I have been interested especially in the interplay between law and ethics with respect to the acquisition and maintenance of museum collections. The Code of Ethics adopted by the International Council of Museums (ICOM) observes that the "illicit trade in objects and specimens encourages the destruction of historic sites" as well as "ethnic cultures," that it "promotes theft at local, national and international levels," and "contravenes the spirit of national and international patrimony."[1] It declares that a museum professional "must warrant that it is highly unethical for a museum to support the illicit market in any way, *directly or indirectly*" (emphasis added).[2] The ICOM Code states:

> A museum should not acquire any object or specimen by purchase, gift, loan, bequest or exchange unless the governing body and responsible officer are satisfied that a valid title to it can be obtained. Every effort must be made to ensure that it has not been illegally acquired in, or exported from, its country of origin or any intermediate country in which it may have been owned legally (including the museum's own country). Due diligence in this regard should establish the full history of the item from discovery or production, before acquisition is considered.
>
> In addition to the safeguards set out above, a museum should not acquire objects by any means where the governing body or responsible officer has reasonable cause to believe that their recovery involved the unauthorised, unscientific or intentional destruction or damage of ancient monuments, archaeological or geological sites, or natural habitats, or involved a failure to disclose the finds to the owner or occupier of the land, or to the proper legal or governmental authorities.

The Code of Ethics adopted in 2000 by the American Association of Museums (AAM) unfortunately is silent with respect to ethical proscriptions regarding a museum's inclusion in its collections of objects that were taken from archaeological sites or were acquired either directly or indirectly through the illicit market. The AAM's policy on collections merely proposes that a museum should ensure its collections are "lawfully held, protected, secure, unencumbered, cared for, and preserved."[3] The code's policy on collections states that a museum must ensure that its "acquisition, disposal, and loan activities are conducted in a manner that respects the protection and preservation of natural and cultural resources and discourages illicit trade in such materials."[4]

The 2000 AAM Code of Ethics does not address the somewhat "problematic" and "questionable" practices on the part of directors of many of the larger and most reputable museums in the United States concerning their amassing of objects from the world's cultural heritage, allegedly for preservation purposes but often simply to enhance their collections.

Despite the fact that archaeologists can construct a history and prehistory for a particular sphere or community through a study of the cultural property of that region, many leading museum officials have been involved, indirectly at least, in the illicit trade in looted antiquities from archaeological sites. A partial justification for this involvement has been the theory that wealthy museums have a better means to curate cultural objects than do source nations with limited resources available for their museums. There still exists a group of theorists who take the position that, because all cultural properties, wherever located, are part of the cultural heritage of humanity, cultural resources should be owned and controlled by those who can best preserve them. Strangely enough, this so-called internationalist theory apparently serves as the justification for many museum directors to maintain within their collections looted, as well as illegally exported, cultural resources.[5] If, in fact, laws have legitimized their methods of collection, they have ignored ethical principles that surely do not.

In December of 2002, officials of eighteen of the leading museums of Europe and North America drafted the "Declaration on the Importance and Value of Universal Museums," wherein they posited a "universality" in their collections.[6] They declared that their museums "provide a valid and valuable context for objects that were long ago displaced from their valuable source" and postulated that calls "to repatriate objects that have belonged to museum collections" must be considered on a case-by-case basis and "judged individually" because "museums serve not just the citizens of one nation but the people of every nation."[7] The directors of these museums have listed "the threat to the integrity of universal collections posed by demands for the restitution of objects to their countries of origin" as one of the most pressing issues facing museums.[8] This indeed is one of the most pressing issues confronting museums, but some members of the museum community view the issue in a different light. Some would contend that directors of the "universal" museums are attempting "to establish a higher degree of immunity from claims for the repatriation of objects" in their collections and would view their "presumption that a museum with universally defined objectives may be considered exempt from such demands" as "specious."[9]

Two recent cases in the United States illustrate the questionable and somewhat alarming position of some members of the AAM regarding the international trade in art and antiquities. The AAM itself openly acquiesced in the view of the internationalists that cultural resources are commodities that should be salable on the international market when it stated its position in the first of these two cases. In *United States v. An Antique Platter of Gold*,[10] the AAM submitted an amicus curiae (friend of the court) brief supporting the actions of an art collector (who also was a benefactor of the New York Metropolitan Museum of Art) in importing into the United States a looted third-century B.C. Phiale.[11] The Phiale was taken from an archaeological site in Sicily, was exported in violation of Italian laws, and was imported into the United States in violation of its customs laws.[12] Pursuant to a 1939 Italian law, an archaeological item is presumed to belong to the state unless its possessor can show private ownership prior to 1902.[13] The Italian government sought the assistance of the U.S. government in investigating the circumstances of the Phiale's exportation and requested that it confiscate the Phiale for return to Italy. The district court ruled that the Phiale must be returned to Italy. On appeal, the AAM filed its amicus brief wherein it urged the appellate court not to give effect to the cultural patrimony laws of other countries. The AAM asserted: "American museums have a deep and longstanding interest in, and commitment to, the responsible collection and exhibition of cultural objects of all countries and civilizations." It declared that "American museums have supported, and will continue to support, all responsible efforts to further the preservation and conservation of cultural objects, and to combat their destruction, looting and theft."[14] However, it then asserted that the decision of the district court (wherein the district court ordered the forfeiture of the Phiale and its return to Italy) "threatens the ability of U.S. museums to collect . . . and make available for public exhibition objects from around the world" that are "the subject of *sweeping* foreign cultural patrimony laws" (emphasis added).[15] It declared that these cultural patrimony laws "are, in significant respects, antithetical to fundamental principles of U.S. law and public policy." It expressed concern that, should the decision of the court below not be reversed, "countless objects" in museum collections would be in peril.[16] The AAM maintained that the decision of the court would "have a profound impact on the law governing all museums and their ability to collect and exhibit cultural objects." It then declared that American museums were "compelled" to urge the court to reverse the decision of the court below.[17] The AAM took the position that the district court committed "fundamental error" in "its automatic enforcement of Italy's patrimony law." The AAM opined that the "unprecedented procedure permitted the U.S. government" by the court made the U.S. government a "surrogate for the Italian government."[18] Curiously, the AAM described the "efforts of some nations to claim ownership of all objects discovered within their borders" as a "more parochial view of cultural property," one that would "directly challenge the 'common cultural heritage' philosophy" upon which, it stated, "our museums and society are founded."[19] The AAM declared in its amicus brief that "cultural patrimony laws are fundamentally inconsistent with the United States' treatment of its own cultural property and with our underlying system of private property."[20] It further stated that "the effect of the indiscriminate application of these laws will be to jeopardize existing museum collections and the future ability of our museums to continue to collect and exhibit cultural objects for the public."[21] The AAM concluded, in its amicus brief, that, should the decision of the district court (that the Phiale must be returned to Italy) be affirmed, that decision "will amount to a judicial fiat . . . that often will preclude *responsible* museums from acquiring cultural objects from other countries" (emphasis added).[22]

The substance of the AAM's position, as set out in its amicus curiae brief in *Antique Platter of Gold*, is that there should be no limitation on the looting of archeological sites. This astonishing position was reasserted by leading members of the museum community, albeit not by the AAM specifically, in the most recent of the two cases. In *United States v. Schultz*,[23] respectable and prestigious members of the museum community joined in the filing of an amicus curiae brief supporting the activities of a well-known art dealer who was convicted for transporting knowingly stolen Egyptian antiquities. The art dealer, Schultz, was indicted for "conspiring to receive stolen Egyptian antiquities that had been transported in interstate and foreign commerce" in violation of the National Stolen Property Act (NSPA).[24] Schultz contended that the objects he had taken were not stolen within the meaning of the NSPA because, he claimed, they were not owned by anyone and, thus, could not be stolen. The prosecution, on the other hand, showed that the Egyptian government owned the antiquities pursuant to a patrimony law known as "Law 117," which declares that all antiquities found in Egypt after 1983 are the property of the Egyptian government. Evidence in the case showed that an individual (Parry) smuggled an ancient Egyptian sculpture (the head of Pharaoh Amenhotep III) out of Egypt by disguising the figure in plastic and plaster.[25] Schultz later paid Parry a substantial fee to serve as his agent to sell the sculpture. The two men created a false provenance for the sculpture, claiming that it had been brought from Egypt in the 1920s and had been maintained since that time in an English private collection, which they called the "Thomas Alcock Collection." They prepared fake labels for the sculpture, which were designed to appear as if they had been printed in the 1920s. After a jury trial in the U.S. District Court for the Southern District of New York, Schultz was convicted of conspiring to receive stolen property that had been transported in interstate or foreign commerce under the NSPA.[26] The case was appealed to the Court of Appeals for the Second Circuit. Amicus curiae briefs supporting Schultz were filed with the Second Circuit by dealer groups and by a newly formed "Citizens for a Balanced Policy with Regard to the Importation of Cultural Property." The newly formed organization is a group of twenty-seven individuals that includes nine present or former museum curators, members of museum boards, and counsel for museums. The group represented that their interest in the case was their "abiding commitment to the preservation of cultural heritage and the continued existence of a national policy with regard to international trade in cultural property that balances the legitimate but often conflicting interest of archaeologists, art dealers, collectors, museums and our national government."[27] In their brief, the group stated that the indictment of Schultz has "shook the American art world" and, with it, members of their group. The group contended that, if the NSPA covers claims of ownership based on foreign patrimony laws, "our nation's cultural policy is at stake."[28] The Second Circuit Court of Appeals apparently was unimpressed with the group's argument as it affirmed Schultz's conviction.

In 1982, Congress ratified in part the 1970 UNESCO Convention on the Means of Prohibiting and Preventing the Illicit Import, Export and Transfer of Ownership of Cultural Property by its implementing legislation, the Convention on Cultural Property Implementation Act, which became effective in 1983.[29] At that time, members of Congress noted that the demand for cultural artifacts had resulted in the irremediable destruction of archaeological sites and objects. They expressed concern that this demand was depriving situs countries of their cultural patrimony and the world of important knowledge of the past.[30] Some members of Congress noted that the United States had become a principal market for artifacts of archaeological or ethnological interest and of art objects and that the discovery of stolen or illegally exported artifacts in some instances had strained severely the United States' relations with the countries of origin, some of which were close allies of the United States.[31] The Cultural Property Implementation Act, which was enacted to ratify in part the 1970 United Nations Educational, Scientific and Cultural Organization (UNESCO) Convention, provides that, when a participating nation makes a request to the United States for import restrictions on cultural property from that nation, because the requesting nation contends the cultural patrimony of the nation is in jeopardy from the pillage of its cultural properties, the president may enter into a bilateral agreement with that nation to apply import restrictions.[32]

In 2000, then-Senators Moynihan, Roth, and Shumer introduced a bill[33] that would have amended the Cultural Property Implementation Act to curb the president's ability to comply with the 1970 UNESCO Convention. Sponsors of the bill were concerned that art dealers were not members of the

Cultural Property Advisory Committee (CPAC). The CPAC recommends to the president whether import restrictions should be adopted. The bill would have imposed significant administrative burdens on the CPAC, for it would have required input from collectors and traders of cultural property before the president could comply with requests of foreign nations that the United States prevent the importation of their illegally exported cultural treasures. The bill would have required requesting nations to submit evidence to the CPAC reflecting contemporary pillage before import restrictions could be imposed. It would have changed the status of committee members to provide that all would serve in a representative capacity and would not be considered to be special government employees to whom conflict-of-interest provisions apply. Sponsors of the bill wanted the CPAC to consist of eleven members representing four categories of interested parties: museums, archaeologists/anthropologists, dealers, and the public. They wanted a provision that would define a quorum to include at least one member from each category. In addition, they wanted the act to be amended to provide that the president could not act without a recommendation from the committee. Because, to have a quorum, a member from each category would have had to be present, the effect of such a provision would have been that dealer representatives could have prevented the CPAC from acting by refusing to attend meetings of the committee. As the CPAC could not act, so the president could not act. The Metropolitan Museum of Art presented a position statement in which it lent support to the "thrust" of the bill, particularly the provisions that would have required nations seeking import restrictions to provide more information about the material they sought to protect and the provision permitting outside parties an opportunity to provide comments on the findings and recommendations of the committee before the president could act on the committee's recommendations. The museum also supported the provision clarifying that all members of the committee would serve in a representative capacity and would not be considered special government employees. Even though the museum's position paper affirmed its support of principles of the 1970 UNESCO Convention and its deep sympathy "with the problem faced by many countries with regard to the looting of antiquities and destruction of ancient sites," the paper expressed support of administrative restrictions that would have made it impossible to enforce principles of the 1970 UNESCO Convention. Fortunately the Moynihan bill was not enacted. My concern is that the museum community did not come out in force to oppose it and that officials of one of the most prestigious U.S. museums endorsed it.

Members of the CPAC are appointed by the president and serve staggered three-year terms. Curiously, in July 2003, an entirely new committee was established. The eleven appointed members (all appointed in 2003) included three international sales experts and three members of the public.

In 1995, the International Institute for the Unification of Private Law (UNIDROIT) Convention on Stolen or Illegally Exported Cultural Property was adopted in Rome. The convention provides a substantial benefit for owners whose property is stolen by its attempt to tighten the market so as to avoid the present easy passage of stolen goods into the licit market. The United States has not ratified this convention. Among the chief opponents of its adoption in the United States are some leading members of the museum community. The Parliamentary Assembly of the Council of Europe regards the 1995 UNIDROIT Convention as an important contribution to the preservation of cultural heritage of humanity and fully endorses it. It calls upon members of the Assembly to work toward ratification of the convention in their own parliaments.[34]

Cultural patrimony is inalienable, and cultural objects have their greatest value to society when they remain, and can be studied, in their place of origin. All nations, as well as the international museum community, must accept, either based simply on a "moralistic" theory of what is right and justifiable or on the recognition of a crucial necessity to protect and conserve the cultural heritage, that nations, and museums, must join together to help protect and preserve each country's treasures. Such protection and preservation does not translate to a right to take another country's cultural patrimony. It is peculiar indeed that many leading museum officials have not encouraged such a national demeanor and even have condoned, indirectly at least, the trafficking in cultural treasures. Museum officials must begin to follow a stricter code of ethics with regard to their acquisitions. Provisions of the Code of Ethics adopted by the International Council of Museums should provide the example for all museums.

Another example of the failure of many museums to subscribe to and follow ethical principles in their accessioning policies is the past and continuing failure of many leading museum officials to acknowledge that museums should not acquire nor retain Holocaust-looted artworks. It is my opinion that the museum community's tolerance of museums having Holocaust-looted artworks in their collections represents participation in the "crime against humanity" symbolized by the Holocaust. Many leading museum officials continue to refuse to return looted Jewish cultural property that became a part of their collections either as a result of the museums having purchased the property through the international market or having received such property through donations from art collectors who acquired the property in the illicit (or licit?) market.[35] Although many museum officials have begun to recognize a moral obligation to return Holocaust-looted artworks in their museum collections and have offered to open their collections to the Jewish community to determine what works were indeed stolen and, thus, should be restituted, overall the process of returning looted Jewish cultural property has been slow.[36]

Two important recent cases involving rights of possession to Holocaust-looted artworks illustrate the current thinking of courts that society can no longer sanction the use of legal theories to justify the continued possession of property illegally taken by the Third Reich.

In *United States v. Portrait of Wally*,[37] the United States is seeking forfeiture of an Egon Schiele painting, *Portrait of Wally*, which was brought into the United States to be exhibited at the Museum of Modern Art in New York and which was on loan from the Leopold Foundation in Vienna. The facts in the case established that the painting was taken from Lea Bondi Jaray, a Viennese Jew, when Germany annexed Austria in 1938 as part of the "aryanization" of property owned by Austrian Jews.[38] Bondi went to the Belvedere Museum in Vienna after the war and claimed *Wally* as hers, but received no reply. Dr. Rudolph Leopold, a collector of Schiele paintings, later visited Bondi in London to ask for her help in buying Schiele paintings and mentioned that *Wally* was hanging in the Belvedere even though it belonged to her. Bondi then asked Dr. Leopold to explain to the Belvedere on her behalf that the painting was her property. Dr. Leopold subsequently acquired *Wally* from the Belvedere and did not tell Bondi. She discovered he had obtained *Wally* in or about 1957 when the painting was featured in a catalogue for an exhibition and Dr. Leopold was listed as the owner. In 1994, Dr. Leopold sold *Wally* to the Leopold Museum of which he is a director.[39] A federal district judge has ruled, in *Portrait of Wally*, that the United States can pursue its claim that the Leopold violated American law by bringing a stolen painting into the United States and, thus, that the painting is subject to civil forfeiture.[40]

In *Republic of Austria v. Altmann*,[41] the Supreme Court recently affirmed a decision of the Ninth Circuit Court of Appeals that a U.S. court has jurisdiction to hear a claim of a victim of the Holocaust as against the Republic of Austria. Maria Altmann brought a claim against the Republic of Austria for the recovery of six Gustav Klimt paintings the Nazis took from her now-deceased Jewish uncle, Ferdinand Bloch.[42] The Republic of Austria contended it was immune from the jurisdiction of U.S. courts because much of the alleged wrongdoing took place as of 1948, at which time it would have enjoyed absolute sovereign immunity from suit in U.S. courts. It alleged that nothing in the Foreign Sovereign Immunities Act,[43] which was enacted in 1976 and under which Maria Altmann asserted jurisdiction, retroactively divested it of immunity.[44] The Ninth Circuit Court of Appeals had affirmed the decision of the district court that a foreign state is not immune from the jurisdiction of U.S. courts when the issue is whether rights in property were taken in violation of international law. The Ninth Circuit decided that Austria could not expect immunity in light of its complicity in, and perpetuation of, the discriminatory expropriation of the Klimt paintings.[45] It noted that the seizures violated both Austria's and Germany's obligations under the

1907 Hague Convention on the Laws and Customs of War on Land and that Austria's Second Republic officially repudiated all Nazi transactions in 1946. Thus, the Ninth Circuit ruled, and the Supreme Court affirmed, that Austria was not immune from suit in U.S. courts.[46]

There are numerous international agreements in place, some prior to World War II and many others after, that prohibit pillage during military conflicts.[47] Among these are the 1907 Hague Convention on the Laws and Customs of War on Land, which provides that an enemy's property cannot be seized unless the seizure is "imperatively demanded by the necessities of war,"[48] and the 1919 Treaty of Versailles, which required Germany to make restitution of objects taken during the war where it could identify them in territory belonging to Germany or its allies.[49] In addition, in the 1943 London Declaration, the Allies cautioned nations that all transfers of, or dealing with, property taken by the Axis powers could be declared invalid. The Nuremberg Charter included as a war crime the plunder of public or private property during a military conflict. The Nuremberg Tribunal ruled that Germany had engaged in an illegal war of aggression and branded the looting of Jewish property as part of their persecution and, thus, a crime against humanity.[50] The United Nations General Assembly later passed a resolution recognizing the Nuremberg Charter and Judgment as part of the body of general international law that binds all nations.[51]

In 1998, the Washington Conference on Holocaust-Era Assets unanimously adopted principles relating to Nazi-confiscated art wherein the participating nations pledged themselves to identify art that had been confiscated by the Nazis and not restituted and to take steps to achieve a "just and fair solution" with respect to such art. It stated that efforts should be made to establish a central registry of information regarding such art and that alternative dispute resolution mechanisms should be developed to resolve ownership issues. In 1999, the Parliamentary Assembly of the Council of Europe unanimously adopted a resolution that recognized that, while there were moves early after the end of the Second World War to find and return Jewish looted property, much still remains in private and public hands. The Assembly invited the parliaments of all member-states to give immediate consideration to ways in which they could facilitate the return of looted Jewish cultural property. It specifically stated that attention should be given "to the removal of all impediments to identification such as laws, regulations or policies which prevent access to relevant information in government or public archives, and to records of sales and purchases, customs and other import and export records."[52] It provided specifically that entities "in receipt of government funds which find themselves holding Jewish cultural property should return it."[53]

In the Vilnius Forum Declaration, issued at the Council of Europe conference held in Vilnius, Lithuania, in October 2000, governments were asked "to undertake every reasonable effort to achieve the restitution of cultural assets looted during the Holocaust era to the original owners or their heirs."[54] It asked governments, museums, the art trade, and other relevant agencies to provide all information necessary to such restitution.

What should be the role of the international museum community? The Parliamentary Assembly of the Council of Europe has urged the advancement of the recovery of looted Jewish cultural property "before the last of those persons from which it was taken has died."[55] The international museum community should recognize its moral obligation to advance the recovery of this looted property and give immediate consideration to a means that will assure the repatriation of all remaining stolen Jewish cultural property in museum collections. The decisions in *Portrait of Wally* and *Altmann* illustrate that courts may no longer countenance the legal arguments museum directors have relied upon to retain in their collections artworks with Holocaust-related gaps in provenance. If widespread litigation eventually will force U.S. and European museums to return Holocaust-looted art, museum officials should take the ethical approach and return these artworks prior to courts forcing them to do so after long, tedious, and expensive litigation.

Current law provides protections for cultural property, but there are impediments to an effective international legal regime for the preservation of the cultural heritage. Some of the problem is that laws in countries that follow the civil law differ from those in common law countries. In addition, while there are international conventions to provide for the protection of cultural property, many countries have not ratified the conventions either in whole or in part.[56]

Common law countries have more effective legal means of preventing the illicit trafficking in cultural property than do civil law countries. The common law, the English *nemo dat* rule, which is codified in the United States in Article 2 of the Uniform Commercial Code,[57] provides that one who purchases property from a thief, no matter how innocently, acquires no title to the property.[58] The title remains with the true owner. One U.S. court commented that this law "stands as a bulwark against the handiwork of evil, to guard to rightful owners the fruits of their labors."[59] The effect of this rule is that purchasers of stolen cultural property potentially are exposed indefinitely in the United States to claims of true owners. This is equally a problem for museums that have looted property in their collections.

The common law rule contrasts with most civil law states where a possessor can obtain title through a limitations period. Countries whose legal systems are based on Roman law generally permit a period of five years after a theft for a legal owner to recover the goods from an innocent purchaser. After that period of time, the purchaser has good title to the property. Still, the person or entity who purchased the property must have been a "good faith" or "innocent" purchaser for the limitations period to begin to run.

In the United States, in all states except New York and California, a purchaser of stolen cultural property also can acquire good title to the stolen property at the expiration of a statute of limitations on the true owner's claim.[60] However, the statute of limitations does not begin to run until the true owner knew or, by the exercise of due diligence, should have known of the possessor's identity.[61] Thus, there can be a cut-off of a victim's title after a certain number of years as is the case in civil law countries if a court decides an owner has not exercised due diligence in pursuing the owner's claim.[62]

In New York, case law has long protected the rights of owners whose property has been stolen, allowing recovery even if it is in the possession of a good faith purchaser. As the court ruled in *Guggenheim Found. v. Lubell*,[63] the statute of limitations does not begin to run against a true owner's claim until the true owner makes demand of a good faith purchaser for return of the property and the possessor refuses to return it. In New York,[64] and in California by statute,[65] limitation on the time during which a rightful owner can bring a claim to recover stolen property does not begin until the rightful owner asserts a claim to the property and the current possessor refuses to return the property. Courts in New York have decided that this rule is preferable to the discovery rule, which is applicable in other states, because it "gives the owner relatively greater protection and places the burden of investigating the provenance of a work of art on the potential purchaser."[66]

Courts in the United States have "balanced the equities" between a victim of a theft and an innocent purchaser of the stolen property, when victims have brought claims for restitution of stolen cultural property. The courts initially tilt the balance in favor of theft victims because the courts have recognized the extraordinary obstacles persons who suffer from art and other cultural property looting confront in locating their property through the "labyrinth of the international art market."[67] When, as between a dispossessed owner and a good faith purchaser of cultural property, equities are balanced in favor of the dispossessed owner, a higher standard of diligence is imposed on the purchaser. Thus, both for legal reasons and ethical concerns, museum officials must exercise due diligence in investigating the provenance or title to a work prior to its acquisition. This due diligence requirement also should extend to a review of the history of works already accessioned.

Laws in the United States have not in the past prevented purchasers from acquiring good title to illegally exported artifacts.[68] A purchaser's possession of an illegally exported artifact generally was not disturbed in the past if the artifact was not stolen.[69] Still, many countries now have patrimony laws that declare state ownership of all property found at their archaeological sites.[70] After a country enacts such a patrimony law, courts can apply the National

Stolen Property Act[71] to punish encroachments upon what then becomes legitimate and clear ownership rights to imported artifacts, as noted in *United States v. Schultz.*[72] If a foreign country asserts legal title to artifacts located within its boundaries, courts may apply the NSPA to the illegal importation of such artifacts even though agents of that nation may never have physically possessed the artifacts.

While the law is evolving to provide for blanket legal protection for cultural treasures and, as part of this protection, a halt to the illegal trafficking in cultural property, there still are problems. The legal issues relating to claims for restitution of illegally exported cultural property, as well as for Holocaust-looted art, are complex and difficult to administer, principally because of their fragmented nature. There not only are differences in laws in civil law countries from those in common law countries, but there also are differing laws within the civil law and the common law countries. Further, some countries have adopted the international conventions that protect cultural property in whole or in part whereas others have not.[73] When a country or victim brings a claim for restitution of stolen or illegally exported property, legal principles can become barriers to a just and fair solution. An example is the initial, difficult problem of deciding which country's laws apply. To solve this predicament, ethical considerations should predominate and should be applied in the context of a dispute resolution mechanism established by the international museum community to resolve ownership issues relating to artworks and other cultural property in museum collections.

Museums officials must feel an obligation to inform potential claimants of works in their collections that have questionable provenances. They should not employ legal principles, such as burden of proof or statute of limitations defenses, to prevent the true owners the right of redress. If a victim, whether an individual or another nation, can show ownership of a work in a museum's collection, the museum should acknowledge its ethical duty to return the object. Hopefully, in this first half of the twenty-first century, museum officials will come forward and affirmatively endorse and implement the principles set out in the ICOM Code of Ethics so as to prohibit effectively the direct or indirect illicit trade in cultural properties. All museum officials must recognize an ethical obligation to repatriate those objects in museum collections that have been acquired through questionable, if not illegal, means and, thus, should return such objects to their rightful owners. Once this occurs, museums can step forward to take leadership in a more clearly defined and more effective international effort to protect cultural property. Museums then, but only then, will be the respected voice for the protection of the cultural heritage of humanity.

NOTES

1. ICOM Code of Ethics for Museums, 3.2.
2. ICOM Code of Ethics for Museums, 3.2.
3. Code of Ethics for Museums 2000, American Association of Museums, Collections.
4. Code of Ethics for Museums 2000, American Association of Museums, Collections.
5. See Sherry Hutt, "Cultural Property Law Theory: A Comparative Assessment of Contemporary Thought," in *Legal Perspectives on Cultural Resources*, ed. Jennifer R. Richman and Marion P. Forsyth (Walnut Creek, Calif.: AltaMira Press, 2003), wherein Sherry Hutt discusses six theoretical approaches to cultural property law: internationalist, nationalist, moralist, property, scientific, and market.
6. Declaration at www.thebritishmuseum.ac.uk/newsroom/current2003/universalmuseums.html.
7. Declaration at www.thebritishmuseum.ac.uk/newsroom/current2003/universalmuseums.html.
8. Declaration at www.thebritishmuseum.ac.uk/newsroom/current2003/universalmuseums.html.
9. Geoffrey Lewis, "The Universal Museum: A Special Case?" *ICOM News* 57, no. 1 (2004): 3.
10. *United States v. An Antique Platter of Gold*, 184 F.3d 131 (2nd Cir. 1999), *cert. denied*, 528 U.S. 1136 (2000).
11. Brief of Amici Curiae American Association of Museums, et al., In Support of the Appeal of Claimant Michael H. Steinhardt, prepared by Weil, Gotshal & Manges LLP, New York, Attorneys for Amici Curiae.
12. The country of origin of the Phiale was listed on Customs Form 3461 as "CH," the code for Switzerland.
13. Protection of Works of Artistic and Historical Interest, Law June 1, 1939, n. 1089 (law n. 1089/39).
14. Brief of Amici Curiae American Association of Museums, et al., i and ii.
15. Brief of Amici Curiae American Association of Museums, et al., i and ii.
16. Brief of Amici Curiae American Association of Museums, et al., ii.
17. Brief of Amici Curiae American Association of Museums, et al., iii.
18. Brief of Amici Curiae American Association of Museums, et al., v.
19. Brief of Amici Curiae American Association of Museums, et al., xxxiii.
20. Brief of Amici Curiae American Association of Museums, et al., xiv.
21. Brief of Amici Curiae American Association of Museums, et al., xiv.
22. Brief of Amici Curiae American Association of Museums, et al., lix. Despite the arguments of the AAM, the Second Circuit Court of Appeals affirmed the decision of the district court.
23. *United States v. Schultz*, 333 F.3d 393 (2nd Cir. 2003), *cert. denied*, 124 S.Ct. 1041 (2004).
24. 18 U.S.C. § 2315.
25. 333 F.3d at 396.
26. Schultz met Jonathan Tokeley Parry (Parry), a British national, through a mutual friend in 1992. Parry showed Schultz a photograph of an ancient sculpture of

the head of Pharaoh Amenhotep III, and told Schultz that he had obtained the sculpture in Egypt earlier that year from a man who represented himself to be a building contractor. Parry had used an Egyptian middle-man named Ali Farag (Farag) to facilitate the transaction. Parry had smuggled the sculpture out of Egypt by coating it with plastic so that it would look like a cheap souvenir. He removed the plastic coating once the sculpture was in England. Schultz offered Parry a substantial fee to serve as the agent for the sale of the Amenhotep sculpture. Parry and Schultz then set out to create a false provenance for the sculpture so that they could sell it. They decided they would claim the sculpture had been brought out of Egypt in the 1920s by a relative of Parry and had been kept in an English private collection since that time. Parry and Schultz invented a fictional collection, the "Thomas Alcock Collection," and represented to potential buyers that the sculpture came from this collection. With Schultz's knowledge, Parry prepared fake labels, designed to look as though they had been printed in the 1920s and affixed the labels to the sculpture. Parry also restored the sculpture using a method popular in the 1920s. Parry later sold the sculpture to Schultz for $800,000, and Schultz sold it to a private collection in 1992 for $1.2 million. Parry and Schultz became partners in an effort to bring more Egyptian antiquities into the United States for resale, smuggling them out of Egypt disguised as cheap souvenirs, assigning a false provenance to them, and restoring them with 1920s techniques. Parry was arrested in Great Britain in 1994 and Farag was arrested in Egypt. Each was charged with dealing stolen antiquities. Although Parry was arrested, he, with Schultz, continued to obtain Egyptian antiquities. A jury found Schultz guilty, and he was sentenced to a term of thirty-three months' imprisonment. He appealed his conviction. Upon appeal, seven organizations filed amicus curiae briefs in his defense: the National Association of Dealers in Ancient, Oriental & Primitive Art, Inc., the International Association of Professional Numismatists, the Art Dealers Association of America, the Antique Tribal Art Dealers Association, the Profession Numismatists Guild, the American Society of Appraisers, and an ad hoc group called Citizens for a Balanced Policy with Regard to the Importation of Cultural Property. These groups contended in their briefs that permitting Schultz's conviction to stand would threaten the ability of legitimate American collectors and sellers of antiquities to do business. See discussion at 333 F.3d 396–8.

27. Brief of Amici Curiae Citizens for a Balanced Policy with Regard to the Importation of Cultural Property in support of the Appellant Frederick Schultz prepared by James F. Fitzgerald, Counsel, Arnold & Porter, Washington, DC, attorneys for amici curiae.

28. Brief of Amici Curiae Citizens for a Balanced Policy.

29. 19 U.S.C. § 2601 et. seq.

30. 1982 U.S.C.C.A.N (96 Stat.) 4908, 4100. See Paul M. Bator, "An Essay on the International Trade in Art," *Stanford Law Review* 34 (1982): 275–384, in which the author notes that stolen and mutilated art from the jungles of Central America had been traced into some of America's most respectable museums.

31. 1982 U.S.C.C.A.N. 4100.

32. 19 U.S.C. § 2602. The import restrictions would provide that no designated archaeological or ethnological material exported from the requesting nation can be imported into the United States unless the requesting nation has issued a certificate

that the exportation was not in violation of that nation's laws. 19 U.S.C. § 2606. Any designated archaeological or ethnological material or article of cultural property that is imported into the United States is subject to seizure and forfeiture.

33. *Cultural Property Procedural Reform Act*, S. 1696, *Congressional Record* 146, S11,877, daily ed. (December 15, 2000).

34. Council of Europe Resolution 1205, 17 (November 1999).

35. See paper by Owen C. Pell at the Spring meeting of the Section of International Law and Practice on "The Special Responsibilities of States with Regard to Holocaust Looted Art." Pell contends there is a consensus among scholars and nations that a significant amount of Holocaust-looted art remains in the hands of governments, public institutions, and museums throughout Europe and the United States and that Holocaust-looted art continues to be transferred in the art market without identification or notice of Holocaust-related gaps in provenance. Pell notes that victims of Holocaust looting have faced special and significant factual and legal hurdles in identifying and recovering looted art.

36. The AAM has promulgated guidelines for museums concerning Holocaust-looted property. See America Association of Museums, Guidelines Concerning the Unlawful Appropriation of Objects During the Nazi Era, www.aam-us.org/nazi _guidelines.htm. The guidelines request museums to allocate the necessary funds to conduct research on items in their collection that may have changed hands during the period of 1933–1945 and encourage museums to publicize the provenance of these artifacts. Further, several U.S. museums have websites that list works in their collection with gaps in provenance for the years 1933–1945. See American Association of Museums, Nazi Era Provenance, www.aam-us.org/nazieraprov.htm.

The AAM now has established a Nazi-Era Provenance List, which is a new e-mail discussion group for World War II–era provenance research. The list was created to speed the process of identifying objects in U.S. museums that may have changed hands in Europe during the Nazi era by connecting museum professionals working directly on Nazi-era provenance questions with one another and permitting them to exchange information and share best practices. Membership in the list is limited to museum professionals working in this field.

Recently, the Virginia Museum of Fine Arts gave back the *Portrait of Jean d'Abon* by Corneille de Lyon, to art collector Julius Priester's sole heir, Karl Schlinder of Hampshire, England. Schlinder presented evidence, which included a photograph of the painting and a 1950 police report, to show the painting was stolen by the Nazis in 1944 and to prove his claim of ownership of the painting. The museum acquired the painting in 1950 from a gallery in New York. Upon learning the painting was stolen, the museum willingly returned it to Schlinder. The museum board concluded that returning the painting was "simply the correct thing to do." Schlinder's claim was handled by the New York State Banking Department's Holocaust Claims Processing Office, which, since 1997, has represented claimants seeking restitution of Holocaust-era assets at no cost. See discussion at www.vmfa.state.va.us.

In *Rosenburg v. Seattle Art Museum*, 42 F. Supp.2d 1029 (W.D.Wash. 1999), heirs of Paul Rosenburg filed a complaint against the Seattle Art Museum for return of a $1 million Matisse, which was donated to the museum by the Estate of Bloedel. The Bloedels purchased the painting from a gallery in New York in 1954. Heirs of Rosenburg, a Parisian art collector and gallery owner prior to World War II, alleged the painting was stolen by the Nazis and later possessed by the museum. Upon research into the provenance of the painting, the Seattle Art Museum agreed the Rosenburg heirs were the rightful owners of the painting and returned it to them. The museum then filed a third party complaint against the gallery, which sold the painting to the Bloedels, for breach of title, fraud, and negligent misrepresentation. The court initially ruled the museum did not have standing to sue the gallery for defrauding the Bloedels. It noted that the law in Washington provides that transferring ownership of personal property does not transfer thereby a claim for fraud associated with the purchase of that property. However, it agreed to hear the museum's complaint after the museum obtained an assignment of the Bloedels' fraud claim from the Bloedel heirs. The case then was settled.

37. *United States v. Portrait of Wally*, 105 F. Supp. 2d 288 (S.D.N.Y. 2000) and 2002 WL 553532 (S.D.N.Y. 2002).

38. An art gallery owned by Lea Bondi Jaray was confiscated and given to Friedrich Welz. In 1939 Welz joined the Nazi party and visited Bondi at her apartment. He saw the painting hanging on a wall and "insisted" that the 1938 "arayanization" of Bondi's gallery entitled him to it. Bondi later turned over the painting and fled to London. After World War II, Welz was interned on suspicion of having committed war crimes and his possessions, including artworks, were seized by U.S. forces in Austria. See discussion at 105 F. Supp. 2d 289–90.

39. See discussion at 2002 WL 553532.

40. See 2002 WL 553532.

41. *Republic of Austria v. Altmann*, 317 F.3d 954 (9th Cir. 2002) and 327 F.3d 1246 (9th Cir. 2003), *aff'd*, 124 S. Ct. 2240 (2004).

42. Maria Altmann, who resides in Los Angeles, California, filed her claim in a federal court in California in 2000. She alleged the wrongful taking of six Gustav Klimt paintings, valued at $135 million. Maria Altmann had intended to file her claim in Austria, but, because Austrian court costs are proportional to the value of the recovery sought, she could not afford the filing fee ($135,000 to $350,000). See discussion at 124 S. Ct. 2244–45.

43. 28 U.S.C. §§ 1602–1611.

44. Maria Altmann asserted jurisdiction under § 2 of the Act, 28 U.S.C. § 1605(a)(3), which expressly exempts foreign governments from immunity in certain cases involving "rights in property taken in violation of international law."

45. 317 F.3d at 965.

46. 317 F.3d at 965. The Supreme Court held that the exception to immunity under the Foreign Sovereign Immunities Act applies to conduct, like the Republic of Austria's alleged wrongdoing, that occurred prior to its enactment in 1976.

After the Supreme Court decision, the issue of restitution of the Klimt paintings to Altmann was referred to the Austrian mediation panel. In January of 2006, the panel ordered the Austrian government to return the paintings to Altmann.

The heirs of Kazimir Malevich, the Russian artist, have filed suit in the U.S. District Court in Washington, D.C., *Malevicz, et al v. City of Amsterdam*, Civil Action No. 04-0024, against the City of Amsterdam to recover fourteen valuable Malevich artworks. The complaint sets out the history of how the City of Amsterdam, through its Stedelijk Museum, acquired the historic legacy of Kazimir Malevich. When Malevich's work was condemned by the Nazi regime as "degenerate" art, the works were hidden in the basement of the Berliner Kunstausstellung, where they had been on display and where they remained until Malevich was forced to flee Nazi Germany. After the Berlin exhibition ended, several of the pieces were loaned to the Stedelijk. Some were loaned to the Museum of Modern Art in New York and the Busch-Reisinger Museum at Harvard University. The Malevich heirs have been attempting to recover the artworks from institutions around the world. The Museum of Modern Art and the Busch-Reisinger have returned the works they had in their collections to the heirs. The City of Amsterdam, however, has refused to return any of the works in its possession to the Malevich heirs.

Recently a Restitutions Committee appointed by the Dutch government recommended that the Dutch government return more than 200 old-master paintings to the heir of Jacques Goudstikker, a Dutch Jewish dealer and collector who fled Amsterdam ahead of advancing German troops in 1940. The Dutch government announced in February of 2006 that it would return the paintings because, as Medy van der Laan, the Dutch deputy culture minister, stated, returning the works was the morally correct action. See Alan Riding, "Dutch to Return Art Seized by Nazis," *New York Times*, February 6, 2006.

47. See Pell, "The Special Responsibilities of States with Regard to Holocaust Looted Art." Pell cites *The Nurnberg Trial*, 6 F.R.D. 69, 122, 157–58 (1946).

48. 1907 Hague Convention, Article 23 at 2301–2.

49. 1919 Treaty of Versailles, Section II, Article 238 (June 28, 1919).

50. *The Nurnberg Trial*, 6 F.R.D. 69 (1946).

51. Pell, "The Special Responsibilities of States with Regard to Holocaust Looted Art."

52. Council of Europe Resolution 1205 (November 1999), 11.

53. Council of Europe Resolution 1205 (November 1999), 12.

54. Vilnius Forum Declaration, 1.

55. Council of Europe Resolution 1205 (November 1999), 5.

56. The United States has ratified in part the 1970 UNESCO Convention on the Means of Prohibiting and Preventing the Illicit Import, Export and Transfer of Ownership of Cultural Property. Congress enacted the Convention on Cultural Property Implementation Act, 19 U.S.C. §§ 1601–13, in 1982, effective in 1983, to implement part of the 1970 UNESCO Convention. The act provides that, when a participating nation makes a request to the United States for import restrictions on cultural property from that nation, because the requesting nation contends its cultural patrimony is in jeopardy from pillage of its cultural properties, the president may enter into a bilateral agreement with that nation to apply import restrictions on all cultural property taken from that country.

Congress enacted implementing legislation in 1980 for U.S. participation in the1972 UNESCO Convention for the Protection of the World Cultural and Natural Heritage. 16 U.S.C. § 470a-1. The implementing legislation was part of 1980 amendments to the National Historic Preservation Act, Pub. L. No. 96-515, 1980 U.S.C.-C.A.N. (94 Stat.) 6406. Pursuant to this convention, the United States lists properties of cultural significance within the United States in a "World Heritage List."

The United States has not ratified the 1954 Hague Convention for the Protection of Cultural Property in the Event of Armed Conflict nor the 2002 UNESCO Convention for the Protection of the Underwater Cultural Heritage. (Pursuant to the 1954 Hague Convention, cultural property bears a distinctive emblem, a blue shield, during military conflict to facilitate its recognition. Cultural property being transported and bearing the blue shield is immune from seizure. Monuments bearing the blue shield are subject to special protection during a military conflict.)

57. *Nemo dat quoid non habet.* [He who hath not cannot give.] The *nemo dat* rule is set out in Article 2 of the Uniform Commercial Code at 2.403.

58. See *Menzel v. List*, 267 N.Y.S.2d 804, 819–20 (N.Y. 1966), in which a New York court stated that the "principle has been basic in the law that a thief conveys no title as against the true owner."

59. *Menzel v. List*, 267 N.Y.S.2d 804, 819–20 (N.Y. 1966).

60. In *O'Keeffe v. Snyder*, 416 A.2d 862 (N.J. 1980), the Supreme Court of New Jersey commented that a possessor has the right to retain property except as against the true owner. As the court stated, the only imperfection on a bona fide purchaser's claim is the original owner's right to repossess the property. According to the New Jersey Supreme Court, once that imperfection is removed, the possessor should have good title for all purposes.

61. In *O'Keeffe v. Snyder*, 416 A.2d 862 (N.J. 1980), the New Jersey Supreme Court ruled that the statute of limitations on a suit to recover stolen paintings would begin to run when the true owner "discovers, or by exercise of reasonable diligence and intelligence should have discovered," facts that form the basis of rights of owners whose property has been stolen to recover property even if it is in possession of a good faith purchaser.

62. In *O'Keeffe v. Snyder*, the court decided that an innocent purchaser should be protected from an owner who "sleeps on his rights." 416 A.2d at 857. Thus, the New Jersey Court would place "due diligence" requirements on the true owner. In more recent court decisions, courts have shifted the "due diligence" requirement to the purchaser of valuable cultural property. See, for example, *Autocephalous Greek-Orthodox Church of Cyprus v. Goldberg*, 917 F.2d 278, 294 (7th Cir. 1990) and *Guggenheim Found. v. Lubell*, 569 N.E.2d 426 (N.Y. 1991).

63. 569 N.E.2d 426 (N.Y. 1991).

64. *Guggenheim Found. v. Lubell*, 569 N.E.2d 426 (N.Y. 1991).

65. California has adopted a three-year statutory limitation period that begins to run at "the discovery of the whereabouts of the article by the aggrieved party." Cal. Civ. Proc. Code § 338.

66. *Guggenheim Found. v. Lubell*, 569 N.E.2d at 431.

67. See discussion in Robert E. Madden, "Steps to Take When Stolen Art Is Found in an Estate," *Estate Planning* 24 (1997): 459–64.

68. See discussion in *United States v. McClain*, 545 F.2d 988, 996 (5th Cir. 1977).

69. *United States v. McClain*, 545 F.2d 988, 996 (5th Cir. 1977). In *Peru v. Johnson*, 720 F. Supp. 810, 814 (C.D. Cal. 1989), the court noted that restrictions on the export of certain artifacts are concerned with protection of such artifacts and that such restrictions do not imply ownership. The court commented that possession of such artifacts is allowed to remain in private ownership and that such objects may be trans-

ferred. The court characterized an export restriction as an exercise of the police power of the state. It stated that such restrictions do not create ownership in the state. See also *Jeanneret v. Vichey*, 693 F.2d 259 (2nd Cir. 1982).

The general rule that export restrictions do not prevent a possessor in another country from acquiring good title to such artifacts can be qualified by statutes or treaties. For example, in the United States, the Pre-Columbian Art Act, 19 U.S.C. 2091–2095, provides that any pre-Columbian monumental or architectural sculpture or mural imported into the United States in violation of the act is to be seized and is subject to forfeiture under the U.S. customs laws. The Convention on Cultural Implementation Act, 19 U.S.C. 2601 et. seq., provides that import restrictions will be placed on designated archaeological or ethnological material exported from a nation which requests such restrictions. If such objects are imported into the United States, they are subject to seizure and forfeiture.

70. For example, the trade in antiquities became illegal in Italy in 1939 with the enactment of the Law for the Protection of Works of Artistic and Historic Interests (law n.1089/39). Under this law, all archaeological objects belong to the state unless they were in private ownership prior to 1902. Further, only the state (or a private citizen by special permit) can conduct excavations.

As noted in *United States v. Antique Platter of Gold*, 184 F.3d 131 (2nd Cir. 1999), *cert. denied*, 528 U.S. 1136 (2000), the Egyptian government has declared ownership of all its archaeological artifacts pursuant to its Antiquities' Protection Law 117, which was adopted in 1983.

The 1932 Act with Respect to Antiquities in Greece provides that all antiquities belong to the state. Individuals cannot acquire ownership of antiquities.

In 1926 the Republic of Turkey declared in force and effect a 1906 decree that all antiquities found in or on lands in Turkey were owned by the Republic. Also, in 1926, the Republic adopted a Turkish Civil Code which remains in effect today. Article 697 of the Turkish Civil Code declares that antiquities found on Turkish land are the property of the Republic.

71. 18 U.S.C. §§ 2314–15. The NSPA provides that it is a felony knowingly to sell or receive stolen goods in interstate or foreign commerce.

72. *United States v. Schultz*, 333 F.3d 393 (2nd Cir. 2003), *cert. denied*, 124 S.Ct. 1041 (2004).

73. See discussion in note 56 of U.S. ratification of the international conventions.

5

Connection, Recollection, and Museum Missions

Sherene Suchy

The invitation to write a chapter on museum philosophy for the twenty-first century arrived during a turbulent period of change. I had just finished a book about change management in museums and was preparing to launch it internationally. In the middle of this excitement, my beloved father passed away unexpectedly. This meant relocating from Australia to the United States to act as coexecutor for the family estate. Unexpectedly, the experience offered complex challenges similar to those confronting museum directors. We needed to develop a team with a purpose and philosophy to achieve our estate management goals.[1] This was a serious responsibility, weaving together material and intangible heritage to account for and complete our parent's life journey. We had to make decisions for an estate and collections in a house that resembled a museum without the benefit of registrars, curators, public programmers, conservators, or a manager!

Museums were an integral part of the process. Surprising insights about museums, memory, meaning making, and missions will be shared in this chapter. The insights illustrate the importance of social capital and the social-emotional experience as an underlying philosophy for museums in the twenty-first century. Linda Ferguson, an audience analyst with the Australian War Memorial in Canberra, suggested most museums shy away from contested topics and issues to avoid emotions focusing on history and facts.[2] Emotions do get in the way of dealing with issues but we'll see that, without social-emotional connections, museums become irrelevant.

MEANING MAKING, MISSION, AND MUSEUMS

Death is a major life event. It asks us to assess and reassess the nature of our relationship with the person who is no longer part of our lives in a physical way. It also leaves us with the peculiar task of making sense of the legacy they left. In my case, this meant making sense of a complex family collection (artwork, glass, books, and memorabilia) and the need to create a mission to manage a family heritage project. The collection reflected our parents' combined lives plus the connections and recollections of our grandparents—hence, the title to this chapter. Readers are advised to substitute the name of their organization wherever the word family appears.

Many organizations, particularly museums, function like families. Elaine Gurian, a museum consultant based in the United States, reflected on this metaphor during the 2004 American Association of Museums annual meeting. Described as the "mother of museums," Gurian described how those of us who love museums are integral to the museum family and that we need to let conflicts over source of income (consultants) fade away.[3] Gurian also described the museum's mission as creating contest and context for topics to help visitors develop new insights. Insight happens when we *see* something that arouses an emotional response *and* we are allowed time and space to reflect and meditate on why this makes a difference to us. As described in *Leading with Passion*, learning how to *see* the outer world through art is similar to learning to see the inner world through psychology.[4] We make pictures in our mind's eye, to see destinations for our selves and our organizations. What we see is what we bring to life. Our inner social-emotional perspective shapes our life mission and ultimately the missions we create for our organizations.

Kate Johnson, an educator with the Minneapolis Institute of Art, described museum missions as a process of getting people to *look* carefully, no matter what the topic or object.[5] Reflective thinking and an inner dialogue engage memory to complete patterns. Connection and recollection is about making the best match available in memory. Memories are reconstructed every time we remember. We only recall what we *see* through visual thinking strategies that connect and construct personal meaning. David Anderson, a learning specialist with the Museum of Anthropology at the University of British Columbia in Canada, described measuring visitors' memory seven, fifteen, and twenty years after visits to a cultural site.[6] Out of seven research factors, sociocultural identity was the dominant theme for all museum visitors. The social-emotional aspect of the visit dominated any memory of the exhibitions. Visitors remember who they were with at an exhibition and the quality of the socioemotional connection but very little about the actual exhibition. Deep and lasting memories are anchored in socioemotional connections. Anderson concluded that who we are mediates what we are able to see.

Universities, libraries, and museums are unique organizations. Their missions revolve around intellectual, cultural, and social capital. Delicate to create and sustain, social capital is the trust relationship that must be in place before any serious economic exchange can take place.[7] This was evident in several discussions at the 2004 American Association of Museums annual meeting. One museum advocate described missions as a series of trust relationships with the public, interwoven with complex expectations about truth.[8] An audience analyst with the Australian Museum in Sydney promoted the museum's mission as a learning center reputed as a source of trustworthy information, reliability, credibility, and authority.[9] An art educator at Northern Illinois University observed the trend in contemporary museum missions toward education, and that educators all want to create the same thing—a lasting memory.[10] What are the implications for museum missions when social capital makes the most memorable visitor experience?

CREATING A CONTEXT FOR CHANGE

Successful museum directors in *Leading with Passion* demonstrated the influence of socioemotional connections on change management. Their description of a four-fold change-management role influenced my role as an estate executor. Similar to a museum director, I was entrusted with family heritage (material and intangible). We had to find a way to manage wisely with a shared philosophy and an agreed purpose. We had to learn how to stay grounded in turbulent emotional waters and to accommodate different ways people adapt to change. To shape a meaningful mission, we had to figure out what our family stood for, in our heart of hearts. Despite conflicting views, my mission focused on justice and fairness—to be of service to the family, rather than self-serving. And, similar to a museum, the integrity of the mission was tested again and again.

Fulfilling our mission started with the first part of the four-fold change-management role described in *Leading with Passion*—representing the family story so it honored the way our parents lived out their lives. The same holds true for a museum. Missions are fulfilled in the way the museum's story is represented internally and externally. Our father's passion for collecting spawned stories in the local community about a packrat. This public persona or identity disguised a profoundly different personal purpose. Sue Sturtevant, a health project manager with the Department of Cultural Affairs in New Mexico, reflected on how identity involves what other people think of us—our inner sense of self-worth shapes identity.[11] People and organizations construct identity through the stories we tell. In my case, we needed to connect, recollect, and construct stories that reflected the integrity of our parents' real purpose or mission to sustain vital community support. The same holds true for museums.

The second change-management role focused on creating a context where others could give their best. Our identity as a family had changed without Dad at the center of the relationship wheel. We had lost our director. This change created an identity crisis and unpredictable challenges. Like any team, the family was often at odds as we sorted through conflicting and competing agendas. The team had different gifts and skills to contribute. There were power struggles over who controlled what part of the process and misperceptions about intentions. Borrowing from Esther Orioli's research on emotional intelligence, intentionality is an ability to act deliberately, on purpose, saying what we mean and meaning what we say.[12] Like any team, it took time to align intentions with the mission to create a context where we could give our best. This was never perfect because alignment is never static.

Acting as an ethical entrepreneur was the third change-management role. We had to balance the mission with highly emotional attachments to parts of the family collection and astute asset management to fulfill legal obligations. This role challenged deeply held value systems. Probing questions were raised about priorities. How do we measure heritage value? How do we honor emotional attachment in a way that's fair for all? How do we assess and weigh contradictory values? As I became clearer about my ethics, other's ethics became less clear. There were occasions where it felt like others exercised unethical entrepreneurism at the family's expense.

Nurturing relationships of trust with a range of key stakeholders was the fourth change-management role. Stakeholders included family members and professionals such as the attorney, accountant, financial advisor, estate sales manager, art auctioneers, insurance companies, and the local community or public. We built on the social capital our parents left as their legacy within their community. The local community was one of our key stakeholders. Their ongoing goodwill and trust enabled us to work toward fulfilling our family mission. The same holds true for museums.

CONNECTION AND RECOLLECTION
SHAPES IDENTITY

Connection and recollection is a delicate process. Connection embraces the way we approach relationships. Connection creates support by sharing our real self, expressing care and appreciation, and revealing emotional vulnerability. It relies on trusting others to be trustworthy and to treat us fairly. Recollection is a process of drawing together again things that have been scattered. Recollection is recalling ideas, composing one's thoughts, remembering, and reminiscing for meaning making. The process for our family is reflected in the museum family. It is a creative challenge—finding ways to connect and recollect for insights, meaning making, and memories.

Family estate management, like museum management, is an emotional roller coaster. It's a potent mix of magic and misery. In the same way museums have extraordinary directors and staff, we had extraordinary parents. International travel was a major influence on the family and reflected in the collection. Artifacts we had all forgotten surfaced from dusty footlockers and boxes with labels from Germany, Japan, Iran, Morocco, Greece, England, and regional United States. Family stories were remembered and shared with each piece that came to light. There was magic and pleasure in remembering. We helped each other fill in the memory gaps hoping that, like mortar between bricks, we could shore up the family foundation. We learned to appreciate the different ways we each remember the same event. A pleasurable memory for one person was painful for another. Recollection helped us appreciate the interface between our personal identity, the various places we lived, and family history. We discovered painful differences. For some, our most valuable heritage rested in the stories, not the objects used to tell the stories. For others, the exact opposite was true.

Unfamiliar collections and more boxes surfaced as we cleared the family museum. We had no stories for these objects. It became apparent that, after we lost our mother to cancer, Dad had devoted himself to a renewed interest in collecting paintings, books, and beautiful glass. He nurtured himself with visual beauty, surrounding himself with collections for a sense of security and well-being. Jacqueline Melega, an educator with the Georgia O'Keeffe Museum, described how, through the arts, we develop a greater sense of self—that creativity and self-expression is important for wellness.[13] Dad's passion for collecting fulfilled a deeply felt need for socioemotional connection and, we believe, contributed to his longevity. He became defensive if challenged about the increasing volume, saying it was more productive than sitting on a bar stool! Few people knew the deeper purpose for the expanding collection. Dad was actually buying out estate sales for close friends to financially assist surviving spouses. He also bought out volunteer firemen auctions and church basement rummage sales as a form of community development. Although he loved art and celebrated beauty in all forms, his main mission revolved around social capital—making and keeping trust connections within his community.

The sheer volume of the collection left the family with major decisions. Like a museum, we questioned whether we were prepared to carry it as family heritage or share it in the public domain. We needed help if we were going to release it, and this is where museums played an important role. I would like to acknowledge various museums that played a part in this journey: the Hood River County Historical Museum, the Museum at Warm Springs,

Portland Art Museum, the Evergreen Aviation Museum, the Maryhill Museum, the Denver Natural History Museum, and the Basque Museum. Although often difficult to connect with, museum curators helped clarify collection puzzles so we could make important decisions. We also worked with commercial curators to weigh up art auction values versus precious family heritage. The commercial curators spoke candidly about the importance of connecting and sustaining relationships based on mutual trust. Our connection was tested several times to ensure our mission of justice and fairness stayed aligned during difficult economic decisions.

For example, Dad was a distinguished pilot with the U.S. Air Force. His high altitude flight suit was definitely a collector's piece. More importantly, it had deep sentimental value. No one in the family could think of a way to display and honor the suit until we talked with a curator at an aviation museum. Sensitive to our emotional dilemma, the curator encouraged us to donate the suit along with Dad's extensive archive of documents. This created a project that drew on my old journalism skills. The outcome was a small book called *Wind Beneath Their Wings: A Family Memory Making Workbook*. It was a creative approach to documenting provenience as well as creating a connection between the collection and family recollection.

Jennifer Ellison, a Ph.D. candidate at Carleton University in Canada, described the value of including journalists in exhibition development teams. Journalists have a way of engaging local communities through meaningful narratives because they are not afraid of emotions.[14] Journalists look for the human-interest angle, honoring the emotional side of life because it engages the hearts of others. Journalists encourage emotional responses so viewers can answer an important question: why does this matter to me? The best stories are about transitions in values over time and how we become better people. A story is often more relevant than an object. In our family, stories were part of our healing process. Museums were partners in the process.

MUSEUMS AS SITES FOR HEALING

Museums were a valuable professional and personal resource during this turbulent transition. They offered a life jacket to ride the waves of change. On a personal level, membership with an art museum provided an opportunity to reconnect with paintings my father and I had enjoyed together on previous visits. As companions, we used to move from room to room sharing reflections, seeking out images that touched our hearts. Mihaly Csikszentmihalyi described incorporating museums into a life-management strategy in his research on flow and peak performance. He said cultural institutions are places of undiscovered psychological significance, used by some people to create meaningful order out of life's confusing changes.[15]

What put museums on our social-emotional radar screen? While all museums manage valuable cultural, intellectual, environmental, and financial capital, it was social capital that put museums on our radar screen. Dad and I enhanced our relationship through the pleasure we shared on our visits to museums. We enjoyed the social experience, investing economic capital knowing we would be happy with the return. Without Dad, I continued to invest, but in a different way. The museum's after-hours music program provided a safe, creative context with friends in a new city.

Achieving our estate management mission, with museums as unwitting partners, had a few delightful surprises. One county history museum offered its exhibitions as a way of connecting with the community where our parents lived out their lives. The museum's stated mission was preserving yesterday's heritage for tomorrow. The museum fulfilled its mission on the first visit. As I rounded a corner in the museum with the chair of the board of trustees, a display case caught my eye. A concert program highlighted by a spotlight celebrated an orchestra conductor who played in the community over fifty years ago. I recognized the conductor's name because his successor had been my violin teacher. This recollection led to a reconnection with my teacher who still conducted a local symphony. Our connection led to a donation of musical instruments from our family estate to a youth orchestra, thanks to the museum's founding mothers who had the foresight to save concert programs. Like the text panel in the Basque Museum in Boise said: "The oldest women in the family kept the families together. They had some kind of guiding light." Several months later, we had another opportunity to connect and recollect with this museum through the loan of our grandmother's quilt for a quilt exhibition. Our mother's friends in the local community restored the antique quilt. This led to an article in the local newspaper celebrating the museum's exhibition and the ties that bind quilts and communities together.

SENSING SOCIAL CAPITAL

After months of interaction with museums for professional and personal reasons, it became easier to sense which museums valued socioemotional connections and social capital. Clues surfaced through informal audits and content analysis on museum communications, for example, the visitor interface, team meetings, annual reports, and membership magazines. Museums consciously creating social capital seemed to use a distinctive "co" word vocabulary: commitment, codes, consumers, councils, cooperation, coordination, cohesion, collaboration, coaching, consultation, communication, complexity, constructive, conservation, cognition, contemplation, collection, connection, control, context, consideration, compassion, and competition. Social capital was reflected in observable behavior in the organization's internal culture—*the way we do things around here*. After visiting museums, I use the following questions to sense connection:

Context. How did we physically find this museum? Where did they advertise? What was the main message promoted? Did the message have meaning making for us? Why? Where was the front door? Was it a friendly entrance? How friendly were the reception staff and security guards? Was the lobby area daunting or human scale? Did we feel safe in the museum? If not, what broke the connection?

Communication. How easy was it to navigate communication channels in and around the museum (face to face, phone, printed material, website, and signage)? How did staff respond to interpersonal communication? What tone was used? What tone was used in exhibition text panels? Did signage help us navigate the spaces? Did we feel at ease in the museum? If not, what broke the connection?

Creativity. How creative was the museum in its presentation and programs? Did we feel a deeper appreciation for creativity (human and nature)? Did we feel prompted to express our own creativity? Did we feel inspired? If not, what broke the connection?

Collection. Was the collection brought to life with stories? Did the stories connect objects to people for a greater sense of humanity? Did we feel inspired enough to buy a memory of the collection with an investment in a postcard, catalogue, print, book, sponsorship, or membership? If not, what broke the connection?

Celebration. Was there a sense of mystery? Did we feel connected to life in all its rich diversity? Did the museum celebrate this life force through the visual arts, music, dance, and storytellers? Were we invited to celebrate and did we? If not, what broke the connection?

Cuisine. Was there a restaurant? Did it offer creative and nourishing food? How was the service? How did the ambience feel? How were the prices? Did we feel content with the cuisine experience? If not, what broke the connection?

Community. Was the museum sited in the *heart* of the community? How did we know? Did we know more about the local community as a result of visiting this museum? Was there a space within the museum where we could sit and feel like we belonged? If not, what broke the connection?

CONCLUSION

Managing a family's estate heritage is mirrored in the way museums manage our collective cultural heritage. Our family fulfilled its estate management mission for fairness and justice with joyful and painful insights. On the joyful side, never underestimate the value of socioemotional connections. On the painful side, document life stories while key players are still alive. Objects don't create stories. Stories are created through the connections we create with people who make, use, trade, give, buy, sell, steal, love, neglect, store, reject, rediscover, and restore objects.

In my case, museums provided enriching platforms to connect and recollect around collections (family and museum). Visits to museums in the last year of Dad's life provided precious opportunities for him to review eighty-six years of adventure. Biography is particularly important for older people. It is an obsession in the last stages of life, when people start reviewing their life. They want to make sure the legacy they are leaving is intact. While we are glad for those memories and subsequent partnerships with museums, there is a deep regret. We should have written the stories down while we had a chance. Raking through memory to find provenance is a tough call. We brought our socioemotional connection to museums, but we didn't have tools to make the most of the experience for meaningful memory making.

Kit Grauer and Jill Baird, teachers of cultural identity with the Museum of Anthropology at the University of British Columbia, describe using memory books and visual journals to create and record important personal learning.[16] The journals facilitate memory making through writing and image making in community education programs. The programs are designed to fulfill the museum's cross-cultural mission. First Nations people facilitate public programs with children, visiting the museum with sessions on weaving, plant walks, and story telling. In their words, this facilitates a more open social circle, allowing participants to teach each other who they are, expanding social-emotional filters to create more emotionally enriching social connection.

We need more of this philosophical approach in museums for the twenty-first century. Museums play a unique role in our communities. Although the term social capital evolved out of economic studies, I admire the definition offered by the Dalai Lama. He described our basic nature as social beings and our interdependency as a fact of life: "Meaningful human dialogue can be achieved only through mutual respect or mutual understanding in a spirit of reconciliation."[17] Claudine Brown, an arts programmer at the Nathan Cummings Foundation in New York, suggested that part of a museum's mission involves creating a context where we can describe our human struggles: "Out of this we create a group biography. We change the world as a group, not as single individuals."[18]

Like museums, our family will be retelling stories for years to come, making sense of the legacy our parents left. We cannot put the clock back but we can wind up the future. There is an opportunity window open for museums to consciously create social capital, making meaningful emotional memories with, not for, visitors. Connection ensures the museum's relevance. In the end, relevance is the museum's mission for the twenty-first century.

NOTES

1. Hugh H. Genoways and Lynne M. Ireland, *Museum Administration: An Introduction* (Walnut Creek, Calif.: AltaMira Press, 2003), 24–25.

2. Linda Ferguson, *Contested Sites: The Role of Museums in Contemporary Societies* (presentation, American Association of Museums annual meeting, New Orleans, LA, May 7, 2004).

3. Elaine Gurian, *Contested Sites: The Role of Museums in Contemporary Societies* (presentation and speech, American Association of Museums annual meeting, New Orleans, LA, May 7–8, 2004).

4. Sherene Suchy, *Leading with Passion: Change Management in the 21st Century Museum* (Walnut Creek, Calif.: AltaMira Press, 2004).

5. Kate Johnson, *Memories Are Made of These: Visitors' Cultural Identities and the Museum Experience* (presentation, American Association of Museums annual meeting, New Orleans, LA, May 8, 2004).

6. David Anderson, *Memories Are Made of These: Visitors' Cultural Identities and the Museum Experience* (presentation, American Association of Museums annual meeting, New Orleans, LA, May 8, 2004).

7. Francis Fukuyama, *Trust: The Social Virtues and the Creation of Prosperity* (London: Penguin, 1995).

8. David Carr, *The Promise of Cultural Institutions* (Walnut Creek, Calif.: AltaMira Press, 2003), 109–125.

9. Linda Kelly, *Contested Sites: The Role of Museums in Contemporary Societies* (presentation, American Association of Museums annual meeting, New Orleans, LA, May 7, 2004).

10. Elizabeth Vallance, *Memories Are Made of These: Visitors' Cultural Identities and the Museum Experience* (presentation, American Association of Museums annual meeting, New Orleans, LA, May 8, 2004).

11. Sue Sturtevant, *Building Museum Identity through Community Partnerships* (presentation, American Association of Museums annual meeting, New Orleans, LA, May 9, 2004).

12. Esther Orioli, *EQ Map Interpretation Guide* (San Francisco: Essi Systems, Inc., 1996), 8–16.

13. Jacqueline Melega, *Building Museum Identity through Community Partnerships* (presentation, American Association of Museums annual meeting, New Orleans, LA, May 9, 2004).

14. Jennifer Ellison, *Contested Sites: The Role of Museums in Contemporary Societies* (presentation, American Association of Museums annual meeting, New Orleans, LA, May 7, 2004).

15. Mihaly Csikszentmihalyi, *Flow: The Psychology of Optimal Experience* (New York: Harper and Row, 1990), 235.

16. Kit Grauer and Jill Baird, *Memories Are Made of These: Visitors' Cultural*

Identities and the Museum Experience (presentation, American Association of Museums annual meeting, New Orleans, LA, May 8, 2004).

17. Renuka Singh, ed., *The Dalai Lama: Live in a Better Way* (New York: Penguin Compass, 1999).

18. Claudine Brown, *Contested Sites: The Role of Museums in Contemporary Societies* (presentation, American Association of Museums annual meeting, New Orleans, LA, May 7, 2004).

6

Museums and Restlessness

Jean-Paul Martinon

The central question of this book (what underlying philosophy/mission should museums pursue in the first half of the twenty-first century?) calls for a prediction, the revelation of a secret unbeknown to museums. It calls for a prescriptive utterance that will determine or shape their future. *This is* the underlying philosophy that museums should pursue in the future. And the future is short. This book refers only to the first half of the twenty-first century, a mere forty-four years from 2006. This invitation to prediction raises a number of questions: From which horizon of expectation does this question arise? Are forty to fifty years the maximum length of time a museum's mission statement holds currency? How and from where does one make a statement about the future of museums? Who is entitled to prophesize, predict, or project what will happen to museums in the future? What conception of the future is needed to make such a prediction? What does it mean to predict the future of an institution that retains as its main task that of preserving a heritage *for the future*?

Considering these issues, the only response that can perhaps be put forward to the central question of this book is this: If there is one single "thing" museums should pursue in the first half of the twenty-first century, it is to stop acknowledging that they have a future. Museums have no future and will still have no future in 2050. To address this issue in a satisfactory manner would require a lengthy analysis that cannot be included in such a short chapter.[1] The only argument that this chapter can put forward is, therefore, this: Museums have no future because they can no longer sustain a historical conception of the future; they can only sustain an (a)historical conception of restlessness. How to begin thinking in those terms?

My remark that museums have no future is deliberatively provocative. I am not implying here that museums should be closed or that museums are no longer relevant. I do not imply either that it is impossible to make predictions or that there are no longer any prophets, accountants, or cultural commentators capable of making predictions or projections. Practical decisions have to be made, and these are always based on a certain prosopopoean[2] vision of the future. On the contrary, when I write that museums have no future, this simply means that museums are no longer in a situation to assert what they understand by time and that one can no longer think of the future the way art historians and museum curators formerly thought of the future in the nineteenth century.

The nineteenth century understood time as already interpreted, as a social and historical phenomenon. It defined the future within the context of notions such as succession, periodicity, or duration. As such, the future was conceived as a temporal category within a predetermined structure. It was always a future-present, one that depended on a strict temporal and historical (linear) logic that clearly established what was in the past and what lay (ahead) in the future. The future was one element within the dominant linguistic mode of the time—the narrative. To put it extremely briefly, it conceived the future as another social or historical time (distant or not) that situated itself in the present.

As one of the key institutions of the nineteenth century, the museum was at the center of this structured definition of time. The traditional temporal ideology of the museum was to situate itself in relation to both a past, which it preserved, and a future into which it projected the past it contained. In this way, it turned time into a grand narrative of progress, an inexorable movement that led the visitor through a continuous series of galleries. Inside these arcades, art was segregated into specific and clearly defined movements, orchestrated by a few protagonists. And within this self-creating chain with clear points of rupture and continuance, the future was the unquestioned extension of the grand narrative, one that could only be understood as the continuation of these periodicities and discontinuities. The old teleological process[3] could only lead to projections, predictions, and prophesies.

Today, the museum is forced to think of the future outside of these dusty categories. Beyond the empirical necessities of financial constraints and issues of maintenance, the museum must think of a finer kind of future. The only future it can contemplate today is that of the setting into motion of difference, that which opens itself, that which comes. If the museum is serious about the presentation of its collection, the preservation of "the past," its history, then it must think of the future quite simply, but most definitely, as the opening of space itself, what the philosopher Jacques Derrida understands by *l'à-venir*, the "to-come."[4] This is not "the future" of museums;

this is the museum as it deals with the unravelling of temporality. It is what, inside, but also outside of the museum, in an unidentifiable location, space takes from itself—the way space distances itself within itself and takes place. In other words, it is that which, in the museum, opens space—the space of the work of art, the space of and for the viewer. This has nothing to do with the endless expansion of collections or the museum's ability to open up new galleries, but, rather, concerns the space the museum fosters to maintain its activity, to generate its own distinctive experience. This has also nothing to do with succession, duration, or extension, and certainly not with beginnings, middles, and identifiable ends. This has to do with the unfolding or the exposure that takes place *at every instant*, at every showing. It is the disjointing of temporality here *or* there in the gallery, no matter what or to whom it is exposed.

When thinking of the museum in relation to this unfolding of temporality, one is in fact not thinking of the future (utopian or dystopian) of the museum per se, but of its event, what Derrida understands in another context by the "non-contemporaneity with itself of the living present."[5] This is the only thing a museum can truly understand as its future: that which is to come, the unstable and unidentifiable unfolding that is immanent to the museum's creation and experience.

If the museum abandons its old concept of the future, if it takes into consideration this unravelling of temporality, then it becomes an occurrence or an event that can never form or prefigure a closure (the death of museums) or a presence (a stable or an identifiable museum). The museum is an institution that can only conceive itself as an unstable and unidentifiable form of exposure (in the sense of both display and revelation). The reason for this is simple: The museum is an institution that positions itself at the juncture of endings and openings. I use here the words "openings" and "endings" in order not to confuse them with origins and closures.

On the one hand, the museum is only concerned with the manner in which art or artifacts are "ended." As the International Council of Museums made clear, the museum's function is to acquire, conserve, research, communicate, and exhibit, for purposes of study, education, and enjoyment, material evidence of man and his environment. As such (and on a Foucauldian note), its main role is to bring an end to the errancy of works of art.[6] Everything ends in the museum, and the museum is therefore an institution of endings. This is what made Antoine Quatremère de Quincy and Paul Valéry so famously miserable—museums are mausoleums, repositories of carcasses of bodies that were once alive, whether attached to a cult or as part of an artistic process.[7]

On the other hand, the museum is the place where both the artwork and the viewer also depart. It is the place where, for the viewer, the imagination is let loose, where the world is placed between parentheses in order to pursue a voyage into another world—past, present, or future. It is also the place where the artwork acquires the legitimacy that will open it to a myriad of interpretations to come. The museum is the place of critical and curatorial journeys and trajectories.[8] This is Marcel Proust's well-known argument that the museum *continues* the work of the artwork and that, through the encounter between architecture and art, we find ourselves, as viewers, curators, or art historians, always on an open road where one never knows where one is going.[9]

Right there, on this unstable and unidentifiable spacing of temporality, the museum reveals itself as a dialectical institution. Such a claim should not be seen as referring to the traditional sense of the word "dialectical,"[10] in the way used, for example, by Walter Benjamin in his *Theses On the Philosophy of History*.[11] As is well known, the museum is an institution of the nineteenth century. Unlike the Cabinet of Curiosities, in which objects were assembled randomly, the museum follows a dialectical model that sees its collections either organized chronologically (narrative) or thematically (image), but in all cases through a methodological approach intended to establish either truths or uncertainties. In this way and at its most banal, semantic level, the museum is essentially dialectical. Through its series of rigid or flexible frameworks where time and space are isolated, placed in parentheses, in other words, "aestheticized" by the curator, the museum attempts to make sense of the art or the objects it houses. This is also true of the most avant-garde of museums or public galleries such as, for example, Le Palais de Tokyo in Paris, where the encounter with the work of art supersedes issues of authorship or display. Whatever its function, the museum's aim is always that of making the logos play or work.

Beyond this basic understanding, the word "dialectical" should be understood here, following a tradition first inaugurated by Jean-Luc Nancy, as a word that marks or shapes the difference between openings and endings, a marking that has no proper destination except the sublation[12] (*aufhebung*) to which it is bound. Nancy's interpretation of the term inaugurates a new reading of Georg Wilhelm Friedrich Hegel, one that understands the dialectical, not as an act intended to resolve a contradiction logically, but as an act of receptivity that is also a formative process.[13] Instead of a rigid interpretation of the dialectical, Nancy took up the more plastic[14] (Hegel's *plastische*) interpretation of the word, one which rescues it from the museum of dead ontotheological monuments. The word "dialectical" conceived through the Hegelian prism of plasticity is crucial in the way it disturbs any systematicity, the possibility of teleology itself. The dialectical not only becomes supple and flexible (plastic arts), but also violent and sudden (plastic explosion). The dialectical intertwines the contradictory forces of the teleological and the contingent[15] in an act of deferment.

I have used here this revised interpretation of the word "dialectical" not only because it is at the heart of the museum process, but also because it is inseparable from the future. In her book, *L'Avenir de Hegel*, Catherine Malabou takes up this inaugural reading by Nancy and proposes to reject the usual understanding of Hegel's conception of time. For Malabou, Hegel never perceived time as a "now" amidst a series of "nows," a time in which the future is always a "future-now." Malabou sees Hegel's time as an instance of dialectical differentiation that can only determine itself momentarily, that is, "now." In this way, Malabou refuses to reduce Hegel's time to a continuum of instants. Because it "is structured by several 'nows,' it has the ability to differentiate itself from itself."[16] Hegel therefore understood time not so much as what appears here or there, but as what constitutes a state of "separatedness" and negation that never marks a repetition or a closure. By proposing this interpretation, Malabou's aim is to reject Martin Heidegger's claim that Hegel only understood time in its vulgar sense, that is, as homogeneous and empty. Hegel's time becomes not a point or a time that can only pass or be reiterated or recuperated, but an instantiation of difference. It is, therefore, no longer a time defined by closure (the end of history), but a time necessarily open to the future, to what distances itself from itself, a time that effectively confuses the future and time.

On this unstable and unidentifiable spacing of temporality, the museum turns dialectical (plastic) in the way it brings together, isolates, and restores works of art within its walls, not in an attempt to provide a final eschatological[17] view of aesthetics, history, or humanity, but in order to perpetuate and/ or dislocate the language that animates it. In other words, its role is not to provide a teleological ending to these perceptions, but to constantly present and/or challenge the usual perception of works of art. In this way, the museum does not represent an origin for the work of art (where it acquired meaning), nor does it represent its death (where the artwork loses its original meaning, the one established by the artist in the studio or in its original location by the temple or church). By being located at the juncture of endings and openings, the museum is necessarily involved in a process that sees the constant deferral of works of art (in or out of the storeroom or gallery space). In this way, the museum presents itself through the double bind that informs and justifies its existence—the constant rehanging of art or the constant advent of something new. As such, it positions itself in relation to both the foreseen and the unforeseen—the future as a predictable entity and the future as radically other and, therefore, as an instance that can only be determined in its immediacy. The museum places its treasures right on this process of deferment, this instantiation of space that brings together, *at once*, the teleological and the contingent, that which curators and viewers expect but can never imagine coming.[18] This explains why it is never possible to actually pin down or determine what museums are because they are always at a center of their own redefinition, presenting themselves only in their estranged momentariness. The movement of the museum is one that sustains itself through and with the tension it manages to withhold between its own determination and its annihilation into the universal.

This does not mean that the museum is engaged in a process of eternal rebirth. There is no reference here to a temporality of suspense or to a configuration pregnant with tensions.[19] The museum can no longer be seen as engaged in a temporality of incompletion, of return, a cyclic temporality that extends across the ages. Rather, both the museum and the artworks are engaged in a plastic process, which has no proper destination except the sublation (*aufhebung*) that animates it. When thinking of an art object in the museum, one is not thinking of it as engaged in a reliable process where past informs the future, but on the unstable and unidentifiable opening that is immanent to the creation and the experience of these artworks. In this way, like there is no center to the structure and no origin to trace, there is no stable ground for the museum dialectical process. This does not mean that works of art or museums can only exist in the hell of absolute and infinite relativism. Their plastic character reveals that the abyss they represent, an abyss where interpretation nosedives at every occasion, can only be a true abyss. It is a true abyss because it suppresses the absence of abyss that prevents it to drift into itself. In this way, the dialectical process ruling the museum still manages to shape a history, to plasticize itself into the periodization of what has been sublated.

What we are left with is not the museum as a solid entity, located on a prescribed and self-defining site, declaiming or holding forth the truthfulness of its long-established values. The museum is engaged in a performativity of its own, one which can never establish any form of presence. By being situated at the juncture of endings and openings, by plasticizing itself (molding/dislocating), the museum is in a permanent "state of conjugation," always about to be declined, derived, or inflected. For this reason, the museum is always in a state of dispute and contestation. The museum is not a monolithic monster that rules like a despot over various constituencies. The museum is not conservative, but argumentative in the sense that it always seeks to challenge that which enters the plastic process—that which it first rejects as other (site-specificity in the 1960s, for example) and then welcomes as the same (off-site projects today).

If the idea that the museum is dialectical (plastic) in the sense explored by Nancy and Malabou is acceptable, then how to qualify its operative mechanisms or its future? Not unlike the archive, there is a spectral messianicity at work in the concept of the museum.[20] The museum, following Derrida's famous interpretation of the archive in his commentary on Yosef Yerushalmi's monologue with Freud, is also tied to the very singular experience of the promise.

Until the nineteenth century, the museum promised to be the keeper of a nation's heritage and to educate the masses. This dual character can be found, for example, in the mission statement of the South Kensington Museum (now the Victoria and Albert Museum in London), which stated both the necessity to expand the collection constantly (enlarge the nation's heritage) and the imperative to keep a policy of low admission charges and late opening hours for the working classes. As such, the main imperative of the museum was essentially messianic. However, and this is what marks the change from the time of Walter Benjamin, this power is no longer redemptive. The education of the masses no longer rescues them from their miserable existences. Today, the museum offers only experiences, and the spectator wants only to be impressed. As such, the museum has lost the redemptive quality that society endowed it with at its creation.

In a time when time has ceased to represent something fixed and stable, something reliable pointing to a single direction, the only thing a museum can do is to maintain this promise in a state of radical indecisiveness. The museum does not promise the perfect world of art or that, one day, there will be no more museums. The museum's promise is a promise without determinate content. In order to understand this, we may turn to Derrida's careful rephrasing of Benjamin's messianism.[21] Derrida's messianicity without messianism represents the continual commitment to keep open the relation to the other. This promise is crucial as it prevents any presence from being closed around itself. The museum always says to artists and viewers: "Yes, come. There is (a) future here." In this way, all action performed by the museum is ruled by the promise, a vacuous promise, of an always postponed education. As Ernest Laclau remarked in his review of Derrida's *Spectres of Marx*: "We can do away with the teleological and eschatological dimensions, we can even do away with all the actual contents of the historical messianisms, but what we cannot do away with is the 'promise,' because the latter is inscribed in the structure of all experience."[22] The museum, as the institution safeguarding a heritage for the future, is at the center of this noneschatological and nonredemptive promise.

This messianic dimension of the museum does not therefore depend on any form of messianism. It does not know what art is, but it keeps the promise that the museum is the place where the answer is. And the museum insists that this can happen at any time, to the viewer at any visit and to the artist on the occasion of a commission, an exhibition, or a purchase. In this way, the museum places itself as the type of institution that allows its existence to be always defined by the other. Its identity always comes from the other, that is, from the future. The way it recuperates artistic practices (for example, feminist or non-Western artistic practices in the 1980s and 1990s) shows that the museum constitutes itself on the pretence that its reason to *be* comes exclusively from the outside, from the other, from that which has not yet been created or entered into its process.

The messianicity of the museum is to allow the other to come. The museum's messianic power is to withhold the certainty that it will always be able to expose itself to the absolute surprise, to the radically new. It always wavers between an "it is coming" and a "is it coming?", between a call and a response. Contrary to common understanding, the museum is not an archival institution in the sense of a repository of past events. Because it is engaged in the daily business of staging performances and catering to an ever-increasing audience, the museum is always positioning itself within a performative structure, always engaged in its own event. Not unlike the archive, the museum is always tied to the "question of the future, the question of the future itself, the question of a response, of a promise and of a responsibility for tomorrow."[23] In this way, the museum maintains its promise not between a teleological opening onto the contingent (what Benjamin referred to as revolutionary chance) and a messianic *cessation* of happening (the eschatological or the—perpetual—Last Judgement[24]), but between its plasticity and a messianic *structure* of happening.

Considering this situation, can the museum still hold a sense of the temporal and of its role in respect of the future? Without past and without future, the museum can only remain permanently on edge. It can no longer articulate itself in any other way, but as in a state of restlessness. This does not mean that the museum or the works it houses are always desperate to leave its site, to leave La Gare Saint Lazare and literally go on journeys to Balbec.[25] Restless simply means "unable to be still." The museum is unable to be still *on site*. The fact that it is restless *on site* and not in relation to or in the direction of *other sites* is crucial as the site itself is the emblem of modernity. It defines the museum as the only structure that the Western world knows to organize itself, its art, its histories, and ideologies. The Musée d'Orsay in Paris epitomizes this site: it was a site of departures; it is still a site of departures, only, now, no one physically ever departs. In this way, and against Proust who understood time as a stream, a modeled or modulated duration, the museum offers thrills and uncertainties, states of excitability and disappointments, that never amount to a journey as such. On these busy sites, the museum is what it does. Its act is that of keeping a promise, of keeping "the door" open, and of repeating and/or returning the call "yes, come." The aim of this double act is to maintain the tremor that animates it, the deferment or the differentiation that leads the museum to maintain itself as museum. It is through this act, through this restlessness, that the museum plasticizes history and that historiography takes place.

NOTES

1. I am currently finishing a book, titled *Of Times To Come*, that addresses these issues in detail.

2. In the sense of a figured or calculated future.

3. As is well known, the museum often presents history in a teleological fashion, that is, as a series of articulated frameworks that advance by themselves and have a single unifying destiny.

4. Jacques Derrida, *Archive Fever: A Freudian Impression*, trans. Eric Prenowitz (Chicago: University of Chicago Press, 1996), 68.

5. Jacques Derrida, *Spectres of Marx, The State of the Debt, the Work of Mourning & the New International*, trans. Peggy Kamuf (London: Routledge, 1994), xix.

6. See the opening pages of Michel Foucault, *Madness and Civilization: A History of Insanity in the Age of Reason*, trans. Richard Howard (London: Routledge, 1993).

7. Antoine Quatremère de Quincy, *Considerations morales sur la destination des ouvrages de l'art* (Paris: Arthème-Fayard, 1989); and Paul Valéry, "The Problem with Museums," in *Degas, Manet, Morisot*, ed. Douglas Cooper and trans. David Paul (London: Routledge and Paul Kegan, 1972).

8. Theodor Adorno, "The Valéry Proust Museum," in *Prisms*, ed. and trans. Samuel and Sherry Weber, 175–77 (Cambridge: Cambridge University Press, 1981).

9. Marcel Proust, *Within a Budding Grove*, trans. C. K. Scott Moncrieff (London: Chatto, 1960), 310–11.

10. In the sense of the tension or the contradiction between two conflicting or interacting forces, elements, or ideas. In Walter Benjamin's case, between a theological and a Marxist conception of history.

11. Walter Benjamin, "Theses on the Philosophy of History," in *Illuminations*, ed. Hannah Arendt and trans. Harry Zohn (London: Pimlico, 1973).

12. The Hegelian verb "*aufheben*," usually translated with "to sublate," is used in the sense of "to raise," "to hold," "to lift up." The term "sublation" refers here to the necessary process by which something is never left to rest.

13. Jean-Luc Nancy, *The Speculative Remark (One of Hegel's Bons Mots)*, trans. Céline Surprenant (Stanford, Calif.: Stanford University Press, 2001); and Jean-Luc Nancy, *Hegel, The Restlessness of the Negative*, trans. Jason Smith and Steven Miller (Minneapolis: University of Minnesota Press, 2002).

14. The word plastic is derived from the Greek "*plassein*," which means "to model" and/or "to mold." As an adjective it is what is malleable and what has the power to mold.

15. The word "contingent" is used here in relation to what is dependent on or results from a future as yet unknown.

16. Catherine Malabou, *L'Avenir de Hegel, Plasticité, Temporalité, Dialectique*, trans. Jean-Paul Martinon (Paris: Vrin, 1996), 29.

17. That is, a view where aesthetics, history, and humanity arrive at an end.

18. For the importance of the words "at once," see Jacques Derrida, "Le temps des adieux: Heidegger (lu par) Hegel (lu par) Malabou," *Revue Philosophique de la France et de l'Etranger* 188 (1998): 6. Translated by Jean-Paul Martinon.

19. Jean-Louis Déotte, "Rome, the Archetypal Museum and the Louvre, the Negation of Division," in *Art in Museums: New Research in Museum Studies: An International Series*, ed. Susan Pearce, 215–32 (London: Athlone Press, 1995); for a more comprehensive analysis of the relationship between Benjamin and Nietzsche, see Jean-Louis Déotte, *Le musée, l'origine de l'esthetique* (Paris: L'Harmattan, 1993).

20. The concept of "spectral messianicity" is explored by Derrida in *Archive Fever*, 36.

21. Derrida's reading of Benjamin's messianism can be traced back to Khôra 1995, *Specters of Marx* 1994, Marx and Sons 1999, and most recently in *La philosophie au risque de la promesse* 2004. Jacques Derrida, "Khôra," in *On the Name*, ed. Thomas Dutoit and trans. Ian McLeod (Stanford, Calif.: Stanford University Press, 1995); J. Derrida, "Marx and Sons," in *Ghostly Demarcations, A Symposium on Jacques Derrida's Specters of Marx*, ed. Michael Sprinker and trans. G. M. Goshgarian (London: Verso, 1999); and J. Derrida, "Questions à Jacques Derrida," in *La philosophie au risque de la promesse*, ed. Marc Crépon and Marc de Launay (Paris: Bayard, 2004).

22. Ernest Laclau, "The Time Is Out of Joint," *Diacritics* 25, no. 2 (1995): 90.

23. Derrida, *Archive Fever*, 74.

24. For an analysis of how W. Benjamin's *Last Judgement* can be repeated ad infinitum, see Ian Balfour, "Reversal, quotation (Benjamin's History)," *Modern Language Notes* 106 (1991): 622–47.

25. Proust, *Within a Budding Grove*, 311.

7

Philosophy and the Ends of the Museum

Donald Preziosi

> Everything of significance to museology has already been said.

Everything or every issue that can be adequately (or inadequately) (re)presented in a museum has already appeared, or is about to appear under conditions we can surely specify in advance. We inhabit a world where virtually anything can be contained in a museum, and where virtually anything can convincingly (or not) serve *as* a museum. Even expanding our definition of museology so that a museum becomes a *when* rather than a *what* seems to bring little relief from the contemporary (but it's been there all along) problem—philosophical no less than institutional—that constitutes the museum in the first place, or at the end of the day. The question that requires our attention is the most basic one, effectively obscured by the discourses in and about the museum, namely: What kind of world is that? What kind of world is prescribed, defined, and proscribed by the museum? How has it come about, whom does it service, and whom does it do a disservice? Can it possibly have a future, which is dissimilar from a present, which is inescapably an allomorph or predictable fractal version of all its pasts?

At least three decades have been devoted to celebrating, ignoring, and/or regretting the putative ends, rebirths, or aftermaths of art, art history, or museology, or the endlessly celebrated returns to or flights from "art" or "the object," or the rediscoveries (or the putting behind us) of aesthetics, fetishisms, social histories, formalisms, and contextualisms, and the endlessly contorted reformatting of "relations between" the perennially specious

69

antitheses of "subjects" and "objects"; after all this, what remains? Why yet another forecast of museological "philosophies" or ideologies? Isn't the ideological project, which naturalizes the idea that a museum is the "practice" of a certain theory or philosophy, the problem in the first place?

It is notable that, in professional museum literature over the past few decades, there has been virtually no projection of the institution's future missions or philosophies that has not been more of the same, or not simply better, versions of the safely familiar. Its future continues to be conceived almost exclusively in an instrumental manner—as technically more refined versions of public edutainment and infotainment, or as more "responsive" and "representative" versions of whatever forms of social and cultural diversity seem to be required in increasingly more diverse communities, cities, and countries.

There seems to have been, at least among "insiders" or museum professionals, an endemic, across-the-board abandonment of critically engaged and historically responsible attention to fundamental questions about the functions and social and political roles of museums. The disjunction between the "external" critical and philosophical literature relating to museums, museology, and collecting and that emanating from "within" the profession is very great and growing.

This dismal situation is not sudden but has been building over the past several decades. It has been punctuated periodically by conferences and publications devoted to projecting the museum's future(s), in both utopian and dystopian modalities; the museum's present is articulated as the future anterior of what it shall have become. In 1999 a major international conference was held at the Tate Museum in London (now the Tate Britain) on the future of the museum institution (specifically the "art" museum). What the large audience was presented with, with one or two academic exceptions, was a parade of talks by museum curators and directors vying with each other over the size of their budgets and endowments, complete with power point presentations charting the economies of newly expanded and upgraded facilities. The conference moderator (shortly to assume the directorship of the new Tate Modern museum) pointedly refused to engage questions or comments from participants onstage or from the (increasingly frustrated and vociferous) audience members on the floor—many of them prominent museum professionals, collectors, artists, critics, and academics—regarding more substantive issues about the institution and its roles and missions. Indeed, any comment or remark even remotely "theoretical," "critical," "historical," or "philosophical" was either pointedly ignored or loudly overridden and smoothed over in boilerplate platitudes.

Yet, in fact, the "philosophical future" of the institution was being articulated in plain sight: as a technical evolution; as a future defined simply by technological "excellence" in "delivering" cultural "content" (of whatever kind) to public constituencies; and constituencies envisioned as fundamentally similar to those crafted for other consumerist media, other modes of public entertainment, or sport. The philosophy of the museum in the twenty-first century articulated so poignantly at the Tate by the major directors of the world's major museums was being written, quite literally, in stone—a content-free and ethically vacuous philosophy of "excellence." Yet the philosophy of twenty-first century museums articulated in London at the end of the last century was not a new jargon but a very old one—a politics of hypercommodification and super-hyped consumption, written in an upgraded and "globalized" (that is, neofeudalist) fantasy language of corporate accountancy. The language at a cursory glance seems new, but the underlying syntax replicates existing hegemonic relations of power.

Nothing has changed in the half-decade since that remarkable (and, perhaps for the sake of the intellectual reputation and integrity of the organizers, safely unpublished) conference, which was called "The Future of the Art Museum." It simply articulated the facts of institutional power—that the train of museological progress as currently redefined had already left the station. The implication was clearly that anyone with any sense would scramble to climb aboard or risk being run over or left behind in the builder's dust of recapitalization, reconstruction, and refurbishment.

After several decades of extensive critical discussion and public debate in many countries, and in light of there having been more published on the museum in those decades than in the entire previous history of the institution, nothing has changed; nothing of substance has happened. Museums have instead learned to present more effectively than ever a façade of change and progress without, in any significant way, altering existing relations and structures of power or deviating from the scenarios and dramaturgies of identity politics and the commodification and fetishization of the modern self. Museums seem to have needed to be seen as having changed while avoiding any more than cursory engagement with the critical, theoretical, and philosophical literature of the past several decades dedicated to the institution of the museum and the profession of museology. While reading any expert insider literature in professional journals is often a lesson in provincial thinking in a larger vacuum, the literature of museology seems almost pathologically isolated and disengaged.

New museum architecture is an apt metaphor for this philosophical disjuncture and sleight of hand—one thinks of Frank Gehry's Weisman Museum in Minneapolis, his immediate precursor to his Bilbao Guggenheim, or of Daniel Libeskind's (in progress) addition to the Denver Art Museum. Such architecture is all delightful (or infuriating; ultimately it doesn't matter which) eye-candy packages for the same old spaces; the same old white cubes or cuboids; the same old modes of display and demonstration; and the same old consumerist fetishizations of celebrity artists and historical personalities, of "movements" and "schools" and "ethnicities" and "periods" and "themes" and "identities"—what was once aptly termed old w(h)ine in new bottles. In a sense, newly articulated "missions" or "philosophies" for museums have been similarly disappointing, masking museological practices that in fact are fundamentally unchanged since the early nineteenth century. Having been invented as an instrumentality of the modern nation-state in the forging of identities and the invention of heritages, the public museum institution has never failed to fulfill or perpetuate its original ideological, philosophical, or political functions.

The disjunction between the critical, historical, and theoretical literature on museums and professional practices and methodologies remains vast. Reading the latter literature can induce a feeling that the museum is a stable, known institution and practice, that those in charge are fully cognizant about theoretical and political developments in the wider world, and that anything amiss with the institution can be rectified instrumentally and technically—mo' better museology.

The rhetorical substrate of professional museum practice is perhaps best exemplified in a recent article in the *Guardian* newspaper[1] by the current director of the British Museum, arguing against the return by his museum of artifacts to their countries or peoples of origin. The article (unhappily and embarrassingly called "The Whole World in Our Hands") was yet another in the wake of a recent joint statement by directors of nearly two dozen major museums from Los Angeles to St. Petersburg articulating their pointed refusal to respond to the increasingly vociferous claims by various countries to return patrimony taken over the past several centuries by a variety of (legal and illegal) means.

Yet one reads the essay by the director of the British Museum, Neil Mac-Gregor, with not a little sadness in the face of its obscurantist claim that "controversies over ownership obscure the British Museum's purpose." If the artifacts in the museum (whose foundations, like those of most major civic museums in Europe and America, are sunk quite deeply into the soil of not a few enduring "controversies" over identity, ownership, plunder, and patrimony) are indeed "part of a story that is not only national," then surely such stories are as justifiably and as appropriately "told" from Athens, Baghdad, or Beijing.

What precisely can it mean, today, to presume that the function of a museum is to "tell stories"? Whose stories, told for whom by whom, and to what ends? To be sure, the foundations of great national museums such as the Louvre were explicitly connected to the reeducation of a peasantry in the techniques, protocols, and ceremonials of citizenship in a republic where patrimony was staged as collective (civic) rather than exclusive (royal and ecclesiastical), and every newly minted citizen could "share" the grandeur of a collective (and equally newly minted) history of the Republic and its people by literally walking through that "history" represented by its relics. To what extent have museums today deviated substantially from this original national-ideological agenda and mode of story telling?

For much of its life, the British Museum (among not a few others in Europe and America) was organized to foreground very particular "stories" about Greco-Roman and mid-eastern civilizations in their relationships to others, past and present, not least in relation to a British nation that, no less than France, Germany, Italy, and a few other places, not so incidentally staged their modern identities as inheritors of that from which they would wish to be descended—Greece, Rome, Babylonia, and Egypt woven together in a "Newer" Testament "story" of European national patrimonies. In such stories, the French Republic emerges as the reincarnation of the Roman Republic, or London, Stockholm, Berlin, or another becomes the new Athens.

MacGregor's claim that the British Museum "was in large measure removed from the political realm" is patently false in so many ways as to be hilarious were it not so sad. His claim for the British Museum's "worldwide civic purpose" echoes the notoriously disingenuous joint public statement made by directors of some two dozen museums noted above rejecting the burgeoning effort by many countries and peoples to have their (mostly plundered) patrimony returned.

In claiming support for his contention that his institution is a "community of interpretation," MacGregor misses the point of Edward Said's quoted remarks about "the terrible reductive conflicts that herd people together under falsely unifying rubrics like America, the West, or Islam."[2] He would have us thank our lucky stars that "we are the British Museum and not a French one," given the French "reliance on a Catholic model of authority," which (as we are presumed to know, he writes, "looking from London") "denied intellectual liberty." Where the "conceptual French wrote a book" (Diderot's *Encyclopedia*), "the empirical British collected things and put up a building."[3] Never mind that empirically and/or conceptually-minded Europeans of many countries were all doing such things for centuries before the founding of the British Museum, namely writing books and putting up buildings to display their stuff. And Richard Lenoir and the late eighteenth-century founders of the Louvre wrote with candor about the intellectual, cultural, political, and educational functions of the new museum institution they put together, as well as about the idea of a museum in the modern nation more generally.[4] Lenoir's book and its "mission statements" would be perfectly in place in any modern museum director's five-foot reference shelf.

In raising the persistent problem of the museum's refusal to return the Parthenon sculptures (the *Elgin Marbles*) to Greece, MacGregor sidesteps the obvious and increasingly voiced argument that, if indeed these sculptures are "part of a story that is not only national," there is no plausible reason why this story is more legible in London than in Athens. By dismissing international calls for the return of the Parthenon sculptures as "political," MacGregor's argument reads embarrassingly like the jingoistic responses still current in the press to critiques of George W. Bush or Tony Blair as being "partisan" and hence unworthy of notice or comment.

Questions of what should or should not be "held in trust for the world" and when and where and by whom and for how long are very serious ones indeed, not to be dismissed by spurious arguments that only "world museums" (pick your favorite) offer us chances to, as he puts it, "defeat the simplifying brutalities which disfigure politics" around the world.[5] One might very well wish it were true that what he claims to be museums' "civilizing influences" were more effective than they currently are allowed to be, trussed up as they are by the cultural politics of hypercommodified infotainment, edutainment, and containment to which we have allowed ourselves to be in thrall. The rearticulation of the missions and purposes of museums and related institutions can only effectively be carried forward by engaging with (rather than avoiding) the actual complexities and contradictions of their histories as key instruments in the fabrication and maintenance of modern nation-states, cultures, and peoples.

INSIDE AND OUTSIDE THE MUSEUM

Given the ostensible parameters and protocols of the call for contributions to this volume, I am being given to imagine myself as one of a group of contributors situated "outside" a (museum) "profession" and "looking in," as a "scholar who has written books about museums but who [is] trained and work[s] in other disciplinary areas." In accepting the generous invitation to contribute to the collection, I am nonetheless placed, however provisionally, and according to the self-admittedly tentative nature of the editorial formatting of the volume, in a curiously dichotomous relationship to those "looking from within the profession."

You might then expect, quite rightly, that I would immediately question not only my "outsider" status (and its implicit second-class position in contrast to "insiders" presumed to speak '*dans le vrai*,' as Michel Foucault once put it) but also the very logic of "inside" and "outside" a "profession" and institution. The institution is neither singular nor homogeneous, but rather inherently heterogeneous and diverse, and which was philosophically and ideologically contested, historically, in its foundational assumptions.

Not only is "the museum" a heterogeneous phenomenon "internally," it is at the same time historically inseparable from a variety of "external" practices, disciplines, and professions with which it evolved in coordinate fashion over the past three centuries since its modern establishment as a social technology essential to the identity and evolution of the European nation-state.

It is necessary to begin any consideration of the issues and problems raised by this collection by calling into question the purported "exteriority" of museums and philosophies; that is, the presumption that, on the one hand, we have an institution, the museum, and, on the other, a "philosophy" or "mission" to which the former might adhere or aspire. The fact of the matter is that museums have been recognized quite explicitly, since their modern foundations two and a half centuries ago, *as* philosophical, ideological, social, and political practices. A museum is not the "practice" or "reflection" or the "representation" *of* (a) theory; it *is* a theoretical (that is, philosophical, ideological, political) practice. It is not "related to" philosophy as practice to theory; it *is* theory as practice. It is, in short, an epistemological technology for producing knowledge and fabricating worlds, in a dual relationship—(1) to things unsaid and unseen, and in relationship, (2) to an audience of viewers choreographed in space so as to generate knowledge as the dynamically-evolving relationship between "subjects," "objects," and "object-lessons."

All of this at base is fiction; the stuff of fiction making and *artifice*: in (re)presenting the historically "real," the institution functions precisely as theater, as dramaturgy and stagecraft in the service of creating the "effects" of the (historically) real. "Philosophy" is not external to this existential set of circumstances, nor the ghost in the museum's machine, but it is the machinery in its practice. At base what has been and remains at stake in museology, art, art history, art criticism, and aesthetics is the *paradoxically simultaneous possibility and impossibility of representation as such*. The museum, in its social role as a "representational" artifact, is at the crux of this paradox, which informs equally the very underpinnings of modernity itself, and its possibilities and prognoses.

CONCLUSION

I want to conclude these brief remarks by leaving you with the accompanying images. The first (figure 7.1) is Edward Cruikshank's remarkable image, published in 1851, of the world's first great international exhibition, the "International Exhibition of the Arts and Manufactures of All Nations" at the Crystal Palace, in London's Hyde Park, which opened on May 1, 1851, and closed October 15 of that year. Cruikshank's satirical image, entitled "All the World Going to the Great Exhibition of 1851," situates the Crystal Palace (and by extension the Britain it emblematizes) astride the world, absorbing all the world's cultures and peoples into one bright, completely prefabricated, infinitely expandable taxonomic artifact, whose lightness and

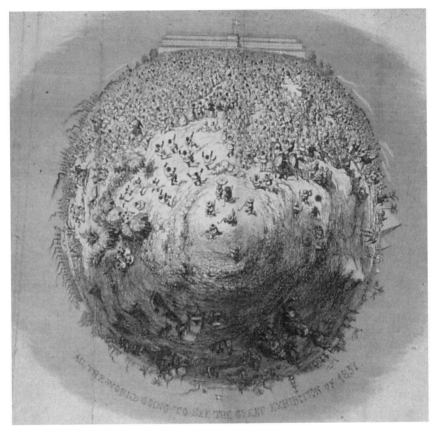

Figure 7.1. Crystal Palace, London 1851

openness so brilliantly rendered invisible and obscure Britain's (and Europe's) colonial investments, whilst reordering social and cultural differences and incommensurabilities into a new universal order melding aesthetics and ethics in the commodity. This was the common ground of Queen Victoria (who visited it sixty times) and Karl Marx—the crèche of commodity fetishism (and several other modern fetishisms as well); the glass and iron blueprint of the ultimate, final museum, the museum at the end of the mind; the most distant imaginable horizon of any likely or probable universal history of art. Figure 7.2 is a contemporary view of the interior.

Victoria played a key role in vivifying this massive exhibition of "the arts and manufactures of all nations" in her daily progress through the countless aisles of art and craft and invention, divided into regional and national pavilions, very like the window displays of department stores in Europe and

Figure 7.2. Crystal Palace Interior: Central Transept

America later in the nineteenth century. Trailed by great crowds each day, her very glance of interest in an object of any kind contrived (as a prerogative of royal privilege) to elicit it as her property. She thereby performed the ideal phantasm of consumption.[6]

We have never left the Crystal Palace. Everything that has been written about museums, museology, art, and art history for the past century and a half carries with it the watermark of this astonishing philosophical artifact—this mentifact scripted in and as iron, glass, and air. The building's vast interior—it was the world's largest building in the nineteenth century—was of such proportions as to create its own blue haze, whose brightness obscured the central fact of the exhibition: the fetish (or factish) that is the modern commodity, each linked to its maker's nationality, race, class, and ethnicity as its "style." It is in this sense that the museum is a mode of working with and on things, a way of using things, in certain (theatrical) ways of world making, and a philosophy as such. Having achieved its institutional apotheosis in the Crystal Palace, the museum's history came to an end.

What then does it mean, today, to *deny* that this "history" is over by continuing to generate futures that can only ever be reiterations and replications of the same?

We need to reconsider where we stand, and what we stand for.

NOTES

1. Neil MacGregor, "The Whole World in Our Hands," *The Guardian*, July 24, 2004, Review section, 4–6.

2. MacGregor, 4.

3. MacGregor, 4.

4. MacGregor, 4.

5. MacGregor, 6.

6. Discussed at length in Donald Preziosi, *Brain of the Earth's Body: Art, Museums, and the Phantasms of Modernity* (Minneapolis: University of Minnesota Press, 2003), 92–115.

8

The Moral Obligations Incumbent upon Institutions, Administrators, and Directors in Maintaining and Caring for Museum Collections

Michael A. Mares

I trust & believe that the time spent in this voyage, if thrown away for all other respects, will produce its full worth in Nat: History. And it appears to me the doing what *little* one can to encrease the general stock of knowledge is as respectable an object of life as one can in any likelihood pursue.

> Charles Darwin in a letter to his sister about the voyage of the *Beagle*[1]

My appeal is, then, to every museum director and to every curator responsible for the proper use as well as the safe preservation of natural history specimens. Many species of vertebrate animals are disappearing: some are gone already. All that the investigator of the future will have, to indicate the nature of such then extinct species, will be the remains of these species preserved more or less faithfully, along with the data accompanying them, in the museums of the country.

> Joseph Grinnell[2]

What is education? Properly speaking, there is no such thing as education. Education is simply the soul of a society as it passes from one generation to another. Whatever the soul is like, it will have to be passed on somehow, consciously or unconsciously, and that transition may be called education. . . . What we need is to have a culture before we hand it down. In other words, it is a truth, however sad and strange, that we cannot give what we have not got, and cannot teach to other people what we do not know ourselves.

G. K. Chesterton[3]

The Smithsonian Institution is the principal repository of our nation's collective memory and the nation's largest public cultural space. It is dedicated to preserving, understanding, and displaying the land we inhabit and the diversity and depth of American civilization in all of its timbres and color. It holds in common for all Americans that set of beliefs—in the form of artifacts—about our past that, taken together, comprise our collective history and symbolize the ideals to which we aspire as a polity.

Commission on the Future of the Smithsonian Institution[4]

Natural history museums are facing the same fate as the dodo, the passenger pigeon, and other extinct animals whose remains they preserve. . . .

James Owen[5]

I selected these five quotations because they encompass much of the range of what museums do and have done, how they have been viewed, and how they are coming to be viewed. The fact that the quotations were made over more than a century and a half speaks to the continuity of museums and their collections. Museums are forever. Permanence is the sine qua non of all museums. On my research on South American mammals, I routinely work with specimens that Charles Darwin collected on his famous voyage. His specimens are still preserved in the Natural History Museum in London. I cannot handle those specimens without thinking about him, his journey, and all that came of it. Indeed, I will often read his notes and learn interesting things about how he caught this or that animal that I am studying in that great museum.

One of the species I study is a small desert mouse in the genus *Eligmodontia*. Darwin collected one of the first of these animals (a type specimen) in Bahia Blanca, Argentina. He had been gathering small branches from shrubs in the desert on the evening of Wednesday, October 3, 1832, in order to make a fire to cook dinner. He noted: "This little animal does not appear to agree exactly with any of the subgenera of Cuvier.—It was caught Octob. 3d at Monte Hermoso in B. Blanca.—In bringing at night a bush for fire wood, it ran out with its tail singed.—So probably it inhabits bushes:—In sandy hillocks near the sea—it could not run very fast: it is a male: after skinning the head it has a much more elongated appearance than it had in Nature."[6]

Museums began with collections, but it may be more accurate to say that collections begat museums. The urge to collect is an ancient one, with the earliest collections being recorded at about the time that great civilizations arose thousands of years ago. The word "museum" has its roots in the Mouseion of Ptolemy at the great Alexandria Library more than two millennia ago,[7] although vast collections also were included with burials in the pyramids of Egypt dating back about five millennia, and animals and plants were depicted in the earliest rock art dating back to Cro-Magnon people more than forty millennia ago.[8] Indeed, collecting is one of our most human traits, whether it is done to recall places we have been; to learn from the past; to see our humanity connect across the ages with other peoples through the objects they produced, utilized, and treasured; to assemble burial goods that will accompany our ancestors, relatives, and leaders to hoped-for better worlds; or to understand the world of which we are a part, a world that changes at a scale that defies understanding over the short life spans of humans.

Consider, for example, that only eight years after Columbus discovered the New World in 1492, Vicente Yañez Pinzón, on a journey of exploration to South America in 1500, returned to Spain with a specimen of a South American opossum, an extraordinary animal whose uniquely odd appearance underscored the newness and strangeness of the expanding globe and provided the first mammal specimen collected from the South American continent.[9] The specimen was given to King Ferdinand and Queen Isabella.

Since that time, museum researchers and collectors have surveyed the rich South American biota and shown that the tropical rain forest is one of the major repositories for life on earth. The South American rainforest, which has been likened to the lungs of the planet, harbors many more species that remain unidentified than species that have already been named.[10] The number of unidentified species in the tropical rain forests of the New World may number in the tens of millions, whereas only about 1.7 million plants, animals, and organisms of all types have been described to date for the whole world.[11] Moreover, new species continue to be discovered daily, many of them from the continent where that opossum was collected more than 500 years ago.[12] Explorations also have been underway in the deserts of South America where new species and even genera of mammals are being discovered in the arid habitats of the continent.[13]

Such explorations are not limited to the New World. Modern explorers are going into habitats across the globe and discovering new organisms daily. Most biologists believe that the species that have been described to date represent the tip of the iceberg of biological diversity.[14] Each new species, when discovered, becomes a part of the natural history collections of museums. In fact, in order to be accurately described, each new species must be compared with specimens that are already in museums and that extend back through time to the beginning of taxonomic research. Without this comparative database, one cannot describe new species effectively. Museum collections are thus the foundational database of life, present and past.

Museums throughout the world dutifully preserve, maintain, and study these specimens, adding to our information on the past and current status of organisms and their habitats. The collections of biological materials also permit us to document recent changes that are occurring due to such massive forces as global climate change, human-induced habitat conversion, pollution, extinction, and the general habitat fluctuations that are a part of the rhythm of nature. They also allow us to describe sudden and massive changes buried deep in the history of the earth. For example, when Luis Alvarez and colleagues published their theory that the extinction of the dinosaurs had occurred as the result of a massive asteroid collision with earth about sixty-five million years ago,[15] it was a collection of geological ocean bed cores that had been maintained at the University of New Orleans for decades that provided the hard evidence of a widespread layer of iridium and other impact products that supported the asteroid theory.[16] Once again, collections, whose function could not be foretold when they were made, were used to support a cutting-edge theory that has changed the view of the history of life on earth and led to a new appreciation of celestial dangers that lurk in deep space.

In 1732, Carl Linnaeus began the practice of naming species using two Latinized names. Although extensive natural history collections did not begin with Linnaeus—known today as the father of taxonomy—he was certainly a collector. Indeed, the medically trained Linnaeus almost died when he was shipwrecked on one of his field trips to the wilds of Lapland in 1732.[17] As a professor of botany in Sweden, he arranged to have his students accompany trading ships and voyages of exploration as ship's naturalists, collecting plants as they sailed around the world. One student, Daniel Solander, sailed with Captain Cook on his famous voyage in 1768. The extensive collections of plants made by the botanists Joseph Banks and Solander immediately following the "discovery" of Australia led to the name of Botany Bay being given to the first anchorage of Captain Cook's ship, *Endeavour*.[18] These naturalists returned to Sweden with plant collections to be described by Linnaeus.

When Darwin embarked on the voyage of the *Beagle*, a journey that would literally change the world with his publication of *On the Origin of Species* in 1859, his main task was to collect organisms. He was constantly chasing down and pressing, pickling, or cataloguing the new animals, plants, and rocks that attracted his attention. These were dutifully shipped back to London where they became part of the British Museum of Natural History. Darwin's travels and collections provided the grist for his mill as he developed his theory of evolution, a view of the development of life over time that changed the world and helped move humanity from the dark ages of ignorance into the more challenging, if not always more comforting, world of science. Darwin knew, even as a young man of twenty-three, that his specimens would be preserved forever in his nation's national museum. The vicissitudes and dangers of his four-year long voyage would not be in vain. Moreover, he knew that science changes over time, so his specimens and all of the information they contained would find new uses for later generations. They could only increase in value. He knew that he was collecting the fundamental data of nature as he found it in the early nineteenth century. Those data would not change over time, but they would provide an irreplaceable resource of nature discovered, collected, and described on the global voyage of *H.M.S. Beagle.*

With all of his brilliance, not even Darwin could not have predicted just how valuable his museum specimens would become with the passage of time. Later centuries would witness the destruction of habitats, global climate change, global chemical pollution, the initiation of a human-induced mass extinction, the rise of new and deadly diseases associated with habitat destruction and increasing human population density, and the development of new techniques and technologies based in genetic research, biology, chemistry, physics, and computers that would allow an ever increasing amount of data, and more precise data, to be extracted from museum specimens than anyone living in the early 1800s or even mid-1900s could have predicted. The billions of specimens carefully gathered and preserved over centuries at enormous expense and sacrifice would become the only data that humanity has available to chronicle our changing world over time. Natural history collections provide fundamental information on species and their environments across the habitats of the world and even across the seemingly impenetrable barrier of time.

In effect, collections have become time machines that permit us to view earlier periods of a world that no longer exists. The habitats Darwin visited are no longer there. In some cases, the animals and plants he studied no longer exist. The world has changed irrevocably. Thanks to the work of natural history museums—as well as the thousands of collectors who have explored most of the habitats of the globe in search of organisms to become a part of museum collections—those organisms that Darwin and others worked so hard to collect are still available to study. Each specimen in a natural history museum reflects the time and place of its life, whether it is a dinosaur that lived 110 million years ago or a fern that was collected this morning. Each year we find new ways to extract additional information from these specimens, information that tells more and more about the time and place of each organism. Taken together, the natural history collections of the world are a resource nonpareil about the history of life and mankind's place in, and effect upon, the biosphere. The world's biological collections cannot be duplicated, replicated, or replaced. As time is one of the major characteristics of each specimen, and as time moves in a single direction, each point in time, once past, cannot be recovered.

Try this simple exercise: Collect some leaves from a tree growing in your yard today. That is simple enough to do. You have now made a collection that reflects not only the species of tree, but its genetic code, its internal physiology, the contaminants in the region, the overall climate during the time those leaves were produced, the season, and other factors that reflect the place and time of that tree. Now collect leaves from that same tree again, but collect them yesterday. Finally, as it is an old tree, and as a final exercise, collect some leaves from that tree in 1904. Can you do it? Of course not. How can you go back in time and collect leaves a hundred years ago or even yesterday?

But wait! It turns out that your species of tree is an ideal bioindicator for chemical contaminants that were released into the environment in 1940 and appear to be involved in the possible extinction of several species associated with your tree. Can you document when these chemicals reached the leaves of your tree? Can you collect some insects off the tree in 1939, 1940, and again in 1941, or bird nests that were built in the tree during those years, or eggs from those nests so that we can see how this contamination spread? Can you collect predaceous birds or carnivorous mammals that preyed on the smaller organisms living in your tree in 1940 and see how they were affected by the contaminants? Once again, you cannot do this.

However, there is a way to go back in time and compare organisms, not only for chemicals, but for bone density; gene sequences; hair quality; feather contamination; radiation levels; leaf function; coexisting prey, predators, and competitors; environmental quality; general climate; and a host of other factors that accumulate and leave traces as organisms carry on their daily lives. You have available for your use a time machine of life that extends across billions of years to a world that existed before life began. As noted: "Our natural history museums are sentinel observatories of life on Earth, peering over its past 3.8 billion years and assaying its present condition."[19] Museum collections provide precisely these kinds of data, and each year they provide more data, more sophisticated data, and more important data. Not only are the data in collections invaluable, they are also irreplaceable, in part because you cannot go back in time to make a collection. As a nation, we have likely spent tens, if not hundreds, of billions of dollars and thousands of centuries of person-years amassing and protecting the greatest storehouse of the biological history of our world. That storehouse resides in the collections and museums of our country, whether in private museums, government-related organizations, such as city, county, state, or national museums, or within university museums. Biological collections in museums are the *only* source of accurate data about organisms that have existed in the past. Books, journal articles, field notes, anecdotes, newspaper reports, and all of the various mechanisms people use to communicate information across time have little value when hard data on organisms are needed. Only collections provide the foundational data that do not change. Publications can be filled with errors, identifications may have changed over time, and other factors may have affected the accuracy of the printed or spoken word. But if a scientist needs to examine a specimen that accurately and unambiguously represents its time and place, this can only be done in a museum.

Today that irreplaceable storehouse, which has been protected and cared for at such great cost and sacrifice for centuries, is being threatened by people who do not understand it, cannot appreciate it, and are unable to shoulder the enormous responsibility of caring for it. The lifetimes of effort of countless scientists, scholars, educators, researchers, students, collectors, and supporters of museums and collections over more than two centuries are now threatened by hapless ignorance, mean-spiritedness, arrogance, fiscal meanness, or well-meaning ineptness. In some cases, perhaps especially in university museums (although museums reporting directly to political entities are not excluded here), we have given over the ultimate responsibility of protecting our collections to good-hearted, back-slapping administrators who look good, interview well, and moved onto the administrative track early in their careers—often without becoming important scholars in their own right. They have little experience or interest in museums, culture, heritage, or science. They are bean counters with advanced degrees, capable of managing a budget—often by adhering to "business principles"—but incapable of making the hard decisions necessary to protect the priceless materials in collections and museums from being lost forever. One reason among many that they have trouble dealing with museums is that museums do not fit a business model. They never have and they never will. Try as they might, bean counters can neither understand this nor accept it.

How did this situation come to pass? How could we have fallen so far so fast in our societal love and appreciation for culture and learning? For university museums, I believe it has occurred in part because money has been allowed to become the primary measure of importance on a campus. If you bring in more money than a colleague, then your work is more important than your colleague's. If you bring in less, you are a less important person. If your unit garners huge grants, it is more important than a unit that attracts less money. Bottom-line thinking by bottom-line administrators is destroying the natural heritage infrastructure of our universities, their museums, and their collections. It is also undercutting scholarship. Bottom-line thinking by government entities is accomplishing the same end for their museums.

John F. Kennedy's comments on poetry are apropos here: "When power leads man towards arrogance, poetry reminds him of his limitations. When power narrows the area of man's concern, poetry reminds him of the richness and diversity of existence. When power corrupts, poetry cleanses." Ah, poetry. How many of us see the need for more poetry in our lives? How many of our administrators see the need for more poets on campus? Not many, I would wager. Poetry does not yield high overhead or require a great deal of equipment. Few grants support poetry. Even the Pulitzer Prize pays only $10,000, not enough money to buy a teaching microscope, and no overhead either. Things have changed greatly over the last several decades on many campuses, and not for the better.

Substitute the word "culture" or "museum" for poetry, and you can feel a sense of how and why collections that were protected at all costs in the past are faring poorly today. Clearly poetry, museums, culture, and scientific awareness of nature are all related. A respect for one bespeaks a respect for the other. Who would say, "I love poetry, but I hate museums," or "I feel that cultural awareness is vital, but museums are not," or "I feel a deep respect for the collective heritage of my nation, but I hate museums"?

At the dawn of World War II, L. V. Coleman wrote: "Good college and university museums are found on the whole in the good colleges and universities. . . . To be sure not every one of the campus museum[s] . . . marks a progressive institution, but the colleges and universities having these museums are as a class the top, and the institutions with no museums at all are in the class of the backward colleges."[20] Indeed, the first public natural history museum to be founded was the Ashmolean Museum at Oxford, perhaps the world's greatest university.[21] Sadly, this respectful view of museums no longer obtains, and we are the poorer for it at all levels, from that of the individual, through the collective souls of our institutions, to society at large. We wear our ignorance with button-busting pride.

Consider, for example, a small university in a small town near the geographic center of the United States during World War II. The university was the University of Oklahoma; the town, Norman. The University of Oklahoma had begun its natural history museum in 1899 during territorial days. Oklahoma hoped to become a state and, like most new states, it viewed having a museum as an important signpost of cultural and scientific development.[22] Surely this raw territory would soon merit statehood, and the development of a museum would help the process along. Between 1899 and 1942, the collections of the university had grown enormously to encompass several million objects.

In 1942, however, the United States was engaged in a great global conflict, where the very survival of liberty was threatened.[23] Despite these dark days, the federal government established the Committee on the Conservation of Cultural Resources Planning Board "to promote measures for the protection of books, . . . works of art, museum objects . . . and other cultural resources."[24] It was recognized that, even with the demands of war, if proper care were not exercised "by . . . museum directors . . . [they could] contribute to an even greater peril to our cultural resources than enemy attacks."[25] Norman, with its two military bases, was considered a potential target for enemy attack, and a committee was established to determine ways to protect the museum's collections. Museums throughout the world were engaged in similar exercises in preserving their heritage in the face of perceived dangers (Norman never was attacked) or in response to very real dangers (all of the natural history and cultural collections in the British museums in London were moved to isolated farms or mines before and during the blitz—they survived largely unscathed).

During this period, the fear about possibly being bombed, which was felt in many towns and cities in the United States, was not totally unfounded. Japan, for example, launched 9,000 balloon bombs during World War II, and 1,000 of these reached the United States, killing a number of people in the Pacific Northwest.[26] As improbable as an attack on Norman might seem, steps were taken to ensure that the University of Oklahoma's museum would be safe. Aute Richards, chair of the zoology department, wrote an article about the museum and the war and how he hoped that the present state of alertness in Norman would protect the museum and its collections. His words have meaning today, though they were written more than a half-century ago.

> In civilized nations everywhere the monuments to the past and the accumulations which display the riches of nature have always been highly regarded previous to the present world conflagration. Now every effort must be directed to the successful prosecution of the war efforts, but we must look also to the peace to come and to the continued development of the arts and sciences of civilization to the end that there will thus be created a nobler world than that of the past. Institutions which have played their parts in the achievements of whatever is estimable in our present lives must be preserved for their future contributions. Of these the museums stand in a high place; they are like light houses which mark the courses toward the safer future havens.[27]

How has the previously unquestioned respect for museums and their mission fallen so far on so many campuses? Why have those lighthouse lights marking the course toward safer havens been dimmed?

In the 1990s I had the honor of serving on the Commission for the Future of the Smithsonian Institution. Such commissions are established only every fifty years to assess the continued development of America's national museum. As part of our job, some of us were asked to travel to London and meet with each director of the many "national museums" of Great Britain that are located in London. Our most memorable meeting was with Neil MacGregor, director of Britain's National Gallery of Art. We had been asked by the Regents of the Smithsonian to consider whether or not the Smithsonian should charge admission to its exhibits. In London, some museums charge admission, whereas others do not. Mr. MacGregor was eloquent in defending his institution's decision not to charge admission. "We are a trust of the people," he said. "Therefore they own these great works of art. How can you charge the owner to see his own artwork?" He went on to point out that people need to spend time with great art, and in his museum there are examples of some of the greatest art in human history—Rembrandt, da Vinci, Velazquez, Renoir, Monet, El Greco, Van Gogh, Michelangelo.[28]

How sacredly is this trust taken by the museum and its administrators? Today, on the sixtieth anniversary of D-Day, the story I relate should have special meaning. During World War II, the various British museums moved all of their collections into mine shafts, farms, and other places outside London where the precious heritage of Great Britain and much of the rest of the world would be safe from destruction by Germany's air assaults. The city was under nightly bombardment. German bombers and, later, buzz bombs would fall on different parts of the city. London was totally blacked out. Tens of thousands of people were killed, and tens of thousands more were injured, their homes destroyed. But the English people needed symbols of normality to help stiffen their resolve against Hitler's onslaught. One sign of normality, one connection with the best side of humanity, were the great pieces of art in the British Museum. Although the museum had been emptied of its art—as the area around Trafalgar Square where it is located was a favorite target of German bombardiers—it was decided that the people of London needed to have a great work of art from their museum on exhibit even during the most horrific assaults by the Nazis. Each month, one dazzling and precious piece of art was hung in the otherwise empty museum, where it was visited by tens of thousands of people, who found sanity in art to help counteract the insanity that surrounded them. They used the beauty and permanence of the best in mankind to escape the ravages of the worst of our species.

Museums clearly enrich our lives. They inform; they entertain; and they teach both children and adults. In museum collections we can see both our mortality and our immortality. Museum collections provide hope of our rebirth, as we observe the spark of wonderment in our children's eyes as they contemplate artifacts and specimens from other cultures and other worlds that have gone before. These facts have been recognized by those responsible for the development, protection, and maintenance of museums throughout much of history. This is no longer the case for many museums.

Hilde Hein, a philosopher and another contributor to this book, wrote the following of museum collections:

> The world, in all its complexity, appears as a gigantic museum, a treasure house whose content changes continually, reflecting the thought that defines it and inviting its further refinement. Like the world, museums are sites of ideated expression, where things are kept, and the thoughts that inhabit things are

transmitted from mind to mind and generation to generation. Museums are places to muse in comparative freedom and security. Inside the museum visitors can contemplate objects imaginatively, partaking of the histories of their creation, function, and meaning. We may think of museums as enclosures that encapsulate portions of the world—more physical, symbolic, real, or fictional "stuff" than any finite mind can encompass. . . . Whether we conceive the world as one or many, singular or plural, constant or changing, museums multiply narratives. They are collections of collections—momentary worlds comprising the matter of prior worlds. Philosophers conjecture how worlds are generated out of one another. Museums bring us experientially into the presence of just such alternative ways of world making.[29]

When the great appreciation for museums and culture that has been shown throughout history is considered, the present state of affairs of many museums is almost inexplicable. Museums and collections have come to be underappreciated or unappreciated by administrators at all levels, including within the museums themselves! As noted, I believe that money is the driving force, but it is not the lack of money that lies at the root of the problem, as some administrators would suggest.

An example of how important it is for administrators to possess an appreciation of culture, collections, museums, and heritage is illustrated by comparing two museums—the University of Nebraska State Museum and the Sam Noble Oklahoma Museum of Natural History. About half the states in the nation have a state museum, and about half of these are located at a university.[30] All states and museums differ in fundamental ways, but such museums face similar challenges.

Nebraska lies in the northern Great Plains. It is primarily a grassland state, but there are treed foothills of the mountains in the west, and overall the state has a rich cultural, biological, and geological history.[31] The state had a population in 2000 of 1.7 million people (ranked 38th), with a mean annual income of $26,804 for 2002, making it the 22nd poorest state in the nation.[32] Agriculture and ranching (with associated food processing) are the major industries. The state has seven public universities offering at least a master's degree, and its flagship university is the University of Nebraska at Lincoln. The University of Nebraska State Museum is on the University of Nebraska campus in Lincoln. The museum was founded in 1871. Its collections total more than 13 million specimens and artifacts, making them twice as large as those of Oklahoma's natural history museum. The museum has a number of buildings, some of them quite old and of a substandard quality, although the main museum building functions well for exhibits, collection storage, and research. Each year about 225,000 people visit the main museum and its branch museums—the Ashfall Fossil Beds State Historical Park near Orchard, the Trailside Museum near Crawford, and the Larsen Tractor Test and Power Museum on the agriculture campus in Lincoln. The museum's annual budget was $3 million in 2003, which supported a staff of forty-four full and part-time personnel.

Oklahoma lies in the southern Great Plains. It is also primarily a grassland state, but there are mountains in the east and south-central parts of the state and upland plateaus (mesas) in the far west. Like Nebraska, Oklahoma, too, has a rich cultural, biological, and geological heritage.[33] The state had a population in 2000 of 3.5 million people (ranked 27th), with an average annual income of $23,026, making it the 40th poorest state in the nation.[34] It is thus much poorer than Nebraska. Agriculture, oil, and ranching are the major industries. The state has twelve public universities offering at least a master's degree, and its flagship university is the University of Oklahoma. The Sam Noble Oklahoma Museum of Natural History is on the University of Oklahoma campus in Norman. The museum was founded in 1899. Its collections total more than 6 million specimens and artifacts. The University of Oklahoma completed construction of a new, state-of-the-art museum building in 2000, moving out of eleven old buildings whose quality was atrocious, including having collections stored in former horse barns.[35] Since the new building opened in May 2000, 900,000 people have visited the museum (with traveling exhibits and world wide web visitors totaling several million more over this same period), for an average of 225,000 in-house visitors per year (the same as Nebraska). The museum budget (including funds kept at the university level for maintenance costs) is about $4 million, which supports a full and part-time staff of 140.

Both of the natural history museums in these two states are broadly similar. Both have had to respond to challenges in recent years. Both have been subjected to various reductions in support over the last decade. However, it is instructive to examine the most recent challenges faced by the two institutions, which both occurred in 2003 (as state economies are generally related to the overall U.S. economy). Generally, the reason given for cutting back on support for museums and collections within a larger organization—whether a university, or city, county, or state governments—is financial exigency. For example, in response to the recent fiscal "crisis," the University of Nebraska State Museum was reduced greatly in size and scope. In a letter from University of Nebraska Chancellor Harvey Perlman (written for him and in his name by Prem Paul and Herbert Howe) to various museum professionals from around the nation who had written to him opposing the elimination of curatorial and staff positions at the museum and the closing or eliminating of museum collections, Perlman wrote:

> As we know you will be pleased to learn, we have received a number of emails in response to this proposal and hope that you will understand our need to respond in a generic manner to the concerns that have been raised.
>
> To put this in perspective, the University of Nebraska-Lincoln is now facing

our fourth budget reduction in a year. The total cumulative reductions we have made or are proposing to make will be nearly 19% of our state-aided budget. In all previous cuts, with careful effort, we have been able to avoid significant reductions to any academic units, including the research divisions of the Museum. However, that is no longer an option available to us. All that is left, other than mandated services, are academic programs. The question we now face is not whether to cut academic programs but rather what programs do we cut? Clearly, these are choices that we would prefer not to have to make, but our Governor and Legislature seem determined to force us to make these decisions.

There is no question that eliminating these programs is a tremendous loss to the University of Nebraska-Lincoln, the state and, indeed the nation. No one in campus leadership wishes to make these choices. Indeed, we recognize that we are proposing the elimination of preeminent programs, but unfortunately that is the case for whatever cuts are proposed.[36]

This type of reasoning is common at all levels where museums have been scaled back or eliminated. Consider the Nebraska case further, however. The museum was founded in 1871. Over the next 133 years, thousands of scientists, collectors, students, and ordinary Nebraska folk worked to build their natural history museum into one of the finest state museums in the nation. They worked through freezing winters and dust-blown summers. They worked through the Indian Wars, World War I and World War II, Korea, Vietnam, and the first Gulf War. They survived the depression of 1873–1896, the panic of 1907, the recessions of 1910 and 1913, the panic of 1914, the Great Depression of the 1930s, the oil shock of 1973, the energy crisis of 1979–1982, the junk bond collapse of 1987–1992, and the dot com bubble of 2000.

That's a pretty good record of survival for a museum in a small state. Nebraska has been blessed with a rich Native American heritage, a remarkable fossil mammal history that lies buried in its soil, and some of the richest grasslands in the world. It is an amazing piece of America, and its geological, biological, and cultural histories provide an endless array of valuable material, which any museum would be proud to have in its collection. Such objects have been preserved in the State Museum and protected and studied through all of the economic and geopolitical vicissitudes detailed above.

Enter Mr. Perlman, whose actions were much more destructive than either the Great Depression or the Japanese balloon bombs. Is Nebraska's economic situation worse than it was in the Indian Wars or the Great Depression? Hardly. Is the economy of the United States worse than it was during the Great Depression, World War I, or World War II? Not likely. Yet the Nebraska museum managed to ride through those vast economic challenges, and even flourish over the years. In 2004, however, in the richest nation on earth, the museum had finally met its match. It was greatly damaged, purportedly for financial reasons.

I do not believe that the large cuts imposed on the museum (a 49 percent budget reduction) were made solely for financial reasons. In all state universities, the proportion of state funding that makes up the overall university budget has plummeted over the last several decades. Most state universities now receive less than 25 percent of their overall budget from the state. The rest of the money comes from federal and state grants and contracts, private funds, earned income, tuition, and other funds. Thus, if the University of Nebraska's state budget were cut by 19 percent, as Mr. Perlman noted in his letter, that would be perhaps 19 percent of the 25 percent of the overall university budget provided by the state, or about 5 percent of the entire university budget. This is a serious cut, but hardly a case for jettisoning major collections and curatorial personnel and gutting an outstanding museum, which had been in place for more than 133 years.

In my opinion, the cuts at Nebraska were made because the administrators responsible for the continued existence of the museum—very likely at all levels of the university and state bureaucracy—did not understand the importance of a museum to its people and its place. They also did not understand why museums and collections must be maintained at all costs. Permanently. Eliminating museums is not an option. That is the moral mandate that was given to universities, state governments, and the federal government by citizens, scientists, scholars, students, collectors, administrators, and politicians across the centuries. Unlike Jack Kennedy, Nebraska's administrators were simply incapable of hearing the "poetry" of the collections.

The Nebraska museum came into existence before General Custer was wiped out at the Little Bighorn. It is an old and a great museum, as I wrote to Chancellor Perlman in a letter that alerted him to the long-term mistake I believed he was about to make:

> State museums contain the tangible heritage of the people of that state. University museums translate that heritage into information and new knowledge. The work of the curators is a requisite to develop exhibits, to serve the public with fundamental knowledge about the materials in the collections, to train new specialists in museum studies, to provide a fundamental database on the biological and cultural underpinnings of the state and region, and to provide experts to answer the questions posed by undergraduate and graduate students, and the general public that are related to the valuable collection resource.
>
> The Nebraska State Museum has a long and noble history. It was founded almost a half century before Oklahoma's museum was established and has done a good job of protecting Nebraska's priceless collections, conducting research, educating museum professionals, publishing and interpreting research conducted on the collections for exhibit use and for the increase of scientific knowledge and public edification in Nebraska and throughout the world. There is no doubt that the museum's buildings could be in better shape, its programs more extensive, and some of its personnel could be more productive, but that is fre-

quently the case. You and I both know that quality varies across any organization, whether one is considering faculty, support staff, or administrators. Nonetheless, the answer to any perceived problems related to management or productivity is not to dismantle the organization. One must remember that a museum is a permanent institution. It holds the treasures of the state in trust for the people of the state, and it does so in perpetuity. It is this quality of permanence that must be considered when pondering reductions in budgets or personnel.

It is my assessment as a museum administrator, a faculty member, a curator, and an expert with national and international experience on museum operations, that it would be a mistake for the University of Nebraska to eliminate curatorial and collection support personnel in the State Museum due to a system-wide budget shortfall. It is folly to think that the reputation and all operations of the organization would not be seriously and negatively impacted. I know of no university natural history museum in the United States that is able to operate effectively without curators and collection support personnel. Indeed, those few that have tried to do this have fallen far below the level of mediocrity. To eliminate the very engine of creativity and expertise that drives the collections—the heart of the museum—is to doom public programs and exhibits in the coming years. No museum of quality has been successful with this strategy. None. . . .

The University has a moral and fiduciary obligation to care for the heritage of the people of Nebraska. It cannot meet this obligation by eliminating the very positions that are responsible for the care, growth, and development of these collections, materials that are the permanent and priceless treasures of the State of Nebraska.

Clearly this plan was developed without much input from museum experts. I hope you have not been misled by advisors who have suggested that such sweeping changes can be made without compromising the quality of the museum's programs, for they can not. Both the exhibits and the children's programs will be severely affected by the proposed changes. One simply cannot continue to enjoy the eggs if the goose is killed, yet that is precisely what this plan proposes. Moreover, the proposed changes mock the legal obligation that was granted by the people of Nebraska to the University to care for their heritage for all time. Universities and their museums have a moral obligation not only to balance the books, but to serve future generations of their public. Like it or not, you, the University, and the Museum, are the keepers of Nebraska's heritage. It is easy to meet your responsibilities in this area during times when funds are readily available, but the true test of meeting one's duty occurs when times are difficult. Now is one of those defining moments when mettle is tested.

[T]he decision to eliminate these positions for short term monetary considerations will result in long-term damage to the collections, the public programs, the scientific reputation of the museum and the University, and the future use of the heritage of the people of Nebraska. Museums are not merely keepers of the past, but guardians of the future, for people who lose their material heritage lose that bridge of memory that connects the past to the future. They are left adrift without the important foundation of support that is based on an appreciation of their natural and cultural heritage. To harm the museum is, therefore, to harm the future, and to harm the future is to deprive Nebraska's children of their connections to their heritage.

I strongly recommend that you give careful consideration to the full ramifications of a decision to damage the Nebraska State Museum. Such a decision will ring across the years long after you have moved on, for museums reach across the generations. For good or ill, your decision will likely reach well beyond your ability to perceive at this moment. I hope you will permit your vision to guide your decision.[37]

Like Nebraska, Oklahoma's natural history museum also faced a "crisis" in 2003. I had resigned as director of the museum and moved into a research position in January 2003, after twenty years at the helm. The new director, Dr. Ellen Censky, had only been in her position for a month when the University of Oklahoma received a budget cut from the Oklahoma State Regents for Higher Education that would have resulted in a 28 percent cut for the Sam Noble Oklahoma Museum of Natural History and several other university units. The museum had only recently completed an outstanding new building and was exceedingly popular with the public and within the university community. With a new director, it would have been easy for the president and higher administration to mandate these draconian cuts, slicing the heart out of the new museum, shooting it down like a dove that had just taken flight.

But President David L. Boren was not only born in Oklahoma from a long line of native Oklahomans (his father, Lyle, was a U.S. congressman from Oklahoma), he had been a state representative, governor, and a United States senator for sixteen years, before accepting the university presidency. More important, Boren has a deep love for the state's heritage and an enormous respect for the arts, culture, scientific improvement in the state, the classics, and international programs and language studies.[38] He knew that it would be wrong to cut the budget of the museum so dramatically. It could only hurt Oklahoma and the university. He knew that a short-term monetary savings was a poor excuse to destroy more than a century of Oklahoma heritage. He used other funds to save the museum from the enormous projected budgetary shortfall and required the museum to meet the university-wide across the board cut of 10 percent (twice as large as that which was facing the University of Nebraska). No one forced Boren to mitigate the larger cut. However, within any great university there are always "other" funds available. Only in a third-world, government-run university does the state budget constitute the entire budget of the institution. In large universities, such as those of Nebraska or Oklahoma, it is the choices that administrators make on how those "other" funds are used that determine whether organizations such as museums flourish or whether they wither and die.

The responses of the senior administration of the University of Nebraska and the University of Oklahoma were remarkably different. President Boren shouldered his responsibility to protect the museum that had been passed on to him by generations of Oklahoma citizens, university presidents, and scholars across the ages. He chose to save the museum. Chancellor Perlman, facing what was arguably a less dramatic cut than that faced by Boren, chose to devastate his museum.

I do not know Chancellor Perlman personally and am not criticizing him as a person. He is probably a fine gentleman. However, I believe he made a decision that was very shortsighted in regard to the museum. In his hand-wringing letter he almost says, "What were we supposed to do, cut an academic department?" If that truly were the only choice that remained, then the answer is a resounding "Yes!" That is precisely what he should have done. As difficult as it is to eliminate an academic department, it is a fact of higher education that departments come and go, and sometimes return. Various universities have jettisoned everything from departments of fine arts or classics to home economics or languages. It is not an action to be taken lightly, but it is done regularly, often without the driving impetus of fiscal constraints as a motivating force. Departments are not forever.

Museums are *not* departments. Museums must be preserved in perpetuity. It is the reason they exist. It is why generations of supporters, researchers, students, and contributors have placed their materials in these institutions across the centuries. They trusted the museum and its parent organization to protect, preserve, and study these treasures for all time. It is the reason the British government moved its museums to protected places during the German bombardments and the reason museum staff literally risked their lives to save the collections. It is the reason the University of Oklahoma developed a plan to protect its natural history museum should the Japanese or Germans attack Norman. It is why museum professionals constantly work to protect the precious collections against fire, storm, earthquake, vandalism, and terrorism. It is why the people of Oklahoma rallied together against the tide of antitaxation to save their natural history museum by building a great, new museum when the collections were in danger of catastrophic loss.[39] It is why the international community arose as one to help Iraq protect its museums during the 2003 Iraq war. Museums matter.

Museums trump other organizations because they are the only connections in our complex world that reach back through time. They are the precious record of the past that is preserved to serve the needs of future generations. They are the golden thread of our heritage that links yesterday to tomorrow. They are the way we learn about the world. Without them, our cultural awareness, our scientific understanding, and our very sense of self become increasingly impoverished. Museums, especially those with enormous collections and a long history of contributions to their parent institution or state, are, in fact, sacred. They should not have their trip through time stopped by some shoot-from-the-hip transient administrator facing a temporary "crisis" of a budget cut of a few percentage points. To a minor administrator a minor challenge is a major hurdle. His response may be out of proportion to the reality of the threat faced by the organization.

It is the moral obligation of administrators to maintain their museums at whatever cost. If they fail at this task, they not only damage the museum today, but their hasty and poorly reasoned actions become the one thing for which time is not an obstacle. They literally damage the fabric of the past and the future. And although time may not be a barrier to the damage they can wreak, time will hold them accountable. There is a word for people who do not grasp the importance of culture—philistine.[40] Merriam-Webster defines a philistine as "a person who is guided by materialism and is usually disdainful of intellectual or artistic values."[41] Does this sound like anyone who has any responsibility for your museum? If it does, I wish you well. You will have to fight to save your museum, but that is the job of museum professionals. Museums are forever, and no one ever said that the road to "Forever" would be easy.

NOTES

1. Charles Darwin, *Charles Darwin's Zoology Notes and Specimen Lists from H.M.S. Beagle*, ed. R. Keynes (Cambridge: Cambridge University Press, 2000).

2. Joseph Grinnell, "The Museum Conscience," *Museum Work* 4 (1922): 62–63.

3. Gilbert K. Chesterton, *Illustrated London News*, July 5, 1924.

4. Commission on the Future of the Smithsonian Institution, *E Pluribus Unum: This Divine Paradox, Report of the Commission on the Future of the Smithsonian Institution* (Washington, D.C.: Smithsonian Institution, 1995).

5. James Owen, *National Geographic News*, 2004.

6. See news.nationalgeographic.com/news/2004/06/0603_040603_museums.html.

7. Peter Vergo, "Introduction," in *The New Museology*, ed. Peter Vergo (London: Reaktion Books, 1989), 1–5.

8. Henri Oullet, "Museum Collections: Perspectives," in *Museum Collections: Their Roles and Future in Biological Research*, ed. Edward H. Miller, 215–19 (Victoria, B.C., Canada: Occasional Papers No. 25, British Columbia Provincial Museum, 1985).

9. Michael Archer, ed., *Carnivorous Marsupials*, vol. 1 (New South Wales, Australia: Royal Zoological Society, 1982); and Rollin H. Baker, "The Classification of Neotropical Mammals—A Historical Résumé," in *Latin American Mammalogy: History, Biodiversity, and Conservation*, ed. Michael A. Mares and David J. Schmidly (Norman: University of Oklahoma Press, 1991).

10. Robert M. May, "How Many Species Are There on Earth?" *Science* 241 (1988): 1441–49; and Edward O. Wilson, *The Diversity of Life* (Cambridge, Mass.: Belknap, 1992).

11. May, "How Many Species Are There on Earth?"

12. Bruce D. Patterson, "Fathoming Tropical Biodiversity: The Continuing Discovery of Neotropical Mammals," *Diversity and Distributions 7* (2001): 191–96.

13. Michael A. Mares, Janet K. Braun, Ruben M. Barquez, and M. Monica Diaz, "Two New Genera and Species of Halophytic Desert Mammals from Isolated Salt Flats in Argentina," *Occasional Papers, Museum of Texas Tech University* 203 (2000): 1–27.

14. Earl of Cranbrook, "The Scientific Value of Collections," in *The Value and Valuation of Natural Science Collections*, ed. John R. Nudds and Charles W. Pettit, 3–10 (London: The Geological Society, 1997).

15. Luis W. Alvarez, Walter Alvarez, Frank Asaro, and Helen V. Michel, "Extraterrestrial Cause for the Cretaceous-Tertiary Extinction," *Science* 208 (1980): 1095–1108.

16. Benjamin C. Shuraytz, Virgil L. Sharpton, and Luis E. Marin, "Petrology of Impact-melt Rocks at the Chicxulub Multiring Basin (Yucatan, Mexico)," *Geology* 22 (1994): 868–72; Alan R. Hildebrand et al., "The Chicxulub Crater and Its Relation to the K-T Boundary Ejecta and Impact-wave Deposits," Conference on New Developments Regarding the K-T Event and Other Catastrophes in Earth History. Houston, Tex.: Lunar and Planetary Institute Contribution 825 (1996): 49; Richard A. Kerr, "Cores Document Ancient Catastrophe," *Science* 275 (1997): 1265; and Dale H. Easley, "The Death of the Dinosaurs: UNO Department of Geology's Contribution" (2002). http://www.nogs.org/UNO_Dinosaur_Death.htm.

17. Wilfrid Blunt, *Linnaeus: The Complete Naturalist* (Princeton, N.J.: Princeton University Press, 2001).

18. Blunt, *Linnaeus*.

19. Leonard Krishtalka and Philip S. Humphrey, "Can Natural History Museums Capture the Future?" *BioScience* 50 (2000): 611–17.

20. Laurence Vail Coleman, *College and University Museums: A Message for College and University Presidents* (Washington, D.C.: American Association of Museums, 1942).

21. Sidney Dillon Ripley, *The Sacred Grove: Essays on Museums* (New York: Simon & Schuster, 1969).

22. Note that a feeling of pride in cultural attainment, so widely shared at one time, no longer exists as petty bureaucrats jettison cultural organizations if they cost an organization "significant" amounts of money to maintain (significance being determined by the administrators, of course).

23. Aute Richards, "The University Museum of Zoology and Cultural Progress," *The Chronicles of Oklahoma* 20 (1942): 265–72.

24. I have heard of no similar government commission that has been put in place to protect cultural organizations from attacks by al Qaeda, even though attacks within the United States are more likely now than they were during World War II. This speaks volumes for how the importance of culture is viewed at the highest levels of state and national government. Universities are not the only employers of ignorant bean counters. Michael A. Mares, personal observation.

25. Can you imagine administrators saying this in today's climate of bottom-line managers? "They're going to destroy the collections? Good! They'll save me the

trouble." This is a much more likely response in our current anticultural climate. Michael A. Mares, personal observation.

26. Beth Gibson, 1997. "Japanese Attack Mainland America with Balloon Bombs" (Memories by Duane L. Hamilton), *The Courier*, January 1997, East Benton County Historical Society, Kennewick, WA: http://hometown.aol.com/Gibson0817/bombs.htm.

27. Richards, "The University Museum of Zoology and Cultural Progress."

28. Michael A. Mares, personal observation, 1994.

29. Hilde S. Hein, *The Museum in Transition: A Philosophical Perspective* (Washington, D.C.: Smithsonian Institution Press, 2000).

30. Joshua Laerm and Amy Lyn Edwards, "What Is a State Museum of Natural History?" in *Natural History Museums: Directions for Growth*, ed. Paisley S. Cato and Clyde Jones, 13–39 (Lubbock: Texas Tech University Press, 1991); and S. J. Pike and Judith E. Winston, "State Natural History Museums: Results of a Survey," *Association of Systematics Collections Newsletter*, August 2000, 5–7.

31. Paul A. Johnsgard, *The Nature of Nebraska: Ecology and Biodiversity* (Lincoln: Nebraska University Press, 2001).

32. U.S. Census Bureau, quickfacts.census.gov/qfd/states/31000.html.

33. Arrell Morgan Gibson, *Oklahoma: A History of Five Centuries* (Norman: University of Oklahoma Press, 1981).

34. U.S. Census Bureau, quickfacts.census.gov/qfd/states/40000.html.

35. Michael A. Mares, ed., *A University Natural History Museum for the New Millennium* (Norman: Sam Noble Oklahoma Museum of Natural History, 2001); and Michael A. Mares, "Museum Director: Seventeen Years in the Vortex," in *A University Natural History Museum for the New Millennium*, ed. Michael A. Mares, 99–121 (Norman: Sam Noble Oklahoma Museum of Natural History, 2001).

36. E-mail letter from Harvey Perlman to Michael A. Mares, March 18, 2003.

37. E-mail letter from Michael A. Mares to Harvey Perlman, March 17, 2003.

38. David L. Boren, "Reflections on the Dedication of the Sam Noble Oklahoma Museum of Natural History," in *A University Natural History Museum for the New Millennium*, ed. Michael A. Mares, 1–4 (Norman: Sam Noble Oklahoma Museum of Natural History, 2001).

39. Michael A. Mares, "Oklahoma's Newest Museum," in *A University Natural History Museum for the New Millennium*, ed. Michael A. Mares, 5–8 (Norman: Sam Noble Oklahoma Museum of Natural History, 2001); and Michael A. Mares, "Miracle on the Prairie: The Development of the Sam Noble Oklahoma Museum of Natural History," *Museologia* (Portugal) 2 (2002): 31–50.

40. Michael A. Mares, "Did We Help Create the Crisis in University Natural History Museums?" *The Newsgram*, Mountain Plains Museum Association Newsletter, November 2003, 22–23.

41. Merriam-Webster Online, www.m-w.com/dictionary/philistine.

9

As Long as the Grass Will Grow: My Teaching Philosophy

Charles Dailey

> *"As long as the grass will grow"* is my own teaching philosophy. I began
> in the Museum Field in 1956—and no one knows my name—but my
> students will. *That is my goal.*

I was the museum director for over twenty years, I wore a tie, I cared very
deeply for my staff, and I was quiet. I have gone to American Association
of Museums (AAM) and American Association for State and Local History
(AASLH) meetings, listened, and taken notes, which were filed in my expan-
sive museum resource system. My wife and I spent a year on a Vespa in Western Europe visiting museums from Yugoslavia to Italy to Finland. My wife
photographed the museums, and I wrote notes.

My wife, Carol, and I were "hippies" in 1962 looking for the perfect place
to contribute to the world. We picked Santa Fe because it was small, beautiful, and had different cultures, which were so beautiful. The Hispanic, the
Indian, and the White lived side by side. The Museum of New Mexico
(MNM) system of museums, the Museum of Navajo Ceremonial Art (Wheel-
wright Museum), the School of American Research, and the Institute of
American Indian Arts Museum were in Santa Fe.

I was with the Museum of New Mexico as the head designer for the state.
Because of a lack of funds for the exhibitions department at the MNM from
1964 to about 1970, I went to the Santa Fe Plaza area and found "hippies"
who had "dropped out of life." They loved museums. I would offer them
lunch if they would help clean floors, paint walls, do wiring, plaster, carry
artwork, and install exhibits. Year after year these youngsters did a large part

of the work on exhibits from the Palace of the Governors to the International Folk Art Museum. The ability to select a person, train them to work for you, and have it work is the educational philosophy that I tried. My workers—men and women—came from all of America. Never did we have a person who felt "used" or "unappreciated." Never did a person take advantage of the museum or of its abilities. I never had a person who did not pour his or her heart into a project. This is when I began to develop a "way to teach" young people. One aspect that I always looked for was a person who had common sense as well as intelligence.

The Institute of American Indian Arts (IAIA) in Santa Fe was a chance to work with Native American students from Alaska to Florida. Each student had the most wonderful history and legacy. I was wise enough to accept the job as faculty and director of the museum. I was janitor, painter, electrician, exhibitionist, curator, and teacher—and, of course, director.

My wife had taught me honesty, humility, and hard work. I was very excited to work with my students. When they painted, I painted. When they washed floors, I washed floors. I am not a perfectionist, but rather just a person who takes pride in doing humble things. Students liked that. When exhibits were done, even when I did most of the work, I would always say the "students did a good job." I never take credit for anything, but I always accept the blame.

When an exhibit is being prepared and we are washing floors, I talk about the chemicals, the steps of washing, the corners, and the waxes. Then we wash the floors. When lighting is to be done, we will work out problems in the shop with lights, filters, grills, grates, and then go to the exhibit area. We make mistakes in the shop and then go to the gallery and do it correctly.

In the collections, we had 6,000 items. Nothing was identified, nothing done. Sitting down on the floor, we worked out a system of scale models on good "storage" for paintings and sculpture. We discussed, argued, changed ideas, and then did the second phase. The IAIA Museum now exists as it does because of student scale models.

The students sat on the floor discussing what experiences they wanted the tourists to have when they walked in the door. Students from Canada, California, Delaware, Florida, the Southwest, and Oklahoma discussed these problems. We decided on the present introduction area for the IAIA Museum. We now have a "quiet orientation room" with a waterfall in the center of the circle, and the room has a quiet introduction of flute music. It is the students' idea.

Students work in classes for two hours a day, two days a week, with three hours of reading for lecture classes. In studio classes they have two days of three hours in class, with three hours of reading and homework. Sometimes I have to get after students to not be late; sometimes they are absent. When exhibitions come, however, students and I have worked until two or three in the morning, and then we have come back the next day to complete the project. With pizza and coke, the world could be changed in an exhibition gallery.

In the past ten years, the IAIA Museum has become a Bachelors of Art program. Students earn some thirty-plus credits in the museum field. We provide experiences in exhibitions, collections care, and administration. All of our students do research as well. We conclude the Associate of Fine Arts (AFA) two-year program with a course called "Museum Development I." This course forces the student to completely design a hypothetical museum of their tribal affiliation with all of the rooms required by a "typical" museum. Students design the rooms they want, hallways, heating, ventilation, and air conditioning systems, loading areas, collections needs, and exhibition spaces in a building they want. Each person prepares the scale model and the written document that explains the different rooms.

I do not teach architecture, so the room is not a consideration. What we want is that the student act as "director," so the student designs a space to fit his or her needs. The student designs and builds to his or her needs. The next day the student will be the collections person, or the exhibition person, or the janitor. To complete the project the student assembles this collection of jobs together in a building. The second thing of importance is the environment. Each student has a close relationship to wind, heat, snow, rain, and water. This has to be represented. A workbook must accompany this experience of the model. The workbook must begin with the mission, bylaws, articles of incorporation, collections policy, and staff positions, and each room is listed and covered with electrical needs, flooring, walls, furniture, equipment, and lighting.

If I were to design my own museum structure, I would begin with the board of trustees, then the director, and continue down to the responsible departments. The Native American student, however, will have a number of people "above" the board—the earth, water, sky, the elders, the clans, the tribal members, the plants and animals, and so on. This changes the nature of the director's responsibilities. We explain each of the tribal directions as the student feels they should be. Each of these "elements" must be reflected, and some paragraph or page will explain what the museum must "do" to be responsible.

For Museum Development I, the student will have to design *one* of the following sections of the model: collections, exhibitions, or administration. One of the sections must be completed in scale and covered thoroughly in the workbook.

At the end of the four-year program, the student will return to the workbook and model done two years before. They will then have to complete the project. All rooms will be completed; all of the workbook will be done. For the last semester with Museum Development II, one student's workbook was over ninety pages long. Next semester it will be longer.

In 1969 the Bureau of Indian Affairs had some 169 tribal groups that wanted to build cultural centers. Only two of these museums were run by Indians. In 1989, we did another survey, and there were over 269 tribal groups wanting assistance to build or renovate tribal cultural centers. In 1989 there were nine of these museums run by Native Americans! And seven of these centers were run by IAIA alumni!

We are not in a hurry. Many Native Americans are finding places of assistance today all across America.

In 1971 I asked students where they "came from." Each of the students had his or her own stories about Mother Earth. Nobody's family came across the Bering Strait. We want our young people to have their own legends; we want them to believe in what they think. If they came from the stars like the Osage Indians, then they will put that in their museum.

American Indians include over 500-plus groups. They are as different as the "French" and the "Germans." Even among the nineteen Pueblos of the Rio Grande Valley, each of the small tribes is different. There are even differences in languages of tribes just fifty miles apart.

In 2003, I was fortunate to attend the AAM conference in Texas. I went with two students who wanted to attend. I only went to a few of the workshops but spent most of the time reading books at the AAM bookshop. I tried to get new titles to add to the modest library at our museum. In most of the classes we teach, we now will ask the student to buy at least two books as reading. The plethora of books is wonderful for the young student. I challenge the students today, yesterday, and tomorrow to be the ones who will "write their own books" on museology, to make themselves heard—to be able to gently say the things in one's heart and to be read by a person 100, 1,000, or 10,000 miles away and think about what you want people to know.

We have assembled over the past fifty years essays, magazines, writings, and notes from conferences, audiotapes, and discussion notes, which cover every aspect of museology. The IAIA museum studies program has a wealth of materials from the International Council of Museums, AASLH, AAM, the Mountain-Plains Museums Association, and some of the other museum associations in America. All of these publications are cut up and sorted into categories—docents, exhibitions, research, collections, and conservation—and filed. At any moment we can stop and see what has been written or said for over fifty years! Attendance problems, labeling, lighting—all of these categories have been discussed. This is the wonderful aspect of the assembled categories. We like the files because we do not have to look at directories or bibliographies discussing the writings in some source.

I have mentioned that my wife was a photographer. When we visited America and every country in Europe, we photographed. My wife photographed in the Louvre, in Finland, in Yugoslavia, and in Germany. We were arrested in the Louvre photographing the security system! We can just think of any subject and select slides stored in vertical files on any aspect of museology! I have over 80,000 slides on museums, and there is an equal file system at the IAIA Museum. Many years ago I was at the Smithsonian Institution's National Museum of Natural History. I was photographing the *Tiger Pouncing on the Deer*. As I was photographing the habitat group using a tripod, someone on the floor upstairs apparently was moving a file cabinet, and it hit the floor. The ceiling plaster fell on me and the habitat group, covering us with a layer of plaster. I photographed the scene before and after the accident. It was six minutes before the guards arrived to ask the children not to play with the plaster! So when I discuss "security systems," it is easy to illustrate the best and worst!

In 1971 the IAIA Museum got its first video system. My wife and I recorded every show broadcast for over forty years that had to do with museums. I cut and pasted video programs on personnel, exhibits, collections, conservation, zoos, and everything else. When I teach, I will sing, I have my old "sayings," I will show slides, videos, or movies, and I will lecture. I will do anything that is necessary for people to remember. Classes have ranged from independent study projects with one student to larger classes of some ten or fifteen students. The IAIA tries to keep class size small. It helps us to work on a system of individual projects so that we can work with individuals to guide them. I have had classes of thirty students in European art survey courses, but prefer a dozen students who challenge each other in daily activities and grow together.

I expect students to be in class, to think, to react, to question, to work, and to get excited. Because we are in Santa Fe and only sixty miles from Albuquerque, we take field trips frequently. These are on Fridays and are extra time that students must spend.

We are also only thirty miles from Los Alamos. We take a field trip there every fall. Many of my students are conservative, some are peaceful, and some are very radical. I try to get the student to be responsible for whatever beliefs they have. When I was in college, my professor told the class to read *Mein Kampf*. I had just gotten out of the Marine Corps and wrote on the paper "NO." He wrote a note to me and asked me, "If you hate something so badly—then what do you hate?" I did not know. So in lectures I tell students that they must be wise, and, if they dislike "something," then tell me what is bad about the thing and act wisely. When students visit Los Alamos and see the atomic bomb, they would be wise to know what is good and what is bad. They should be able to criticize with wisdom.

I teach Native students. I am very quiet and humbly a hard worker. I do not ask my students to do anything that I would not do. I work with them constantly. One of the reasons the IAIA has a museum studies program is quite simple. A tribal group may have 3,000 people in the community. They want a museum. In America today we would just look for someone in our community who has a bachelor's degree in history or art and ask them to be the director. In our tribe, we don't have the numbers. The person who has the bachelors degree is already working. We don't have extra people. Just get someone who is "an artist," "a history buff," or "who doesn't have another job." We began to train young people for two years—to get an AFA and then return home. This worked for many years. Now we are a four-year college with a museum studies degree. Our students are exceptional.

I had the opportunity to enroll at the University of Colorado. For two years I worked full-time as a uranium miner in the afternoon and evening shift, then got the chance to work for Dr. Hugo Rodeck, the director of the University of Colorado Museum. I was in his first museum theory class in 1956, and it tied in my artistic work, my love for hard work, and my enthusiasm. Dr. Rodeck was my hero, for he believed so strongly in museums! His daughter, Jean Rodeck, was already with the National Park Service. By classwork, by enthusiasm, by leadership, our class of eight students became dedicated to the idea of museums. No person could ever get a greater and more positive boost than by Jean Rodeck and Hugo Rodeck!

When we began our museum studies program, we wrote to Leicester University, to Winterthur, to the University of Colorado, and to the University of Oklahoma asking for their college catalogs. In 1970, we received some twenty letters from Europe and America. My wife and I had just returned from a year traveling and visiting museums in Europe. We then traveled for six months in our old hippie car in America, Canada, and Mexico, visiting museums. We photocopied the materials we received on courses offered everywhere. We separated them into four categories—administration, collections, exhibitions, and research. We thought of what we would like to learn in each of these areas. My wife and I knew Native people, had visited several reservations, and were knowledgeable about Native peoples. We then separated "world museums" and their needs and listed these, and then looked at "Native museums" and their needs and listed them. Tying these together, the two fit beautifully. For our "Introduction to Museums," we listed the development of world museums and separated the categories of information into times. Then the needs of "Indian museums" were separated as well and formed the junction.

The museum studies faculty leads in the teaching of students at the IAIA. The faculty is supported by the personnel at the IAIA Museum in downtown Santa Fe. At the present time we rely on the exhibitions staff, the collections staff, and the educational department staff.

Because I had worked for almost ten years at the Museum of New Mexico, we have a wonderful relationship with the MNM. The Museum of New Mexico has been overwhelmingly supportive with demonstrations, visits, workshops, and lectures for our students. The associate director, John McCaffrey, has consistently supported our program for many years.

We require students to do two internships for the bachelor's degree. The Museum of New Mexico has always supported the possibility of accepting our young people. In 1995 the IAIA Museum had hired a new director for the IAIA Museum. He was a very fine person, but his goals for the museum were to make it "world class." He would not let my students work on exhibits any longer, and they could no longer work with the permanent collections. After a couple months of this, the IAIA Museum students bought T-shirts and had them printed with the image of the front of the IAIA Museum and the words "This IS My Museum." They wore these t-shirts for about a month, and the director of the museum was asked to resign. This is pretty powerful for students to go to the aid of the organization and ask it to change!

The National Museum of the American Indian of the Smithsonian Institution is led by one of the members of the IAIA board of trustees. Richard West was a powerful force as a board member in the early years of the IAIA. When Richard West was a trustee, he made regular trips to the IAIA Museum to see exhibits and to see what students were doing. The Smithsonian Institution is working with the IAIA to contact alumni in collections, exhibitions, and administration as possible employees.

At the beginning of this chapter, I alluded to the words "as long as the grass will grow." At the end of this essay I affirm my quiet and very humble contribution to assisting my young people to be able to "stand up and tell their stories—as long as the grass will grow." Perhaps the anthropologists can prove by "digs" here and there and tell us when the "Bering Strait" was used. My students are not just "obstinate" and "listening to the wind." We listen to stories; we know that animals and birds talk. We know that the grass grows on the plains, and the great trees have "led us before."

When we visit a reservation, if we are quiet and sit under a tree and think, we can "still hear the grass grow." We do not hear "rock music," but just the sound from the rustle of trees and know that the old people can feel the "grass" and the "wind" even yet. This is the philosophy that I have, and continue, to teach to my museum studies students at IAIA. I hope that it is a philosophy that will serve them and their museums well in the twenty-first century. I also hope they will share this knowledge and philosophy with others so that it is passed onward as the wind moves the grass, as in waves on the ocean continuing forever. Thank you for letting me speak of my "teaching philosophy."

10

Science Centers: Creating a Platform for Twenty-first Century Innovation

Lesley Lewis and Jennifer L. Martin

The Ontario Science Centre (OSC) opened to the public in 1969 as one of the first of a new generation of science "museums" around the world. These new institutions were not collection based but were designed to actively engage the visitor through hands-on, interactive experiences. They paved the way for a new approach to learning by utilizing exhibits, programs, and demonstrations that made science and technology accessible to everyone.

Many people have linked the development and success of science centers to a Chinese aphorism variously attributed to Lao Tsu (604–531 BC) and Confucius (551–479 BC).

> I hear and I forget
> I see and I remember
> I do and I understand

First Ten Years,[1] a publication written to comment on the first decade of the OSC, reflects on the development of a new model of visitor engagement.

> Let visitors touch the exhibits. This exciting and original concept came after hours of deliberation and experimentation and its adoption has been responsible for the Centre's tremendous success. . . . The most successful exhibits are those based upon the curiosity of people about themselves. What does my voice sound like? How do I hear? How good is my balance. . . . When a child asks if he can see something, he is really asking if he can touch. Taizo Miake (Chief Designer) wrote about this phenomenon: "The Science Centre can focus on that

special and unique quality of human interest that must see with their own eyes, touch with their own bodies. In many cases the visitor is a component of the exhibit, the missing link required in order to make it work."

Two decades later in 1999, while celebrating its thirtieth anniversary, OSC reflected on its past and looked toward the future. The world had changed significantly since 1969. We were now living in a time where the "brand" of interactive engagement developed by the science center was found in retail stores and restaurants; children and adults can explore the world of science on the Internet; science magazines for the layperson are widely available; and there are television programs, and even television channels, devoted to the world of science and discovery.

LOOKING TO THE FUTURE

In our quest to determine what new unique role we could play in society, we conducted a series of research projects. That research told us that our visitors had a clear sense of what we offered. The words used to describe what we offered included: trusted; authentic; neutral (that is, unbiased); communicators; and knowledgeable about science and technology.

Science and technology communications had been at the core of our work for thirty years. We had provided a dynamic, involving, and safe environment for young people, and their families, to learn. Perhaps our greatest strength had been that we made the complex simple and in so doing engaged people in science.

Against that backdrop, the Ontario Science Centre, like many other science centers, museums and art galleries around the world entered the twenty-first century challenging itself on how to further engage the public.

One of our self-imposed challenges was to increase the level of engagement with a traditionally difficult audience for our sector to reach. In their teen years, young people turn to peers for entertainment, rejecting many of the activities they have previously enjoyed with parents and families. They only return to institutions like science centers in their twenties, or perhaps not until they have children themselves. And yet, it is in these same teen years that youth are making their most significant career and life decisions. We wanted to play a role in this, and realized that in order to do so we would need to change.

We began to speak to youth, to explore their interests. Not surprisingly perhaps, we learned that young people today are not so different from earlier generations. They want to make a difference in the world but, unlike previous generations, today's youth have technologies to allow them to connect with their peers on a worldwide basis and the potential to actually fulfill that goal. Our ability to explore these technologies and thereby engage with teens in a whole new way was seen as a key strength in connecting with this audience. Simultaneously with this, we became increasingly aware that the focus of governments around the world was on innovation and the importance of innovation to global competitiveness. We began to explore the unique niche that a science center can occupy in expanding the confidence in, and capabilities for, innovative thinking by our public audiences. A country can only succeed in being innovative if innovation is truly embedded in its culture. From these two seemingly disparate threads, a vision for a new model for engagement at the Ontario Science Centre began to emerge.

DEVELOPING A NEW MODEL
OF ENGAGEMENT

Today, in 2006, the Ontario Science Centre is extending the aphorism that has guided it for thirty years.

> I hear and I forget
> I see and I remember
> I do and I understand
> *I create and my mind opens*
> *I innovate and the world opens*

Our focus will continue to be on science and technology but the approach we will use will foster creativity and innovation in a broad array of disciplines. Our goal is to move from being an attraction-based place to visit, to being a leader in building relationships beyond the site, beyond the visit. We want to make a real difference in the lives of all children and youth, not just those with high potential who are often the focus of specialized science center programs. We want to shift our audience from visitors to *participants*, gaining confidence through our activities to be creative problem solvers. We will strive to ensure that science and technology are viewed as equally essential to twenty-first-century culture as museums and art galleries. But to accomplish these goals we had to approach our work in a different way. We had to become more innovative. Ultimately, our inspiration came from Einstein's statement that "the problems that exist in the world today cannot be solved by the level of thinking that created them."[2]

Science centers are uniquely positioned to provide a window for the public to understand and explore the latest developments in science. As the world faces increasingly complex scientific issues, this role has never been more important. However, physical exhibits rarely lend themselves to the type of flexibility required to address rapidly changing views in science and ongoing advances in technology. We had to expand our thinking to contemplate the nature of the experiences we could provide that would keep our visitors at the forefront of science, while engaging them in activities that are relevant on an individual scale.

As we met with leaders from corporations, research institutions, and educators, they confirmed that science centers can and must increase their role in helping the public to understand the issues and outcomes of today's scientific research. Working with these same partners, we are developing experiences that will contribute to a better understanding of research, ignite creativity, encourage problem solving and collaboration skills, teach the importance of risk taking, and promote science literacy.

All of this is about much more than simply developing new experiences. It's about a change in our thinking about informal science, discovery, and communication. It's about changing the model of how a science center develops and presents information in partnership with others. It's about our visitors becoming true participants with us in the process of science. Institutions such as ours have an important role to play in the cultivation of creative citizens, engaged in the exploration of science and technology and prepared to create new solutions to the challenges the world faces.

At the OSC, diverse activities and programs will encourage visitors of all ages to develop problem solving, teamwork, and communication skills. We will expose young people to the attitudes, skills, networks, and tools that will enable them to become the drivers of a culture of innovation—today's informed citizens and tomorrow's research scientists.

Who are the major audiences for this new approach?

- Members of the general public interested in life-long learning to enhance skills and expand their knowledge and understanding of the world;
- Young children, whose intellectual abilities are most flexible;
- Parents who want to help their children learn to seek out new solutions;
- Teachers who want to foster an innovative spirit in their classrooms;
- Businesses who want to rejuvenate their approach to innovation through hands-on, team-building experiences; and
- Teens and young adults who are seeking skills and confidence and want to make a difference in the world.

Embarking in a major new direction requires a window of opportunity as well as the inspiration to test new waters and break old ways of doing things. The Ontario Science Centre promoted these concepts to funders and supporters who have joined in making this project a reality. The initiative is called Agents of Change, and it is already radically changing the way the Centre engages with visitors, partners, and staff.

CREATING A PLATFORM FOR CHANGE

The mission of the Agents of Change initiative is:

To ...
Spark creativity, inspiration, innovation and change.
By ...
Joining participants and partners with the Science Centre to create unexpected, unbelievably cool experiences, relationships, networks, environments, and enterprises.
So that ...
People generate new ways of seeing and thinking about themselves and the world.
New questions. . . . New solutions. . . . New possibilities.

A series of goals have been established to assist us in achieving this far-reaching mission:

- To increase public awareness of the importance of innovation
- To foster the attitudes, skills, and behaviors that enable innovation (including creativity, risk taking, problem solving, and collaboration)
- To build understanding of the process and products of innovation
- To provide access to current science and technology research and discoveries
- To encourage critical thinking skills
- To introduce young people to career opportunities in science and technology
- To revitalize the Ontario Science Centre and continue its evolution as a leader on the world stage of science centers
- To reposition the Ontario Science Centre within Canada's infrastructure for science and technology as an important node for information dissemination and discussion
- To create new, deeper, and ongoing relationships between visitors and the OSC

To achieve these ends, we cannot work alone. We are working with leading-edge academic and corporate researchers, bringing together their research with our proven ability to make complex subjects accessible. As one example, we have formed a strong partnership with DuPont Canada. As our "knowledge partner," they have committed over eight years to provide us not only with financial support but, even more importantly, with expertise. DuPont scientists are working with our science communicators in developing innovative programming for our visitors. DuPont business strategists have helped us to question and redesign our development processes. DuPont in turn is learning new ways to spark creativity and innovation in its own organization. We anticipate such content partnerships as being key to our success. But we will not relinquish our control over the actual visitor experience.

A SERIES OF CHALLENGES

The development team has faced enormous challenges. Is it truly possible to influence the attitudes, skills, and behaviors of an individual through his or her engagement with a science center? If we can, then how do we create a platform for twenty-first-century innovation? What are the physical and dynamic conditions necessary to enable this to occur?

Very early on in this period of questioning it became clear that fundamental to this development was the concept of working *with* our audience, not following typical processes to create exhibits *for* them. This significant turning point in our thinking owes its genesis to discussions we had with teenagers, as noted earlier.

Further, these experiences need to be much more process oriented than outcome driven. Processes, such as new knowledge or ability that are transferable to situations well beyond the walls of a science center, can be taken away from a "visit." The fact that a quickly rigged-up contraption to transport water from one point to another might actually fail is much less important than the innovative thinking, rapid prototyping, and collaboration it took to try out the idea in the first place.

The development team has been taking the processes of innovative thinking to heart, redressing their own approaches to exhibit development, and collaborating with the audience at virtually every step of the way. Testing of concepts, piloting loose frameworks for activity, engaging visitors and visiting professionals (teachers, corporate executives, academic researchers, etc.), and rapidly expressing ideas in physical form have all become new modes of development for the staff involved in this work. It is fun, it is fast, and it is uncertain. However, through rigorous documentation of trials, and a freedom to step well out of the normal bounds of their professional roles, the development team has succeeded in creating "platforms for agents of change."

Each of these platforms, together comprising well over 30 percent of the existing exhibition space within the science center, is focused on a specific subset of innovation skill strategies. As an example of the level of partnership involved on this project, we worked closely with DuPont Canada to adopt a strategic process that tightly focused our thinking on these strategies. There is overlap and some redundancy in this framework, ensuring that different engagement and learning styles are attracted to and comfortable with the types of activities and content being addressed.

The entire suite is broken out into seven areas, each ranging from 3,000 square feet to over 16,000 square feet. A significant, central location in the building is dedicated to a cluster of these areas, with two located elsewhere. The seven areas are:

Hot Zone—Here visitors explore current science and emerging technology through multimedia presentations, engaging interfaces, and live updates by Science Centre staff and experts "behind the headlines."

Visitors are able to encounter real-time field diaries from scientists on location across the globe. Several scientists and physicians from the Centre for International Health, Faculty of Medicine, University of Toronto, have agreed to provide journal entries while in the field in such places as Burkina Faso and Dar es Salaam, Africa.

The Hot Zone development team also is focusing on creating on-site and web-based opportunities for youth to express and share their views on "hot" science and technology. Discussions are underway with Carleton University, School of Journalism, and Ryerson University, School of Broadcasting, to explore mechanisms for their students to contribute to Hot Zone content.

Challenge Zone—With a focus on encouraging collaboration and risk-taking, the Challenge Zone invites visitors to use everyday materials to solve a relevant scientific challenge within a specified time limit. Extensive pilot testing, with over 4,200 participants in loosely fashioned development sites in existing exhibition halls, has had a significant influence on understanding the conditions necessary to make visitors feel comfortable with the prospect of sharing their ideas in a problem-solving environment, and working with others who they may not have ever met.

Citizen Science—Citizen Science provides opportunities for visitors to become citizen scientists, contributing observations and data to real research projects set up and led by scientists. As part of pilot testing, visitors have been able to help monitor the health of the large wetland adjacent to the Science Centre through a series of sensors and web cams that visitors can access via a computer on-site or online.

The Citizen Science development team has collaborated with Parks Canada, Wildlife Habitat Canada, several universities, museums, and other organizations interested in enabling community and citizen-based environmental monitoring. The team also has worked with TVOntario, Environment Canada, and the Royal Botanical Gardens on a program called "Sightings of Spring." Young participants in grades 1–5 from across Ontario tracked the coming of spring by making observations and posting them on the Internet.

Media Studios—This area of approximately 3,500 square feet features a variety of media tools through which visitors can discover what happens when the boundaries between technology, music, fashion, art, and science are blurred. The development team has worked with MIT Media Lab in Boston and with York University, Institute for Research on Learning Technologies, Seneca College, and Ontario College of Art and Design to explore ways to collaborate on the design and development of novel experiences.

Material World—Material World will demonstrate that materials are both the enablers and the products of innovation. Visitors are encouraged to employ all their senses to manipulate and explore the characteristics, applications, and potential of both new and common materials in unusual and often surprising ways. Experiences will range from demonstrations on new materials, a chance to try out unusual materials in the "Materials Testing Zone," and exhibits illustrating the often circuitous routes taken by innovators as they develop new materials.

KidSpark—At over 16,000 square feet, this is a dedicated learn-through-play area for children eight years and under. Over thirty open-ended, interactive experiences in six themed areas foster creativity, problem-solving abilities, and early innovation skills by focusing on the processes of discovery and experimentation.

To ensure that young visitors are getting the most from their KidSpark visits, senior interns in early childhood education (ECE) from Ryerson University are working with Science Centre hosts on the floor to facilitate interaction among children, caregivers, and the experiences. ECE interns have both learned from and enhanced the KidSpark experience. Fotini Fokidis, an ECE intern, says of her KidSpark experience:

> As an educator guiding children, sparking their curiosity and challenging their minds is always a rewarding ideal. At the Ontario Science Centre I was able to accomplish just that. It was very rewarding to know that children were amazed by the capabilities I helped bring out in them. KidSpark has given me the opportunity to spark the curiosity in myself.

Grand Central—This final area of the Agents of Change revitalization is an inspirational starting point and end point for an OSC visit. Through sensational art installations, visitors are invited to explore the creative edge of science and technology. The initial vision for this space includes large artworks that take full advantage of the magnificent space. The Grand Central development team is collaborating with experts and artists in related fields and is outlining the process for partnership with artists who will contribute to the experiences in this area.

BECOMING MORE INNOVATIVE OURSELVES

All of this work could not have occurred had we not seriously and rigorously questioned our development and design processes. After all, which comes first, the innovative organization or the innovative visitor experiences? In truth we have found that there is no serial answer to that question, as both process and product influence each other as well as the culture of our organization.

Nevertheless, at this stage of the work, as we stretch to reach our most significant goal of becoming a platform for twenty-first-century innovation, we have found the following elements to be critical:

Question past practices—Don't dismiss every skill or process that has led your organization to its present stage, but don't rely on them either. Changing processes can be unnerving and difficult to describe, but by sticking to this ideal we have looked anew at our work, and have gained new skills by shifting the emphasis off some stages of development. We have added entirely new steps along the way, such as pilot-testing concepts before even making an exhibit list for prototyping.

Play—Laughter is a great indicator of how comfortable people are expressing new ideas. In a playful environment, only ideas fail, not people.

Change the language—We have purposefully changed language to illustrate that we are working differently. For example, we speak of participants, not visitors, and of experiences, not exhibits.

Make mistakes—One of the fundamental characteristics of innovative thinking is the ability to take risks. How can we create environments for participants to be innovative, if we don't allow staff to make mistakes? In fact, we have a saying in the development teams: "Learn to love the crash."

Move people around—Changing processes and practices is more successful if people are moved out of their traditional environments into new locations. Their point of view literally changes when they start working in a different location, with different team members.

Document—How else can one repeat success, if the process is not documented? Oral traditions can be valuable, but they are not transferable. Spread the wealth of knowledge by capturing it in the moment. We use everything from digital images on the fly during pilot testing, to simple, one-page frameworks to document the thinking and inspiration behind an idea.

Read—There is a wealth of information available on innovation. The business press is thick with it, and the research into innovation in the social sector is increasing daily. These experiences and thoughts have helped with so much of our work to change processes, sometimes by simply providing a new word or phrase to describe what we are hoping to achieve.

Celebrate—While this would seem self-evident, it can easily be forgotten in the rush toward deadlines and during frustrating budget-crunching meetings. Remember, this is new work; people are putting their heart and soul into trying uncertain and untested ideas.

As this experiment in innovation unfolds, we are learning daily that we are at once on the right track and still learning as we go. It is a remarkable experience. We are confident that the role of science centers in the twenty-first century is changing, and we are truly creating a platform for twenty-first-century innovation.

NOTES

Permission to reprint this essay is gratefully acknowledged. Copyright © 2004 Centennial Centre of Science and Technology.

   1. Ontario Science Centre, *First Ten Years* (1979).

   2. The *Expanded Quotable Einstein* collected and edited by Alice Calaprice (Princeton, N.J.: Princeton University Press, 2000) describes the quotation as "possibly by Einstein."

11

Renewing the Social Contract at Berkeley

Douglas Sharon

A HIDDEN TREASURE

On January 2, 2003, I became the first full-time director of the century-old Phoebe A. Hearst Museum of Anthropology at the University of California, Berkeley. During the negotiations that eventually led to my appointment, the following excerpts from the Biennial Report (1999–2001)[1] of my predecessor Professor Patrick V. Kirch caught my attention:

> Since assuming the responsibility of the Hearst Museum directorship, in 1999, not a day has passed when I have not been reminded of the incredible value—and I refer here to the cultural, aesthetic, scholarly, and scientific, not merely financial value—of our holdings. Yet these vast collections, which quite literally would be impossible to acquire anew even if an institution had unlimited financial resources, have for too many decades been under-appreciated and under-utilized. It is true that researchers from around the world know of our collections and come here to do original scholarly work with these materials. It is also the case that Berkeley faculty curators use the collections extensively in their teaching and research, and that each year hundreds of Berkeley students benefit from direct exposure to artifacts which can speak to them—as mere textbooks cannot—of ancient civilizations and diverse cultures. Yet to the broader public of the Bay Area, to the ethnically diverse citizens of California, to the national and international worlds of art and culture, the Hearst Museum remains too little known, its resources appreciated by too few. . . .
> The pending centennial celebration of the Hearst Museum's founding, in 2001–2002, provides an opportunity not just to reflect on one hundred years of

collecting, research and teaching with the collections, but to dream of the future. To this end the museum's curators and staff devoted much effort during the past year to developing a long-range strategic plan. Meeting for a day-long retreat in January 2001, a strong consensus emerged that the Hearst Museum should set its sights high, to build upon its incredibly rich collections and proud history of research, by expanding its role in public education and outreach. The strategic plan resulting from this retreat and follow-up planning sessions is ambitious to be sure, and would aim for nothing short of a transformation of the Hearst Museum: from a "hidden treasure" known and valued by a small group of researchers and students, to a significant cultural force within the Bay Area and California.

VISION

What really captured my imagination was the opening section of Professor Kirch's "A Vision for Transformation" in the *Long-Range Plan: 2001–2010*:

It is early in the fall semester, 2011, a decade after the Hearst Museum of Anthropology celebrated its centennial and began to enter a phase of institutional transformation. A rush of physical and verbal energy emanates from an excited 6th grade class, engulfing the Egyptian Civilization gallery, one of five permanent exhibition halls that have put the Hearst Museum on the cultural map of the Bay Area. Assisted by a trained docent, their teacher points to the exquisite 4th Dynasty Stele of Prince Wepemnofret, the best preserved example of its kind in the world, reinforcing, as only such a real artifact can, the brilliance of early Egyptian art. Nearby, in the Hall of African Cultures, a group of high school students is diligently taking notes on the wonderful diversity of Yoruba and Ivory Coast sculptures and carvings, part of the world-class collection of African material culture preserved by noted Berkeley anthropologist William Bascom. In addition to the beautiful objects on display, this class accesses the full range of African objects in the Hearst collections, through touch-screen computer consoles situated throughout the gallery. These windows on the collection provide digital images of hundreds of additional specimens not on exhibit, as well as offer additional explanations, bibliographic materials, and links to related web sites throughout the world.

Strolling through the spacious exhibit halls, with their state-of-the-art steel and glass cases, artifacts of feather, shell, wood, ceramic, and metal, all brilliantly illuminated with fiber-optic lighting, and the entire complex climate-controlled for maximum conservation, the viewer takes in the breadth and quality of objects representing world cultures spanning thousands of years. The viewer reflects that just a decade earlier these collections—among the greatest in the nation—were almost entirely hidden away from public view, moldering in the basements of more than four UC Berkeley buildings. Only recently, with the completion of the university's new museum complex in downtown Berkeley, has the Bay Area public been able to finally appreciate the legacy of Phoebe Hearst, the visionary UC regent who sent expeditions around the globe to obtain what she knew would be "a great educator" for the people of California. Moreover, the Hearst collections, now displayed in a physical home befitting their world-class quality, are attracting national and international attention. Always known to serious researchers, they are now being discovered by thousands of visitors to Berkeley, who stroll along the Addison/Oxford Street "arts corridor."

Meanwhile, the museum's vast systematic collections are also inspiring a renaissance in undergraduate teaching and graduate research on the Berkeley campus. With the museum's 3.8 million objects now on-line in a fully-searchable database system, incorporating vital provenience data and links to other databases and research materials (such as the museum's extensive photo and field note archives), some 25 faculty curators from more than 10 departments make extensive use of collections in teaching, while many graduate students are discovering that entire new research avenues can be addressed from systematic collections acquired decades earlier. Teaching has been greatly enhanced by new dedicated museum classrooms in Kroeber Hall, outfitted with proper lighting, digital cameras, display cases, and binocular microscopes for examining and recording artifacts. Week by week, a steady stream of undergrads have the privilege of learning, first hand with the real thing at their fingertips, in courses ranging from the civilizations of the Greco-Roman world, to ancient Peruvian cultures, to the history of ancient trade routes as determined by chemical analysis of obsidian, to the study of Native California languages (using the museum's extensive collection of early sound recordings).

Behind the scenes, in the museum's collections storerooms and staff work areas, there have also been significant improvements over the past decade. The old cramped, seismically-unsafe, basement storeroom of the Women's Gym, infamous for its rank smell of chlorine from the adjacent swimming pool, is but a memory recalled by the older staff. Now, with collections consolidated in Kroeber Hall and the Marchant Building, and with all storerooms climate controlled and with state-of-the-art fire suppression systems, the threat of potential seismic disaster (not to mention creeping decay from humidity and temperature swings) no longer haunts the museum. Two full-time professional conservators carry out their work of repairing old damage to priceless objects in a well-equipped laboratory, aided by interns from the new Museum Studies Program.

This is a vision of a future that *could be*—if the University of California at Berkeley were to recognize and avail itself of the unique educational and outreach opportunities offered by its holding of one of the nation's greatest collections of world cultural artifacts. At the same time, this is a vision of a future that *must be*—if the University is to meet its fiduciary responsibilities of caring for a priceless and irreplaceable resource, a resource it holds in trust for all the citizens of California.[2]

THE SOCIAL CONTRACT

On September 10, 1901, the University of California Board of Regents created a Museum of Anthropology at Berkeley.[3] This action came largely at the urging of Mrs. Phoebe Apperson Hearst, the first woman to hold a seat on the board, and a major patron of the young university. For some years prior, she had been actively building a substantial collection of antiquities and artifacts, financing expeditions to Egypt, Italy, Greece, Peru, Guatemala, and Mexico and purchasing objects from cultures around the world. With the founding of the new museum, she turned these priceless collections over to the university. Over the next few years Mrs. Hearst continued to support both the museum and the Department of Anthropology, headed by Alfred Kroeber. Her patronage ultimately resulted in a legacy of some 260,000 stunning artifacts and antiquities, which form the core of the Hearst Museum collections.

In a letter dated July 24, 1900, sent to Director Stewart Culin of the University of Pennsylvania Museum, Mrs. Hearst wrote the following concerning the establishment of the Museum of Anthropology at the University of California:

> In looking at the true object . . . in centralizing collections, which, as I take it, is the dissemination of knowledge among the many, not the pride and possession by the few, I think . . . that most real good can be done by placing in the distant West the collections referred to as a nucleus of what may one day become a great educator. . . .
>
> My purpose now is to turn my every effort to giving the people of California every educational advantage in my power to secure.

Nearly a century after Mrs. Hearst articulated her vision for the Museum of Anthropology as a "great educator," the American Association of Museums (AAM) firmly and emphatically established the preeminence of the educational mission of museums and their responsibility to make collections and programs relevant and available to diverse audiences. The landmark document published by the AAM in 1992, entitled *Excellence and Equity: Education and the Public Dimension of Museums,*[4] called for fundamental changes in how museums see their public service mission. The three key elements of change included (1) commitment to education as central to public service; (2) inclusiveness that welcomes diverse audiences; and (3) dynamic, forceful leadership from individuals and institutions.

In the *Long-Range Plan 2001–2010,* the Hearst Museum curators and staff wholeheartedly endorsed the University of California's long-standing commitment to excellence and diversity and the tenets of AAM's *Excellence and Equity.* The vast and varied collections of the Hearst Museum from around the globe support cross-cultural interpretive programs, which other museums must stretch to provide. In order to expand this programming and to accomplish the overarching goals in the *Long-Range Plan 2001–2010,* the Hearst Museum must undertake a mission-driven capital campaign to reveal to the public the "hidden treasures" of the Hearst Museum. To prepare for this major fund-raising effort, a foundation of private support must be laid through the "Diversity—Cultural Arts—Antiquities" program[5] as outlined in the next few pages.

DIVERSITY—CULTURAL ARTS— ANTIQUITIES PROGRAM

Mission: *To collect, preserve, research, and interpret the global record of material culture, so as to promote understanding of the history and diversity of human cultures.*
Goals established in the strategic long-range plan were:

- continued excellence in serving faculty research and university students;
- new exhibit galleries that match the quality of the collections;
- expanded public programs and increased community consultation;
- use of digital technology for preservation, access, and control;
- revised governance structure; and
- diversification of financial resources emphasizing private support.

Starting with my first day at work in January 2003, I spent several months using my training as an ethnographer to conduct participant-observation of the Hearst Museum's programs, policies, and practices. After taking some time to thoroughly understand the current situation at the Hearst Museum, under the rubric "Diversity—Cultural Arts—Antiquities," I formulated the following objectives:

- Diverse public education and outreach
- Accessible and user-friendly collections
- Coordinated research and publishing
- Museum studies curriculum development
- Endowment building initiatives

There are a few guiding principles to use in developing short-term tactics for "friend-raising."

- *Use what you have to get what you need*—through an active exhibition and public programs calendar, highlight the value of the collections as much as possible to attract support for developing the museum.
- *Strengthen existing relationships while supplementing them*—loyal members and friends of the museum, faculty curators, campus administrators, and previous donors provide a solid base upon which to build.

It's all about people, not about their money. Strong relationships will lead to strong financial support.

- *Do not duplicate existing efforts but build upon them*—utilize expertise of university relations staff and other campus fund-raising professionals.

With principles established, tactics may then be pursued:

Tactic One—Develop an ambitious program of exhibits and public programs that shows off the museum's assets to attract increasing numbers of people, to bring in new members and donors, to provide opportunities for publicity, and to validate the fact that the Hearst Museum is worthy of substantial support. These exhibits and public programs are the first priority for initial fund-raising efforts. Despite its astonishingly deep and multifaceted collections, and Mrs. Hearst's vision of its broad public education function, the museum has been underutilized as a public and community resource for generations.

Tactic Two—Increase community outreach and support by developing and expanding contacts and significant collaborations with cultural institutions and key groups within the diverse East Bay multicultural and arts community. As part of this effort, develop high quality programs and materials for local teachers and students as well as a well-trained docent corps.

Tactic Three—Develop strategic alliances and joint fund-raising opportunities with the public schools, with Native Californian tribes and other heritage communities, with other museums through traveling exhibitions, and with media outlets such as public television stations and print publishers. Diversifying the audience for museum programs and serving the heritage communities that are represented in the collections will only be possible through these partnerships. If the collections and programs continue to be located exclusively on the Berkeley campus, the long-range goals will never be accomplished. Alliances should also be formed with local companies and corporations that can contribute in-kind gifts for museum programs and events.

Tactic Four—Reach out to the campus community—one of the most ethnically diverse communities to be found anywhere. By engaging current undergraduates in museum programs, long-term relationships can be established which will bear fruit in the future. It takes a long view to undertake this short-term tactic, but this audience is so readily at hand that to miss what is virtually under our noses would be a grave mistake. These are the leaders of tomorrow. Get them interested in the Hearst Museum today.

STRATEGIC INITIATIVES

Diversity—Cultural Arts—Antiquities

We have embarked on an ambitious three-year program of changing exhibitions and public programs to increase our role of service to the campus and the broader community under a newly launched initiative, "Diversity—Cultural Arts—Antiquities." In order to fulfill Mrs. Hearst's original vision for the University of California Anthropology Museum as a "great educator" that "disseminates knowledge among the many," a three-pronged approach to public outreach is planned.

1. Implement an ongoing series of changing exhibitions at the Hearst Museum with accompanying public programs and educational materials that involve the community.
2. Extend the reach of the Hearst Museum by promoting museum-based education to the broadest spectrum of the population through exhibits designed to travel to communities where art and artifacts of the quality of the Hearst collections are rarely exhibited.
3. Make a lasting record of the knowledge gained by curating the collections for public presentation through an articulated program of research and publication distributed through a variety of formats including books, catalogues, compact discs, and the museum website, and through replicable programs.

University Museums/Hotel Complex

We were very pleased to learn that the university administration is committed to helping the Hearst Museum reach out to the public through the use of our collections. We are indebted to former director Patrick V. Kirch for bringing the hidden treasures of the Hearst Museum to the attention of all the top campus administrators as he started the negotiations for additional exhibition space. His eloquence about and persistent promotion of the Hearst Museum are now bearing fruit. One major project related to public outreach is the development of university-owned property on the edge of campus that will become a university museums and hotel/conference center complex. A substantial new exhibition space (25,000 gross square feet of space) for the Hearst Museum is being incorporated into the plans for the downtown complex.

We are proposing to the campus administration that, after renovating our current galleries and classrooms and relocating our entrance on Bancroft Way, permanent galleries be installed at the downtown location to highlight our major collections: Ancient Mediterranean Civilizations (Egypt, Greece, and Rome), Latin America, Native California, Africa, and Asia/Oceania. The addition of permanent gallery space in downtown Berkeley will greatly enhance the Hearst Museum's ability to serve the local community and school-age visitors.

On November 21, 2003, the *San Francisco Chronicle*[6] had this to say about the project:

Berkeley and UC officials announced a bold plan Thursday to dramatically change the city's core and give downtown more uptown credentials—high art, a high-rise hotel/conference center and a showcase for UC's buried treasures of anthropology. . . .

In a breakthrough for often-strained town-gown relations, the effort pleases both sides with a doubling of the city's arts district, badly needed hotel rooms and meeting space for campus visitors, and the promise of up to $1 million in hotel tax revenue for the city.

Institutional Advancement and Reorganization

In March 2003, we hired an experienced fund-raising development professional. The recruitment was the number one priority of this administration. We must diversify the mix of resources supporting the museum due to ever decreasing funding from the state. The first major development activity, solicitation of support for the "Diversity—Cultural Arts—Antiquities" program, recently resulted in underwriting of this important three-year initiative by the William Randolph Hearst Foundation.

After careful consideration and in light of our strategic initiatives, we have reorganized the public outreach staff of the museum along functional lines. By reorganizing the exhibits and education staff, we have been able to hire members of the staff team who bring with them new talents and skills to help advance our collective vision for the public outreach mission of the museum. Key new personnel in graphic design and museum education will enhance the look and reach of all of our public programming.

PHILOSOPHY

Finally, in terms of overall philosophy the following statement by Margery Wolk[7] encapsulates what I believe is a truly relevant orientation for a museum of anthropology in this new century.

I hope anthropology is now mature enough to accept its responsibility to the world outside the academy. We must no longer hide behind the usual excuses. "Hey, I am just doing basic research"; "I don't get involved with governments, mine or anybody else's"; "My work isn't relevant to social problems"; "I do theory, not practice"; "Far be it for me to . . ." We already are being asked about the point of our rushing around the world asking all these annoying questions if our findings are not useful either to the people we work with or their descendants. And if we want to be sure that our research will be used responsibly when it reaches the public domain, we had better lay out its implications ourselves.

We need to metaphorically sit down together and start thinking about what our larger responsibilities are as a discipline and how we can meet them. We need to reflect on and write about the reasons for the exponential growth of the gap between the haves and have-nots in China, Africa, the US or wherever we have expertise. Can we debate it in friendly nonjudgmental terms? Should we write about it with informed passion? Why has religion been so divisive, bringing war and grief to so many despite its promises of the opposite? What does civil liberty mean in different settings? Can we explain the implications of these differences in terms that even Congress can understand? Are there ways humans might organize themselves that would allow them to live peacefully and enjoy basic freedoms? Could we describe that organization in a way that will not immediately inflame those entrenched in a labeled politics? Could that be accomplished before we destroy the planet with weapons or make it uninhabitable by pollution? Shouldn't we make space in our Annual Meetings for such discussions—not presentations, but discussions of topics such as these?

Anthropology is a discipline being challenged from many sides to either become something more than it is at present or else fade away. Not all of us want to become advisers on the human condition, but anthropologists nonetheless are in a unique position to speak both generally and specifically about human behavior in most areas of the world. If anthropology is to have a future, we must accept our responsibilities now to use our research wisely, ethically and with political sensitivity.

SHOW AND TELL

On September 16, 2004—Mexican independence day—the Hearst Museum launched *Tesoros Escondidos: Hidden Treasures from the Mexican Collections*, the inaugural exhibit of the three-year "Diversity—Cultural Arts— Antiquities" initiative. The display includes 250 objects, most of which have been in storage for over 100 years. The print media response has been very encouraging with three, full-color articles from Bay-area newspapers. The following quote from the *Oakland Tribune*[8] captures the essence of the exhibit:

"Tesoros Escondidos" sheds light on pieces ranging from everyday items, such as chocolate stirrers carved from a single piece of wood, to religious objects, including a ceremonial arrow used by shamans praying for rain. The works represent Mexico's population, made up primarily of Indian peoples, the majority mestizos—people of mixed Spanish and Indian heritage—and the Hispanic elite.

The article goes on to quote the exhibit's curator, Ira Jacknis: "Because this collection hasn't been seen, I wanted to take the opportunity to be as diverse and representative as possible."

The die is cast, starting with the showcasing of a culture that has strongly influenced western America. I think that Mrs. Hearst would be pleased to know that her legacy is at the heart of this initiative to reconnect with the people of California.

NOTES

1. Patrick V. Kirch, *Biennial Report* (Phoebe A. Hearst Museum of Anthropology, Berkeley, Calif., 1999–2001), 2.

2. Patrick V. Kirch, "A Vision for Transformation," in *Long-Range Plan: 2001–2010* (Phoebe A. Hearst Museum of Anthropology, Berkeley, Calif., 2001), 1.

3. University of California Board of Regents, Minutes of September 10, 1901, Berkeley, Calif., 1.

4. American Association of Museums, *Excellence and Equity: Education and the Public Dimension of Museums* (Washington, D.C.: American Association of Museums, 1992).

5. Phoebe A. Hearst Museum of Anthropology, *Program Plan: Oxford Street Site* (Berkeley, Calif., 2003), 6–10.

6. Charles Burress, "Berkeley Unveils Big Plans to Build," *San Francisco Chronicle*, November 21, 2003, 19.

7. Margery Wolk, "Future of Anthropology: An Ethnographer's Perspective," *Anthropology News* 43, no. 6 (2002): 7.

8. Monique Beeler, "Olé," *Oakland Tribune*, October 5, 2004, 1.

12

Museums and (In)Justice

Jennifer Eichstedt

From 1997–2001, my co-researcher/author, Stephen Small, Associate Professor of African American studies at University of California, Berkeley, and I researched over 130 plantation museums/tourist sites in several Southern states. We toured these sites to discover, document, and understand racialized representations of the enslaved and enslavers in the plantation-tourism industry. In addition to these sites, we also extensively toured local, regional, and state history museums and state tourism centers. The plantation research enabled us to show how whites construct and use stories that valorize whiteness, while simultaneously avoiding, whitewashing, denying, and misrepresenting brutalities and oppressions committed against racialized "Others." That work, like my dissertation[1] before, demonstrated to me the deeply white-supremacist[2] shape and texture of contemporary United States society. In this chapter, I want to demonstrate that the racialized representations found in the plantation museums align with representations found in the larger, contemporary social world, to consider how to approach these representational strategies from a racial justice perspective, and to raise the question of moral responsibility and museum ethics.

In 2002, the Smithsonian Institution Press published our book, *Representations of Slavery: Race and Ideology in Plantation Museums*.[3] Our primary focus was on plantation museums in Virginia, Georgia, and Louisiana, although we also conducted research in five other states (Florida, South Carolina, Alabama, Mississippi, and Tennessee). Based on this research we argued that most of the sites that we explored tell a story of American history that is white-centric, male-centric, and usually elite-focused, and that these sites primarily erase or minimize the presence, labor, and lives of enslaved Africans and African Americans. These sites construct and maintain public white racial identities that both articulate and reinforce the idea that whites created "freedom," democracy, and epitomized the idea of hard work. African Americans and their labor are presented as virtually incidental to the growth of the South and, by extension, the United States. These racialized, representational strategies and practices, although altered through time, are directly linked to the ideological strategies created during the period of enslavement. These strategies were developed in order to legitimate white enslavement of other human beings and demonstrate the moral worthiness of master-enslavers. That variations of these representational strategies are still employed today suggests the degree to which they are accepted and normalized parts of white culture. Further, these strategies continue to exist because they help meet a continuing need of whites to understand ourselves as morally worthy in the face of ongoing oppression of all peoples of color and, in particular, African-descent peoples. We also explored thirty black history sites found in our three primary states and considered their representations of African-descent peoples and whites. I do not discuss the representational strategy of "counter-hegemonic narratives" that we discovered in these sites in this chapter, but instead refer you to our book.

In the following pages I will describe the racialized regimes of representation that we discovered and demonstrate how they are linked to similar strategies found in the larger cultural domain. I'll then return to a discussion of the moral, ethical, and racial (in)justice implications of these strategies.

TYPOLOGY

Professor Small and I developed a typology of representations that included the following categories: symbolic annihilation and erasure of African peoples while aggrandizing lives of white enslavers; trivialization and deflection of suffering of African-descent peoples while framing white enslavers as moral and hardworking; segregation and marginalization of knowledge of enslaved peoples even as a central focus on white lives is maintained; and relative incorporation of lives of African-descent people into the story of white life. Each of these rhetorical or organizing strategies positions discussion of enslavement and those enslaved in different ways.

Sites that employ "symbolic annihilation and erasure" as their primary organizing strategy effectively erase slavery and those who were enslaved. The presence, labor, struggles, and contributions of African Americans are symbolically annihilated. Over 60 percent of all sites primarily used this representational strategy. The second category, "trivialization or deflection," reflects those sites in which slavery, the enslaved, or African Americans are mentioned, but primarily through mechanisms, phrasing, and images that minimize and subordinate them. Narratives and pictorial images that serve to demonstrate the benevolence of plantation owners, and the affection of "faithful slaves" for these plantation owners, dominate this pattern. The third strategy, "segregation and marginalization of knowledge," is found at those sites that include information about enslaved peoples presented through separate tours and displays that visitors can choose to see, or ignore, depending on their desire. "Black history" or "slave life" tours vary in format and content, take place less frequently than the "main" white-centric tours, and are less likely to be advertised. These sites develop information about slavery, enslaved, or African American history beyond minimal levels, but do so in ways that maintain separate pathways to knowledge, with the pathway for these issues being subordinated to the regular tour. The fourth category is "relative incorporation." At the few sites that fall into this category, the topic of enslavement and those who were enslaved are discussed throughout the tour. These sites are much more likely to raise issues that disturb a positive construction of whiteness and that challenge the dominant themes that each state tends to present about its own history. Finally, we constructed a residual category that we note simply as "in between." The sites that fall under this heading are those sites that have moved beyond the first three categories but are still quite conflicted in their representations of enslavement and enslavers; they incorporate more information than many sites but do so in a way which still valorizes whiteness and trivializes the experience of slavery.

As I noted above, the racialized regimes of representation at work across these sites are effective because they articulate existing racialized ideologies, images, and allocations of resources that construct African Americans, and African American experiences, as inferior and white Americans and white experiences as superior and more worthy of consideration and focus. These racialized regimes of representation therefore both articulate and reaffirm the racialized mythic life of the dominant white public in the United States and resonate with national and regional, collective white memories and senses of identity. A prime example of this is the practice of symbolic annihilation. Symbolic annihilation, the erasure of peoples of color, is seductive in its normalcy in a white supremacist system. What and who matters are whites—people of color may be included, but primarily in ways that are peripheral to whites. Symbolic annihilation is the museum equivalent of both outright erasure and denial of black suffering at the hands of whites in modern culture. In many (53 percent) of the sites we toured, African-descent people were mentioned less than three times, although they often constituted between 50 to 95 percent of the plantation's population. When enslaved people were mentioned, euphemistic language, such as "servants,"[4] "they," or even "employees," was used to speak of them. Most frequently, the work they performed was simply erased through the use of passive language; such

practices are still common today as the epitome of "hard work" is often represented as the white (usually male) chief executive officer of a company and
not the workers on the factory floor, making or serving the food, or washing
the dishes. Public stories continue to be primarily individualistic in focus;
wealth is seen as something that individuals have because of their own effort,
while the transgenerational transference of wealth and poverty[5] is buried
under stories that valorize those at the economic top. At plantation museums, the fact that enslaved peoples created the vast bulk of white enslavers'
wealth is likewise excluded from consideration.

The strategy of trivialization and deflection of suffering and work, found
at 29.5 percent of all sites, is similarly linked to dominant tropes that exist in
the larger culture. For instance, plantation tropes that focus on threats of
slave rebellions, thievery (of food, spices, and time), or the "loyalty" of
enslaved people to their master-enslavers mesh well with contemporary stereotypes that depict African Americans as dangerous, lazy, or needing to be
led by whites, as well as contemporary, new-Right discourses that deflect
attention away from the suffering of blacks and instead frame whites and the
South as "victims" of preferential treatment for blacks and other minorities.[6]

Trivialization is a successful representational strategy because it meshes
with long-standing racist constructions of African Americans. Ed Guerrero,
who traces the ways that African Americans were/are represented in film,
argues:

> In almost every instance, the representation of Black people on the commercial
> screen has amounted to one grand, multifaceted illusion. For Blacks have been
> subordinated, marginalized, positioned and devalued in every possible manner
> to glorify and relentlessly hold in place the white-dominated symbolic order
> and racial hierarchy of American society.[7]

The representations found in plantation museums closely align with these
Hollywood images. As in Hollywood, the framings found in most plantation
museums focus on white romance and glory compared with the servile or
potentially dangerous behavior of enslaved African Americans. Stories of
possible theft connect to contemporary public imagery of blacks as dangerous, dishonest, and basically problematic. This imagery was begun during
the period of enslavement, rose to a fever pitch after legal enslavement ended,
and continues to this day.[8] When a specific site tells a story, it must be
understood as being located in a web of stories, told at other plantation
museums and other racialized sites, as well. When a visitor hears the story
of possible theft once, it may not have a continued effect. However, when
you consider the framing of these stories within the larger context of racialized imagery, the interpretation cannot be assumed to be without effect. As
Stephen Weil notes, "In general, the impact of museums on their visitors is

not of the one-shot or 'Eureka!'' kind but something far more subtle, cumulative over repeated visits.''[9] If visitors to a plantation museum generally visit more than one site (which our experience attending multiple sites in the same region and seeing the same visitors move from plantation to plantation suggests), it becomes a snowballing message—whites, even then, had to guard against the thieving tendencies of blacks.

At the other extreme are the stories that referenced the loyalty of blacks, and framed the enslaver at a particular plantation as a "good" owner. It may be the case that most sites represent stories of loyalty and service because those are the stories that the master-enslavers memorialized in letters, diaries, and oral tradition. That is, these few stories may be the only "documented" stories that sites have and so those are the ones that are retold to visitors. The problem is that, in the absence of any other representations, these ones that celebrate loyal "servants" and grateful (or shiftless) "slaves" suggest that such behaviors were representative of those who were enslaved. It must also be remembered that the representation of "loyal slaves" and "good masters" found at these sites does not exist in a vacuum; instead, it is situated within the context of continued imagery of mammies, servile "Uncle Toms," and shiftless "coons" produced from the 1850s through the present moment.[10] Today the representations in mass media are less direct, though "blacks as criminals" is still prevalent.[11] There are also numerous "buddy" films where the secondary character is black; the *Lethal Weapon* series is a prime example. Another framing of loyalty or service to whites is found in the significant number of films where a black man occupies a role as spiritual advisor, cipher, for a white lead; such films include *Bagger Vance*, *What Dreams May Come*, and *Holy Man*. These representations, while they may be seen as flattering by some, are problematic because the white person, and his or her spiritual transformation, is what matters.

The third pattern or strategy, that of segregated knowledge, resonates with other segregated ways of "knowing" (and controlling) African Americans. Such segregation is found in knowledge production and consumption that relegates learning about blackness to a specific month (black history month) or body of literature (African American or ethnic studies) that largely is not incorporated into the white-centric knowledge base. This exclusion is linked with material practices of housing segregation[12] and work segregation.

The final category, relative incorporation, is representative of the struggles some white institutions are going through as they attempt to incorporate "diverse" voices. The tendency is to maintain a white-centric organizational strategy while adding in stories of racialized others (similar to the "add and stir" approach of superficial multiculturalism), which is problematic as it does not disturb the basic premises of white supremacy. A few sites within the relative incorporation category have done a better job of trying to shift the actual terms of the debate to make it clear that the very fact of slavery makes problematic any attempts to valorize specific white enslavers—even if they are traditionally presented as "heroes." However, how to really disturb traditional, white-centric framings appears as unclear in these sites as it is in larger white public venues and discourses. While there are academic and activist analyses and discourses that shift these debates (see, for instance, post-colonial feminisms, critical race theory and critical race feminisms, and multicultural feminisms), these analyses have largely not moved into the public sphere. Instead, we have very conflicted public discourses, where there is some acknowledgement that there are incidences of "racism" (usually presented as idiosyncratic versus systemic) at the same time that so-called cures for racial inequality are presented, which primarily focus on so-called cultural deficiencies of people of color. Additionally, in public spaces, there is still a perception that even acknowledging "race" is undesirable. Instead, many whites believe they should be color-blind—which usually means turning a blind eye to existing racial injustice.[13] Given these larger issues, it is not surprising that there are very few representational strategies in plantation museums, originally created as celebratory spaces for the white enslavers, that disrupt white-centrism. This, however, does not allow museums off the hook. As Hilde Hein notes, "Historians and museum scholars, working at semiotic meta-levels, discover narrative veins within their collections and extract their meaning for visitors by applying epistemically effective exhibition strategies to them. *Museums thus bear multiple responsibility for their collection and reassemblage of items that represent intended stories*"[14] (emphasis added). To go further, it is not only that museums are responsible for the stories they tell but, as Ivan Karp asserts, "Museums and their exhibitions are morally neutral in principle, but in practice always make moral statements.[15] If we agree that museums are always making moral statements, while bearing the legitimating seal of providing public "education," then we have an obligation to explore the moral and ethical implications of museum, and, in this case, plantation museum, practices.

MORALITY AND ETHICS

My starting point in thinking about the ethics of these museums has been a belief that museums do occupy an important site of public education[16] and exist as a potential dialogic space of critical reflection. In fact, museums may be able to help create "healthy communities,"[17] and "make a positive difference in the quality of people's lives."[18] Given this, museums need to be cognizant of the ways they are part of ideological apparatuses that make and legitimate social meanings. All museums need to ask "who" is envisioned as the community that is served? Which people's lives are being positively affected? In terms of education, what should we educate people *for*? Why should people know, or have exposure to, various experiences? Will it make them better people? Better citizens? Better in what way? Toward what end? I suggest here that a legitimate goal is the creation of a racially (and socially) just world. Such a world, I believe, would be a world where all peoples are valued, where they are able to fully create and discover who they are, where all people are treated with respect and dignity, where people have true access to decent housing, healthcare, education, work, and the construction of complete, and therefore necessarily complicated, representations of themselves.

So, what does this have to do with museums? Museums are in a powerful place to effect people's understanding of the social world in which they live. Even if the museum is focused on the past, as historic museums are, it is imperative to remember that knowing the past is essential to understand the present and create a livable future. Museums, if they matter at all, matter *precisely* because they help to create a picture of the past that helps people understand the present and prepare for the future. Continuing to use frameworks that largely exclude African-descent people from the full web of humanity, while centering white enslavers as highly moral, is, I believe, profoundly immoral. The immorality, however, goes far beyond the specific curators, staff, and others who work at these museums; as with most whites, they are expressing the cultural and material advantages of whiteness, which they have been taught to embrace, if only subconsciously. The immorality expressed through these sites, as well as most white sites, is quite broad and deep. It is part of the very foundation of racialized life in the United States.

However, again, the fact that the larger society continues to operate from an immoral position does not mean that museums should not strive to create more just representations and meanings. A social, and racial, justice perspective requires that we ask whose lives are enriched by certain representations, and whose are damaged. It seems a truism, given what we've already covered, to say that white stories of white history are valorized by the representational regimes used at plantation museums. The fact that white history is valorized does not mean that whites are not damaged, a point to which I'll return below. What seems indisputable is that African Americans are injured by the continuing one-sided representations told at most plantation museums. Lack of accurate information is a form of abuse. The over 80 percent of plantation museums that either engage in symbolic annihilation or trivialization are contributing to a world in which white people devalue their African American brethren. Continuing the telling of untruths, distorting experiences, and so on constitutes victimization. It is harmful to both the target and the nontarget or perpetrating group. It is harmful to the target group (in this case African Americans) because all African Americans have to bear the cost of stereotypical representations that frame them as dangerous, criminal, and hypersexual. Works by many noted scholars, researchers, and public intellectuals speak to the damage to self-esteem, as well as the emotional and physical cost (such as increased hypertension, heart disease, liver disease, and so on), of warding off negative stereotypes. These stereotypes affect how whites, and other non-blacks, approach and interact with African Americans regardless of social class.[19] African Americans bear a horrible cost of the misinformation that is presented about them; plantation museums are complicit in the perpetuation of this misinformation.

The horrific costs to African Americans, and the maintenance of a system that exacts these costs, have huge ethical and moral implications for the non-target, or white, population. If whites, as a group, are continually recycling and spreading misinformation, and participate in a material hierarchy that privileges whites to the cost of all others, then the foundation of whiteness, and its expression in the modern moment, is profoundly immoral. Ironically, these racialized stories were and are constructed precisely to frame white history, indeed the very category of whiteness, as moral.

The fact that white Americans have constructed stories that present us as good and deserving is not shocking. In fact, when I've presented this research (and current research on California and Arizona mission museums), someone will always point out that the "winners" of any struggle are the ones who write history, not "the losers." In other words, the winners tell the story in a way that makes them look good, and we should not be surprised that our research bears this out. We were not surprised at what we found, but the extent and, at times, the unrelenting white valorization flies in the face of public white claims about the degree to which whites are held accountable for racism and continually berated about the "sins of the past." Instead, the sins of the past were presented as largely nonexistent or at least normal and understandable.

Recent work on the construction of national and group memory certainly demonstrates the practice of groups/nations framing themselves positively.[20] However, seeing oneself, or one's group or nation, as in relatively uncomplicated and positive ways becomes more difficult than usual when there is a history (and present) of oppressions, violations, and systematic violences. In such a case, the humanity or morality of the perpetrators is very likely to be called into question. If perpetrators and descendants are not willing to look at what is required for true reconciliation and recompense, then they have to construct stories that not only frame themselves and their ancestors in a good light, but that frame the victims, or "losers," in a negative light. The victims must be shown, if shown at all, as having been deserving of their treatment. Some countries, such as Germany in relation to the Holocaust, and South Africa in relation to apartheid, have been required to account (at least partially) for the injustices committed in their countries. In the United States there has been no corresponding large-scale recognition either of the depth of tragedy that was over 220 years of slavery, and another ninety years of legal segregationist practices, or the genocide of indigenous Americans. This relative silence from dominant institutions allows for the continuation of problematic, racialized (and racist in outcome) imagery and feeds into the dehumanizing stories that buttress social whiteness.

CONCLUSION

When museums are complicit in telling inaccurate, and very one-sided, stories of a past shattered by great atrocities, they undercut any claim to an ethical foundation they might make. Given that museums are often seen as "educational" spaces (many of the plantation museums we visited host school tours designed to teach state and local history), it is imperative that they not only look for the most obvious ways in which they might be presenting problematic images, but go deeper and consider the very lens through which they look. Whiteness, white-centrism, white power/normalcy, continues to shape many museum practices today. This is not a problem if people are up front about the role of their museum in furthering a specific power agenda. However, if museums frame themselves as being about the betterment of *communities* and *people* in some generic sense, there is a formidable obligation to consider the ways that representational strategies work to recreate an unjust world. Using an explicit lens of racial justice should stop many museums, and certainly all plantation museums, in their tracks so that they consider what they are doing. Racial and social justice are issues that should not be seen as luxuries that only some should think about. Given the ways that inequalities in education, housing, wealth, and so on not only continue, but increase, ignoring the links between how we construct knowledge, and a core vision of humanity, seems dangerous and, yes, immoral. I encourage us all to look deeply at the practices, both institutional and interpersonal, in which we engage and be very clear about the vision of the world that we want to enact. And when we create images that further the devaluation of millions of human beings, we should not be surprised when we are asked to account for our behavior. It is time for all of us to look closely at our actions and their consequences and face up to where we fall short in creating a socially and racially just world. If we do not, we are doomed not just to irrelevance in the world, but to being rightly understood as not only participants in the system that produces immense inequalities, but as participants who then stand silently allowing the carnage to continue.

NOTES

1. Jennifer Eichstedt, *Maintaining and Challenging White Privilege: Multiculturalism in an Arts Community* (PhD diss., University of California at Santa Cruz, 1995).

2. I use the term "white supremacist" in the same vein as Joe R. Feagin, Eduardo Bonilla-Silva, and others. White supremacist refers not to explicitly racist organizations such as neo-Nazis or white power groups; instead it refers to the system of power where whiteness is consistently preferenced, advantaged through the systematic workings of social institutions, ideologies, and everyday practices. This advantaging, or racial privileging, carries a substantial material and ideological cost for folks of color and damages the moral underpinning of white life.

3. Jennifer Eichstedt and Stephen Small, *Representations of Slavery: Race and Ideology in Southern Plantation Museums* (Washington, D.C.: Smithsonian Institution Press, 2002).

4. We understand that enslavers themselves used the language of "servants" to mask the reality of enslavement. This term was considered more "polite" than referencing slavery. However, the use of such language to mask oppression in the past is not a legitimate reason to continue to use it today. The use of the term in the past, and its role, could be discussed as part of an educational campaign.

5. Melvin L. Oliver and Thomas M. Shapiro, *Black Wealth/White Wealth: A New Perspective on Racial Inequality* (New York: Routledge, 1995).

6. Cheryl I. Harris, "Whiteness as Property," in *Critical Race Theory: The Key Writings That Formed the Movement*, ed. Kimberlé Crenshaw, Neil Gotanda, Gary Peller, and Kendall Thomas (New York: New Press, 1995); Joe R. Feagin and Hernan Vera, *White Racism: The Basics* (New York: Routledge, 1995); Joe R. Feagin, *Racist America: Roots, Current Realities, and Future Reparations* (New York: Routledge, 2000); George Lipsitz, *Possessive Investment in Whiteness* (Philadelphia: Temple University Press, 1998); and David T. Wellman, "From 'New Political Linguistics' to Anti-Affirmative Action 'Minstrels'," *Socialist Review* 26, nos. 1–2 (1996): 147–54.

7. Ed Guerrero, *Framing Blackness: The African American Image in Film* (Philadelphia: Temple University Press, 1993), 2.

8. See Anti-Defamation League, *Highlights from an Anti-Defamation League Survey on Racial Attitudes in America* (New York: Anti-Defamation League, 1993); Feagin, *Racist America*; and Robert M. Entman and Andrew Rojecki, *The Black Image in the White Mind* (Chicago: University of Chicago Press, 2000).

9. Stephen Weil, *Making Museums Matter* (Washington, D.C.: Smithsonian Institution Press, 2002), 64.

10. Kenneth W. Goings, *Mammy and Uncle Mose: Black Collectibles and America Stereotyping* (Bloomington: Indiana University Press, 1994); Jean Muteba Rahier and Michael Hawkins, "'Gone with the Wind' Versus the Holocaust Metaphor: Louisiana Plantation Narratives in Black and White," in *Plantation Society and Race Relations: The Origins of Inequality*, ed. Thomas J. Durant Jr. and J. David Knottnerus, 205–20 (Westport, Conn.: Praeger, 1999); and Patricia A. Turner, *Ceramic Uncles and Celluloid Mammies: Black Images and Their Influence on Culture* (New York: Bantam Doubleday, 1994).

11. Anti-Defamation League, *Highlights from an Anti-Defamation League Survey on Racial Attitudes in America*.

12. Douglas S. Massey and Nancy A. Denton, *American Apartheid: Segregation and the Making of the Underclass* (Cambridge, Mass.: Harvard University Press, 1993).

13. Eduardo Bonilla-Silva, *White Supremacy and Racism in the Post-Civil Rights Era* (Boulder, Colo.: Lynne Rienner Publishers, 2001); David T. Wellman, *Portraits of White Racism*, 2nd ed. (New York: Cambridge University Press, 1993).

14. Hilde Hein, *The Museum in Transition: A Philosophical Perspective* (Washington, D.C.: Smithsonian Institution Press, 2000), 31.

15. Ivan Karp, Christine Mullen Kreamer, and Steven D. Lavine, eds., *Museums and Communities: The Politics of Public Culture* (Washington, D.C.: Smithsonian Institution Press, 1992), 14.

16. Susan Porter Benson, Stephen Brier, and Roy Rosenzweig, eds., *Presenting the Past: Essays on History and the Public* (Philadelphia: Temple University Press, 1986); Lisa C. Roberts, *From Knowledge to Narrative: Educators and the Changing Museum* (Washington, D.C.: Smithsonian Institution Press, 1997).

17. Weil, *Making Museums Matter*, 206–7.

18. Weil, *Making Museums Matter*, 60.

19. Ellis Cose, *Rage of the Privileged Class: Why Black People are Angry and Why White People Should Care* (New York: HarperCollins, 1993); and Joe R. Feagin and Melvin P. Sikes, *Living with Racism: The Black Middle Class Experience* (Boston: Beacon Press, 1994).

20. Iwona Irwin-Zarecka, *Frames of Remembrance: The Dynamics of Collective Memory* (New Brunswick, N.J.: Transaction, 1994); David Lowenthal, *The Heritage Crusade and the Spoils of History* (Cambridge: Cambridge University Press, 1998); Jeffrey K. Olick and Daniel Levy, "Collective Memory and Cultural Constraint: Holocaust Myth and Rationality in German Politics," *American Sociological Review* 62 (1997): 921–36; and Barry Schwartz, "Frame Images: Towards a Semiotics of Collective Memory," *Semiotica* 121, nos. 1–2 (1998): 1–40.

13

Open Minds: Inclusive Practice

Helen Coxall

> Being inclusive in museums means not excluding anyone. It means being accessible to people in general. Barriers to inclusivity lie in people's mind-sets. Museums strive to be accessible to a general audience just as the mass media do. But we need to challenge the notion that aiming at that general audience—"the man in the street"—is not being exclusive.[1]

I wrote this at the turn of the twenty-first century. Reading it again raises questions that require answers in order to write this chapter. What is inclusive practice and how can it be achieved? To answer these questions I want to distinguish between the various aspects of inclusive practice and to discuss examples that illustrate them. I have selected projects at a city museum, national museums from different countries, and a university museum. The examples are chosen for their relevance to aspects of inclusivity, and are not intended to be a survey. I believe aspects of inclusive practice are:

1. serving communities;
2. consulting with audiences and communities;
3. collecting and interpreting;
4. collaborating with external bodies;
5. working across disciplines;
6. staffing and training; and
7. mainstreaming diversity awareness.

TARGETING AUDIENCES

Aiming exhibitions at "the general public" can be exclusive as this usually assumes an audience of "average" intelligence, white, sighted, and able-bodied with English as a first language. "Average" is a tyranny. How can you aim at an average reading ability when the potential audience includes school children and adults and people with English as a second language? How can you assume a consensus of viewpoint when the potential audience includes visitors from abroad and indigenous populations of many different cultural backgrounds? I use the word "potential" advisedly because by assuming a "general" audience those that do not fall into the assumed notion of the "general public" are effectively excluded. Not surprisingly, therefore, the actual audience is unlikely to match the potential audience in these museums.

The key to inclusive practice is relevance. For example, when dealing with "other" people's objects, curators are dealing with those people's culture, history, and way of life. In this context I am using the term "other" to indicate any culture that is likely to be misrepresented if seen from a purely monocentric perspective.[2] These objects hold a special relevance for the people whose cultures they represent but also for any visitor who has a human interest and curiosity about the objects in the collection. When objects are removed from the original context of their use and placed in a museum environment, they can be robbed of their biographies and, therefore, their relevance to visitors. It is commonly acknowledged now that audiences can be excluded by interpretive text written in inaccessible, complex language. However, even accessible text describing an object's derivation can be exclusive if the cultural perspectives of the creators are not represented, or the language of the group is not referred to or used in some way. A people-centered approach to interpreting objects is necessary to relevant, inclusive practice.

> Once objects have arrived in a museum, they become exhibits in an "alien" environment. Enabling voices from the past and present to be heard has the effect of reinstating the objects, and with them, the people who made, used and valued them before they arrived at the museum.[3]

Purely "object-centered" approaches to interpretation are less common today and tend to occur when dealing with objects from previous centuries, which having been documented at the time of acquisition are more likely to adopt a monocentric viewpoint. It can be less time consuming to focus on the information that the museum already has and the staff's own expertise than to seek a fresh viewpoint. But there are often people who are descendants of those who made or used the objects who would be able to provide insight into the significance that these objects hold for them now. Alternatively they may have suggestions about different ways of using the objects within the context of the museum.

So why do we bother when it is impossible to reach all potential audiences? Well it is not impossible. We need to have open minds about the purpose and responsibility of museums. By consulting communities, we facilitate interpretation while serving the community concerned.

> The way forward is to take time to trace people at source and "in the field" rather than just focussing on internal concerns of collection and "receive" stories; also to relax control of interpretation in order to enable people to tell their own stories. This will enable people to articulate the way the objects were (and still are) viewed by those people to whom they once belonged, and to enable a global, rather than mono-centric perspective of history.[4]

The Museum of World Culture, Gothenburg, Sweden

The new Museum of World Culture offers an excellent example of how inclusive practice can be incorporated from the outset with a new museum. This new museum, which opened at the end of 2004, inherits the old Ethnographic Museum's extensive collection but is taking a different approach to interpreting ethnographic objects. Its aim is "to be a meeting place that will make people feel at home across borders, build trust and take responsibility together for a shared global future in a world in constant change."[5] Its program of exhibitions, conferences, and events is designed to allow multiple voices to be heard on controversial subject matter. There are to be no permanent displays; instead the museum will develop temporary thematic exhibitions that contribute new perspectives on relevant current topics. One of the first deals with HIV/AIDS as a global concern to make the subject comprehensible on an intellectual and emotional level. *African Voices* critiques stereotypical images of Africa from a postcolonial perspective in collaboration with the National Museums of Mali and of Kenya. For both of these exhibitions, Gothenburg University was involved as a partner for the research. Artist Fred Wilson worked on installations based on the museums collection.

Jette Sandahl, director of the Museum of World Culture, explained methods of targeting specific audiences for each temporary exhibition. An initial focus has been with communities in Gothenburg that have their cultural origins in the Africa Horn area. The method of working illustrates the open attitude to collection research that the museum is taking. Within a European Union–supported project, the museum, and a number of other agencies in the Gothenburg area, liased with a group of twenty-five people originally from this area of Africa with different qualifications and skills and enlisted their help to research and document information on the museum's collections from this part of the world. In return, these individuals got support for additional education, job training, trainee positions, consultations on setting up their own businesses, or other consideration. Museum staff and project participants worked together on supplementing the existing documentation of the Africa Horn collection with the more personal information and stories that the project participants brought with them, from their own, their parents', or grandparents' memories and from living history. The appeal and meaning of this oral history and reminiscence work has varied with different people within the group. A number of them created an elaborate project of their own, dealing with identity, migration, and the African Diaspora, to form a major, separate section within the *African Voices* exhibition.

By consulting specific audiences, the Museum of World Culture, in collaboration with outside agencies, has made the interpretation of its objects more relevant to those audiences while expanding the notions of others to new perspectives.

The Imperial War Museum, North Trafford, England

This is an example of an inclusive initiative that is aimed at serving particular communities and broadening the diversity of the museum volunteer workforce by collaborating with outside bodies. Three years ago, Imperial War Museum North set up a new initiative with a grant from the European Social Fund. Deborah Walker, the head of Learning Access and Outreach, and her team have been training disadvantaged people from the local vicinity (Salford, Trafford, and Manchester) on their volunteer program. Participants targeted are lone parents, returners to work, and young people at risk of exclusion—the latter are mainly male and as young as fourteen-years-old. Participants are offered customer care training and taught basic computer and office skills. They also have the opportunity to take the National Vocational Qualification (NVQ) in Cultural Heritage at level 2. It was soon discovered that this was too advanced for many who had poor literacy skills, so the local College of Further Education in Salford began working in collaboration with the museum to teach a pre-NVQ of basic skills.

When they join the museum's volunteer workforce, they sign a letter of agreement, which commits them to a minimum of time per month. The longer-standing volunteers eventually take part in the museum's introductory talks and assist the interactors who work with school groups. Currently the museum is investigating continued funding to enlarge the training program. They want to open it to less disadvantaged individuals who could work as mentors or offer basic skills support to the original group. They also want to take volunteers from the bank of veterans from the Second World War and onwards to train them to be part of the Leaning Access team and to take on students to do work placements within the Learning and Access program. This will relieve the pressure on time for this very ambitious program of basic skill training for disadvantaged local people. Two hundred people have been in this program over the last three years; many have moved on to paid work; and fifty are still working at the museum. The Learning Access team leader recalled with delight how a young trainee with dyslexia had told her that he had been successful at an interview for a full-time job and had been told he had the best customer-care skill of all of the applicants.

Western Australian Museum—*Western Australia: Land and People*

I chose this example to illustrate the importance of the somewhat neglected, but very productive, aspect of inclusive practice—working across disciplines within organizations.

Western Australia: Land and People is an exceptional achievement. It is the first multidisciplinary permanent exhibition of its kind in Australia and probably in the world. Funding was supplied in part through partnership with the Western Australia Lotteries Commission. Specialist museum staff from across disciplines of history, anthropology, archaeology, natural sciences, earth sciences, education, and design worked closely with each other and with their communities. Together they interwove a range of social, cultural, and environmental issues to portray the emergence of the distinctive Australian landscape and the complex interaction between people and place from prehistoric times to the twenty-first century. The Western Australian museum is in Perth, where 1.3 million people from more than seventy-five different cultural backgrounds live. It is a modern industrialized society on the site of one of the most ancient landforms in the world. How this came about and how the environment and the people have shaped each other are the major themes of the exhibition. By integrating natural science and history, the exhibition was able to trace the complex stories of:

- a broad view of Western Australia's environment and society;
- the emergence of the current landform and the first people;
- European invasion and the resulting clash of peoples within an "alien" landscape;
- the spread of settlement and the effects of land clearing on the economy, the natural environment, and the Aboriginal people;
- the area's renewable and nonrenewable resources and the social impact of their exploitation;
- the postwar urban growth, the creation of a multicultural society, and the impact of urban growth on the landscape; and
- a range of environmental and social issues and the options for the future.

Not only was the making of *Land and People* an inclusive process (within) inside the museum, involving all departments, it was also an inclusive process outside the museum. Before planning the new gallery the museum conducted two surveys to assess visitor opinion. Once past the planning stage, they worked closely in consultation with the local indigenous Nyungar people. This information helped to shape the exhibition focus—the Western scientific approach compared with Aboriginal people's ways of understanding and working the land. Interestingly scientists discovered that the memory of the separation of nearby Rottnest Island from the mainland as recorded by fossil records also was recorded in Nyungar oral tradition. By collaborating with and continuing to work with their local communities the museum team has been able "to look at Perth through the eyes of the Nyungar people, post war immigrants and long-term Anglo-West Australians. Throughout the emphasis is on understanding the actions of the past in the context of their times, reaching a better understanding of themselves in the present in order to look toward the future."[6]

This example illustrates how working across disciplines and consulting with local communities has informed the interpretation of *Land and People*, thus enabling museum staff members to best serve their local communities. It fulfills several categories of inclusive practice listed above and is an excellent example of inclusive practice for the twenty-first century. The advantage of having a gallery that has involved staff from many different departments is that this inevitably also has a lasting impact on general awareness of mainstreaming diversity in the museum's program as a whole.

COLLECTING AND INTERPRETING

The Western Australian Museum's Department of Anthropology works with indigenous people to maintain collections, prepare exhibitions, and conduct research on indigenous cultures from Australia and overseas. The ethnological programs have focused on compiling a representative sample of Aboriginal cultural material spanning the timeframe of European colonization. Recently this effort has been targeted toward the acquisition of material that documents contemporary Aboriginal society in urban and regional areas. Projects have included the development of the Aboriginal Gallery, *Katta Djinoong*. The introductory statement for the *Katta Djinoong* gallery is of interest here in relation to interpretation. Often the impact of how we contextualize exhibitions is not sufficiently considered; main introductory panels play a key role in this respect.

"Katta Djinoong: First Peoples of Western Australia"

Welcome to this exhibition about the longest living culture in the world. We invite you to share aspects of our culture. Many of us, the people of Western Australia—have joined with the museum to present a glimpse of our culture and history. Katta Djinoong means to see and understand us.[7]

This introduction both welcomes all visitors, and testifies to the museum's confidence in enabling the people's own voice to be heard. Hearing voices like this ensures that visitors have the opportunity both to hear a viewpoint that they may feel is speaking on their behalf or it may be one that is new to them. It takes courage on behalf of curators to relinquish their hold on their exhibitions. The more closely museum staff work with their own communities, the more trust is established to make this possible. There have been some notable successful examples of museums doing this in many places. I am sure you can think of others known to you.

Similarly, artists have increasingly become involved in making interventions into museum displays as a way of reinterpreting collections. New York artist Fred Wilson's installation *Mining the Museum* in the Maryland Historical Society's collection in 1991[8] and Chris Dorsett's intervention *Snares of Privacy and Fiction*, at the Pitt Rivers Museum in Oxford, England, in 1992, have had far-reaching effects.[9] They raised the awareness of both artists and museum staff to the possibilities of rereading hidden histories and opinions not previously being addressed by the museum's interpretive methods.

SO WHAT IS INCLUSIVE PRACTICE?

Petrie Museum of Egyptian Archaeology

I have selected this case study as it embraces all seven aspects of inclusive practice. The Petrie Museum at University College London (UCL) houses internationally important collections of ancient Egyptian material collected by the Victorian archaeologist Flinders Petrie, a professor at UCL from whom the museum takes its name. A fund-raising initiative to move the collection from its two rooms to a three-story building is in progress. Two years ago the museum received a Heritage Lottery Fund (HLF) grant for a two-year outreach project, *Egypt in Africa*, to look at repositioning Egypt in both an African and a modern Egyptian context. This funding enabled the museum's director, Sally MacDonald, to appoint two part-time outreach workers (an African Caribbean youth worker and an Egyptian Egyptologist) to work with the African Caribbean, Sudanese, and Egyptian communities in London in order to modify resources to better address those audiences.

A vital role of the outreach workers was to organize discussions with African Caribbean and Egyptian people, as well as to arrange study days for potential Sudanese and Egyptian audiences. Some really interesting information has come out of these sessions, which has been built into the early plans for the presentations in the new museum. The idea that modern Egypt should be represented alongside ancient Egypt has come across very strongly, as has the necessity of not avoiding contemporary conflict. Thus, although these outreach workers are on temporary contracts, their work will have a lasting impact on all audiences.

They also have concentrated on helping the museum review its mainstream resources by looking at what the museum is doing from a different perspective, which has similar longer-term implications. For example, they have been reviewing the *Key Stage 2* education pack (for seven- to twelve-year-olds) and are currently piloting a new pack entitled *Egypt in Africa*, which is being tested with school groups and is proving very popular. They are reviewing the museum's handling boxes to make them more thematic and to include modern alongside ancient objects—a modern Egyptian office key to compare with ancient Egyptian and Coptic keys and prayer beads alongside amulets.

The whole staff team is working toward a view of Egypt for the new museum displays. Views of ancient Egypt vary (conflict) from the Egyptian to the African to the white European perspective. So they are negotiating the museum's position on this with the help of the outreach workers and are working on a statement to be included in the school packs.

> Within the race debate, ancient Egypt has become a terrain contested by three mutually inclusive views.
> 1. Modern Egyptian—the ancient Egyptians are the same group people as the modern Egyptians.
> 2. Afro-centric—the ancient Egyptians were black Africans who were later displaced by Macedonian, Roman, and Arab conquests.
> 3. Euro-centric—the ancient Egyptians were ancestral to modern Europe.[10]

The Outreach Work

Okasha El Daly is an Egyptian Egyptologist, which is very unusual. He trained at UCL and his Ph.D. is in medieval Arab perceptions of ancient Egypt. He has shown that medieval scholars drew on Egyptian writings and had an understanding of Egyptian hieroglyphs long before European scholars did. Today, the way ancient Egypt is represented in the Arab world is very distant. It is not taught in schools, and the majority of people who live in the country surrounded by ruins know very little about them. Okasha is respected because he is a Muslim and an Egyptologist and has been doing great work with the media in the Arab world, speaking about the Petrie Museum and about outreach work, which is an unfamiliar concept there. As a result, the museum now has many links with Egyptians both in London and in Egypt. In London, he has worked mostly with adult community groups organizing consultation days for the Egyptian Cultural Bureau and the Nubian Society and events such as those that foregrounded Egypt and Palestine during refugee week.

Being a youth worker, Kenneth John has focused on how to communicate the museum to new audiences. He has used his contacts with youth workers in local authorities to bring in groups. Since starting, he has been representing the museum on several bodies such as the Mayor of London's Commission for African and Asian Heritage. Kenneth works with "looked after" young people and in supplementary schools. He takes handling boxes to the groups and then encourages them to come back to the museum, often for evening events, which means the museum staying open late one day a week to accommodate his groups who cannot attend in the daytime. He had stalls at a conference for a London schools project for the black child and has helped African and African Caribbean groups to apply for lottery funding.

Thus, the way the outreach work has developed is opportunistic, capitalizing on both the skills and experience of workers and on opportunities that have arisen. The museum is applying for an extension to the HLF funding for three years to develop further ways of embedding the outreach work into everyday work and teaching practices at the university in order to diversify its staff and student population. A mentoring scheme for African and African Caribbean students is already in place at the university. New audiences are starting to visit the museum for tours, but there are ways that this could be followed up to maintain interest that could ultimately diversify the student body in the archaeology/heritage professions.

The museum used an increase to its core funding to establish a positive action traineeship. They advertised in an African/African Caribbean newspaper for someone with personal experience of ethnic concerns to undertake a part-time work placement at the Petrie with a subsidized part-time place in the M.A. program in museum studies at UCL for two years. When the present incumbent finishes, the traineeship will be renewed. This is a positive, long-term step to diversify both the student body, the staff body, and ultimately the profession as well.

The museum has also managed to raise a small grant from the university's equal opportunities fund to translate the main general information pages on its website into Arabic.[11] This fund also gave money to run diversity awareness training for museum staff, which went very well. The next step is to run a training program for the volunteers and for the Friends of the Museum.

We are glad we have been able to be more responsive to deployment of the two outreach workers allowing them to use their own experience, abilities and contacts and to respond to needs as they saw them arise. Ultimately this is just a project and I would feel much happier telling you about this if they were established staff.

Sally MacDonald, Director.[12]

CONCLUSION—THE WAY FORWARD FOR THE TWENTY-FIRST CENTURY

In conclusion, I would like to refer to and quote from *Holding Up the Mirror*—an initiative that investigated how London's museum sector was responding to the needs of its diverse communities, looking particularly at issues of ethnicity and racism in 2003. This research indicates that the number of museum staff and museum governors from ethnic minority backgrounds falls far short of reflecting the diverse communities that London's museums serve.

> Some institutions do not feel that social or cultural inclusion strategies are relevant to them if they are located in non-diverse areas. A proportion of museums cannot conceive of barriers for any communities because they assume their museum is 'for everyone'. Institutional awareness is therefore closely linked to an organization's commitment to social inclusion, awareness of audience, and new audience development. . . .
>
> Cultural diversity work has mainly been confined to individually funded education events, exhibitions and outreach projects . . . but equality of practices should influence all activities ranging from front of house procedures to collecting policies, interpretation and permanent exhibitions.[13]

The report also makes interesting observations about collecting. "Incomplete records and catalogues/finding aids are a significant problem. . . . A lack of knowledge by curators of their own collections is a major barrier to taking diversity work forward."[14] Rather disturbingly, many museums assumed that only those collections that specifically reflect the minority ethnic communities themselves would be relevant to those communities, which demonstrates a lack of appreciation of ways of making diverse cultural issues globally relevant. Over a third of museums failed to record the ethnicity of an object's donor, for example, thus losing the opportunity to make vital connections.

Holding Up the Mirror makes a case for change from business, legal, ethical, and intellectual standpoints and concludes:

> We need to be aware that we bring our own prejudices and judgments to ways in which we interpret and present objects and the stories they tell. Contemporary and retrospective collecting and the recording of associated information needs to be representative of our diverse communities to provide future generations with the materials they will need to interpret the past.[15]

NOTES

1. Helen Coxall, *Inclusivity: The Disability Directory for Museums and Galleries* (London: The Council for Museums, Archives, and Libraries, 2001).

2. Helen Coxall, "Speaking Other Voices," in *Cultural Diversity: Developing Museum Audiences in Britain*, ed. Eilean Hooper-Greenhill (Leicester, UK: Leicester University Press, 1997).

3. Helen Coxall, "Whose Story Is This Anyway?" *Journal of Museum Ethnography* 12 (2000): 87–100.

4. Coxall, "Whose Story Is This Anyway?"

5. Museum of World Culture, Gothenburg, Sweden. For more information see www.worldcultures.se.

6. *Western Australia: Land and Freedom* mission statement. For more information see www.museum.wa.gov.au.

7. *Katta Djinoong: First Peoples of Western Australia*—the Western Australian Museum's gallery of Aboriginal culture and history. For more information see www.museum.wa.gov.au.

8. *"Snares of Privacy and Fiction"* (1992)—an exhibition devised by British artist Chris Dorsett with contributions from contemporary artists, musicians, and writers who produced objects, images, sound works, and texts that intervened with the ethnological collections at the Pitt Rivers Museum, Oxford, England. Colonial collector General Pitt Rivers donated his ethnographic objects, which form the original core of Oxford University's ethnology collection at the museum named after him.

9. *"Mining the Museum"* (1991), an installation by artist Fred Wilson at the Maryland Historical Society. He introduced references to important African Americans from Maryland whose histories were significantly absent from the collection. Equally significantly, he renamed paintings from the collection and displayed slave shackles alongside silver objects, drawing attention to those whose work had created the wealth to purchase the silver.

10. Petrie Museum statement as supplied by the Petrie Museum of Egyptian Archaeology's director, Sally MacDonald.

11. General information pages on the Petrie Museum's website in Arabic. See www.petrie.ucl.ac.uk.

12. Statement of the Petrie Museum, supplied by the Petrie Museum of Egyptian Archaeology's director, Sally MacDonald.

13. Helen Denniston Associates, *Holding Up the Mirror: Addressing Cultural Diversity in London's Museums* (London: London Museums Agency, 2003), 6. See www.londonmuseums.org. *"Holding Up the Mirror* is a project and publication that is committed to working with the sector to ensure that the capital's museums and galleries embrace cultural diversity and place it at the heart of their core values and services." Helen Denniston Associates, *Holding Up the Mirror*, 6.

14. Helen Denniston Associates, *Holding Up the Mirror*, 6.

15. Helen Denniston Associates, *Holding Up the Mirror*, 16.

14

African American Museums in the Twenty-first Century

Christy S. Coleman

For well over a century, mainstream white museums throughout the United States and other parts of the world have presented exhibitions about various ethnic groups. Prior to the 1960s, these exhibitions took the form of anthropological or natural history themes that predominately displayed cultures of Native American or African groups. More often than not, these displays depicted the peoples in early Common Era diorama environments or at best as "noble savages," with the underlying implication being these were dead cultures and societies. A reflection of their times and lingering notions of white superiority, these exhibitions often reinforced stereotypes rather than illuminated the dynamics of depicted peoples' values and beliefs or cultural expressions. Displaying works of art by peoples of color was a very rare phenomenon. A handful of African American artists had their works displayed in major museums in New York City and Boston, most notably Romare Bearden, Jacob Lawrence, and Aaron Douglas. Exhibitions featuring Latinos and Native American groups usually featured so-called craft or traditional works. This methodology continued well into the late 1960s, and some would argue even later.

Prior to 1950, there existed about thirty museums at historically black colleges and universities and libraries that collected and preserved the history and culture of African Americans. These institutions amassed large collections of materials on the African Diaspora, the black experience in the United States, and provided venues for artistic works of all types. In addition to these museums, a number of historical societies, reading groups, and history clubs were established in black communities across the country as a way to preserve cultural heritage and teach others about the contributions and accomplishments of African Americans. The first black museums operating as independent nonprofits were the African American Museum in Cleveland (1956), the DuSable Museum of African American History in Chicago (1961), and the International Afro American Museum in Detroit (1965).

The social and political upheaval of the 1960s created a shift in the academic community that gave birth to the social history movement. As a result, a few museums (particularly art museums) began to take notice and produced exhibitions that spoke to the growing diversity of artistic thought, expression, and historical impact. Simultaneously, African Americans began to demand that their stories be told from their own perspective. It was no longer acceptable to be the "subject" of exhibitions; rather, they demanded to be the voice. Throughout the country, cultural centers and museums devoted to teaching African American history and displaying creative and performing arts sprang up. Most of these new museums were founded by grassroots groups seeking to establish a place where they could tell their stories and celebrate their accomplishments. The museums became symbols of validation and community pride. Among those early founders were individuals who had achieved some level of financial success or political clout and wanted to "give back" to the communities from which they came. These new museums often functioned with minimal budgets, small or nonexisting collections, dedicated volunteers, and a few professional staff. The early museum prospered in the energy of self-expression. By positioning themselves as antiestablishment, many were able to draw their communities to a series of exhibits, festivals, performances, and lectures that were as far ranging as celebrating black inventors to exploring social ills that the community battled. Unlike mainstream museums, there was nothing shameful about doing an exhibit about rats and how to combat them, or teaching people how to organize themselves against those who preyed on migrant workers. These lectures and programs were deemed just as important as exhibits on historical figures and works of art.

For over a decade these organizations prospered, in that they attracted fairly strong audiences, became important community institutions, and always seemed to be a step ahead of the mainstream in identifying new and emerging talent and educational trends. Whether deliberate or instinctive, this open-minded perspective spawned innovations in presentation and funding. Whether converting an old Winnebago into a mobile museum and traveling to neighborhoods, caravanning church buses to exhibit openings, or coordinating live performances to complement paintings, each museum found a way to make its few dollars stretch. Their base communities supported them with bake sales, spaghetti dinners, and penny drives. But oftentimes this was not enough. Due to the predominately grassroots nature of the support, many of these museums found themselves in dire financial straits when their base communities suffered economic difficulties. The bottom line was that, when the nation's economy caught the proverbial cold, African American communities got pneumonia and their institutions suffered right along with them. Ironically, financial success within the community could have an equally damaging effect. With growing integration in housing and in the workplace, the financial success that some African Americans experienced did not necessarily translate into more support for black cultural institutions. For upwardly mobile African Americans, the museums were no longer seen as relevant or academically challenging. It must be noted that improved financial position also led many to pursue associations with mainstream institutions for the perceived cachet. The resulting loss of support caused many African American museums and cultural centers to operate to the brink of collapse, or shut down entirely. But like their communities, black museums proved a resilient bunch.

By the 1980s, a number of African American museums founded in the 1960s were still operating, but not as the grassroots entities they once were. Of the survivors, most managed to gain financial support from municipalities or state government. But the new infusion of dollars often called for a new paradigm for operations. The grassroots gave way to the "professional" and with it a perceived battle for the souls of these organizations. The public drama often took on ugly and damaging tones. The founders of these organizations became the wronged party, while the newly appointed boards and museum-trained staff became the "sellouts." While there may be some truth behind the perceptions, discussions about the museums in Detroit, Washington, Chicago, and other cities were dominated by conversations about the controversies, not the impressive exhibitions and programs offered by each. Ultimately, the real truth was the museums were evolving.

In order to survive, African American museums had to seek other revenue streams outside of the community base. To be successful, they had to grow audiences. This environment placed the museum's leadership in the precarious position of articulating a vision that may or may not match that of the founders, but rather addressed the changing needs of the community served. They also had to conform to certain standards regarding collections, operations, and exhibitions. Did these dynamics actually corrupt the stories being told? Probably not, but perception can be more damning than reality. Most of these museums did not have mission statements, let alone collection policies or operating procedures. In order to be competitive in the grants arena, these issues needed to be addressed and the facilities to sustain it all had to be modified or built. While there were certainly foundations and granting agencies that rewarded ethnic museums for their creativity, and the edgy stories they displayed, they were often penalized for the behind-the-scenes operations or activities.

While most within the black community agreed (if only in principle) that preserving historical artifacts and documents was important, transforming the museum to address that need was often difficult. Take, for example, the museum-trained staff that worked to develop a collections policy that specified exactly what the museum would accept or pursue. They often faced the dilemma of telling a potential donor (and community member) that the material did not fit the policy, or that the pieces currently in collection needed to be deaccessioned. From this exchange, the word spread throughout the community that the museum had become too "bourgeois." Hence, it is no longer of the people. Ergo, if not of the people, then they no longer need or want grassroots support. Making matters worse, many of the professionals coming into leadership positions were not from the host communities and were deemed as outsiders. Being African American was not an automatic badge of acceptance for many communities and their museums. But these brave professionals (pioneers in their own right) persevered to help the museums grow even in the most hostile environments. They challenged their organizations and communities to reach beyond their successes and address their shortcomings. Their success led to an explosion of new African American museums throughout the country in the 1990s. According to the 2003 survey of African American Museums, nearly half of all African American museums or newly preserved historic sites were established in the 1990s. It is also interesting to note that the majority of these new museums were public or quasi-public institutions. They were established by a governmental body or appointed commission that provided funding to conduct feasibility studies, programming initiatives, and finally the buildings themselves. A handful could easily be considered vanity projects, created to appease or recognize the accomplishments of community icons. Some were built to ride the wave of cultural tourism and economic development. But the federal government also greatly increased the number of historic sites through the National Park Service, a considerable number of which were tied to the Underground Railroad and Civil Rights movements. The long-term problem for most of these new sites is that very few were properly capitalized to support them into the future. The notion of "build it and they will come" spread so quickly that few noticed that, as these facilities were being built, an alarming number were closing down.

In the meantime, more established Eurocentric art and history museums experimented with programs and exhibits about aspects of the African American experience. History museums in particular were encouraged to diversify their stories and audience by funders. There was also increased pressure from African Americans that their stories become part of exhibitions and tour offerings of these mainstream museums. Many African Americans felt that failure to incorporate black history at these museums and sites was akin to perpetuating a public fraud. By the 1980s, battles were waging at such venerable sites as Mount Vernon, Monticello, and state historical societies. Throughout the South, visitors demanded a more complete history that included addressing slavery and segregation, each a national trauma that continues to plague the American psyche. For the small few that opted to pursue the topics as an integral part of the presentation or exhibition, a new public trust was created with the institution; for those that did not or relegated the histories to special observances, audiences sharply declined. While there was some success for mainstream museums, most history museums throughout the country continued to grapple with how to depict African Americans. The dilemma of how to portray a people and history that is fraught with conflict and injustice stifled many to the point of inaction. Still others chose to present exhibitions about safe icons that had been identified by the African American community itself, like Harriet Tubman, Frederick Douglass, or movements like the Harlem Renaissance. Very few addressed the stories of Nat Turner, the bombing of Black Tulsa, Marcus Garvey, or the rise of black nationalist groups. Art museums had greater success showcasing works by African American artists that depicted their diverse experiences and perspectives. Ironically, successful showings in art museums and strong integrated programs at leading historical sites encouraged a feeding frenzy for all things black in the late 1980s and 1990s. Artifacts, art, and other material culture had become highly sought after and valuable. The irony was that African American museums that relied on contributed or moderately priced material now had to buy it at exceptionally high rates. More often than not, they did not have the resources to acquire them.

With black history and culture seemingly everywhere in the 1990s, the leadership of African American museums were required to develop a new set of skills that mirrored the phenomenon that was occurring in the museum field as a whole. It was no longer acceptable for the director to simply be an academic, artist, or an educator. He or she also needed to be a major fundraiser, visionary, business manager, project manager, political savant, and grassroots advocate. The problem was and is that many of the institutions, though vastly changed since the 1960s, were still challenged by inadequate facilities, partially managed collections, inexperienced staff, shrinking finances, declining audiences, and increased competition from unlikely sources. For directors of newer museums, they had to manage institutions through the exuberant openings where earned revenues and fund-raising support is high to the down cycling and settling into standard operations. With no track record of long-term operational trends, aggressive or unrealistic forecasting could prove disastrous. Against these backdrops, many directors sought to shift focus to the "back of the house" to shore up operations. For those in aged facilities, a number of capital campaign projects began. When possible, they invested heavily in capacity building initiatives designed to improve collections management and business operation systems. For the fortunate few, some directors tried to slowly address pay imbalances to attract and retain good, experienced staff. Others began hiring consultants of all types to help them run the business side of their museums. But few managed to catch on to the fundamental question of audience—who do we serve, how do we reach them, and how do we retain them? For those that did, a number of projects took place with considerable degrees of success.

Ever diligent to find new opportunities, several African American museums became involved in partnerships designed to expand audiences and share resources. Some aligned themselves with school districts by directly tying their offerings to curriculum requirements. Many also offered training programs for teachers and in-school programming. The goal was to increase student visitation and to strengthen credibility in the academic community. This is perhaps one of the most successful partnerships available. It strengthens teachers' skills and makes the museum a must-see for their students. Another form of partnership that evolved in the late 1990s is the collaborations between black museums and mainstream museums or universities. The primary idea behind these arrangements was that both could share and grow audiences by lending a level of credibility to the other. Whether partners were mainstream museums or universities, the bottom line was that these partnerships were generally imbalanced and, therefore, failures in many respects, regardless of whether or not the exhibit or project was completed or had good attendance. With significantly greater resources, both in terms of capital and personnel, the larger institution inherently controls the relationship. More often than not, when funding for the project came from an outside source, those funds were held by the larger organization. Generally, the African American museum had to give accounting for funds required to complete its phase of work in a highly scrutinized environment. And while this is not necessarily a negative, the fact is that operating differently can carry the implication of operating poorly. An example offered is the case of the African American museum that partnered with the historical society to present a major exhibition that was too large for either to accommodate.

They agreed to share the exhibition and worked diligently to prepare all advance materials. The historical society had a practice of charging its members for all preview receptions. The African American museum did not charge its members. The historical society had a practice of sending out notices for its receptions eight weeks in advance; the African American museum time frame was three weeks. With regard to the exhibit content, the African American museum wanted to supplement the show with additional label copy and a few pieces from its own collection. They contacted the originating institution for permission to do so. The historical society found this unacceptable and insulting. While on the surface these do not seem insurmountable issues, they in fact nearly destroyed the exhibition and created an even greater rift between the institutions. The historical museum felt that the African American staff was unprofessional by not meeting the deadlines that the historical museum had preset. The African American museum felt that the society's staff was condescending and inflexible. Although the African American museum asserted itself in these arrangements, their perspective was dismissed due to the imbalance of financial resources. But what ultimately killed (or at least severely wounded) the relationship was a profound difference in organizational culture. The fact is that, more often than not, African American museums function as family businesses, in that emotions can run high, leadership may or may not rest with the director, and there is a strong expectation to mentor and guide young professionals coming into the institution. In addition, the base audience served has different expectations.

Most who work in African American museums will assert that their work is more than a job or career. For them, it is a highly personal and emotional calling. They are what they do. For example, an exhibit about George Washington that is less than stellar will seldom be met with calls to white curators accusing them of being race traitors. But if an exhibition about George Washington Carver depicts him in a less than favorable light, the likelihood of a black museum curator receiving such a call is almost guaranteed. The pressure of knowing that your racial identity or cultural allegiance can be called into question is something that few can fathom. But those who work in African American museums deal with it consistently. For many, their work potentially has a direct impact on the community with which they identify. They know that many people who attend African American museums will never set foot into mainstream museums. And while the same may be said of white visitors not attending African American museums, the truth is that, on the whole, African American museums enjoy on average an audience that is at least 20 percent non-African American. Mainstream museums considered successful at diversifying audience are lauded when they reach 10 percent!

Again, herein lies the big question. Who is the audience for the African American museums, especially in the twenty-first century? Answering this is critical as we consider the future of black museums. There are certainly diehards who will assert that the African American museum exists first and foremost to serve African Americans by telling their stories and sharing their accomplishments in their voice. And here is the problem. Since the 1960s, the African American community has changed significantly. One of the most dramatic changes relates to family structure. Prior to the 1960s, more than 80 percent of African American children were born to two-parent (married) households. According to the 2000 U.S. Census, that number is sharply reduced by more than 20 percent. Neighborhood enclaves, churches, and other family support structures have eroded. As the majority of black museums are in urban areas, the issues of illiteracy, unemployment, and violence have a profound impact on operations and creative direction. There is also a greater financial divide within the black community. While there is a thriving and growing black middle and upper class, more working-class African Americans are falling into poverty. The black urban experience is something to which a growing number of suburban and rural African Americans simply cannot, or choose not to, relate. While working-class blacks may not have monies to give to museums, those of upper incomes choose instead to contribute to organizations where there is a perceived cachet attached to having their names listed as donors. The urban working poor are concerned with fulfilling life's basic needs and tend to expend their leisure dollars more toward entertainment venues. With these and other dynamics at play, the African American museum finds itself in a position of wanting to address the needs of the least, but being financially supported by those with the most. The museum is placed in the precarious position of trying to serve both interests.

While there is always great fanfare and pride when black museums open, the unfortunate truth is that most African Americans have not embraced black museums by including them in their regular charitable-giving habits. Many will answer a call during periods of crisis, but sustained annual financial support to the museum is not something that is done in the same manner as giving to churches, United Negro College Fund (UNCF), or the National Association for the Advancement of Colored People (NAACP). Museum giving is viewed as a good thing to do, but it has not taken on the full cultural significance of the previously named organizations. This situation has forced many black museums to look beyond their traditional base by expanding geographic regions and assuring non-African Americans that their museums are welcoming to them.

As we move through the twenty-first century, there are many that are again asking the question, what is the role of the African American museum? Is it still a needed or viable institution? Given all the dynamics that have impacted these museums in the past, the role is needed now more than ever. Even though there are mainstream museums that are depicting African American history and culture (and rightfully so), there are still no better voices than the originals. Therefore, a strong argument can be made that African American museums are indeed viable and important. But the successful African American museum in the future will be one that is well funded so that it can take risks with the culture and history that is portrayed. They are and will continue to be the starting point and incubator of significant dialogues about the state of the black community. They can continue to be places of experimentation and they can reach out to new and expanding audiences without having to apologize to themselves or others for doing so.

There must be a "Sankofa Principle" at work, meaning that stability in the future requires some forward thinking while looking back.

Among the things that made African American museums successful in the 1960s was that they celebrated the accomplishments of their community while also turning an eye to the darker chapters of the collective American past and its impact on the black community. Today, there is a tremendous opportunity for these black museums to look inward and explore the pathologies that continue to plague our communities. When will we see exhibitions and forums about the impact of drug culture on the black community? Will there be examinations of the disproportionate incarceration of black males and the continuing disparity that exists in the criminal justice system? Equally compelling could be an exhibition that challenges visitors to consider the difference between making money and building wealth within the African American community. These and many other topics have the potential to galvanize the museum's relationship with the community and the other organizations that offer services or support the community's successes or problems. Expanding on the idea of an exhibition on drug culture, consider, for a moment, collaborations with treatment centers, law enforcement, and faith congregations. Students could be encouraged to make documentaries with the assistance of local filmmakers, poets, writers, etc., while filming the stories of users, dealers, or victims of associated violence in neighborhoods or area hospitals. Imagine the opportunity to critically consider the festering effect of drugs through the eyes of a child—a child who now has been given a creative outlet to examine the world around him or her in an immediate and compelling way. This is not to suggest that the only stories worth presenting must deal with community pathologies. But it is suggested that the successful African American museums in the twenty-first century are responsive to the needs, questions, and interests of the primary community it serves. The museum must be prepared to go deeper in its celebrations of individual accomplishments, artistic vision, and cultural events. It must be prepared to delve into those sustaining and strengthening characteristics that make the accomplishments achievable and examples for duplication. An example for consideration centers on the Rev. Martin L. King Jr. Imagine the impact on students who have the opportunity to read his early college essays on the plight of blacks in America, which are very radical for the time. The fact that he was only twenty-six years old when he led the Montgomery bus boycotts is very inspiring for young people. Unfortunately, he has been frozen in time with his "I have a dream" speech. But his writings and speeches on poverty in America, his antiwar sentiments, and many others are incredibly dynamic and give a richer view of this remarkable man. By taking a global story and making it significant locally, a black museum in the Northeast can explore this further by finding local congregations that provided money and shoes for the walkers to support their efforts. They may discover that some of their community members actually went south to provide medical care or register voters. Similar possibilities abound in communities across the country. Reclaiming that sense of creativity and defiance of the 1960s will certainly give new energy to the museums' offerings.

The successful black museum in the twenty-first century is one that is able to sustain itself while articulating the importance of community, cultural memory and expression, and preservation of African American materials. With fervent effort, black museums must convince their communities and base audiences that collection and preservation are critical to the community's well being. But convincing is just half of the equation; they must also get them to actually believe it, because belief yields action. This is no small feat, but it is critical that black museums become a part of the "must give" category in the black community first. With increasing pressure from outside funding sources and governments, the best way to demonstrate importance is when the base audience is engaged on a variety of levels with the institution. Many black museum colleagues are hearing, "What is the black community giving and how are they participating?" Imagine the impact if African Americans expanded their charity so that not only were faith (religious affiliations), education (for example, UNCF or the alma mater), community (for example, Urban League), and civic engagement (for example, NAACP), but also museum and cultural endeavors included in regular giving patterns. With sustained support the museum could thrive and position itself as the center for a diverse black community's life.

With more black museums being planned in the first decade of the new millennium, clarity of mission, audience, and programming is paramount for each organization, whether it has been in existence for forty years or four months. The future well-being of these museums is directly tied to their ability to sustain themselves and do the kind of programming that appeals to their chosen demographic. Essentially, the key to solvency is relevancy. Black museums are well positioned to reclaim or expand their base audiences, become community centers of discourse (going beyond the AAM Civic Engagement treatise), and maintain their core function as repositories of community culture. The void is waiting to be filled and black museums must gain the substance to fill it.

15

Learning by Looking: The Future of Museums

Franklin W. Robinson

Recently, I was asked to speak to a group of alumni at their fiftieth reunion about what the world of art and museums will be like fifty years from now; a distinguished geologist and an equally distinguished astronomer were asked to share the podium with me. In a sense, my two colleagues, as scientists, had an easier task than mine, as science is, to a great degree, a progression—we know more than we did fifty years ago. In art, that isn't true. Someone once said to T. S. Eliot, "We know more than the old masters," and he replied, "Yes, and they are what we know." Or as Ezra Pound once said, "Art is news that stays news." For example, wonderful though contemporary art can be, is it really "better" than Rembrandt or Michelangelo? Could anyone looking at Art Nouveau in 1903, or Picasso's Blue Period, have predicted Jackson Pollock's drip paintings or Mark Rothko's "walls of light," executed fifty years later? Could anyone in 1950, looking at Rothko and Pollock, have predicted Andy Warhol's Brillo boxes, or performance art, where an artist bites his leg or masturbates in public, or what we often have today—video installations, Internet art, and piles of rocks in the gallery? So, like Sam Goldwyn, I don't like to make predictions, especially about the future, but if I have to, here goes.

- There will be many more museums. Most American museums have been founded since 1970, and the flood tide shows no signs of letting up. This is because, especially in a democratic age, everything that people are interested in is considered worth preserving, so we have museums of beer cans and barbed wire. Art museums in particular are caught in this egalitarian, pluralistic dilemma—we should preserve everything, but we should stand for, and teach, the best.

- Today, European and American museums are the leaders of the profession, a profession we created; in a few years, that will no longer be true.
- Contemporary art will be what fills most of the museums, for two reasons. First, there are over half-a-million people in this country who define themselves as full-time artists, and who knows how many others are part-time. Second, the art of the past is finite in quantity, and much of it is slowly decaying in attics or garages, or being absorbed into museum collections. So contemporary art is what is available.
- Technology will take command, at least in part. We are already immersed in palm pilots, distance learning, virtual exhibitions, and digitized collections. This can only grow, not because it is a fad, but because it really does make art more accessible and easier to study, aside from many other functions, such as preservation, security, and reproduction. Artists themselves will use technology more and more, and museums that do not keep up with them will be left in the dust.
- Education is the core mission of museums today, and that commitment will become more and more important, from kindergarten to old age. Today, we have many university museums; in the future, we may reverse that and start speaking of museum universities. The Getty in Santa Monica is already a campus. Museums have for decades been focused on lifelong learning, learning outside the classroom, and so they are in a unique position to provide this opportunity on a greater scale.
- In tandem with this deepening commitment to education will surely come a greater emphasis on collaboration. This is already happening; for example, in Ithaca, New York, a town of 29,000 people, the eight museums have come together in a loose, informal consortium called the Discovery Trail; we collaborate on exhibitions, education, publicity, and Discovery Month (May). Joint projects in the future will bring together, hopefully, not just art, science, and history museums, but also theaters, symphony orchestras, dance companies, social agencies, and corporations.

What will artists do? I don't dare predict that, but the context that artists will work in will surely change.

- The world of instant communication means that we already can keep up to date with what is happening this week in Tokyo, Calcutta, Lagos, and Buenos Aires. Soon, the hot young videographer in Helsinki will be in Denver the following week. Recently, the Johnson Museum, in Ithaca, copremiered a video exhibition; the show opened the same day in New York City, Seoul, Reykjavik, and Krakow.

- I've already mentioned artists' interest in technology. Aside from all of those spectacular possibilities, and the opportunity for globalizing whatever they create, technology will challenge the very idea of the "original," as, with nanotechnology, we will be able to reproduce the *Mona Lisa* perfectly, atom by atom; you can have your own world-famous masterpiece above your sofa.

With all this technology and globalization, will, in fact, the original disappear, or will it become even more precious? Will artists, and what they create, become more homogenized, or will they become more eclectic and eccentric, synthesizing even more streams of consciousness and streams of culture into their work? Will museums still help us remember the past, and will artists still mirror the present? Let's hope so.

All these attempts at prediction bring with them obvious, related questions:

- How big should museums be? How big should their collections be, or the size and number of the buildings on their "campus"? How big a staff do we need? What should be the relative sizes of different departments—fund-raising versus curatorial versus education versus publicity and marketing?
- How many museums should there be? Can there be? How many do we need? How many can we afford? How many "boutique," single-collection or single-focus museums should we have? Can some museums be rolled together? Is the history of the three-tined fork as important as the history of the butterfly—or Mr. Smith's collection versus the American Museum of National History? If we say that every human soul is unique and irreplaceable, then every work of art—the product of that soul—is unique and irreplaceable. And yet, and yet. . . . Can we preserve it all? What is quality? How can we make distinctions? What are our criteria?
- How expensive can we get? We have capital expenses, operating expenses, special projects, such as exhibitions and publications, and, most expensive of all, acquisitions to the permanent collection. How much of this can society take? How vulnerable can we make ourselves to the vagaries of the economy? How many museums are building up their endowments? What, or who, will be our new sources of funding? If the economy turns down, can we really justify taking money that might go to the poor or the sick or the elderly? Are we moral institutions?
- Are we populist or elitist, or, somehow, both? What will be our true value to society in the future? As a place where we can see the original,

the real thing? As a place for intellectual growth and spiritual refreshment? As a place that provides a kind of social glue, in a world that is increasingly disparate?

Whatever happens, the arts will, I hope and assume, remain what they have always been—our best map and guidebook to the changing state of our souls, both individual and collective.

16

A Plea for Silence: Putting Art Back into the Art Museum

Didier Maleuvre

The enjoyment of criticism often takes away the pleasure of being moved by truly beautiful things.

Jean de La Bruyère

Museums are places dedicated to preserving and offering artworks to the appreciation of present and future generations. To this purpose, they aim at creating optimal conditions for the viewing of art; they identify which objects warrant seeing and admiring; they carry on the message that human lives can profit from gazing at beautiful objects. "The museum has to function as an institution for the prevention of blindness in order to make works work," says philosopher Nelson Goodman.[1] All interested parties agree that museums want to open the eyes of visitors. Where consensus breaks down is on the matter of deciding what counts as really seeing artworks. To some people, genuine seeing means knowing an artwork part and whole. To others, true sight will be to map out how a specific work intersects with its era and society; or how it punctuates the artist's psychological development; or again how it illustrates or critiques esthetic history. That museums are dedicated to the appreciation of artworks is indisputable. What constitutes true appreciation of art, however, is a matter of tireless dispute. Hence the matter of what an art museum is or should be really amounts to answering this most difficult question: what do artworks essentially want of us?

The time seems past when the art lover could respectably discuss whether there should be art museums at all. This debate was entertained throughout

165

the birth period of the art museum in the nineteenth century but was finally
laid to its grave by art itself when, round the avant-garde period, artists
began making artworks unabashedly destined to the museum. John Dewey's
call to liberate art from the museum in *Art as Experience* (1934) is preempted
by Marcel Duchamp's first readymades (for instance *Bicycle Wheel*, 1913),
which depend entirely on being seen in the company of museum holdings
for their artwork status. Right or wrong, museums today are the natural
environment of artworks—a balance, which, as I argued elsewhere, probably
comes out beneficial to art.[2] By their prominence, pomp, and solemnity,
museums still gallantly proclaim the respect and attention that great art
requires. Turn art loose into the street and it will likely founder in the noise
and distraction of modern life. No artwork, however compelling, stands a
chance next to the giant, digital glitz of Times Square. I recall seeing some
years ago an exhibit of artworks on loan from The Hermitage at a Guggenheim venture unhappily housed in a Las Vegas casino. The arrangement
between high and low was mutually favorable: The Venetian casino topped
its turgid chintz with the finishing touch of real cultural capital; and the
Guggenheim philanthropically brought artworks where the masses play—
thus democratizing art, civilizing the indolent, and in the bargain keeping
the museum in the public eye. Of course this could be a wholly personal
failing of mine, but I cannot recall my eyes ever managing to adjust to the
paintings, so small and startled they seemed in the hysterical splendor of a
casino, within earshot of clanging slot machines, overcast by the decorative
explosions through which the visitor had to stumble to reach the exhibit.
Meditation lost the fight against organized distraction. The day taught a simple truth: art requires a bit of peace and a bit of quiet, a corner where one
can take time and be gentle and attentive.

This lesson is a warning to those who still dream of breaking artworks out
of the alleged necropolis of museums. An artwork that, as Dewey dreamed,
could hold the attention of a passerby would have to be louder than our
aggressively loud and distracting public ways. Everyday life today is in the
grip of generalized esthetic commotion where commerce, information,
advertising, and propaganda pull the senses hither and thither, blanketing
every square inch of available mental space. Everywhere the dazzle of fast
and loud electronic media fights for our eyes and ears, keeps the mind on
nervous alert, sampling everything but tasting nothing. For taste requires
time and "the society of the spectacle," to use Guy Debord's expression,[3]
conspires to leave the viewer no time—no pause for thought in the sensory
onslaught. Artworks designed for today's public space now have to imitate
the gigantism (for example, the steel walls of Richard Serra) or the gaudy
impudence (for example, Claes Oldenburg) of the advertisement that
increasingly sets the template for what qualifies as esthetic experience—to

wit, it must be big, it must be loud, it must stun the intelligence. Sensation nowadays is not what unfolds the senses, but what stuffs them.

Now, given that noise seems to be winning the battle over silence in society and given also that art requires not a quick noisy connection, but acts of prolonged quiet attention, it appears that in the right circumstances (suitably away from gambling casinos, for instance) art museums still probably provide the best haven for art. That we need speak of artistic safe havens suggests that our culture is inadvertently inhospitable to art. This uncongeniality does not come from a conflict of values. Every modern secular nation is generally proud to sponsor the arts, which, as it cannot officially fund religion, is among its few available means to show commitment to higher values, transcendence, civilization. But a conflict persists between art and society, and it stems from the kind of beings we have become. Modern life breeds habits of perception—fast, utilitarian, goal-seeking, overstimulated, clashing, discontinuous—that are at odds with the quiet daydream and pause, the sloweddown pulse of consciousness, through which artworks reveal themselves. What are most anachronistic about art museums are probably their silence and the comparative freedom of pace and movement they give the visitor. Alone among the organs of entertainment that compete for the individual's free time (amusement parks, film and television, package tours, sports), the museum does give free time—freedom to loiter and tarry, to indulge the long double-take, the retracing steps, the dreamy pause, the regress and ingress of reverie, the wending progress that is the dress of genuine mental engagement. It is a tempo of consciousness disarming to the modern audience conditioned to fear open-ended silence as a forerunner of boredom. The commercial media implants the belief that a well-adjusted mind is an excited mind—alert, on the ball, eager for fast stimulus. Silence, by contrast, is the slippery slope of depression, a dip into mental recession, idle time, and therefore money wasted.

The image that rules over modern life, the image that shapes our visual intelligence, is the flashing image—television, the cinema, the roadside billboard, the commercial break. It is an image whose power of persuasion rests on quickness. It spares no time for understanding and acquaintanceship. Its aim is to impress, to daze, and to intimidate. The flashing image is onedimensional—it presses one point, one impression. Unlike the work of art, it is not an image that asks to be inhabited or invites the ripening work of active understanding. The modern image pulverizes on impact. It flashes up on the screen, delivers its punch, and vanishes before intelligence has a chance to ask questions. This is the image (the image as stun-gun) that now shapes our relation to experience. Likewise, the visual news media brings the world to our notice in the style of the advertisement—the message, which brooks no reply or dialogue. That this creates apathy in the viewer has often been observed. But the tyranny of the flashing picture has equally changed our relation to images. In particular it has damaged our capacity to sustain a long, patient, probing conversation with them.

The difficulty that faces the museum visitor today is not that he or she does not know enough about art; the problem is that looking at an image has been made equal to being grabbed by it and getting the message. Under the conditioning of a quick-image society, we forget that images can also be landscapes—long in traveling through, slow to unravel, as deep as the horizon—and not just signposts. This experience is now jeopardized by the selective, truncated mode of knowing typical of hurried, technological society: the quick scan, the plucking of data, the looking only for what is wanted. Indeed museums upset our normal consumption of images because they ask us to take time in seeing them. The artistic image is landscape, not signpost. It invites venturing-into, following, cultivating, unfolding. It probably moves too slowly for our speed-addled brain, for an age in which to say that a book or movie is "slow" is basically to advise against it. Perhaps, like the Dickensian or Tolstoyan novel, paintings belong to an era when spending an hour gazing at a canvas matched the slow pace of acquaintance in a society not yet caught by the fever of fast connections, instant data-delivery, and ready-made contact.

Reckoning with this decay of attention in our time, artists of the last thirty years have taken to making art that is less to be contemplated than understood. A case in point is conceptual art. It consists of artworks that work like intellectual riddles. They require astuteness and savvy and a viewer fluent in politics and esthetic history, who is asked less to lose herself or himself in the work than decode its message. Like the commercial image, such artwork is more informative than transformative: it asks us to "get it." Its appeal lies in tendering a message to one's intelligence—hence, in keeping to the safety of meaning. For it is always easier to ask "what does this object mean?" than "who and where am I in this object?" The first is a demand that the artwork speak to us; the second acknowledges that we need to dwell and find our own place in the object. The commercial image, however, has trained us to think that seeing an image amounts to receiving a message, which more or less lowers all imagery to the level of behavioral prompt. This training in passiveness and recipience is what today sets the greatest obstacle to the continued appreciation of art.

Art requires more than smartness and cultural savvy. Art is first of all a practice of contemplation, the ability to dwell on details, to linger over the minute and the unimpressive, to attend to what is there, especially when what is there does not stridently tug at our sleeve, like advertisement, or admonish, like the propaganda billboard. Art requires active, generous attentiveness. It is the opposite of, for instance, fireworks, which extort our attention by bang and bluster. The Dutch still life is a good example of the artistic sensibility—to give one's uttermost attention to a few nothings, the curl of

an orange peel, a chalice, a knife, a drop of dew glistening off an apple. This
is a world of slowness and silence normally brushed aside in the human bustle. It is quiet and humble and obvious. And yet, given time and attention, it
unveils a cornucopia of realities, impressions, and thoughts. To reach this
wealth, we must agree to pause, to embrace the time of objects, which, like
the artwork, live in the slow time of natural growth and decay.

> The sources of art will be learned by him who sees how the tense grace of the
> ballplayer infects the onlooking crowd; who notes the delight of the housewife
> in tending her plants, and the intent interest of the good man in tending the
> patch of green in front of the house; the zest of the spectator in poking the wood
> burning on the hearth or in watching the darting flames.[4]

The philosopher suggests that the origin of art is extra-artistic; it begins with
not scholarship, but everyday observation. He who takes time to notice has
begun cultivating art. So much of ordinary vision is shallow, perfunctory,
and narrowed by prejudgments and concepts. To notice things afresh a sort
of listlessness and vacancy are needed, an absence of purpose to quiet the
cerebral bustle. Like moral intelligence, artistic vision lies in noticing things
other than ourselves—a housewife at work, a man watering his lawn, a fire
in the hearth. Observe that each of Dewey's examples involves an act of
observant tending and disciplined practice. The budding art lover begins by
noticing those who heed and take care—the cook, the gardener, the household servant, the athlete, they who attend to the fine detail, the precise ges-
ture, the just balance, the right presentation. Genuine seeing is a form of
cultivating. It is the opposite of taking. It consists in enhancing and high-
lighting what lies outside of us.

Seeing, however, is a silent slow-paced art, which, like much of Dewey's
examples, savors of a bygone age. The eye today is conditioned to pick out,
not to delve; our gestures are trained not to tend, but to operate, to obey
signals, to drive, and be driven by machines whose time is fast, nearly instantaneous, though never spontaneous. The visual education of today's young
is set by the videogame and the music video. It rewards single-focus action
and, unlike the picture-book of old, thwarts unguided creative wanderings
of the eye and mind. Stepping into an art museum today feels like crashing
into an anachronistic time zone. Its universe is still that of the bored child
looking out the window, the gardener tending his garden, or the athlete
rehearsing his pitch. The museum is slow, listless, meticulous, and too quiet.
This seems so not because museums are silent (in truth they are alive with
chords and discords), but because the world has grown very garrulous and
busy in contrast. To gauge how much visual and aural noise crowds our
senses—indeed to measure how much we now accept distraction as the normal mode of perception—it is enough to set side by side the typical nine-

teenth century complaint about museums and that of today. The former vituperated against the cacophony of artworks in excessive supply; the latter oppositely confesses nervousness at the silence and paucity of stimulus. The fogy of yesteryear was overwhelmed by sensory overload; the week-ender of today feels abandoned, unassisted, and unsolicited by strangely phlegmatic objects. The contemporary spectator is a born consumer. His natural environment is the *wunderkammer* of commodity culture where he is wooed, cajoled, and sweet-talked by the image industry. Pictures come to him (rarely he to them) bearing promise and flattery, jockeying for his interest, his chuckle, his delight, for the moment when, finally warmed over, he reaches for his wallet. The consumer expects service; he is used to receiving. So what is he to make of those museum masterpieces that do not jingle and chime for his attention? How is he to deal with so much silence? He feels like an unwanted guest. He does not know how to *give* his attention because he is accustomed to having it ransomed out of him. A customer pays the admission price with the expectation to receive in equal measure; this is how entertainment works. Now, the art museum requests him to pay but, once inside, he, not the pictures, is asked to supply the effort. This is an incomprehensible situation.

This misunderstanding is the great problem of art curators today. A great deal of the curatorial effort nowadays seems to go toward reassuring the visitor. The public art museum is being transformed into a public-relations trek where artworks are held in illustration of historical, sociological, or psychological lessons. Museums are increasingly places *about*, rather than of, art—indeed, places about history, in which artworks are taken to be the visual enablers. Artworks are becoming signposts, like the commercial image. Thus it is not rare to see art exhibits organized around social issues, where artworks are skimmed like documents of other times, customs, and politics. To bring art out of its silence (as though silence were not the contemplative background of artworks but some sort of moral lichen eating them up), curators see it necessary to tell people what to notice, what to look for, what to appreciate, what to learn, and what to remember—all of which turn the viewer into a receiver, the suitor into a customer, the explorer into a tourist. The volume of explanations is crowding out the artistic works. The small biographic note next to the painting now extends into regular placards, pseudointeractive CD-ROM displays, and portable audio guides that lead, cue in, and monitor the spectator throughout the visit. Beauty and its rewards (gratitude, joy, the kindness in understanding, the solace, the clarity, the sense of moving upward, of participating in something great and precious) all take second place to the anthropology lesson. The museum is thus another channel of information, a "medium" of temporary exhibits where artworks appear as events and novelties, which, like commodities, trigger reflexes of urgency and "must-see" among the public.[5] "If present trends continue," the great art historian E. H. Gombrich predicted, "public relations and education are likely to loom ever larger in the future of our museums than they did in the past."[6] No matter our feelings about this development, it behooves us to reflect on why a man who dedicated his life to scholarship would feel alarm at the agglutination of learning onto the works of art.

Obviously a scholar like Gombrich cannot be assumed to have favored a raw, emotionally unreflective appreciation of art. He, all of people, knew how much knowledge enhances our sense and experience of artworks. Nevertheless, he raises a point of caution about turning the museum visit into a school trip. His warning is probably on a level with that of André Malraux, who somberly reflected that art appreciation in the twentieth century was "growing more and more intellectualized."[7] When intellectuals themselves deplore intellectualization we know to take their concern seriously. Perhaps there is something about art that, in the end, commands admiration over explanation. So, at any rate, concluded the great art critic John Ruskin: "You sent for me to talk to you of art; and I have obeyed you in coming. But the main thing I have to tell you is that art must not be talked about. The fact that there is talk about it at all, signifies that it is ill done, or cannot be done."[8] The role of criticism is to point to distant summits, not to measure their heights. The task of critics and curators is to convince us by example that our lives will profit from climbing the distance on our own. "Our attitude to the peaks of art," Gombrich opined, "can be best conveyed through the way we speak about them, perhaps through our very reluctance to spoil the experience by too much talk."[9] Of course art quickens the intelligence. It urges us to translate our impressions into words, ideas, debates. To an equal extent, however, it invites us to silence.

What is this silence made of? What's inside it? And what claim does it have to speak better about art than all the lectures and explanatory notes and CD-ROMs and audioguides that earnestly strive to enhance our delight? To answer this question is tricky business because it is contradictory to convey with words the substance of a wordless experience. Let us instead sketch it by negative inference, evoking what gets left out when we do speak about art.

A viewer who listens to an audioguide commentary may be discerning aspects of a painting he would not have otherwise made out; his ability to look and explore alone, however, is overshadowed. On the uneasy feeling that he ought to know more about art, and that its appreciation depends on adequate knowledge of esthetic history, he gives up his nascent reflections to the standard speech of another. His gaze is relieved of making and losing its own way through the artwork. His attention is weighed with reasons and abstractions. Just when he had the chance to know a work of art, he settles for the ersatz of merely knowing about it. This is not to deny that "knowing-about" can foster attention. After all, very few people would become art lovers if, sometime in their life, no one had shown them why artworks are worth looking at. No art seeing goes absolutely free of cultural mediation. However, presentation loaded with explanations may end up eclipsing where it seeks to highlight. Explanations are abstract, intellectual, and generalizing. It does confirm my observation of Manet to be told that he studied Velasquez; but put this explanatory tidbit ahead of my observation and it will, as it were, tame the art piece. Likewise it may in fact forestall or trivialize my serious exploration of *Starry Night* to be told that its painter lived in an insane asylum. Information relieves me of having to notice on my own, to sketch and refine my thoughts. It dilutes the particular moment into general, common knowledge. It inhibits experience, which consists not in being told, but in grappling with particulars. Personal, physical encounter tends to lead us deeper into the substance of things; it forces us to share their time, rhythm, and inner density. He who only surveys the world has no deep appreciation because appreciation requires treading the path of physical life. It calls for acquaintance. Aesthetic experience is a venturing into the sensate world—matter, form, density, substance. It is an experience in incarnation, not abstraction. Somehow the art museum must mirror what is properly aesthetic about art—that is, that it requires physical acquaintance.

Unlike theoretical knowledge, acquaintance is lived through. It brings the knower and the known closer together because the act of obtaining knowledge is woven into the object of knowledge. Acquaintance is development, growth, change; it admits false starts, blind alleys, groping boredom, bafflement. It is no service to the visitor to spare him or her this labor. Any great work of art, and not just the firebrand modernist piece, should cause confusion. To see a great work of art is to behold its singularity, which therefore upsets habits of viewing and thinking. The educationalized museum tries to save the visitor this initial upset because to disconcert the customer is a verboten of the merchant and public relations mentality that holds public institutions, and not just the museum, under its spell.

Of course education has a place in the museum. Artworks do have the power to enlighten and broaden and lift the mind. To this extent, a customer-friendly style of exhibition can go a long way in making new converts. The problem is that it distorts the nature of art appreciation. Art appreciation is an apprenticeship, not a body of facts. In appearance it seems like the audio-guide democratizes esthetic access on the faith that anyone, given the right help, can enjoy the venerable artwork. In reality, it patronizes the visitor who is assumed to need the words of a critic to appreciate what she would not otherwise see. In reality, artworks require no more or less than the introduction normally given to persons. We do not want to be told *everything* about a new acquaintance. A preemptive scientific fact-sheet or résumé would spoil what we know to be the living worth of experience, which is that a person or object is not merely known but discovered; that the nature of a person or object is not factual but experiential; that the process by which an object or person lets itself be known and unveiled is essential to who or what they are. Moreover it is a process by which we also unveil and discover and *become* who we are. We are defined just as much by what we know as by how we come to know. And all worthwhile knowledge involves becoming, the braid by which subject and object influence each other along the road of acquaintance. But acquaintance takes time, patience, even the lulling edge of boredom. It is likely that the first-time visitor will see precious little in the paintings—glumly distant portraits, dumb-show gestures in period costumes, long-faced saints or, down in the twentieth century wing, finger-painting splotches. This bafflement, this lack of fast-and-easy connection, is not to be wished away—to do so degrades the potential agent of knowledge in each visitor to the status of recipient.

This training in recipience and passivity conforms to the modern myth (cobbled together of pseudoscience and psychology) according to which art is easy, ready of access, subjectively pliant. It is, of all mental activities, the one closer to the native, childlike heart of people. It should therefore be fun. In appearance, the explanatory notice or audioguide seems to explain something; in reality it is there to soothe. In most cases, the information is irrelevant or tautological: irrelevant because the word generally pales out of significance when set in too near juxtaposition with the thing; tautological because the so-called explanatory note often consists in transcribing the obvious, such as the fact that, for instance, this painting blends reds and browns, or favors blurred strokes over lines. The achieved effect is less informational than psychological. It colludes with the blurring of distinction between art and entertainment—an unfortunate fusion in which the educational museum is regrettably caught. Museums today are bafflingly split between the rhetoric of their façade, which proclaims the majesty of art, and their public-relations system, which denies that loftiness.

Of course the education-minded curator is correct: art excludes no one. In practical terms, this truth means that the art institute should remain, or go back to being, free of charge. It is a paradox that, while advertising the belief that art is for all, the ever heftier fee at the ticket office denies this conviction. Art's exclusiveness should never be a socioeconomic matter—though it is sheer wishful thinking to pretend that, in cultural terms, art is not elite. It is elite because it takes dedication and thoughtfulness to become an art lover. Just as no Johnny-come-lately becomes a professional baseball player after one throw, an art lover is not made overnight. That museum-going was traditionally the pastime of the upper class stems simply from the fact that the rich had more time on their hands. But being rich does not give a person more sensibility or insight into art. In fact there is nothing about art that especially recommends it to the monopoly of the moneyed elite or

the knowing elite. Quite the opposite. Art by nature dislikes polish and pru-
dence—the qualities by which one acquires and keeps capital, fiduciary or
cultural. Art is never classical. It is not for the mind shaped by status quo.
What looks classical over time was usually outlandish to contemporaries.
Giotto may look staid to the modern eye but, as Girgio Vasari observed, it
was his untutored ways, his complete ignorance of "the proper style," that
opened him to discovery.[10] This leap beyond the tried and tired is another
reason why, in fact, we should be wary of treating artworks as historical lessons. The genuine artist opens a road that leads out of, not into, his age. Do
artists create in order to make their public feel safe and educated? Does
Picasso paint in order to teach about modern art? Of course, one becomes
more cultured from the company of art. But this culture is not knowledge
of facts; it is about developing a sharply personal quality of experience, of
perception, of empathic attunement for fine shades—all things which one
gets by *practicing*, not receiving, them.

The duty of art museums lies in presenting the works in a spirit akin to
that in which they are made. Other museums pay this courtesy to their
objects. Museums of natural history inspire respect for the nature that creates the whale or brontosaurs; anthropological museums work sensitively to
honor the worldviews and ways of life indigenous to various cultures. Likewise the art museum should see to it that works of art are appreciated in the
same spirit that created them. Their creation is, after all, their original milieu,
by which we should mean not just the social background, but in fact the
artwork's power to break with tradition. Of course no artwork arises sui
generis. But an artist is a creator and not a mere chronicler owing to some
unique waywardness of personality that grants the audacity, irreverence, or
curiosity to leap into surprising realms of expression. Indeed the work of art
is both exclamation and interrogation mark; it surprises and it baffles. This
is so because the artist followed his or her willingness to be disarmed before
the forms arising from his brush. Should the viewer be sheltered from this
aptitude for surprise that creates the great work of art? Surprise is the opposite of the theoretic, knowing, confidently expert attitude sibilating in the
headset of the audioguide. Surprise comes to whomever does not shy away
from bewilderment, which means anyone unafraid to walk without prejudgment. This open disposition assumes the silencing of the inner and outer
voices that warn about the encounter even as it is happening. The art
museum fulfills its duty by making clear that some objects are important; it
does not need to expatiate upon how to verbalize their importance (that is
the business of universities). No musicologist would dare speak during a
concert performance. Artworks are owed the same sort of tact. In talking
too much, the museum dulls the artwork's real thrust—that of having chosen
action over explanation, matter over theory. In any case, all the explaining

and lecturing ends up sounding apologetic, the symptom that high culture feels in need of ingratiating itself to the court of business and entertainment.

Too much knowledge given too soon or in the wrong circumstances blunts the chance of wonder. Artworks, like the potential friend or beloved, need not come with their curriculum vitae. For to be given reasons to admire is a reason why one will never completely admire (who, today, can still feel unbullied affection for the *Mona Lisa*?). Of the things that are explained to us we can only feel interest but not wonder. "Interesting" is what can be tamed by knowledge. "Interesting" is the kiss of death by which the indifferent shut the voice of passion and novelty. To make art "interesting" is as irrelevant as to suppose a bullfighter is "interested" in the charging bull, that the concert pianist is "interested" in the piano, or that a race car driver is "interested" in the road. Artworks are not "interesting"; they are wild and restless and sometimes callow; they are amazing, stunning, unexpected, unexpectable, violent, demanding, and transformative.

Coming before a work of art should be an encounter, not an appointment. A museum visitor is asked to *perform* a work of art, not learn about it. Going to the museum is not a visit, it is a pilgrimage, by which is meant that we go there not to genuflect, but to *bring* something, to offer ourselves, to communicate and not just get information. Artworks require us to *perform* them, to enter them, to move in time with them. The audio lecture pulls the artwork into the realm of information (acquisition of facts, cultural veneer, sophistication, etc.); it depresses the initiative of genuinely giving one's attention and not just the lending of one's ear—the kind of curiosity that seeks reimbursement in the form of "interesting" factoids. It is true that to be shown why an object is beautiful can open us to other people's taste and thus widen our sense of the beautiful. But beauty is a cold, academic form if the beholder does not find it alone. Beauty explained is beauty lost. It intrigues the intellect but causes no wonder. What is explained to us by others is rarely wondrous because already comprehended; only that is wondrous which shatters prejudgment. The task of a museum is to maximize the conditions wherein a person can experience wonder, which entails losing one's bearings. No guide should lead a wanderer. Teaching someone how to lose his or her way is contradictory. At best can that person can be encouraged. Perhaps the ideal museum should dare be unmapped—a terra incognita.

In summary, the difficulties before the museum are external and internal. The *external* challenge comes from the decay of mindfulness in our speed-rattled lifestyle. Seeing art requires a depth and length of attention that is out of date in the age of attention deficit. The *internal* challenge comes from the measures taken by modern curatorship to palliate this anachronistic shock: liven up the silence; turn the artworks into information booths; keep the mind jazzed up, excited—techniques through which we seem to admit that artworks nowadays need to be alluring if they are to be found beautiful. I do not know that, given the blanket rule of the electronic media, our seeing is doomed to become ever more nervous and distracted. Some unforeseen change may yet turn the tide. Meanwhile, it remains that a museum's duty is with the artworks and the experience enshrined in them—attention, contemplation, silence, mindfulness. Should these values be now in disuse, then let art museums run the risk of seeming anachronistic. In fact, protecting their archaic quietness need not hurt their popularity. For if what wins over a modern audience is shock and sensation, then what better jolt than to hush the halls? The best way to teach our noisy age about art may yet be to turn up the sound of silence.

Of course this advice is likely to sound foolhardy to curators embattled by financial pressures and trustee boards that demand box-office return. Nevertheless, it is advice nourished by the optimistic faith that art's lesson is not accommodation to social conditions, but power to change them. Art serves its social purpose by blasting the encrusted ways of society. From art, the museum must draw the courage to pull, not just follow, the surrounding mindset.

NOTES

1. Stephen E. Weil, *Rethinking the Museum and Other Meditations* (Washington, D.C.: Smithsonian Institution, 1990), 54.

2. Didier Maleuvre, *Museum Memories: History, Technology, Art* (Stanford, Calif.: Stanford University Press, 1999).

3. Guy Debord, *The Society of the Spectacle* (Detroit: Black&Red, 1970).

4. John Dewey, *Art as Experience* (New York: Perigee, 1980), 5.

5. Roger Silverstone, "The Medium Is the Museum: On Objects and Logics in Times and Spaces," in *Towards a Museum of the Future*, ed. Lauro Zavala, 161–76 (New York: Routledge, 1994) (analyzes the phenomenon of the art museum as sorting station).

6. E. H. Gombrich, *Ideals and Idols: Essays in Values in History and Art* (London: Phaidon, 1979), 198.

7. André Malraux, *The Voices of Silence*, trans. Stuart Gilbert (Princeton, N.J.: Princeton University Press, 1978), 14.

8. John Ruskin, "The Mystery of Life and Its Art," in *Selections from the Writings of John Ruskin*, ed. John D. Rosenberg (Boston: Houghton Mifflin, 1963), 340.

9. Gombrich, *Ideals and Idols*, 163.

10. Girgio Vasari, *The Lives of the Artists*, trans. Julia Conaway Bondanella and Peter Bondanella (New York: Oxford University Press, 1991), 17.

17

Values, Advocacy, and Science: Toward an Empirical Philosophy for Zoo and Aquarium Leadership

Terry L. Maple and Suma Mallavarapu

Replete with priceless living collections, American zoos and aquariums have been increasingly subjected to government regulation and the close scrutiny of concerned citizens and animal rights activists alike.[1] This oversight is energized every time a zoo or aquarium suffers a highly publicized accident or loses a treasured member of its collection. If the problem spins out of control or the exposure leads to a loss of public confidence, leaders may be toppled and new leaders may emerge, or, in extreme cases, the institution's future may be at risk. The much-maligned Stanley Park Zoo in Vancouver, B.C., was closed by a public referendum in 1993. In this instance, local government concluded that it could no longer defend city zoo practices from citizen criticism. In our opinion, the Vancouver authorities took the easy way out; admittedly, it is costly in time, effort, and money, but all flawed zoos and aquariums can be fixed. However, there are no "quick fixes" in the zoo business, and a community must sustain its commitment if the institution is expected to achieve total operational excellence. To succeed in a sea of competitors, zoos and aquariums must exceed public expectations for quality and, frankly, they must stand for something. As stewards of many of the earth's rare and endangered species, zoos and aquariums can no longer be regarded as simply a fun, family experience, although learning at the zoo or aquarium should always be fun. Indeed, if zoos existed only for local amusement, the community would be singled out by its critics as "exploiters" of wildlife.[2]

It seems to us that the interests of the community and the institution itself are best served when zoos and aquariums promulgate proactive standards, ethics, and shared values that are derived from a deeply ingrained organizational and community commitment to quality. The 213 zoos and aquariums that comprise the American Zoo and Aquarium Association (AZA) have monitored operating quality since 1985, when an accreditation process was implemented for all member institutions.[3] The process is not perfect, but it provides for an inspection at five-year intervals by experienced peer professionals who evaluate the institution on a growing volume of objective criteria. Many institutions deploy the accreditation process to influence recalcitrant managing authorities (for example, local governments or non-profit governing boards) to approve critical expenditures or reforms to upgrade facilities, procedures, programs, and standards. This is exactly how the AZA accreditation process functioned in Atlanta in 1984, when the senior author began his service as the reform chief executive of a newly privatized zoological park.[4] To reach its full potential, the Atlanta Zoo needed a push (some would call it a "hammer") from the outside, and the local community needed to be educated about the advancing standards of a profession undergoing nothing short of revolutionary change. After years of infighting, insularity, and indecision, local government and dedicated private citizens reached out to wildlife experts and began to plot a course of action and renewal.

In this chapter we aim to identify strategic opportunities that, if seized, will enable organized zoos and aquariums to succeed individually and collectively in a way that will benefit all aspects of their complex mission. To be recognized as conservation and education leaders, credible seekers and disseminators of newly discovered knowledge, and restorative natural places where families gather to enjoy charismatic wildlife, zoos and aquariums will have to express both passion and wisdom. We will discuss the importance of ethics, standards, and values to the credible operation of institutions accountable to their communities, and we will illustrate the consequences of ethical lapses. We will also assert that creative, dynamic, literate, skillful, and tenacious executive leadership is absolutely essential to meet the challenges of the twenty-first century and beyond. We further argue herein that astute leaders will demand literacy and competence from their employees, at achievement levels far higher than we have needed in the past. This need will be expressed in the recruitment of employees with advanced degrees, especially those with earned doctorates in a variety of scientific specialties from ecology to zoological medicine. By investing in "intellectual capital," it is likely that zoos and aquariums will succeed in solving many of the challenging problems posed by exhibiting, managing, breeding, and saving endangered wildlife. We expect that twenty-first century zoos and aquariums will espouse an "empirical philosophy" based on the systematic acquisition and analysis of business and operational data. A management philosophy based on objectivity and information provides for greater accountability, whether it is a chief financial officer, general curator, or veterinarian who depends on the data. The best zoos and aquariums are managed by managerial empiricists who know how to acquire information, manage it, distribute it, and analyze it. We anticipate that this trend will be pervasive in the twenty-first century.[5]

We suggest further that, by seeking both breadth and quality, zoo and aquarium leaders may have to embrace market and operating techniques that are associated with the entertainment industry and still retain public confidence in the purity of the cause they serve. Future leaders will achieve their goals if they can integrate advanced business methods with a compelling, global conservation vision that resonates with employees, guests, and the greater community at large.

WHEN ZOOS AND AQUARIUMS FAIL

A failed institution doesn't get that way overnight. Instead, it tends to decline gradually, victimized by community neglect, declining public interest, aging facilities, shortfalls in revenue, and waning aspirations. (Unlike zoos, aquariums have frequently failed because of *inflated* performance expectations and the effect of massive debt loads.) In fact, the decline of many institutions is not immediately noticed, as expectations are annually revised downward and risks are no longer taken. Most important, we think, failing institutions often lack for bold leadership. Organizational mediocrity is too frequently a byproduct of institutional reticence, a collective fear of failure, and a kind of "learned helplessness" to impediments, challenges, and marketplace decline. A psychological construct, "learned helplessness" refers to the lethargy produced by events that are no longer predictable.[6] In this sense, as we have applied the principle, an organization so afflicted no longer responds appropriately when confronted by chaotic marketplace circumstances. Conversely, when facing a formidable challenge or opportunity, entrepreneurial leaders respond differently, best illustrated by fellow Atlanta citizen Ted Turner[7] who festooned his desk with a sign boldly proclaiming, "Lead, follow, or get out of the way!"

Looking back on the twentieth century, the vast majority of American zoos and aquariums entered the age with meager aspirations. Like destitute menageries (too often their immediate historical predecessor), these newly emerging city zoos depicted animals as if they were convicted felons, confining them to a life behind bars, doomed to suffer a short, unhappy life of boredom, restriction, and subservience. Exceptions to this dismal trend, in New York, San Diego, and Washington, D.C., were institutions founded by ambitious visionaries. At the end of the century, landscape immersion techniques[8] had transformed the better zoos and aquariums into complex, naturalistic simulations of nature, providing spacious, functional, imaginative, and appropriate living conditions for even the most challenging species. These developments led Robert Sommer, one of the nation's leading environmental psychologists, to conclude that zoos (and aquariums) were the only type of "hard, architectural institutions" (for example, mental hospitals, prisons, etc.) that have to date transcended the condition, transforming themselves into models of "soft" architecture—naturalistic, functional, malleable, and species-appropriate.[9] Not all zoos and aquariums have successfully advanced from "hard to soft," but elite zoos (for example, the member institutions of the AZA) are making steady progress in this direction. Sommer attributed the change to advances in behavioral science, and the zeal with which this new knowledge was skillfully applied by visionary zoo designers.[10]

Indeed, the bases for best practices in the zoo and aquarium are essentially empirical standards honed through years of tedious research. Famed zoo biologist and zoo director Dr. Heini Hediger was one of the first zoo professionals to elevate management and exhibition standards through the judicious application of field and natural history data, systematic observations of individual animals, and objective problem-solving techniques. As Hediger observed: "The standard by which a zoo animal is judged should be according to the life it leads in the wild, under the so-called free conditions of nature."[11]

Regrettably, too many zoo and aquarium curators seem largely ignorant of Hediger's published work. For this reason, the senior author conducted a videotaped interview of Dr. Hediger in Zurich. The edited tapes and a typescript of the interview will soon be available to zoo biologists.[12] One of Hediger's most important observations on design was his recognition that nature was largely curvilinear, not cubic. He considered "the cube" to be essentially "unbiological" and objected strenuously to the prevailing tendency in his time to build cubic animal facilities. Seventy-five years after its publication in the English language, *Wild Animals in Captivity* (1930) is still widely regarded as the finest primer on zoo management ever published.

Hediger was also the first to admit, despite his own successes, that "research is always last in the zoological garden." By this statement, he clearly lamented his own personal struggle to establish science as a higher priority on the management agenda.[13] From Hediger's point of view, a zoo could never provide adequate care for animals unless zoo personnel understood the nuances of animal behavior. Anyone in contact with zoo animals had to learn to observe, listen, and communicate with each and every creature he or she managed (table 17.1). Hediger was one of a small cadre of European zoo directors who were trained in the field of animal psychology,

Table 17.1.   Hediger's "Seven Aspects" of the zoological garden, renamed, recombined, expanded, and prioritized.

- Leadership, Vision, and Finance

- Conservation, Education, and Science

- Animal Welfare, Standards, and Ethics

- Zoo Biology (Art/Science of Management)

Source: Terry L. Maple and M. A. Bloomsmith, *Recruiting, Rewarding, and Retaining Scientific Talent in AZA Institutions* (paper presented at AZA annual conference, New Orleans, Louisiana, 2004).

a specialty Hediger learned from a beloved German mentor, coincidentally a psychiatrist named Robert Sommer. (Upon meeting the American environmental psychologist, Bob Sommer, Hediger was moved to present him with his personal copy of the elder Robert Sommer's German language textbook on animal psychology,[14] a treasure that Bob Sommer has since passed on to the senior author.)

In his Zurich interview[15] Hediger revealed that European zoos were historically allied to entertainment venues (for example, the circus) rather than universities, and, therefore, unlike botanical gardens, zoos lacked a scientific foundation. As a result, even in Europe, scientific zoos were an exception to the norm. In Europe, certainly, zoos and circuses shared a common heritage in their techniques of animal acquisition, exhibition, and management. Hediger himself was an expert on the behavior of animals in both the circus and the zoo, and he wrote about both of them extensively. His own links to academia as Professor of Ethology at the University of Zurich provided encouragement to many of his students who conducted benchmark behavioral studies under his supervision at Zoo Zurich. Some, like Dr. Christian Schmidt, later became his curators and, eventually (in the case of Schmidt, now in Frankfurt), zoo directors in their own right. As long as Hediger remained at the helm, Zoo Zurich valued research, and his legacy of scientific zoo biology continued long after his retirement. Hediger's longevity and prodigious productivity as a scientist/administrator made Zoo Zurich a visible example of innovation, rational animal management, and leadership.

CASE STUDIES IN CRISIS LEADERSHIP

There are many good examples of substandard zoological parks that have been dramatically transformed in the past twenty-five years. One of the first in North America was New Orleans's Audubon Zoo, which began its revitalization process in the mid-1970s under the direction of a young and charismatic visionary, L. Ron Forman.[16] Under Forman's direction the city zoo activated its local citizens through formation of a nonprofit zoological society, eventually transforming the zoo into an effective public/private partnership, a model that stimulated change throughout the zoo industry. Today the Audubon Zoo is one component of a network of zoological facilities including an insect museum, a nature center, an endangered species conservation center, and a major aquarium. Collectively, these facilities operate under the umbrella brand of the Audubon Nature Institute. From the outset, Forman's administration emphasized best business, marketing, and animal management practices, innovation, and a commitment to conservation. A key to its success has been the ability to rapidly raise significant revenue from public and private sources. Bond issues have been approved enthusiastically and repeatedly due to the high degree of public confidence in Forman and his team. In fact, a bond issue on the city ballot in the early eighties to approve public funds for the "Aquarium of the Americas" was supported by a high percentage of the same voters who defeated New Orleans public school bonding.

Public confidence is a key factor in the success of any zoo, aquarium, or museum. In 1984 the City of Atlanta owned and operated a dilapidated facility (on less than twenty-five acres) suffering from decades of public neglect and low operating budgets (less than $1 million allocated in 1984). After a series of management blunders were exposed by investigative journalists, the zoo became an industry pariah and lost its membership in the AZA, an outcome without precedent in the eighty-year history of the organization.[17] The Atlanta Zoo scandal was an international story, resonating with the public due to the mysterious disappearance of some of the animals, including an elephant discovered by the media partially (and apparently hastily) buried in North Carolina.[18] Twinkles the elephant, originally purchased from small change donated by Atlanta school children, became a symbol of the inhumane (and inexplicable) management practices at the zoo in the early 1980s.[19]

The Atlanta Zoo story was a "wake-up call" for the entire zoo profession, an example of what can happen when a zoo is neglected by its community and permitted to drift out of control. Fortunately, the zoo was eventually saved and revitalized by concerned citizens who issued an unambiguous mandate for change. Local government did its part by issuing a significant revenue bond of $16 million, which enabled zoo leaders to proclaim a community commitment to quality. The next bold steps required a new and expanded vision. We asked ourselves in 1984, what in the world could this little zoo become?

CRAFTING A PROGRAMMATIC ZOO VISION

As zoological parks reinvent themselves, they must struggle with their inherent limitations. Both the Audubon Zoo and the Atlanta Zoo, at the outset of their revitalization odyssey, were hampered by their limited acreage and their tiny and unremarkable collections of wildlife. The visionaries who crafted the new Audubon Zoo chose to create a naturalistic zoo with creative balance. It was designed to be good for animals and people, comprised of a critical mass of carefully selected critters that would provide something for everyone to enjoy. Construction of the new zoo commenced in 1977 and developed so swiftly that it attracted the zoo world's national conference to New Orleans in 1981. The remarkable new face of the zoo was showcased to rave reviews and generated hope for other communities seeking to upgrade their own zoos.

The Atlanta Zoo took a more specialized path, owing, perhaps, to the more thorough disclosure of its problems by aggressive media in print, radio, and television, locally and worldwide.[20] Atlanta's zoo had to be thoroughly and completely overhauled in order to demonstrate to its peers that it could provide humane and professional care for the animals it had neglected for so many years. When a new management team was assembled to contemplate and craft its future, staff identified opportunities where the zoo could exert genuine leadership. The new leaders envisioned a zoo that would provide innovations and ideas immediately recognized as new benchmarks. Three programmatic areas of opportunity were thus designated: (1) conservation; (2) education; and (3) science and technology. All of these targets were easily integrated and excellence in each one was a logical extension of the intellectual strengths of potential academic partners in the Atlanta area (for example, Atlanta University, Emory University, Georgia Tech, Georgia State, and University of Georgia). Clearly, the participation of experts in architecture, behavior, reproductive biology, and veterinary medicine was a key factor in elevating the operating standards for Atlanta's zoo. (Three years after losing its membership credentials, the new "Zoo Atlanta" was awarded accreditation by the AZA.) These partnerships are intact after nearly two decades and continue to provide opportunities for achievement and innovation (figure 17.1). Interestingly, both Zoo Atlanta and the Audubon Zoo now enjoy well-earned reputations for their investments and achievements in conservation and scientific zoo biology.

THE ROLE OF ETHICS, STANDARDS, AND VALUES

In 1990 a group of zoo professionals and allied academics formulated a bold plan to conduct a workshop to confront, debate, and perhaps convert some of the zoo world's most vocal critics. The conference was funded by the National Science Foundation and organized through a collaboration of the AZA, Zoo Atlanta, and the Georgia Institute of Technology. Professor

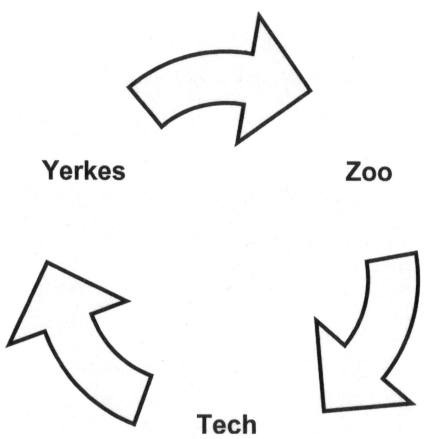

Figure 17.1. **Synergistic relationship among Georgia Tech Center for Conservation & Behavior, Yerkes National Primate Research Center of Emory University, and Zoo Atlanta.**

Source: Terry L. Maple and M. A. Bloomsmith, *Recruiting, Rewarding, and Retaining Scientific Talent in AZA Institutions* (paper presented at AZA annual conference, New Orleans, Louisiana, 2004).

Bryan G. Norton, an environmental ethicist and philosophy professor at Georgia Tech, was the intellectual anchor and lead organizer of this unique meeting.

In spite of decades of progress on exhibit and management standards, zoo and aquarium professionals have suffered the sting of painful (and sometimes personal) criticism from animal welfare and animal rights groups such as the Humane Society of the United States (HSUS) and People for the Ethical Treatment of Animals (PETA). For example, PETA founder Ingrid Newkirk has written:

Let's bring zoos into the '90's by turning them into desperately needed sanctuaries for the poor shackled elephants, bicycle-riding bears and neck-chained chimpanzees who are sold to hunting ranches or put in the back room to die when they are no longer young and pretty. . . . We need to give zoos a very wide berth and a public thumbs down. Until then, I will hate the zoos.[21]

The Atlanta conference on zoo ethics brought together, for the first time, zoo and wildlife experts and responsible, reasonable, and scholarly critics carefully selected to reach an outcome of consensus and common ground. To avoid an unproductive weekend of contentious (and endless) debate, the assembled participants agreed to identify concrete action steps that would significantly upgrade the living standards for zoo and aquarium wildlife. The dialogue produced a series of recommendations submitted to the Board of Directors of the AZA and a highly regarded book, *Ethics on the Ark*, endorsed by AZA and published by Smithsonian.[22]

In spite of this unprecedented moment of rapprochement, many animal welfare/rights extremists continue to denigrate zoos and aquariums and fail to recognize the difference between so-called roadside zoos and the organized, accredited zoos and aquariums of the AZA. A major difference in the two categories is the freely expressed values and standards of AZA institutions (table 17.2). Zoo and aquarium professionals recognize that they must differentiate by more vociferous expressions of their core values, and this has led to a more professional approach to vision and mission statements. Pertinent to our discussion of values is the "naturalistic value" defined by Stephen Kellert:[23]

The naturalistic value emphasizes the many satisfactions people obtain from the direct experience of nature and wildlife. This value reflects the pleasure we get from exploring and discovering nature's complexity and variety. Indeed the satisfactions people derive from contact with living diversity may be among the

---

Table 17.2. Six noble purposes of zoological parks and aquariums.

1. Public Education

2. Field Conservation

3. Animal Welfare

4. Reproduction and Husbandry

5. Discovery through Research

6. Inspiration and Advocacy

Source: Terry L. Maple and M. A. Bloomsmith, *Recruiting, Rewarding, and Retaining Scientific Talent in AZA Institutions* (paper presented at AZA annual conference, New Orleans, Louisiana, 2004).

most ancient pleasures obtained from interacting with the natural world—
particularly the more vivid plants and animals.[24]

Visionary "catch-phrases" also abound. An especially articulate model was
created in the 1980s for the Minnesota Zoo: "Strengthening the bond
between people and the living earth." Variations on this theme have proliferated throughout the industry, but none of them have better captured the
essence of the conservation vision. Museums too reserve the right to express
their values; indeed the public often demands it.

> The real issue is not to purge the museum of values, in all likelihood an impossi-
> ble task, but how to make those values manifest, how to bring them up to con-
> sciousness for both ourselves and our visitors. We delude ourselves when we
> think of the museum as a clear and transparent medium through which only
> our objects transmit messages. We transmit messages too—as a medium we are
> also the message—and it seems to me vital that we understand better just what
> those messages are.[25]

In the zoo and the aquarium, conservation values have gained a stronger
and more active voice. To this end, Zoo Atlanta recently created a center for
conservation, education, science, and technology, naming it the "Conservation Action Resource Center." We wanted it to be known as a place where
the staff and their partners were engaged in "hands-on," action-oriented
conservation projects. The distinction is appreciated by Zoo Atlanta's visitors and donors.

Nonprofit institutions may find it easier to be "ethical," but we are living
in an age where ethics is an important issue for all forms of business. Because
nonprofits are becoming more business-oriented, ethical constraints must be
codified to avoid public rebuke for misconduct or simply poor judgment.
Not long ago, some American zoos were criticized for allowing private hunting ranches to acquire animals no longer needed for the zoo collection.
Clearly, even if they were the unintended consequences of weak disposition
policies, transactions of this kind must be regarded as unethical. The idea
that zoos and aquariums have a "cradle-to-grave" responsibility for their
collections is gaining traction. For many species (for example, elephants,
great apes, and marine mammals), retirement planning is now deemed essential.[26] A spirit of openness now prevails within AZA. It is essential that zoos
and aquariums continue to encourage constructive criticism, debate, and
inquiry from within and without the association if we expect innovation and
reform to advance.

RAISING THE BAR

The last quarter century of zoo and aquarium development is a period in
which institutional operating standards were tremendously and rapidly

advanced. This trend commenced with the revitalization of New Orleans's Audubon Zoo. The two dominating themes of this creative period were wildlife conservation and animal welfare. Indeed, the two were deemed so essential they could generate intense conflict. Scholars at the Atlanta ethics conference debated whether a commitment to species conservation could lead to disadvantages (even mistreatment) for individuals.[27] For example, the greater good of translocating an animal to optimize breeding might bring some measure of discomfort both physically and psychologically to the individual. David Ehrenfeld[28] correctly framed the issue in his foreword to *Ethics on the Ark*:

> Do the rights and welfare of individual animals—this badger, that tortoise—take precedence over the rights and welfare of whole species or even ecosystems; can a hybrid orangutan be sacrificed to make zoo space for a presumably more important orangutan with a genotype closer to that of her wild ancestors? Are zoos playing God . . . ?[29]

Such conflicts are not easy to resolve and may be properly designated "ethical dilemmas." All too frequently, these differences are played out in public debates between zoo experts and those hired by their critics to engage them. Highly trained psychologists and zoologists have argued all sides, and many of these arguments have been captured in print.[30] Animal welfare and conservation are getting greater emphasis in the AZA accreditation process, and the standards for accreditation have advanced steadily year by year. This trend to superior care and relevance among organized zoos and aquariums is worldwide in scope. Regrettably, there are thousands of lesser institutions that are not regulated or aspirational.

Clearly, zoo and aquarium professionals must be able to simultaneously sustain a commitment to both individual animal welfare and conservation, and they must do so in the historical context of the ratification of conservation as the zoo world's highest priority. In most of the cases that we have examined, compromise has been possible, minimizing or avoiding altogether any negative impact of conservation on individual welfare. To achieve acceptable compromise, zoo managers must continue to think outside the box. Since 1993 a common vision has guided the world's organized zoos and aquariums. *The World Zoo Conservation Strategy* was produced by competent leaders and scholars recruited to the task by the World Association of Zoos and Aquariums (WAZA) (formerly the International Union of Directors of Zoological Gardens/WZO). One of the key recommendations in this document was the observation that zoos and aquariums should be enlisted to heighten public and political awareness about the interdependence of life.[31] Furthermore, zoos and aquariums were urged to use their precious collections of living animals to optimize the telling of the whole conservation story.[32] In recent years, there has been a noticeable upsurge in creative media for conservation education in AZA zoos and aquariums. Furthermore, immersion exhibits are now being designed along with sustainable in situ conservation programs, and CLR, Inc. (an American design firm) has pioneered a "zoo campus ecology" program that assumes a twenty-year transition to community leadership in energy efficiency and green architecture.[33]

TRENDS IN CONFLICT

As we enter the twenty-first century, modern aquariums and zoos have committed to naturalistic exhibitry, higher standards for animal welfare, and cooperative field and zoo-based conservation derived from an objective and comprehensive science of zoo biology. This drive to higher quality, breadth, and depth has required increased public and private funding. All great zoos have dramatically increased expenditures on fund-raising, and executive leadership looms ever larger as our communities experience the enthusiasm of rising expectations. However, there is a downside to the emphasis on the bottom line; zoo boards and local governments are looking to the theme park entertainment industry for new ideas. We worry that the infatuation with theme park methods may be a risky step for the zoo profession. The entire museum profession also struggles with the issue of how to interface hot marketing/operating trends and cause-related issues such as conservation, education, and science. As Stephen Weil opines recently:

> Mingled with [this resistance to marketing] also seems to be a sort of fear, a fear that giving the community (the museum's major market) a more participative role in shaping programs might dilute our standards, or cheapen what we do, or leave us open to charges of pandering to the tasteless, the misguided, or the misinformed.[34]

Consider the unicorn. Years ago, Ringling Brothers Circus promoted a traveling unicorn exhibit, showcasing a large, one-horned goat gussied up to resemble the creature of myth and lore. As the circus industry is based on fantasy, it's okay to dress up a goat and call it a unicorn. But zoos and aquariums are in the "truth" business, and would be obligated to identify it as a mere goat. Fantasy enterprises depend upon sleight-of-hand illusions, if not downright deception, in their mission to entertain and amaze their audience. In the history of zoos, it was once a common practice to hide knowledge from competitors. To keep the audience guessing and returning for another look, carnival and circus artists still protect their trade secrets. Zoos and aquariums must be careful not to sacrifice their hard-won credibility for short-term bumps in revenue.

However, it has been clearly demonstrated (in Atlanta and elsewhere) that a zoo or aquarium can incorporate modern, aggressive marketing techniques and still maintain institutional credibility for honesty and objectivity. In fact, zoos today are compelled to study new revenue opportunities as practiced by similar institutions doing it well. An example of having it both ways is the new Disney's Animal Kingdom (DAK), promoted by its ownership as a "new species of theme park." The Disney operating mentality stresses customer service, incorporates strong fantasy themes, and still provides a naturalistic animal park remarkably similar to the African, Asian, and South American wilderness they have targeted for simulation. Disney and its Florida neighbors at Busch Gardens and Sea World have both successfully blended conventional theme park operating/marketing methods and AZA standards and commitments into a coherent operating philosophy. They keep it honest by clearly separating fantasy from reality throughout the park. Disney's "Bug Show" presents vetted bug facts, but the critters are animated. The bugs may talk (and sing), but they also tell the truth! From the beginning both DAK (founded in 1992) and Sea World (founded in 1965) committed to conservation and to science. Currently, both institutions employ Ph.D. level staff with conservation, education, and research responsibilities. In a world increasingly dangerous to people and wildlife, conservation scientists from the zoo and aquarium world should aspire to play an important if not leading role as educators and implementers of conservation programs and policies (table 17.3). In fact, both DAK and Sea World have been effective in marketing their own concern and commitment to wildlife. This builds business and public confidence.

The two cultures, zoo and theme park, often collide with greatest force within smaller institutions. Currently, the bigger zoos and aquariums are doing the heavy lifting in conservation, science, and technology. Among smaller institutions, the lion's share of the "cause" funding goes to educa-

---

Table 17.3.   Characteristics of a "Scientific Curator."

- Earned doctorate or advanced doctoral-level training in a recognized field of science
- Standing in an academic institution (e.g., adjunct, lecturer, or faculty status)
- A teacher, mentor, or collaborator with students and faculty
- Membership in learned societies
- Publications in refereed scientific sources
- Uses systematic data to solve problems
- Computer literate/technically competent

Source: Terry L. Maple and M. A. Bloomsmith, *Recruiting, Rewarding, and Retaining Scientific Talent in AZA Institutions* (paper presented at AZA annual conference, New Orleans, Louisiana, 2004).

tional programs and personnel.[35] Conservation is promoted at this level but not necessarily engaged. Theme park–like revenue opportunities may lead smaller zoos and aquariums to entertain rather than enlighten their visitors. It is highly desirable to do both, but, when push comes to shove, leaders may be forced to decide on guns (entertainment) or butter (conservation/science). How to balance an institution's scarce resources is one of the most challenging problems faced by chief executives. A recent paper in the journal *Conservation Biology* issued some benchmark figures for consideration:

> Only a handful of collection-based institutions commit more than 5% of their operating budget to conservation. Indeed, 10% of an operating budget may be insufficient for a mission. The Wildlife Conservation Society dedicates more than 25% of its total budget to conservation, and that percentage is what we consider a benchmark for collection-based institutions.[36]

In a post-9/11 world economy, the lowest of these benchmarks will be difficult to achieve. As a function of bottom-line strategic thinking, zoos and aquariums in the early part of the twenty-first century will struggle to remain relevant to the global environmental movement. Leadership in conservation is a worthy goal for organized zoos and aquariums, but it cannot be achieved without tremendous growth in the revenue stream. The irony and the paradox is that theme-park methods may be required to reach cause-related objectives. The most promising development of the new century may be the proliferation of a "hybrid operating culture" where noble aspirations drive market and operating zeal. The success of Disney's Animal Kingdom demonstrates the efficacy of blending a family entertainment venue with a global conservation vision. However, an uneasy ambivalence prevails in many of the industry's entrepreneurial zoos and aquariums. Kellert[37] reasons:

> The zoological park seems caught, on the one hand, between the goals of mass entertainment and inexpensive escape and, on the other, public education and conservation. The modern zoo appears to operate at the edge of potential: unsure of what it signifies to most people and uncertain of what it would like to become.[38]

An unfortunate byproduct of the current "identity crisis" is the challenge of recruiting successor-leaders from within our institutions. By and large, zoos and aquariums are producing specialists rather than generalists, and the result is more and more outside chief executive officers (CEOs) recruited from other business and professional sectors. While this may lead us in exciting new directions, it may also lead to a crisis of public confidence, missed opportunities, or major strategic or tactical blunders. Recently, several major American zoos and aquariums have suffered through leadership crises stimulated by flawed recruiting practices. A major issue in the twenty-first century and beyond is the recruitment of a new generation of credible, thoughtful, and creative executive leadership for our zoos and aquariums.

AZA institutions have just begun to struggle with the challenge of workplace diversity. Currently, there are very few zoo and aquarium executives from minority populations. More progress has been made in the recruitment of female executives, with a second and third woman in seventy-five years recently being elected AZA president. Women are entering the field in greater numbers now, so we should expect a growing percentage of women CEOs in the twenty-first century. A more diverse leadership in AZA will doubtless bring substantive changes to priorities, perspective, and strategic aspirations. To facilitate a future of fruitful recruitment, Stephen Weil's[39] thoughtful essay on the optimal attributes of museum leaders should be read by the members of all zoo and aquarium search committees.

CHARISMATIC MEGAVERTEBRATES

An "ethical paradox"[40] is even more challenging than an ethical dilemma. An example of such a paradox is the compulsion to acquire and exhibit the world's largest and most charismatic species in our zoos and aquariums. At the same time, these popular taxa are the most difficult creatures to manage. Worse, many of them do not suffer captivity gladly. Is it ethical to exhibit animals whose home ranges in nature cover hundreds, even thousands, of miles? Is it ethical to exhibit animals that evoke sympathy by their propensity to inactivity, lethargy, and depression? And yet, if we don't find ways to successfully house such creatures, we may be faced with the prospects of a future rescue without experience, knowledge, or hope of saving them. A future war looming in Central Africa could wipe out the last small population of mountain gorillas, and yet no zoo currently exhibits this species. How would we duplicate or simulate their nomadic ways or their specialized diets if we were charged with the responsibility of their salvation?

The zoo's dark, carnival personality longs to exhibit the universe of complex and charismatic creatures; the other, nobler side hesitates for good reason. Professor David Chiszar and his zoo-based coauthors[41] strenuously argue that the *only* justification for zoos and aquariums is public education. But education is not a sufficient justification. Zoo/aquarium animals must be also provided with opportunities to live appropriately, socially, comfortably, and with a reasonable degree of autonomy (or, as we like to say, they must be "living large"). To design and implement such outcomes, zoo and aquarium architects must be innovative, worldly, and exceedingly wise. Naturalistic landscape-immersion was not immediately accepted by the general public, but it has proved to be a tenacious trend. We will stay on this cutting edge if we avoid the trend of edifice building, but backsliding is already evident with the proliferation of major aquariums where enormous sums of money have been spent on the external architecture. CEOs will have to enjoy a high degree of control to ensure that the internal "guts and bolts" of their facilities receive at least equal emphasis and, hopefully, the lion-fishes' share of the resources.

WHY SCIENCE MATTERS

Global conservation debates and decisions require expertise. For zoos and aquariums to be represented at the table for such deliberations, they must continue to recruit well-trained and disciplined conservation, field, and zoo biologists and learn how to reward and retain them. Unlike museums and botanical gardens, zoos and aquariums have been slow to hire scholars. However, in the more successful zoos and aquariums, scholars are abundant and, in some institutions, approach a critical mass. Recent research conducted at Georgia Tech's Center for Conservation and Behavior reveals that scientists in the zoo and aquarium profession are seeking a more supportive environment for their work. One survey[42] of zoo and aquarium scientists reveals that they rated "support from the CEO" as the most important factor contributing to successful scientific programs. Like-minded (and similarly trained) colleagues were also a factor valued by zoo/aquarium scientists. Earlier surveys[43] found that association with universities facilitated productivity, as measured by publications. Clearly, there is a scientific culture required for zoo and aquarium personnel who are expected to conduct serious scholarship. Failure to cultivate this culture may culminate in underachieving scientific units and confound our efforts to answer important questions. The attributes of an academic work climate, namely freedom of inquiry and expression, motivation to publish, and recognition and rewards for disseminating knowledge, should be fostered in every zoo and aquarium (table 17.4).

To further support science, it would be advisable if zoos and aquariums acquired the latest technology for data acquisition and processing and advanced software for scientific applications. The unlimited potential for computerization in every kind of museum setting has been explored in some detail by Maxwell Anderson:[44]

> The growth of wired museums of all kinds may provide a younger generation steeped in this technology with more reasons to connect to us. It seems less likely that it will contribute to our eclipse as institutions than our transformation. Although we may bemoan the extent to which we are different in our contributions to society today from what we were 30 years ago, we cannot return

Table 17.4.   Hubbs-Sea World core values for scientists, staff, and trustees.

- Excellence in original, independent, scientific research

- Public service

- Scientific honesty and integrity

- Safety and efficiency

- Highest standards of animal care and welfare

- Creative and productive workplace

- Common sense

Note: The Hubbs-SeaWorld Institute website provides additional information on the mission and vision of the extensive Hubbs-Sea World scientific programs.

to a time when audiences were tolerated rather than listened to, information was sporadically shared, and amenities were an afterthought. And for that we are without question better institutions.[45]

Computer technology can be applied to monitor facility security, or to simply monitor behavior, particularly during critical events such as an impending birth. Computers can also be deployed to provide interactive educational experiences, and these devices can also supply data on an array of visitor responses including their likes, dislikes, and what they have learned from their visit. When computer technology reaches an advanced stage in zoos and aquariums, they often elect to establish an information technology department. Once this step is taken, the entire organization has reached an important milestone. Zoos and aquariums have cautiously embraced technology, and like their museum colleagues they must grudgingly admit that the challenges of the twenty-first century will demand that every institution be fully "wired."[46] For this reason, computer literacy will become a necessary qualification for working in zoos and aquariums.

There are other ways that scientists can contribute to the success of zoos and aquariums and the profession at large. First, scientists provide a buffer to outside critics, particularly those from humanistic disciplines that find fault with the idea of holding animals "captive." When these critics approach the issue from a philosophical basis (for example, environmental ethics or moral philosophy), the debate may be framed in rational, scholarly argument. Without literate zoo biologists to debate them, welfare/rights critics have the upper hand on zoos and aquariums. However, in public forums with the profession's most able and accomplished scholars at the podium, zoos and aquariums have effectively and persuasively made their case. Scholars are comfortable with open debate and criticism. In fact, the zoo and aquarium profession would benefit from a more candid exploration of its own conflicts and controversies. The recruitment of additional scholars will inevitably lead to a greater climate of openness and peer review, a much needed addition to the zoo biologist's tool kit.

An "empirical philosophy" requires that our values, standards, and ethics will be supported by the facts and findings of conservation and zoo biology and other allied disciplines with an interest in our collections and programs. We contend that animal welfare standards based on behavioral data from the field and the zoo are more effective than platitudes. Certainly, the former are more likely to lead to an effective plan of action. The zoo and aquarium profession is not yet guided by a unified "empirical philosophy," but the merits and applications of sound science have been demonstrated in the publications of zoo and aquarium professionals worldwide. Advances in population genetics and reproductive biology have dramatically improved the breeding record for scores of endangered species collectively managed by zoos and aquariums, but many tough issues remain. The current controversy about best practices in elephant management will not be resolved easily or quickly without relevant data. We must recruit biologists, ethologists, psychologists, veterinarians, and the like who understand the natural history and behavioral biology of these massive, complicated creatures. Only a thorough, objective review of the available data will determine if we can adequately provide for their needs in our zoos. If we are lacking in sufficient data, then additional studies must be commissioned. Science should drive our decision-making process. When we discover gaps in our knowledge, we must seek input from scholarly collaborators. An empirical approach is required to solve this and many other vexing problems in the management and exhibition of zoo and aquarium species.

Unfortunately, we have not achieved critical mass in the recruitment of scientific curators or collaborators. By scientific curators, we mean those who have advanced research training in some specialty, or those who have earned doctoral degrees in a scientific field. There is a clear trend toward the recruitment of scientific curators in the larger zoos and aquariums, but smaller institutions have not yet recognized the need. Zoos and aquariums will be unprepared for future challenges if they fail to aggressively recruit for the attributes of science and technology literacy—the higher the level of training, the better, we believe. Surely the most successful world zoos of the twenty-first century will be those investing heavily in highly competent and competitive scholars who represent the "intellectual capital" of the industry. Science-based management requires a broad base of participation as Donald G. Lindburg[47] notes:

> Zoos today are in many ways prisoners of their pasts, placing local interests ahead of species' welfare, or lacking in comprehension of the diversity of nature, on the one hand, and the creation of viable living environments, on the

other. . . . Some of the best minds in the fields of molecular and population genetics have been utilized in the formulation of captive management plans, whereas the expertise from other academically relevant disciplines remains largely untapped and unheeded.[48]

When zoos and aquariums begin to out-recruit research universities for the best and the brightest young scholars, they will have reached an important benchmark in their struggle to establish a thoroughly empirical operating philosophy (table 17.5).

INSPIRATION, EDUCATION, AND ADVOCACY

The zoos and aquariums of the AZA collectively promulgate exhibition values and standards that are widely supported by their communities. In turn, governments and private citizens vote with their pocketbooks the enormous sums of money necessary to operate highly professional zoological facilities. Although some critics believe that zoos and aquariums are anachronisms unlikely to survive another century of public scrutiny, we foresee a different scenario. As we continue to apply the human imprint to an ever-diminishing natural world, zoos, aquariums, botanical gardens, and other naturalized oases will be sources of inspiration and a reminder of our origins and our essence. Caring for and protecting the living earth will be critical survival tactics and adaptive human values in an increasingly risky twenty-first century. How will we educate new generations to save our good earth? Architect and executive David Hancocks[49] has correctly identified the full potential of the world's zoos and aquariums:

> Zoos have the marvelous potential to develop a concerned, aware, energized, enthusiastic, caring, and sympathetic citizenry. Zoos can encourage gentleness toward all other animals and compassion for the well-being of wild places. Zoos can cultivate environmental sensitivity among their hundreds of millions of

Table 17.5. Number of scientists in leading zoos and aquariums.

WCS:	75	Hubbs/Sea World:	19
San Diego:	35	Zoo Atlanta:	11
National:	31	DAK:	9
Brookfield:	25	Lincoln Park:	8
London:	22	Audubon Institute:	6

Source: Terry L. Maple and M. A. Bloomsmith, *Recruiting, Rewarding, and Retaining Scientific Talent in AZA Institutions* (paper presented at AZA annual conference, New Orleans, Louisiana, 2004).

patrons. Such a populace might then want to live more lightly on the land, be more careful about using the world's natural resources, and actually choose to vote for politicians who care about the wild inhabitants of the Earth. . . . To save all wildlife, to work toward a healthier planet, to encourage a more sensitive populace; these are the goals of the new zoos.[50]

A MODEST PROPOSAL

It may be necessary to plan for a future that requires that zoo and aquarium leaders possess a high level of specialized skill and knowledge and the ability to comprehend all aspects of a complex organization; in other words, the CEO of the future must be both specialist and generalist. Finding leaders with this unique combination of training, experience, and passion will be difficult, but it is not an option if our hard-won momentum is to continue. We must also be prepared to encourage and reward leadership at all levels of the organization. The critical nature of executive leadership has been acknowledged by Weil:[51]

> It is the director [CEO] that we must look to establish a museum's particular truth, its point of view, even—if you will—its taste. . . . The director, after all, does more than simply direct the staff and formulate the museum's various points of view. He also acts as its principal public spokesman. When he expresses a museum's point of view, he must do so in terms that can be broadly accepted as informed and authoritative by all of the museum's various constituencies. He must speak in terms that can command the respect of its board, its staff, its patrons, its visitors, its community, its commentators, and even its critics.[52]

If zoos and aquariums desire such leaders, it would be prudent to begin to produce them through formal training programs. Zoo and aquarium specialists who see themselves as future CEOs will need MBA-type training to provide them with the analytical tools, a global perspective, and the expertise to lead institutions with a multifaceted mission. While AZA is already engaged in disciplinary training for rank-and-file zoo and aquarium employees at its highly successful management schools, it does not yet operate nor cooperate with any existing training programs for CEOs. We propose that MBA-type programs be established by universities, by AZA, or by collaboration that will hone the skills of rising executives within the profession and prepare them to become the next generation of zoo and aquarium CEOs.

As a window into the natural world, at a time when humankind grows increasingly distant from other living things, zoos and aquariums are more popular than ever. The best facilities are restorative, providing respite from the dominance of hard architecture, technology, and noise. In the twentieth century, zoos and aquariums achieved success for people and animals alike. They comprehend how to serve simultaneously the needs of a diversity of social beings, and to measure, as Hediger suggested, the holistic association of "animal and man in the zoo."

Future zoos and aquariums must continue to function as ethical, caring full-service habitats for rare and endangered wildlife. Their patrons will no doubt require justification for constraining and confining such an array of complex creatures, and our zoos and aquariums must be therefore tireless advocates for their wild kin and the remaining protected ecosystems of the world. Global conservation efforts will require proactive institutions with the public confidence that our most effective zoos and aquariums enjoy. To reach their full potential, zoos and aquariums must continue to provide bold and creative leadership while they attract millions of fellow citizens to experience these unique and special settings that so effectively educate, motivate, inspire, and restore.

CONCLUSION

We believe that zoos and aquariums will be held to significantly elevated public expectations in the twenty-first century. To meet these demands, zoos and aquariums must espouse ethical operating values, establish and exceed new performance standards, recruit a literate workforce with advanced degrees, exert global conservation leadership, and identify new, sustainable sources of revenue. Individually and collectively, the highest priority of the next century will be leadership. To this end, we suggest (1) a greater emphasis on formal, MBA-type training for CEOs so future zoo and aquarium leaders will be equally adept at "best business practices" and the science of conservation, and (2) in-house leadership programs that encourage, recognize, and reward leadership at all levels of the organization.

ACKNOWLEDGMENTS

We acknowledge the assistance of Rachel MacNabb in the preparation of this manuscript. Our research is supported by the Charles Bailey Endowment at Zoo Atlanta, and the Elizabeth Smithgall Watts Endowment in the College of Sciences at Georgia Tech. Additional operating funds were provided by the Cecil B. Day Foundation and Doug and Kay Ivester. We thank Dr. Meredith Bashaw, Dr. Joe Erwin, Dr. William Foster, Dr. Lawrence James, Dr. Donald G. Lindburg, Diann Gaalema, Gary Lee, and Jeff Swanagan for their helpful advice and constructive criticism of this manuscript. Suma Mallavarapu is supported by funding from a National Science Foundation Graduate

Fellowship. Dr. Maple acknowledges a special debt to key business leaders in Atlanta, especially Carolyn Boyd Hatcher, Robert M. Holder, Jr., John Mellott, and Robert C. Petty for their special role in shaping his leadership philosophy. In addition to his academic duties, Dr. Maple is Director Emeritus of Zoo Atlanta.

NOTES

1. Bryan G. Norton, Michael Hutchins, Elizabeth F. Stevens, and Terry L. Maple, eds., *Ethics on the Ark: Zoos, Animal Welfare, and Wildlife Conservation* (Washington, D.C.: Smithsonian Institution Press, 1995).

2. Michael Hutchins and William G. Conway, "Beyond Noah's Ark: The Evolving Role of Modern Zoological Parks and Aquariums in Field Conservation," *International Zoo Yearbook* 34 (1995): 117–30; Brian Miller, William Conway, Richard P. Reading, Chris Wemmer, David Wildt, Devra Kleiman, Steven Monfort, Alan Rabinowitz, Beth Armstrong, and Michael Hutchins, "Evaluating the Conservation Mission of Zoos, Aquariums, Botanical Gardens, and Natural History Museums," *Conservation Biology* 18, no. 1 (2004): 86–93.

3. Doherty, 2004.

4. Terry L. Maple and Erika F. Archibald, *Zoo Man: Inside the Zoo Revolution* (Atlanta, Ga.: Longstreet Press, 1993).

5. Kurt Benirschke, "The Need for Multidisciplinary Research Units in the Zoo," in *Wild Mammals in Captivity*, ed. Devra G. Kleiman, Mary E. Allen, Katerina V. Thompson, and Susan Lumpkin (Chicago: University of Chicago Press, 1996).

6. Christopher Peterson, Steven F. Maier, and Martin E. P. Seligman, *Learned Helplessness: A Theory for the Age of Personal Control* (New York: Oxford University Press, 1993).

7. James L. Lundy, *Lead, Follow, Or Get Out of the Way* (New York: Avant Books, 1986).

8. David Hancocks, *A Different Nature: The Paradoxical World of Zoos and Their Uncertain Future* (Berkeley: University of California Press, 2001).

9. Robert Sommer, *Tight Spaces* (Englewood Cliffs, N.J.: Prentice-Hall, 1974).

10. Jon C. Coe, "The Evolution of Zoo Animal Exhibits," in *The Ark Evolving: Zoos and Aquariums in Transition*, ed. Christen M. Wemmer (Washington, D.C.: Smithsonian Institution Press, 1995).

11. Heini Hediger, *Man and Animal in the Zoo* (London: Routledge and Kegan Paul, 1969).

12. Terry L. Maple, *A Conversation with Heini Hediger* (Atlanta, Ga.: forthcoming).

13. Terry L. Maple, "In Memoriam: Professor Dr. Heini Hediger (1908–1992)," *Zoo Biology* 11, no. 4 (1992): 369–72.

14. Robert Sommer, *Tierpsychologie* (Leipzig: Verlag von Quelle and Meyer, 1925).

15. Maple, *A Conversation with Heini Hediger.*

16. L. Ron Forman, *Audubon Park: An Urban Eden* (New Orleans, La.: Audubon Park and Zoological Gardens/Friends of the Zoo, 1985).

17. Maple and Archibald, *Zoo Man*.

18. Francis Desiderio, "Raising the Bars: The Transformation of Atlanta's Zoo," *Atlanta History* 43, no. 4 (2000): 4–64.

19. Elizabeth Hanson, *Animal Attractions: Nature on Display in American Zoos* (Princeton, N.J.: Princeton University Press, 2002).

20. Desiderio, "Raising the Bars."

21. Ingrid Newkirk, "Nature vs. Zoos," www.peta.org. (2004).

22. Norton et al., eds., *Ethics on the Ark*.

23. Stephen R. Kellert, *The Value of Life: Biological Diversity and Human Society* (Washington, D.C.: Island Press, 1996).

24. Kellert, *The Value of Life*, 12.

25. Stephen E. Weil, *Rethinking the Museum and Other Meditations* (Washington, D.C.: Smithsonian Institution Press, 1990).

26. Terry L. Maple, "Strategic Collection Planning and Individual Animal Welfare," in *Journal of the American Veterinary Medical Association* 223, no. 7 (2003): 966–69.

27. Eugene Hargrove, "Zoos in the Twenty-first Century," in *Ethics on the Ark*, ed. B. G. Norton, M. Hutchins, E. F. Stevens, and Terry L. Maple (Washington, D.C.: Smithsonian Institution Press, 1995).

28. David Ehrenfeld, "Foreword," in *Ethics on the Ark*, ed. Bryan G. Norton, Michael Hutchins, Elizabeth F. Stevens, and Terry L. Maple, xvii–xix (Washington, D.C.: Smithsonian Institution Press, 1995).

29. Norton et al., eds., *Ethics on the Ark*, xviii.

30. Norton et al., eds., *Ethics on the Ark*; and B. B. Beck, T. S. Stoinski, M. Hutchins, Terry L. Maple, B. Norton, A. J. Rowan, E. F. Stevens, and A. Arluke, eds., *Great Apes and Humans: The Ethics of Coexistence* (Washington, D.C.: Smithsonian Institution Press, 2001).

31. International Union of Directors of Zoological Gardens, *The World Zoo Conservation Strategy: The Role of Zoos and Aquaria of the World in Global Conservation* (Gland, Switzerland: World Zoo Organization and the Captive Breeding Specialist Group of IUCN/SSC, 1993).

32. Maple and Archibald, *Zoo Man*.

33. Gary Lee personal communication.

34. Weil, *Rethinking the Museum and Other Meditations*, 22.

35. Terry L. Maple, "Toward a Responsible Zoo Agenda," in *Ethics on the Ark*, ed. Norton et al. (Washington, D.C.: Smithsonian Institution Press, 1995).

36. Miller et al., "Evaluating the Conservation Mission of Zoos, Aquariums, Botanical Gardens, and Natural History Museums," 89.

37. Kellert, *The Value of Life*.

38. Kellert, *The Value of Life*, 85.

39. Weil, *Rethinking the Museum and Other Meditations*.

40. W. Conway, "Zoo Conservation and Ethical Paradoxes," in *Ethics on the Ark*, ed. B. G. Norton, M. Hutchins, E. F. Stevens, and Terry L. Maple, 1–9 (Washington, D.C.: Smithsonian Institution Press, 1995).

41. David Chiszar, J. B. Murphy, and W. Iliff, "For Zoos," *Psychological Record* 40 (1990): 3–13.

42. Maple et al. submitted.

43. T. W. Finlay and Terry L. Maple, "A Survey of Research in American Zoos and Aquariums," *Zoo Biology* 5, no. 3 (1986): 261–68; and T. Stoinski, K. Lukas, and Terry L. Maple, "Research in American Zoos and Aquariums," *Zoo Biology* 17, no. 3 (1998): 167–80.

44. M. L. Anderson, "Introduction," in *The Wired Museum*, ed. K. Jones-Garmil (Washington, D.C.: American Association of Museums, 1997); Maxwell L. Anderson, "Museums of the Future: The Impact of Technology on Museum Practices," *Daedalus: Journal of the American Academy of Arts and Sciences* 128, no. 3 (1999): 129–62.

45. Anderson, "Introduction," 32.

46. K. Jones-Garmil, ed. *The Wired Museum: Emerging Technology and Changing Paradigms* (Washington, D.C.: American Association of Museums, 1997).

47. Donald G. Lindburg, "Zoos as Arks: Issues in Ex Situ Propagation of Endangered Wildlife," in *The New Physical Anthropology: Science, Humanism, and Critical Reflection*, ed. S. C. Strum, Donald G. Lindburg, and D. Hamburg (Upper Saddle River, N.J.: Prentice-Hall, 1999).

48. Lindburg, "Zoos as Arks," 212.

49. Hancocks, *A Different Nature*.

50. Hancocks, *A Different Nature*, 252.

51. Weil, *Rethinking the Museum and Other Meditations*.

52. Weil, *Rethinking the Museum and Other Meditations*, 102.

18

Current Trends in Governance and Management of Museums in Europe

Patrick J. Boylan

From Ireland and France in the west to Serbia and Malta in the southeast, many, probably the majority, of the governments of Europe are currently making, or at least proposing, major reforms in the financing, governance, and internal management of public institutions, including museums.[1]

Some of these changes are the almost inevitable consequence of major constitutional changes within the countries themselves, such as the adoption of federal or decentralized structures of national government as in the United Kingdom and France. Others reflect policy moves to disengage the State from some or all of its direct financial and managerial responsibilities, and to achieve major reductions in taxation and hence public spending. The typical consequences include the transfer of state cultural (and many other) bodies to autonomous, self-governing organizations or even full privatization, and to facilitate through financial, accounting, and taxation reforms the development of a much greater proportion of self-generated finance through commercial activities, private or business patronage, and business sponsorship. In addition, there are significant moves towards greater internal decentralization and delegation of management within cultural organizations. In the light of two recent research studies covering seventeen European countries plus some non-European comparisons, this chapter summarizes and compares some recent European trends.

Although the early origins of museums in Europe and many other parts of the world are mainly to be found within the private sector—as institutions created and run by national or local academies and societies, self-governing and self-financing universities, or private individuals—from the nineteenth century onward, national, regional, and local government authorities, in particular, became actively involved in supporting and running former private museums, and in creating and running completely new ones. Consequently, by the early- to mid-twentieth century, in the great majority of "developed" countries across the world (with the notable exception of the United States), museums and related bodies were usually managed within the public sector, whether at national, regional, or municipal authority level. Equally, the public authority concerned has traditionally been regarded as having a major, or even total, financial responsibility for such services.

MOVES TOWARDS SELF-FINANCING

In relation to financial support for culture and heritage, the legal systems and arrangements in countries such as France, the United Kingdom, and Canada used to virtually prohibit any form of income-generating activities on the part of publicly owned museums. For example, income received by French national museums—whether from admission charges, publication sales, or reproduction fees—could not be retained by the institution generating it. Instead, it had to be routed through a special, central government quasi-commercial agency, the *Réunion des Musées Nationaux*, which used the income for general museum purposes such as grants for purchases of specimens and works of art and for major temporary exhibitions. Only rarely would there be any effort to ensure that the income generated by a particular museum was returned to that museum. Of course, prospective private or corporate benefactors could not be expected to contribute to government museums if, as under British rules up to the late 1980s, all money given was going to be deducted from the institution's annual grant the following financial year.

From the late 1970s, in a growing number of European countries, the arts and heritage sector has been calling for their national governments to match U.S. practice in terms of tax and other incentives to encourage private giving and corporate sponsorship. While no country has yet gone anywhere near as far as this, over the past two decades the majority of the twenty-five European Union (EU) countries, and many other countries around the world, are now actively promoting private and corporate financial support for charitable foundations, trusts, and associations.

A French government analysis, prepared just before the enlargement of the European Union from fifteen to twenty-five member states in May 2004,[2] showed that, across the "old" EU countries, business support alone totalled more than 1.11 billion ($1.44 billion), as compared with a total public culture and heritage funding of 29.3 billion ($37.9 billion) (that is, just under 4 percent of total culture and heritage spending), and further compared with virtually no private support for the noncommercial culture and heritage sectors fifteen or so years ago. However, this average percentage masks very big differences. For example, the figure for France (prior to the major reforms of 2003 which started to come into effect in 2004) was only 1.6 percent, while the percentage for Sweden was almost exactly three times that at 4.8 percent of the government support (even though there are still no tax incentives as such at the moment, though businesses may charge the advertising value of sponsorship as a normal business expense). There do not seem to be comparable Europe-wide figures for tax-efficient private giving other than the estimated £256 million ($474 million) for culture and heritage in the United Kingdom in 2002–2003. However, with the development of a range of incentives in most of the countries over recent years, the EU-wide total is likely to be both very substantial—almost certainly already in excess of $1 billion a year—and rapidly expanding.

DEVOLUTION OF GOVERNANCE

The second major international trend is for public sector cultural and heritage institutions and services to be transferred out of direct government control and financial responsibility, with the emergence and acceleration of processes variously described as "devolution," "decentralization," "destatization," or "privatization." In some cases, such as Belgium, France, Spain, and the United Kingdom, this has been part of major national constitutional reforms, particularly the establishment of regional government and the transfer of government services and finances from the central state to new regional parliaments or assemblies and their own ministries or similar bodies. In such reforms, culture and heritage have almost always been among the policies and services transferred to the new, regional level of government. (Within the European Union, the Commission Directorate and the Parliamentary Committee for Culture now has to consider not twenty-five member states, but around sixty autonomous national or regional ministries or their equivalent, while the texts of the latest UNESCO Conventions explicitly recognize that the central governments representing member states may no longer have the constitutional power to enter into binding treaty obligations in areas such as culture or education on behalf of the whole of their country as these functions may be outside their legal competence.)

However, in many countries the rapid expansion of tax and other financial incentives now being offered to museums and similar bodies operating outside the traditional government structure means that there can now be substantial financial advantages in operating both existing and new cultural and heritage institutions through "arms-length," independent bodies with charitable status, whether these are incorporated as trusts, foundations, public charitable corporations, or as not-for-profit *associations* in francophone countries and provinces. Comparisons across a representative sample of major countries suggest that the actual constitutional format adopted is not especially significant, so long as it meets the particular country's legal requirements for charitable status and, hence, qualifies for all available tax exemptions and charitable giving incentives.

INTERNAL MANAGEMENT

The third major trend is towards the internal devolution and decentralization of management within heritage and cultural bodies. Although there are enough examples to show that such necessary cultural and management changes and modernization in fact can be achieved within traditional public service structures and ownership, it is widely argued that such necessary cultural changes and modernization are greatly facilitated by the transfer of the institutions and services out of direct government control to foundation or trust status. Whatever the actual mechanism, such management decentralization and other reforms typically involve shaking off the frequently restrictive rules and procedures of the public service, and empowering not only directors and other top managers but the whole of the staff in relation to the development and implementation of policy and objectives. There can however be negative sides to such changes. Frequently government financial guarantees are withdrawn, leading to the possibility that the new autonomous body could become legally insolvent and have to close down. From the museum staff point of view, the national or local collective agreements on pay, job security, and other guaranteed conditions of employment are frequently lost.

EUROPEAN COUNTRIES

In the space available only brief summaries of four examples (in alphabetical order), covering European countries of very different sizes and constitutional and legal traditions, can be offered.

Belgium

From its independence in 1830 until 1970, Belgium had a constitutional structure based on a unitary, although decentralized, State, but between 1970 and 1993 four successive revisions of the constitution have created and strengthened a structure based on a Federal State built around the country's language-linked communities. Almost all cultural competencies and functions, other than a small number specifically reserved (such as foreign relations, defense, justice, and central taxation), have thereby been transferred to the three, largely self-governing, groupings of the ten provinces—the Walloon Region (predominantly French-speaking), Flanders (predominantly Dutch-speaking), and the bilingual capital region of Brussels.

The residual federal powers in relation to culture and heritage cover only the five major national museums and art galleries, designated as "Scientific Establishments of the State," all in or close to Brussels, but the federal ministry has the power to advise the regions and local authorities on cultural and heritage matters and allocates funds from the National Lottery to heritage projects, such as the funding of monuments, sites, restoration, museum acquisitions, and promotional campaigns.

Although Belgium has gone further than most European countries in decentralizing political and financial responsibility for its museums and other cultural institutions, so far there has been no parallel decentralization or liberalization of their internal management and operations. The dozen or so federal cultural institutions (the five national museums and galleries in Brussels, the national opera house, etc.) remain under the direct control of the relevant divisions of the federal ministry, and their staff are all recruited and employed on permanent civil service contracts by the State, which also is responsible for their salaries and all other operating costs. However, there is currently much discussion of this policy, which is seen by some, if not all, as a serious constraint on operational policy and activities, partly, although by no means only, because of the strict limits placed on staff numbers and functions.

However, the one national-level heritage institution currently managed directly by the French (Walloon) Community, the important Mariemont Royal Museum, appears to be moving towards a dual structure. In this museum, the directly managed main operations of the museum are staffed with civil servants employed by the Community. However, alongside this, the museum now has an autonomous *"caisse"* (foundation—literally "fund"), which raises its own finances for the museum, and which now employs and funds additional staff and activities over and above what is provided by the regional government, giving the museum greater flexibility in addition to greater overall financial security and resources.

A growing trend has been the establishment of joint not-for-profit associations (*Associations sans but lucratif*—"*asbl*") for heritage and similar site management purposes under the general law of associations, rather than the special joint local authority "intercommunal association" provisions. These potentially can have a much wider mandate and are considered to have a much more flexible board and related structure. They can, for example, be established by a single local authority, by another corporate body, or by any two citizens. They may seek contributions of both public and private finance, property, and human resources to the venture, for example, from the association's own members, from public authorities, and from both commercial organizations and other not-for-profit bodies. Such museums and similar organizations are often much more transparent than traditional public service ones in their operation and reporting, as they require formal official approval of their objects, constitutions, and administrative rules and structures, and are subject to public scrutiny, for example, through the regular publication of their independently audited annual accounts and report.

Recognized not-for-profit associations, both general and intercommunal, as well as foundations, all benefit from significant tax concessions including exemption from all business and related taxes, including Value Added Tax (VAT) on sales and services. They also can take advantage of important concessions in relation to employment contracts and employer payroll costs.

Perhaps because of the long and continuing tradition of public sector support for regional and local provision there has been only limited development of the concept of business sponsorship in Belgium. Private patronage and giving are also very limited, in most cases amounting to little more than the mainly very small membership dues of the well-developed network of "museum friends" organizations. However, there is now a marked trend towards linking regional and other public financial grants to devolved and independent museums to formal medium-term (usually five-year) performance contracts, which reflect both overall regional and local objectives and specific targets set by the national, regional, or local government body providing the funds. This is expected to result in significant changes in the management and operational culture in the near future.

France

As is very well known, France has been a very centralized State for centuries, certainly since Napoleon. At the Revolution most of the palaces, monuments, institutions, works of art, and collections of the Crown, the Church, cultural academies, and foundations, and much of the cultural property of the aristocracy, were brought under the direct ownership and governance of the State. The same model subsequently was adopted for the growing number of new cultural and heritage institutions, such as museums, preserved monuments and others that were added to the national inventories and collections after 1789. The buildings and collections were declared to be the property of the State, and, regardless of where the institution or organization was located within France or any of its overseas territories, the professional staffing was provided by a national corps of curators, architects, librarians, archivists, and others. These individuals were recruited by open competition as career civil servants, who were then employed, assigned and reassigned, or transferred at will by the relevant ministry.

Much of the national art collection was decentralized to a network of initially sixteen, now over forty, major provincial museums across metropolitan France to be managed on a day-to-day basis by the city or other municipal authority. However, the central authorities retained a very high degree of control over the professional and artistic policies and operations, not least through the State's direct employment of the Curator/Director and his or her official deputy (plus any other professional staff allocated for the time being to the provincial institution).

"Decentralisation" of functions of the immensely powerful central government was a central theme of François Mitterand's bid for the presidency in 1981 and of the socialist government that followed his election. However, the early measures, carried through in legislation of 1982–1983 and which started to come into operation from 1984, were mainly focused on expanding the competencies and functions of local and regional government rather than transferring powers and activities from the central ministries such as Culture. Nevertheless, the changes in this sector were very significant in the longer term particularly in granting new general legal competencies in the field of culture to all tiers of local government, including the *Départements* (equivalent to counties). The changes also included the creation of new regions with their own elected members, which quickly developed their own regional cultural councils and other organizations in partnership with other levels of local government and with the ministry. Over the next two decades the commitment of local and regional government, and in particular the Departments and Regional Councils, to cultural development and innovation was impressive, so that by the mid-1990s they were together typically providing around half of all provincial expenditure on culture and heritage (mostly in two-way or three-way partnerships with the State or the municipalities).

France had had provision for purely voluntary action in the cultural field since at least the passing of the *Loi des Associations de 1 juillet 1901*, which aimed to simplify and facilitate the creation and management of voluntary associations by, among other things, granting them a legal personality or identity. However, it was not perhaps until the 1980s that this model began to be used extensively within the heritage field, with the establishment of many local, mostly small-scale, site and monument preservation projects, programs of cultural action, such as oral history recording, and the creation of community-based and community-led *"ecomusées"* aiming to preserve and communicate the particular values and character of a defined locality or territory.

In recent years there has been a positive explosion of new cultural, especially heritage, associations and museums, mostly at the local level. A 2003 analysis for the ministry's research and forecasting department of formal notices between 1998 to 2002 in the government's national *Journal Officiel* (where the approval of the constitutions of all new associations must be announced) identified more than 2,000 new cultural associations that had been established during the five years, the majority of them being established largely or mainly within the heritage sector.

More substantial changes were introduced by the third Mitterand government of 1988 to 1992, again under Jack Lang as minister. The decentralization focus shifted away from increasing the cultural competencies and involvement of regional and local authorities to the aim of decentralizing much of the power (and staff) of the ministry itself. Consequently, in the second half of 1991, a rapid succession of laws was passed changing markedly the status and organization of some of France's most famous cultural flagships, including among others the Louvre and Orsay Museums. There were some differences in detail in each case, but the underlying objective was very similar. The aim was to take these institutions right out of the ministry itself and establish them as independent bodies (*Etablissements publiques*) with their own legal identities, governing boards, and financial and personnel management, and with wide powers to operate in the private (and commercial) spheres.

A good example is the new structure for the Musée du Louvre. Although still in receipt of very substantial public funding and subject to certain controls in terms of its financial and other operations, the *Etablissement publique du Louvre* has ownership of the site and buildings, including the major new underground *Carousel du Louvre* commercial center and what must be one of the most profitable underground parking garages in Europe. One of the stated objectives of the transfer from the ministry to foundation/ trust status was to endow the Louvre with a very substantial revenue-producing capital asset in the form of the new commercial development and parking garage, and to allow the new body the freedom to trade in a much more commercial manner.

In contrast with most, if not all, comparable arrangements in other countries, the Louvre's board structure follows that familiar in French private business, centered on the concept of a very powerful President-Director-General. Consequently the Director of the Louvre (who must by law be a qualified and established State curator) is also *ex officio* President of the Board. A combination of around one-third senior staff plus elected staff representatives and two-thirds officials, experts, and prominent private citizens, including academics, patrons, and other benefactors comprise the board. Except for the elected staff representatives (20 percent of the board), the members are nominated by various ministers (mainly the Minister of Culture) and then appointed by formal decree published in the *Journal Officiel*, following approval by the National Assembly, Senate, and other official consultees. The general view is that the restructuring in the case of the Louvre and the other major cultural institutions has been beneficial overall, particularly in liberating the institution and its management from many of the bureaucratic administrative and financial restrictions that applied when it was inside the public service. There also have been major financial benefits, particularly in terms of income from the commercial activities and facilities, and also in relation to income-generation through sponsorship and private patronage.

Most recently France has embarked on what are arguably the most fundamental constitutional reforms for more than 200 years, with the adoption in March 2003 of an amendment to the Constitution of the 5th Republic (1968) to reemphasize that France should be not only a democratic Republic, but also "decentralized." This is based on the principle of subsidiarity, that is, that all functions should be delegated to the lowest tier of government or management that is practicable. Within two months of the final approval of the change by the constitutional court, the first 200,000 civil servants and their services were transferred from central government to regional department or municipal authorities. The current plan is that many tens of thousands of State bodies and establishments, and around 2 million central government employees, will be "decentralized" over the coming two years or so.

While it is likely that in the first instance at least the transfer from the State would be to an appropriate regional, departmental, or municipal authority, these entities might well decide to place them under a different management structure, such as an existing heritage foundation or 1st July 1901 association (perhaps one of the large number of newly created heritage associations and partnerships referred to above), under a new association or foundation established for the purpose, or perhaps a new public-private partnership or joint management. It seems very likely that, as the implementation of the decentralization constitutional amendment is carried forward, similar questions will be asked in due course about the longer-term organization and functioning of some of the small, more specialized, national museums, particularly those for which a complex Louvre- or Orsay-type *Etablissement publique* would probably not be practicable.

A number of important ministries, including Culture, with strong support from the president and prime minister, have recognized that France has been lagging behind other leading developed countries in this area. Consequently, in 2003, France greatly strengthened the law, and particularly the fiscal incentives, in relation to charitable giving, sponsorship, associations, and foundations. Both private benefactors and businesses can now claim a 60 percent tax deduction in respect of altruistic charitable giving (that is, without a personal benefit in return), with a limit of 10 percent of total income in the case of private individuals and of 0.325 percent of gross annual revenue in the case of businesses.[3] The full value of any donation in kind also is deductible within these limits. Sponsorship (including sponsorship in kind such as staff secondments), for which a business receives a measurable benefit, such as advertising, is 100 percent deductible as a normal business expense without limit. The government estimates that these various provisions of the new law could immediately double tax-efficient private funding of eligible areas, particularly culture, education, and research, and expects that these changes, which are now being heavily promoted, will encourage far greater private and business involvement over the coming years.

The government has given assurances that neither the hoped-for increase in charitable giving and sponsorship nor decentralization is intended to reduce the financial engagement of the State with culture and the heritage. Already there are many two-, three-, and even four-way funding partnerships between the central government, different levels of regional and local government, and the private sector, and the ministry hopes to strengthen these by moving where possible from annual budget decisions in relation to state funding to longer-term funding agreements. (It is recognized that this new approach would be very necessary if, for example, a particular monument or other heritage property was to be transferred to a private association or foundation with little or no working capital.)

The Netherlands

There is a long history in the Netherlands of public involvement at both government and municipal levels in both the cultural heritage and contemporary arts fields, with public funding accelerating through the 1980s and 1990s, particularly at the municipal level. Also, there has been a very substantial growth in nongovernmental museums, often very small, local, and established and run by not-for-profit bodies, such as local associations or community councils. Accordingly it is now government policy that each county council should appoint at least one *Museumconsultant*—an experienced museum or heritage professional who is available to advise and support in practical ways local community heritage initiatives and institutions, both public and private, and to promote cooperation between and support for these.

At the national level, the Netherlands has had a policy of decentralization since the late 1980s operating on at least two levels—decentralizing what have traditionally been central government services to regional and local government, and devolving the internal management of central government institutions to their staff. The latter process has been confusingly mistranslated in certain official publications in English as "privatization"—even though the institutions or organizations have not been privatized in the normal sense of the word, for they remain wholly publicly owned and largely publicly financed. Dutch colleagues suggest that a much more accurate translation would be "destatization."

The major national museums and galleries have been given their own appointed management boards under the "privatization" principle. While there is now some flexibility in terms of policy and finance, the government retains close control over most key areas and, in particular, retains ownership of buildings and sites and all collections. The museums are required to meet explicit standards in relation to collections management and conservation, which are set out item by item for each institution in a quasi-contractual medium-term funding agreement signed by the museum and the culture ministry. Also, although much of the institutions' funding still comes from the government, there is a very active program of promoting all aspects of marketing, including all kinds of income self-generation.

The recent introduction of four-year funding plans for the national museums and special government funds is a welcome development. Despite this, the approved national budget for 2004 includes a cut in the annual grants to national cultural institutions and funds by 25 million ($32 million) in 2004, with the prospect of further cuts in future years. A 55 million ($71 million) per year real-terms reduction is planned in total cultural expenditure and subsidies by 2007, largely on the assumption that, under the new organization and management structures, increased self-generated funding will replace government funding. It is not yet clear how this is compatible with the promise of longer-term stability in funding under the four-year agreements.

England

In the United Kingdom a very wide range of organizational, legal, and management structures for cultural sites and museums is found across government, local authorities, other public bodies, the voluntary sector, and the business sector, reflecting in part historical accident and traditions, but also the lack of any clear national policy on either the cultural sector or voluntary organizations. Also, despite its official title, the United Kingdom is far from united. Northern Ireland has had home rule since 1921, and in 1999 both Scotland and Wales were granted devolved government and their own parliament or assembly, taking a wide range of functions, including education, culture, and heritage, largely or wholly out of the control of the national parliament and government. Consequently these notes concentrate largely on England.

The approximately forty government-funded English cultural and heritage organizations have had very different origins, and to some extent still have significant differences in constitutional structure reflecting this history. Some are statutory bodies legally constituted by Act of Parliament or under a special Royal Charter (which has much the same effect), such as the British Museum, the National and Tate Galleries, and the Natural History Museum, while others have been incorporated as companies with charitable status under general company law, such as the National Museums Liverpool and the Horniman and Geffrye Museums in London. A few museums remain constitutionally an integral part of a government department, as with several of the major Ministry of Defence museums.

From the civil service reforms of the mid-nineteenth century through to the 1980s, the staffing, funding, and premises of all national institutions and services of this kind were in effect all integral parts of the public service. Regardless of their actual legal status, whether as a nominally independent trust or similar body, or as an integral part of a government department, staff were recruited and regulated centrally and had permanent positions as part of the Home Civil Service. This status carried with it state-guaranteed salaries and conditions of employment until retirement, when all in professional or clerical grades would receive generous occupational pensions. Any problems in relation to, for example, labor relations would similarly be subject to national policies and practice. In the same way, all of a cultural institution's necessary financial services, including the payment of accounts, payroll management and accountancy, and audit services, were provided by the government. Similarly, the buildings, sites, and other premises were built or purchased, and then maintained, by central government.

However, regardless of their actual legal status and structure, over the two decades there has been a marked convergence in their day-to-day organization and management. All of the central Culture Ministry institutions that were integral parts of the public service, run by civil servants, such as the Victoria and Albert and Science Museums, became independent public foundations. Transferring such important functions from the Civil Service, Treasury, and Property Services Agency to the many national institutions and services themselves has had a profound effect on their staffing requirements. All have had to increase significantly the number, range, and—not least—professional expertise of their workforce, either through the creation of new specialist and administrative positions, or through engaging consultants and contractors to undertake all or part of this work. These positions include both strategic and operational level human resources managers, training officers, pensions scheme managers, finance and marketing staff (accountants, auditors, fund-raisers, and public relations and press specialists), and premises management specialists (for example, surveyors, engineers, and designers).

Then, following some limited experiments with allowing certain institutions to retain the income from trading and charges (rather than paying it all over to the Treasury), in the early 1990s the funding principle was, in effect, completely reversed. In place of the long-standing system under which the government met all the costs, the institutions were instead allocated an annual, cash-limited net grant. (Annual grants have now been replaced by formal three-year funding agreements built around guaranteed cash levels of funding and subject to the achievement of defined performance targets.)

In relation to staffing, it was quickly recognized that, because employee costs represented often the largest part of expenditure, it was necessary for the trustees together with the director or other chief executive officer to take over not only the administrative procedures such as payment of salaries and other employee costs, but also to control these costs and, hence, the staff themselves. All new appointments were, therefore, made by the developed institution itself, and by 1995 all existing staff had been compulsorily transferred out of the Civil Service into the direct employment of the institutions themselves, often with major reductions in their employment rights and benefits. This was in line with a national policy that was very aggressively pursued; it has been estimated that between 1979 and 1997 at least a million general government employees were transferred from the public service into direct employment contracts with either Non-Departmental Public Bodies ("NDPBs"—popularly known as "quangos,"or quasi-non-governmental organizations) or privatized businesses, or to internal self-governing "agencies" within government departments themselves.

Now a number of major local authority museum and heritage services— for example, the long established and highly important city services of Sheffield and York—have been transferred to independent trust/charitable company status, paralleling the transfers of national museums out of the public service. There is currently much interest in this model among both local authorities and the museum profession, and following the apparent success of some of these pioneering museum and heritage trusts it is expected that there will be many other such transfers of local government museums in the relatively near future.

Almost all independently constituted heritage bodies, whether incorporated under an Act of Parliament, Royal Charter, or company law, have charitable status and are entitled to exemption from corporation or income tax and from VAT on their charitable activities, although commercial activities may be taxable in respect of both VAT and trading profits. However, where there are significant trading or similar profits, it is usual to operate these activities through a parallel commercial/trading company, which is taxable in the normal way, but the museum then uses the Gift Aid (tax deduction) scheme to recover the tax paid by the trading company. The amount of tax recoverable can be very substantial; the published annual accounts show that, in 2002–2003, English Heritage was repaid more than £2.5 million of tax paid by its English Heritage Enterprises Ltd. trading subsidiary company.

Following a marked rise in business sponsorship of both commercial and amateur sport through the 1960s and early 1970s, both the arts sector and the 1974–1979 Labour government began to explore ways in which such private funding could be attracted to arts and heritage organizations as well. A voluntary Association for Business Sponsorship of the Arts (ABSA—now Arts & Business) was established in 1976 with support from several leading businesses. The government soon agreed that, within certain limits and conditions, corporate expenditure in sponsoring an arts or heritage organization or project could be treated as legitimate marketing expenditure for the donor company, and hence tax deductible. Then, following much pressure relating to corporate giving generally, the government began to allow businesses to offset a limited amount of charitable donations each year against corporation tax. The principle of corporate tax deductibility has now been extended to the cost or value of donations and patronage "in kind"—such as the loan or secondment of expert staff to assist charitable organizations. Since 1997 the present government has progressively simplified and greatly extended these concessions in successive annual Finance Acts through the single "Gift Aid" scheme open to both individual and corporate taxpayers and covering both regular and one-off payments. Under this scheme, the taxpayer now makes a one-off declaration and the nonprofit organization can then make annual claims for the refund at the standard rate of tax that the donor will have paid in earning the sum donated at the standard tax rate (currently 22 percent) during the previous year.[4]

Over the first twenty-eight years of ABSA, the annual value of corporate support for the arts and heritage sector (sponsorship and charitable giving combined) has risen from just £0.6 million ($1.1 million) in 1976 to £120 million ($222 million) in 2002–2003, whereas tax-effective individual giving has risen over the same period from a few million pounds (mainly National Trust and similar membership subscriptions) to £256 million ($475 million) in 2002–2003. With total public sector grants and related funding of £958 million ($1.78 billion) in the same year, the total charitable giving and sponsorship total of £376 million ($697 million) now represents an absolutely essential part of the operating and development budgets of the sector.

The other major change in the financing of central and local government arts, museum, and heritage organizations and institutions over the past fifteen years or so has been removal of most of the former restrictions on earning income through trading, consultancy, and other commercial activities. Increased trading and commercial activities has produced a very marked increase in the level of external income of almost all major heritage and museum organizations in both absolute terms and as a proportion of total annual expenditure across the sector over the past decade. Today many major national museum and heritage bodies raise an average of around a quarter of their total annual expenditure, compared with a typical level of less than 5 percent prior to the regulatory changes permitting such public bodies to retain their self-generated income rather than hand it over to the Treasury. Indeed one of the new public bodies, the Historic Royal Palaces Agency, now covers not only 100 percent of annual expenditure, but also produces a significant surplus that is devoted to major restoration projects and other developments of the facilities.

CONCLUSION

It is clear that there are major changes in progress in the governance, financing, and management of museums and a wide range of related public bodies, and these changes are likely to accelerate in the face of globalization trends, which are widely seen as hostile to current levels of taxation, public provision of services, and demand competition in the provision of services. These trends are already having profound implications for the museum profession in many major countries, and the days when professionals, and even directors, could work away on their collections and research projects as what I have termed "scholar-curators" are over.

In a growing number of museums, the curators in the traditional sense, once the great majority of the graduate-level staff, are now heavily outnumbered by a wide range of other professionals, not just those who can be regarded as museum related, such as conservators, educators, and exhibits specialists, but also those with a business or related background working in finance, human resources management, premises and security management, marketing, fund-raising, and membership development. Also, even those who still have what might be termed traditional curatorial or similar jobs are now required, as a minimum, to be competent in project, financial, and information management, in relation to their own work and program, and probably competent to manage other staff as well.

Not only does traditional professional training, such as that of postgraduate museum studies programs, need to radically change to make new staff competent to face the pressures arising from the new organizational, financial, and management structures, and cultures, but also most, if not all, current museum professionals at all levels need to have access to continuing education in new skills and techniques, particularly in management and related areas, as part of a very active program of professional development.

In relation to the organization, funding, and management of museums in Europe, currently it seems impossible to predict the future with any degree of certainty. History is little or no help in this. I do not know of anyone who, a quarter of a century ago, came even close to predicting even one of the major changes that has actually affected so many European museums and their staff members over the past twenty years. The nearest was probably Sir Roy Strong, then the Director of the Victoria and Albert Museum, who in a radio interview at Christmas 1980 said that, compared with the financial and other problems United Kingdom museums were already beginning to experience at that time, we would soon be looking back on the apparently difficult 1970s as "The Good Old Days." He was right; by the end of the 1980s, museum closures in Britain were already balancing or even exceeding openings, the number of curators has fallen from around 40 percent of all museum employees in the late 1970s to barely 10 percent today, and every one of more than a hundred museum director positions in British local government has been abolished, to be replaced by senior museum officers at a much lower level of power and responsibility (and usually far lower salaries). Museums have become minor parts of large, new departments covering services as diverse as public housing, consumer protection, economic development, and town planning, and there is no longer a museum voice at the new senior management or political levels.

Analyzing elsewhere world trends in museums over the past 250 years or so, I have identified at least four cycles, each beginning with a period of perhaps twenty or thirty years of creation and growth of many new museums, followed by a period of success and stability, but then there had been a slow decline in interest and support, and eventually many closures.[5] These four cycles roughly dated in turn from the mid- to late-eighteenth century, the period between around 1820 and 1850, the late-nineteenth century through to the First World War, while the fourth, the years since World War II, have been the longest and most remarkable period of all: more than 90 percent of the world's present-day museums have been newly created in these recent years. Of course, some of today's most famous museums date from one or other of those earlier periods and still flourish today—for example The Louvre and the British Museum from the eighteenth century, the London National Gallery and great Berlin museums from the early nineteenth century, while the later nineteenth century saw the creation of, for example, the Metropolitan Museum, the American Museum of Natural History, and many important civic museums and galleries around the world. However, reading old museum directories and research studies on the history of collections, you are immediately struck by the large number of once important institutions that have disappeared, often almost without a trace, except for a few collections or items that have been transferred to another museum.

Some of the significant, but unpredicted, developments for European museums of the past twenty years have included: (1) the collapse of the Communist economic system and rapid decline in the quality of and support for all public services, including museums, in eastern and central Europe; (2) the complete break-up of the Soviet Union, Czechoslovakia, and Yugoslavia, and the fragmentation of many other European countries on decentralized or federal state lines; (3) the sudden promotion and aggressive implementation of free market "economic liberalization" agendas under pressure from some political forces within the continent itself and through outside bodies such as the International Monetary Fund and the World Trade Organization; (4) consequent major ideological changes in both the former Communist countries as well as in many western and southern European democracies, abandoning more than a half-century tradition of "the European social model"; (5) the wholesale withdrawal or massive reduction of government administrative support through quasi- or full privatizations across many public services, including museums and other cultural bodies; (6) rapid moves in a growing number of places to require their cultural heritage monuments and museums to become income-generating profit centers and, hence, substantial contributors of new tax revenues to governments, rather than recipients of tax revenue subsidies; (7) major reductions in, or downgrading of, public service employment, such as those already referred to in relation to museum staff in British local government.

As I have said, nobody had predicted any of these developments, let alone the whole "package," and I feel that the future is likely to be equally unpredictable, and possibly just as surprising. By early 2005, it was becoming clear that a very significant split within the European Union was developing between those governments that want to impose by compulsion the "economic liberalization" agenda of privatization, competition in the provision of public services, and major cuts in both taxation and public subsidies, on the one hand, and other governments that have decided to fight back in defense of the traditional "European Social Model" of the past half-century or more, under which the population expects the country to provide with taxpayers' money most key public services, including the promotion and protection of culture and heritage. This divide widened further with the summer 2005 rejection of the proposed European Constitution by national referendums in France and the Netherlands—two of the original six members—at least in part because the draft Constitution was interpreted as an assault on the long-established European social values.

Indeed, in principle, economic liberalization, being promoted by among others the "New" Labour government under Tony Blair in the United Kingdom and the right-wing conservative, Portuguese president of the Commission of the European Union Jose Manuel Barroso, is already presented as the European Union's official strategy for the decade 2000–2010 as part of the so-called "Lisbon Agenda" adopted in 2000. But behind this is also the International Monetary Fund and the World Trade Organization (WTO). Under the planned WTO General Agreement on Trade in Services (GATS), which is being forcefully promoted by the United States in particular, all public services (including health, culture, and education) would have to be either fully privatized or at a very minimum opened to international competition. Lest anyone thinks that GATS has nothing to do with museums, the current and proposed Guggenheim and Hermitage "franchises" around the world are already being quoted as models for opening up public cultural services to such international competition.

In fact, the European Union (EU) Commission and several governments (including that of the United Kingdom) now insist that comprehensive "economic liberalization" and competition (including privatizations, public-private partnerships, and major cuts in, or total removal of, public subsidies) is already enforceable European policy following the adoption of the Union's "Lisbon Agenda" of 2000 for growth and employment. Certainly these principles are being written into the proposed new EU Constitution, and, in the mid-decade review of the Lisbon Strategy at the European Summit of March 22–23, 2005, a number of States, led by France and Germany, seem to have begun to fight back and successfully demand both a relaxation of the tough monetarist economic policies behind much of the recent public spending cuts, and they went on to insist that the final mid-term review statement should include an explicit statement that economic, financial, and social reforms must be achieved "within the European social model." (The process of national approval and ratification of the EU Constitution is now stalled indefinitely following its rejection in the French and Dutch referendums, as its adoption requires the unanimous approval of all twenty-five member states. With the French and Dutch rejections, and potentially an overwhelming negative vote if and when Britain has its referendum, the Union is now in uncharted waters.) Whether the EU will reverse the trends of the past few years is not at all certain, particularly in the face of economic liberalization pressures from the United States and the World Trade Organization. However, if current trends continue, the European cultural sector including museums will face even greater change and, probably, a continuing decline.

On the much more positive side, over recent years there have been some very welcome improvements, particularly in the internal operations of some European museums, such as the moves towards internal democratization, improvements in management and quality performance, staff training and development, and the finding of substantial new sources of funding to supplement (or, where necessary, replace) falling government or other public support.

However, the fact remains that the longer-term future of many of Europe's museums, from the largest to the smallest, will depend far more on policy decisions made perhaps hundreds or even thousands of miles away in national governments and international organizations, decisions over which even their most senior staff and museum-governing bodies will have little or no influence. Perhaps the insistence on protecting the European Social Model at the March 2005 European Summit will mark the turning of the tide of the neoconservative economic liberalization agenda, and once again taxing those able to pay in order to provide and maintain vibrant public services will become politically acceptable. If so, perhaps we will embark on a fifth cycle of creation and growth in our museums. However, to forecast this would be no more than a guess or, at best, a hope.

NOTES

1. This chapter is based to a large extent on original research by me and fellow researchers of the Option Culture research consultancy, Paris, 2001–2003, on current trends in seven European countries for the French government's Caisse des Dépôts et Consignations under its *Décentralisation* program (*Modes de Gestion des Sites Culturels en Europe*, unpublished report of Option Culture, three volumes, 2003), and my subsequent similar research as part of a team from INDECON Consultants, Dublin, 2004, covering recent and current organization, financial, and management changes across fourteen, mainly European, countries for the government of the Republic of Ireland (unpublished INDECON report, 2004). I have also drawn upon research findings from my UNESCO-funded study of cultural management trends in twenty European countries for my introductory chapter to *Training in Cultural Policy and Management: International Directory of Training Courses* (Brussels: ENCATC & UNESCO, 2004).

2. Admical—Carrafour de Mécénat et d'Enterprise, Paris: *Répertoire de mécénat et parrainage en France*, http://www.admincal.org/default.asp?contentid = 67 (accessed April 28, 2004).

3. Ministère de la Culture et Communication de la France: *Un nouvel élan pour le mécénat culturel*: www.culture.gouv.fr/actualities/politique/mecenat/mecenat.htm (accessed April 29, 2004) and République Française: *Loi n 2003-709 du 1er août 2003 relative au mécénat, aux associations et aux fondations* Journal Officiel n 177 du 2 août 2003 page 13277 texte n 6 (www.legifrance.gouv.fr/WAspad/UnTexteDeJorf? numjo = MCCX0300015L) (May 16, 2004).

4. H.M. Revenue & Customs, *Detailed Guidance Notes, Chapter 3, Gift Aid*. www.hmrc.gov.uk/charities/chapter_3.pdf.

5. Patrick J. Boylan, "Musées Face à la Décroissance [Museums Facing Decline]," in *Perspectives Nouvelles en Muséologie* [New Trends in Museum Practice], ed. Michel Coté and Lisette Ferrara, 17–41 (Quebec: Musée de la Civilisation, 1997).

19

To Members of the Museum Profession

Hugh H. Genoways

Out of necessity my remarks in this chapter are directed primarily to members of the museum profession in the United States. This is the museum community that I know and in which I have worked for the last forty years. It is my hope, however, that some of these ideas deal with issues that are having an impact in the broader museum community worldwide.

There are three important issues that I believe must be addressed by the individual members of the museum profession in the first half of the twenty-first century. Although these issues have a definite practical side, I believe that they also require a fundamental shift in our philosophical thinking. These are issues that will require the active involvement of individual members of the profession to move them forward rather than the changes being instigated by museums as organizations or museum organizations that profess to represent the museum profession. These issues include the role of collections in museums, professional ethics, and professionalization of individuals working for museums.

In the United States there still is not uniform acceptance that a museum profession exists. Victor J. Danilov[1] outlined the controversy, which extends back at least as far as the 1930s. In 1931, Alexander G. Ruthven wrote:

A museum man is a professional zoologist, botanist, geologist, archaeologist, business man, teacher, editor, taxidermist, or some other kind of specialist, working in a museum and having a knowledge of methods of gathering, preserving, demonstrating, and otherwise using data which should be saved. He cannot be a professional museum man, for his institution can only serve the world through the efforts of specialists, in particular fields of knowledge.[2]

Albert E. Parr expressed similar ideas[3] in the 1950s and 1960s.

Laurence Vail Coleman, writing in *The Museum in America* in 1939, countered this idea, arguing that museum work was a discipline of its own.[4] Later, Edward P. Alexander[5] echoed this idea in his 1979 *Museums in Motion*: "The paramount essence of the museum profession is a common cause and goals." In 1988, however, Stephen E. Weil questioned the existence and future of a museum profession:

> Some believe that American museum workers have already succeeded in achieving this status. Others doubt that they ever can. Most, including myself, think that significant progress has been made but that much remains to be done. I think that almost everybody, however, would agree that many important improvements in American museums themselves have come about as a by-product of this struggle by museum workers to gain professional identification.[6]

Danilov's own conclusion was:

> Museum work may or may not be looked upon as a profession, depending upon one's interpretation, but there appears to be little doubt that many aspects of museum work are professional in nature and require specialized training and experience.[7]

Nathan Hatch[8] has described three criteria by which professions can be defined. The first two of these—an occupation that is based on a body of knowledge requiring "extensive academic training" taught at universities and a commitment to public service—certainly fit the museum profession. The third criterion involves a relative autonomy of setting and enforcing professional standards. Although museums and museum organizations have been involved in some setting of standards, little of this effort has been promulgated by working museum professionals.

It is my opinion that there is a museum profession, which was expressed best recently by Hilde Hein, one of the contributors to this volume:

> Such controversy notwithstanding, a professional structure is now in place with national and international representation, numbering thousands of institutions and individuals who communicate regularly among themselves through publications and programs and it has resulted in a de facto profession.[9]

The museum profession may be in its early stages of development, but it is established and there should be no returning to the pre-professional days. Therefore, my further remarks here are directed to those individuals who consider themselves to be members of the museum profession and who are working to move the profession forward.

COLLECTIONS AT THE CENTER

It is time for the museum community to reevaluate the role of collections in museums, and, in my opinion, collections must again be seen as the core of any museum without which its mission can't be fulfilled. Stephen Williams[10] has provided an excellent summary of the museum community's movement away from having collections play a central role in all institutional missions. This real change for the role of collections began with the Belmont Report.[11] The definition of a museum given in the report begins the decentralization of collections in museums. The Belmont Report stated:

> To construct an air-tight, precise definition to cover all American museums may be impossible. What can at least be done is to single out some common denominators. All museums are non-profit institutions. Virtually all are open to the public of all ages, races, religions and conditions. They live by certain ethical and professional standards. They are concerned in one way or another with education. And they perform a function, which no other institution does. These are common denominators which obtain for all qualified American museums.[12]

Even through no "air-tight, precise definition" was possible, the glaring omission of collections as a "common denominator" that characterizes museums was clear to all museum professionals.

The further philosophical marginalization of collections in museums came with the issuing in 1984 of *Museums for a New Century*,[13] a report from a commission of the same name sponsored by the American Association of Museums. In this report, the central role of education is made clear with a recommendation stating, "Education is a primary purpose of American museums." Collections also come in for recommendations in this report, as well as a plea to have "every museum collect carefully and purposefully. Each must exercise care by collecting within its capacity to house and preserve the objects, artifacts and specimen." Also we are told that "museum collections are a national resource which merits a strong federal commitment." The message here would seem to be that education is the primary purpose of museums and that the museum community should be careful that it is not overwhelmed by its collections and, because of the cost, outside help is needed to provide care for existing collections. No museum professional would advocate uncontrolled collecting and they all know that museums are constantly in need of funding, but the juxtaposition of the idea that education is the central mission of museums, and that there should be concern that collections and their care do not overwhelm this mission, clearly places collections in a philosophical second-class position.

Because of the historical and political significance of the Belmont Report and *Museums for a New Century*, the AAM definition of museum was made sufficiently broad so that it can be interpreted in multiple ways to satisfy anyone's desire to be recognized as a "museum." The recently issued standards[14] for participation in the AAM Accreditation program require that museums: "Have a formal and appropriate program of documentation, care, and use of collections and/or objects" and "Have accessioned 80 percent of its permanent collection." These are the sole references to collections in these standards and can be negated with one's interpretation of "appropriate program," which ultimately translates to whatever program is undertaken. The accessioning of a permanent collection is only an issue if a collection exists. The implication of substituting "and/or objects" for collections allows for tremendous latitude. I would expect all museums to have 100 percent of their permanent collections accessioned because this would document the museums' ownership of their collections. Less than 100 percent of the collection may be catalogued, but even here I would hope that the amount would be well over 80 percent.[15] The point that museums "Be essentially educational in nature" is given emphasis as the second standard listed and is sufficiently vague to include public programming, but generally has been interpreted to exclude scholarly research and formal academic instruction.

The introduction to the new standards for participating in the AAM Accreditation program makes several references to the AAM Code of Ethics 2000.[16] Looking slightly beyond the material cited in the AAM website, we see this document make the following statement:

> The museum universe in the United States includes both collecting and noncollecting institutions. Although diverse in their missions, they have in common their nonprofit form of organizations and commitment of service to the public. Their collections and/or the objects they borrow or fabricate are the basis for research, exhibits, and programs that invite public participation.

No clearer statement of the noncentral position of collections in museums could be made. It has led to the illogical situation where noncollecting "museums" such as Children's Museum, Inc., Boston, Massachusetts; Earthplace: The Nature Discovery Center, Westport, Connecticut; Florida Holocaust Museum, St. Petersburg; Health Adventure, Asheville, North Carolina; Louisiana Nature Center, New Orleans; Octagon, Washington, DC; and Coyote Point Museum for Environmental Education, San Mateo, California, are listed among the museums accredited by AAM, whereas old venerable institutions such as the Museum of Vertebrate Zoology, University of California, Berkeley; Texas Cooperative Wildlife Collections, Texas A&M University; and Museum of Southwestern Biology, University of New Mexico, with vast collections of natural history specimens are not even allowed to apply for accreditation because they lack "appropriate public programs."

I am certain that these noncollecting institutions are doing great work and providing a great public service. However, of the five long-accepted functions of museums—collecting, documenting, preserving, researching, and interpreting[17]—these institutions may be doing no more than two, whereas the collecting museums mentioned above are doing at least four and I would argue that they are participating in all five. The question is whether these unaccredited natural history museums are fulfilling an interpretation function by using specimens and artifacts for formal classroom and academic laboratory education, producing publications containing new knowledge, teaching the future museum professionals, and providing educational programs and materials for the public, although they are not exhibiting to the general public in the traditional sense. This picture will become increasingly murky as these institutions produce more and more sophisticated web-based exhibits of materials in their collections.

Why does this shifting concept of a museum matter? Is this an internal argument within AAM and the museum community? This definition matters because it impacts on the resources available to some museums and it is affecting the day-to-day care of collections. Government granting agencies, most importantly the Institute of Museum and Library Services (IMLS), use variations of the AAM definition in their "Eligibility Criteria for Museums."[18] Here are a couple of the most important of these criteria dealing with collections and interpretation:

> Care for and own or use tangible objects, whether animate or inanimate, and exhibit these objects on a regular basis through facilities that it owns or operates; . . .
>
> Be open and providing museum services to the general public (an institution which exhibits objects to the general public for at least 120 days a year fulfills this requirement)

Therefore, you must only "use tangible objects" and don't need to "own" them. Also you must exhibit objects "to the general public," but it is not necessary to do it for more than four months per year. These criteria clearly place exhibiting at the core of museums, and ownership of collections is not necessary. These criteria drawn from those of AAM certainly deny many collecting institutions access to the major funding available through IMLS.

The care and maintenance of collections is an extremely expensive undertaking, including costs for space, staff, utilities, storage equipment, and supplies. As state governments have reduced budgets in recent years, state agencies and universities have felt the full impact of these cutbacks. Museums within these agencies and universities have become prime targets for cuts, especially the collections, which seem to consume resources in disproportion to what they add to the bottom line of the institution. The collections also become a target because their role is not seen as central to the mission of the institution by administrators or many members of the professional community. This has resulted in threats to, or outright closing of, collections and research programs at the Texas Memorial Museum, University of Nebraska State Museum, herbarium of the University of Iowa, Museum of Natural History of the University of Illinois, Vertebrate Museum at Shippensburg State University, and Museum of Michigan State University, among others.[19]

As more bottom-line administrators from outside the museum field take leadership positions in free-standing institutions, these same pressures are developing. All divisions and collections are being asked to add to the bottom line of the museum. In many cases this should be possible for collections, but collections will never add as much or more than what they require for operation. Therefore, it is important that museum professionals make it clear that it is not important for collections to make a positive impact on the bottom line because, for museums, the collections are the bottom line.

I do not want collecting to supplant other museum functions. I do advocate the recognition that collections are at the center of museum functions and that all other functions of museums radiate from the collections. The primary function of museums is using collections to enhance and promote educational programs, exhibitions, research, and preservation functions. As Williams has correctly observed:

> An art museum without a collection is only a *gallery*. A children's museum or a science museum without a collection is only a *discovery center*. A historical society without a collection is only an *affinity group*. A historic site without a collection is only a *local attraction*. A zoological or botanical garden without a collection is only a *nature center*. A museum without a collection is *not* a museum.[20]

So what happens to "noncollecting museums"? Many of these institutions have already formed their own professional associations, such as the Association of Science-Technology Centers, Association of Children's Museums, and Association of Nature Center Administrators. If the American Association of Museums wishes to continue to represent only institutions and to extend the "big tent" of museum organizations to cover noncollecting institutions, it may be time for museum professionals to consider their own professional association. I do not advocate an association of curators, but of all professionals that recognize that the holding of collections and use of three-dimensional objects for programming distinguish museums from all other professional institutions. A new "Association of Museum Workers/Association des Ouvriers de Musée" could speak to issues that impact collections and their use and could set academic standards for those wishing to enter the profession. It could depend on volunteerism—a hallmark of museums—for its organization and advocacy efforts rather than a large, paid professional staff located in one of the most expensive cities in the world. It should be a worldwide organization because problems faced by museum professionals are shared without reference to national boundaries.

ETHICS

Even with my limited understanding of ethics, I have come to wonder why people in the museum profession would have their ethical expectations change as their employment moves from institution to institution. Each museum has its own "code of ethics" as do our national and international organizations. This seems like a confusing array of ethics that confronts museum professionals.[21] Looking to some other professions for guidance, it doesn't appear that the ethics of medical doctors are expected to change if they move their practice from one hospital to another. Lawyers' ethics don't seem to change from one firm to another. In fact there is a whole range of professionals, such as archaeologists, librarians, and pharmacists,[22] in which ethical expectations remain the same no matter who their employers are. So why are museums so different? Are museum professionals more likely to engage in unethical behavior than members of other professions?

So what is ethics? As Robin W. Lovin[23] explains, ethics is a set of values and virtues that unite the members of a profession. Ethics relies on rational thought as a means by which one chooses the highest good through open discourse about such universal values as virtue and justice. Ethical thought prompts us to ask questions about how to achieve excellence in both our private and public lives, thus promoting dialogue. Rational thought enables us to make appropriate choices between right and wrong or, more often, "difficult choices between competing goods."[24]

An example of these difficult choices in museums is the conflict between preservation and exhibition: "The curator's dilemma is the reconciliation of these disparate functions."[25] The true conundrum is this: "Preservation serves the future at the expense of the present. Exhibitions serve the present at the expense of the future."[26] Ideally, with adequate resources to manage objects and artifacts, "the requirements of the public do not normally endanger the material."[27] However, in a world of limited resources, we are compelled to make tough choices between these "competing goods." Perhaps through the pursuit of ethics (and thus rational thought) we may have the capacity to make appropriate decisions in each unique situation.[28]

It is my contention that the codes of ethics of the American Association of Museums, the International Council of Museums, and most, if not all, museums do not serve the true function of ethics, but are rather codes of professional conduct.[29] Codes of professional conduct are certainly important to any profession because they serve as the rules that govern the actions of members, but the museum profession lacks a code of ethics that articulates the values and virtues of members of the profession. Emily Nicholson and Stephen Williams[30] prefer to call these "standards of practice," but I prefer "code of professional conduct." There is no standard set of expectations among institutions and organizations that promulgate these codes; these are rules that govern the conduct of staff members, they are enforceable, and violation of these rules may directly impact a staff member's employment.

As Williams[31] correctly notes, museum organizations that represent the museum community have an institutional orientation and are not oriented toward individual workers in museums or the museum profession. Institutions are more interested in controlling the actions and behavior of their employees than they are in striving for some ultimate goal that may or may not be achieved. It will fall to the individual members of the profession to come forward and proclaim their values, virtues, aspirations, and choices among competing goods. This could be one of the first issues to address for a new "Association of Museum Workers/Association des Ouvriers de Musée."

My coauthor, Mary Anne Andrei, and I previously published what we had hoped would be a statement of ethics for museum professionals, which included the following points:

- Museum workers will strive to maintain as their highest goal serving the public through the enhancement of the search for human knowledge, beauty, and understanding.
- Museum workers will strive to maintain their public-trust responsibilities.
- Museum workers will strive to be guided by their institution's mission in all activities, including collection acquisition and development of public programs.
- Museum workers will strive to conduct their work and programs in a legal and moral fashion and will strive to avoid even the appearance of impropriety.
- Museum workers will strive to identify actions that reveal all discriminatory behavior and will strive to overcome these behaviors by education and active diversification of their institution's workforce.
- Museum workers will strive to aid their institutions to maintain not-for-profit status.
- Museum workers will strive to ensure that the expenses for their operations and programs do not exceed the institution's revenues.
- Museum workers will strive to manage objects and artifacts placed in their care in such a manner as to assure the long-term preservation/conservation of the objects and artifacts.

- Museum workers will strive to maintain their collections and the associated records in an accurate and ordered manner.
- Museum workers will strive to work cooperatively with native groups to provide patrimonial collections care that includes respect for the traditions of the cultural groups that produced them.
- Museum workers will strive to maintain the educational value of their pedagogical objects, but recognize that these objects will receive different use and treatment from those in the permanent collections.
- Museum workers will strive to create and disseminate new knowledge based on research with collections, informal education, preservation/conservation, and new technologies in exhibition and collection care.
- Museum workers will strive to make their public programs available for the education of a broad and diverse audience that is truly representative of the communities they serve.
- Museum workers will strive to involve the most knowledgeable experts available, including representatives of cultural groups when depicted, when planning and implementing exhibits and other public programs.[32]

Each of these values is stated as a work in progress because members of the museum profession can only *attempt* to achieve the end result in each situation; if individuals attained these ends, they would exist in a utopia. These values will not change with place or time, but the ultimate ends they seek may evolve with new technologies, new pedagogical methods, and new understanding of social responsibilities. It should be kept in mind that a focus on progress toward one value, which results in a negative impact upon progress toward other values, might not be judged as ethical behavior. Balance in moving toward each of these values will always be the key goal.

Museum workers are entrusted with the care and use of the very objects—scientific, historic, cultural, and artistic—that represent our humanity. These objects embody the entire spectrum of human behavior and the products of such behavior.

> What makes museum work morally risky is that those objects are often fragile and sometimes irreplaceable, so that it is possible to deprive future generations of an experience by exhibiting objects improperly or disposing of them in ways that makes them unavailable to the public.[33]

We must then strive to avoid even the appearance of impropriety. This may be accomplished through the development of ethical standards based on universal values practiced in all matters through accuracy, honesty, and sensitivity. The root value must be a commitment to serve society as a whole, to serve the highest good.

Museum ethics stated herein would seem to meet the requirements set forward by Williams:

> One of the greatest problems of current ethical codes is that so many apply to the same issues and that many are lengthy documents. In the end it is difficult for an individual to fully understand, endorse, and comply with what is expected. Instead, a code of ethics should be as brief and clear as possible, so that individuals can knowingly and readily practice the intent of the code in question.[34]

The museum ethics stated here consists of 342 words, which is shorter than the statement of ethics of the American Institute for Conservation of Historic and Artistic Works, cited by Williams as a model for others to consider.[35] Hopefully these statements are clear and unambiguous. Other museum workers are urged to come forward in the spirit of open discourse to comment on the ideas presented here and to present their own ideas.

PROFESSIONALIZATION

Every few months an argument will occur on the Museum Listserve concerning what is the best way to enter the museum profession. One group will argue strongly for the status quo, that is, through experience in taking a series of positions in museums with increasing levels of responsibility until one is considered a professional. The second group will argue with equal vigor that the route to take includes academic training through one of the existing museum studies programs. It is my belief that both sides are right and that both sides are wrong. It is true that the tradition has been to enter the museum profession through on-the-job experience, essentially a period of apprenticeship. However, with the maturing of the museum studies programs that came into existence primarily in the 1970s or later, there are a significant number of choices of places to receive academic training in the discipline leading to a career in museums.

I believe that both of these approaches are right and wrong because I believe that, to enter into a professional museum career, both academic training, at least at the masters level, and experience are needed and not one or the other. I expect that there will be an increasing demand for more academic education to enter the museum profession, as museums with reduced budgets and reduced numbers of staff will no longer find acceptable an extended apprenticeship period for each new staff member. It will simply be too expensive, both in time and dollars, especially if museums can access a workforce of people who have paid for their own education.[36]

A question that I often hear asked is: How does one get the required experience even for entry-level positions in museums? There are several routes to get the experience that is so necessary for finding employment in museums and is necessary for the education of future museum professionals. Volunteerism is the first and most important answer. Many museums survive through the use of volunteers to conduct a wide range of activities. Museums will consider volunteer work the same as paid experience. It is the experience and not whether or not money was exchanged that is important. I always advise students to volunteer at a local museum and to put in as much time as possible. This is an excellent way to gain an understanding of what museum work really entails, as well as gaining experience. Another similar route to experience is through a formal museum internship. Many museums offer these types of supervised experiences, and again it does not matter whether these are paid or unpaid.

Demand for a highly trained museum workforce will place increased pressure on the existing museum studies programs and will provide opportunities for the creation of new educational programs.[37] It will become important in the near future to assure that these academic programs are providing a high-quality education. To assure these highest professional standards, an accreditation process almost certainly will be needed. The AAM has set standards for museum studies programs, but it has been slow to enforce these standards. This is another task that probably could be best done by an organization of professional museum workers rather than an organization of museums and, as Hatch[38] indicated, would bring museum workers toward the last step of professionalism.

The need for an educated workforce also will create a need for mid-career training programs. This need will far outstrip the capacity of the current programs and will undoubtedly result in a number of additional onsite programs. This area of educational need will be ideally suited for new methods of delivery through distance learning. This could include Internet and/or satellite technology or some other methods that have not yet been explored.[39] At some point a brave academic program will offer a doctoral degree for students in museum studies. As I have written elsewhere,[40] this may not be a Ph.D., but it can be another degree offered at the same level. Almost certainly, the degree will not be offered in all areas of museum studies, but administration, informal education, and conservation are ready to support such a degree.

The entire museum profession must become far more scholarly. This was even apparent in trying to recruit authors for this volume because those professionals working for academic institutions were far more willing to participate than working museum professionals. The profession must move from the current, word-of-mouth passing of information to an academic approach in which ideas are published, reviewed, criticized, contemplated, revised and restructured, and published again. This process will result in further progress within the museum profession.[41] This type of discourse is best served by scholarly journals, but the current list of journals serving such a purpose is quite short, being limited primarily to several series of the Canadian Conservation Institute, *Collections: A Journal for Museum and Archives Professionals, Collection Forum, Curator: The Museum Journal, Journal of the American Institute for Conservation, Museums Journal,* and *Museum Management and Curatorship.* The American Association of Museums has not taken a leadership position in this scholarly discourse, producing only the trade magazine *Museum News* and books. Enhancing scholarly work concerning museums and museum work should be the top priority for a new organization of working professionals. This would ensure the continued professionalization of museum work.

CONCLUSION

This chapter is a call to action for museum workers to take charge of their profession and its future rather than leaving these issues to museums as institutions or organizations representing museums. Among the actions that museum workers can take include:

- forming their own international professional association;
- working for the recognition that the primary function of museums is using collections to enhance and promote educational programs, exhibitions, research, and preservation functions;
- coming forward and proclaiming their values, virtues, aspirations, and choices among competing goods in forming a true set of professional ethics;
- establishing an accreditation process for museum academic programs to assure they instill the highest professional standards in future workers;
- working toward a more academic approach to the profession in which ideas are published, reviewed, criticized, contemplated, revised and restructured, and published again.

NOTES

1. Victor J. Danilov, *Museum Careers and Training: A Professional Guide* (Westport, Conn.: Greenwood Press, 1994); see also Hugh H. Genoways and Lynne M. Ireland, *Museum Administration: An Introduction* (Walnut Creek, Calif.: AltaMira Press, 2003).

2. Alexander G. Ruthven, *A Naturalist in a University Museum* (Ann Arbor, Mich.: Privately published, 1931).

3. Albert E. Parr, "Is There a Museum Profession?" *Curator: The Museum Journal* 3 (1960): 101–6; and Albert E. Parr, "A Plurality of Professions," *Curator: The Museum Journal* 7 (1964): 287–95.

4. Laurence Vail Coleman, *The Museum in America*, vol. 2 (Washington, D.C.: American Association of Museums, 1939), 418.

5. Edward P. Alexander, *Museums in Motion* (Nashville, Tenn.: American Association of State and Local History, 1979), 233.

6. Stephen E. Weil, "The Ongoing Pursuit of Professional Status: The Progress of Museum Work in America," *Museum News* 67, no. 2 (1988): 31.

7. Danilov, *Museum Careers and Training*, 15.

8. Nathan O. Hatch, *The Professions in American History* (Notre Dame, Ind.: University of Notre Dame Press, 1988), 1–3.

9. Hilde Hein, *The Museum in Transition: A Philosophical Perspective* (Washington, D.C.: Smithsonian Institution Press, 2000), 41.

10. Stephen L. Williams, "Critical Concepts Concerning Non-living Collections," *Collections: A Journal for Museum and Archives Professionals* 1 (2004): 37–66.

11. American Association of Museums, *America's Museums: The Belmont Report* (Washington, D.C.: American Association of Museums, 1969).

12. American Association of Museums, *America's Museums*.

13. Joel N. Bloom and Earl A. Powell III, *Museums for a New Century* (Washington, D.C.: American Association of Museums, 1984).

14. www.aam-us.org/aboutmuseums/whatis.cfm (accessed February 15, 2005).

15. See Williams, "Critical Concepts Concerning Non-living Collections," for a discussion of the difference between accessioning and cataloguing and the function that both processes accomplish.

16. American Association of Museums, *Code of Ethics for Museums 2000* (Washington, D.C.: American Association of Museums, 2000).

17. George Ellis Burcaw, *Introduction to Museum Work*, 3rd ed. (Walnut Creek, Calif.: AltaMira Press, 1997); and Williams, "Critical Concepts Concerning Non-living Collections."

18. www.imls.gov/grants/museum/mus_elig.htm.

19. Robert E. Gropp, "Are University Natural Science Collections Going Extinct?" *BioScience* 53, no. 6 (2003): 550; and Robert E. Gropp, "Expanding Access to Natural History Collections," *BioScience* 54, no. 5 (2004): 392.

20. Williams, "Critical Concepts Concerning Non-living Collections," 61.

21. See Emily G. Nicholson and Stephen L. Williams, "Professional Ethics Revisited," *Curator: The Museum Journal* 45, no. 3 (2002): 173–78, for an excellent analysis of the myriad of "codes of ethics" associated with museums.

22. www.iit.edu/departments/csep/codes/ (accessed on March 1, 2005).

23. Robin W. Lovin, "What Is Ethics?" in *Writing a Museum Code of Ethics*, 2nd ed., 15–20 (Washington, D.C.: American Association of Museums, 1994).

24. Lovin, "What Is Ethics?"

25. David M. Wilson, "Public Interest versus Conservation," *Museum* 34, no. 1 (1982): 65–67.

26. Stephen E. Weil, *Beauty and the Beasts* (Washington, D.C.: Smithsonian Institution Press, 1983).

27. Wilson, "Public Interest versus Conservation."

28. Mary Anne Andrei and Hugh H. Genoways, "Museum Ethics," *Curator: The Museum Journal* 40 (1997): 6–12.

29. Andrei and Genoways, "Museum Ethics"; and Hugh H. Genoways and Mary Anne Andrei, "Codes of Professional Museum Conduct," *Curator: The Museum Journal* 40, no. 2 (1997): 86–92; and Genoways and Ireland, *Museum Administration.*

30. Nicholson and Williams, "Professional Ethics Revisited."

31. Williams, "Critical Concepts Concerning Non-living Collections."

32. Modified slightly from Andrei and Genoways, "Museum Ethics," 10–11.

33. Lovin, "What Is Ethics?"

34. Williams, "Critical Concepts Concerning Non-living Collections," 49.

35. Williams, "Critical Concepts Concerning Non-living Collections," 2004; and American Institute for Conservation, Code of Ethics of the American Institute for Conservation of Historic and Artistic Works, revised (1994). aic.stanford.edu/about/coredocs/coe/index.html (accessed March 2, 2005).

36. Genoways and Ireland, *Museum Administration.*

37. Roxana Adams and Thomas J. Ritzenhaler, *Guide to Museum Studies and Training in the United States* (Washington, D.C.: American Association of Museums, 1999); and Marjorie Schwarzer, *Graduate Training in Museum Studies: What Students Need to Know* (Washington, D.C.: American Association of Museums, 2001).

38. Hatch, *The Professions in American History.*

39. Hatch, *The Professions in American History.*

40. Hugh H. Genoways, "Museum Studies Programs Are Not Prepared for the Ph.D.," *Curator: The Museum Journal* 39 (1996): 6–11.

41. Genoways, "Museum Studies Programs Are Not Prepared for the Ph.D."

20

The Power of Museum Pedagogy

Eilean Hooper-Greenhill

MUSEUMS AS PEDAGOGIC SITES

An understanding of the pedagogic power and potential of museums assumes a new urgency in a multicultural society, where questions of meaning, the character of interpretation, and the significance of the past become of increased importance.[1] Museums have enormous potential as sites for learning and teaching and this has been the subject of detailed analysis by writers involved with museum education.[2] However, there has been little acknowledgement of this from those concerned with the critical analysis of museums from other disciplines. A considerable amount of work has been done from, for example, art historical and sociological perspectives, which focuses on how museums use their collections and exhibitions to produce knowledge,[3] but the responses of visitors to curatorial productions have often been left unexplored.[4] While it is important to analyze how museums produce knowledge, it is equally necessary to explore the negotiation of this knowledge by visitors. It is also important to recognize that the analyses of the ideological framing of museum narratives have not gone unnoticed in museums, and as a consequence some have begun to develop practices that have overtly democratic and inclusive intentions.

Museum technologies involve continual choices about which objects to acquire and display, how to relate objects to each other, and which words and images to use to produce meaningful visual narratives. Through these practices, museums structure histories, geographies, sciences, and arts; and shape perceptions, memories, and identities, influencing views of others and ourselves. Knowledge is not value-free;[5] interests shape the meaning that is

235

constructed about social events in the present and the past, and thus knowledge is always value-laden. These values may inspire or constrain those exposed to them. In museums, as in other epistemological sites, those who interpret artifacts, buildings, and sites do so from their own perspectives, making some viewpoints visible while suppressing others.[6]

Museums frequently have been charged with reproducing narratives and values that privilege those who are already powerful, and indeed this is often the case. One example can be found in the plantation museums in America's south, where history is overwhelmingly presented from the point of view of the slave-owners.[7] On a recent visit to The Myrtles (a plantation "big house" now used as a private museum and bed and breakfast hotel), I was immensely shocked by the tour guide's tales of cruelty and brutality, which were casually (and without comment) interspersed among the exhortations to admire the architectural style and decorative arts that the lives, labors, and deaths of enslaved people had made possible.

But must museums *inevitably* produce narratives that privilege the powerful as some writers appear to propose?[8] And are visitors *always subject* to cultural manipulation, passively accepting the elite views that museums propose?[9] There are two, linked elements of museum culture that suggest other possibilities, and that expose the radical pedagogic potential of museums to empower across the social spectrum. The first is that objects in collections are polysemic, capable of carrying multiple meanings, and the second is that audiences are active interpreters, using their own interpretive communities and repertoires[10] to make sense of what museums choose to do.

Contrary to the views of some museum staff, objects do not speak for themselves. There is no necessary correspondence between meaning and artifact—no essential meaning, no single signification. Objects are spoken; they are given meaning through ideological frameworks and, in museums, through linked objects, texts, and images that focus the direction of signification. In nineteenth-century New Zealand, Maori ancestral tribal wood carvings were physically attacked by Christian missionaries who saw them as "erotic, sinful and evil"; in natural history museums, these carvings constituted evidence of declining native species. These same pieces today, in Te Papatongarewa National Museum of New Zealand, for example, are viewed as artworks, proudly proclaiming tribal power and *mana*.[11] With political, social, cultural, and economic change, the communities of interpretation and the resulting perspectives from which the carvings are seen have changed; the carvings carry different meanings now.

To assign significance to an object means bringing that object into a worldview; for individuals, it means fitting the object into an existing scheme of knowledge,[12] placing it in a meaningful cognitive pattern. Each individual's pattern of knowing, while specific, is built up in and through negotiation with his or her varying significant communities of interpretation and practice.[13] Knowledge is necessarily perspectival (but not relativistic).[14] Different communities of interpretation will assign meaning from different points of view, and these different perspectives, resonating with other discourses in networks of differential power, have social impacts.

Objects may be seen in museums as part of a collection, meaningful because of the light they throw on disciplinary subject areas or on collecting practices, but these are not the only sequences of meaning into which objects can be put. Using what they already know, and their own strategies for interpretation constructed through their individual interests and capacities and their varying interpretive communities, visitors construct their own personal patterns of significance within which to place objects. Thus a visitor to Wolverhampton Art Gallery used his prior cultural knowledge to suggest that a painting (*Stacking the Oak Bark*, by David Bates) showed a Portuguese scene, "because it is one of the few parts of the world where the cork oak grows."[15] At Nottingham Castle Museum, a visitor who was unfamiliar with the relevant Shakespearian play interpreted John Rogers Herbert's painting of King Lear and his daughter Cordelia as "some sort of, you know, religious moment . . . something from the bible. . . ."[16] This interpreter spent some time analyzing the various components of this large painting, speculating about the psychological relationships between the various figures, and the symbolic purposes of the painting, but missed the specific literary references. Objects are given meaning by individuals within cultural and social contexts, using their own systems of intelligibility.[17] Exhibition technologies are used to produce meaning, which is encoded within the displays, but visitors will actively use their own interpretive skills and strategies to make these displays meaningful for themselves. If they do not recognize specific associations and any accompanying texts do not supply them, then alternative (or no) links will be made.

The processes of interpretation are continuous; as Stanley Fish says: "interpretation is the only game in town."[18] The focus of interpretation will of course vary, as contingency demands, but, for most of the time, most people are working to make sense of their experiences as they experience them. From these interpretive activities, meaning is produced and actions are taken accordingly. Most daily situations are designed as communicative; in shops, bus stations, and museums, environments are designed to give information, to enable meaning to be produced and appropriate actions taken. The meaning that is produced is negotiated, provisional, and situated;[19] it is enough to enable understanding and action at that time and in that place, to satisfy contingent curiosity or need related to the specific requirements of the time (to buy a pair of shoes, to catch a bus, to make sense of a display).

The two elements of museum culture discussed above begin to suggest the pedagogic power of museums, and the potential for museums and their collections to enable the negotiation of meaningful learning across societies and cultures. The polysemic character of artifacts means that museums can use their collections to tell multiple stories; the reinterpretation of objects opens up possibilities for bringing new stories to light, re-presenting the events of the past in new ways. The active interpretive processes used by audiences mean that museum visitors are able to use the objects, events, and visual narratives they find as raw materials for constructing their own stories, for their own purposes. And where audiences are used to coauthor museum narratives, new perspectives on old stories may emerge.

MAKING MUSEUMS MEANINGFUL: INTERPRETING AND LEARNING IN THE MUSEUM

There is a great deal of confusion about "learning" in museums. Museums have tremendous potential to inspire learning, but the character of this learning is different from learning in schools, universities, or colleges. The processes of learning in and through museums can be very seductive and powerful and much of this learning does not feel like "education." Where "learning" is equated with formal educational provision and the acquisition of academic knowledge, it is frequently asserted that "education" is not what museums do best. Museums, it is said, are about inspiration—and this is seen as separate from "education."[20] "Education," as an expression, does have academic connotations for many, and this is why the more open and process-based term "learning" has been substituted in recent years.[21] "Learning" is more open-ended and multidimensional, and more focused on the person; "education" appears to resonate with formal systems of qualifications and measurement.

Learning in museums occurs as visitors interpret what they see and do. Visitors experience environments, spaces, collections, exhibitions, activities, and social encounters that are frequently rich, unusual, and impressive, and, as discussed above, visitors engage in a continuous process of interpretation in order to make these experiences personally meaningful. Learning can be described as those processes, which link the known and the unknown, knowledge, and experience in order to produce meaning.[22] Learning is the result of both experience and interpretive processes and is a continuous endeavor.[23] Educational theory tells us that learning is as natural as breathing. The processes of learning occur continually as we use our prior knowledge to negotiate the world, and in doing so we learn new things and challenge, confirm, or deepen what we already know. As Guy Claxton puts it:

> We learn many different kinds of things. We accumulate facts and information and digest this knowledge into opinions. We continue throughout life to

develop know-how; how to use new technology, how to tell a good story. We learn to make new discriminations and learn new preferences. We develop new dispositions, learn new roles and new aspects of character, and broaden our emotional range.[24]

Assigning significance, naming and classifying artifacts, and shaping how things mean are some of the most important and vital of social and psychological activities. Within museums, this process is generally reserved for curators and exhibition-makers, but, when visitors are able to share these meaning-making processes, this can result in a very powerful form of learning. My first example of the power of museum pedagogy is from an evaluation of the impact of the Open Museum in Glasgow. The Open Museum began in 1990; based on partnerships with local communities, this department of the city museum service was responsible for lending small collections or table-top exhibitions to groups, giving people advice on developing collections and exhibitions of their own, and working with community groups to set up exhibitions using objects chosen from the museum collections.[25]

Marie Hopkins was involved over some months in one of the first Open Museum projects. The Wellhouse Women's group, based on a postwar housing estate on the edge of the city, chose artifacts and assembled an exhibition on women in diverse societies. Having curated the exhibition, the women took turns to accompany it as it toured other city venues and, in costume, guided visitors through the displays. In the discussion of her memories of this project, Marie shows the deep impact that the experience had:

> We went to libraries and researched through books. . . . *We were a bit dumb in the beginning*. It took us a while to learn and get into the history and I would say that's because history wasn't out there for us in the first place. Museums were never something we made regular visits to. . . . But now—*I realise you can do almost anything*. It's easy to go out and research. There's always people to help and people to phone up. I couldn't even work an Applemac at the beginning and now I've taught myself. . . . I think I got that through research with the museum. . . .
>
> I'd never really been interested in historical things, but we used some really small Chinese shoes and metal collars from Africa. . . . The Open Museum *made history real for me*. Before that it had been something unreal, like heaven. Next to the Chinese shoes we had a pair of Doc Martens. . . .
>
> It definitely touched my life, that project. We experienced it together, shared it. Three of us got divorced over that period. We were *more independent*. . . . As a group we got together even if it was cups of coffee; even after finishing the exhibition we still spoke about it and it actually gave us more *ideas for future exhibitions*. . . . It's encouraged me to have lots more ideas, some of them I've never got round to doing but I want to. . . .
>
> I know it sounds a bit silly, but it gave me *more energy. I had more interests*.

It gave me something to look forward to. . . . It affected my life-style—being *confident* and going out and being able to tell about the art work. I would go out and do things I wouldn't have dreamt of doing before and . . . doing things I like is making me *happier*.[26]

The interview with Marie Hopkins was carried out about ten years after her involvement with the museum. She has extremely positive memories, and, in her own view, the experience changed her. She developed new skills, new interests, and new confidence in her own abilities. She became more independent, partly through working in a group with a common project. She felt that history was something she could understand and talk about. She became more energetic and happier, and developed ideas about things that she could do. By the time of the interview, Marie had moved from her flat in the out-of-town housing estate to a house with a garden closer to amenities. She had used some of the skills she developed during the museum project to print and make up curtains, and to design and decorate a fireplace and shelves using reclaimed wood.

A second example from a very different project also illuminates the amazingly powerful pedagogic potential of museums. As part of a government-funded museum education partnership between national and regional museums in England, *Understanding Slavery* was developed to address the legacy of slavery through piloting methods and resources for teaching slavery to teenagers as part of their history curriculum.[27] One of the museums, the British Empire and Commonwealth Museum in Bristol, brought together a collection of replica slave items, videos, artists, and actors. The teenagers who visited the museum to take part in this project were involved in four one-day workshops where they handled and discussed the slavery-related objects, took part in role-play activities, visited the galleries where slavery was addressed, and wrote a script for a story to be produced in the recording studio of the museum. Later this was to be performed at school.

Research into the impact of the project involved interviewing three students from a school in inner-city Bristol, which was facing the threat of closure. One girl (we'll call her Lucy) was particularly articulate in her discussion of her experience.

We'd look at objects, [like] slave whips. . . . I was quite shocked. I knew it was cruel but I didn't know how cruel, I never could imagine. . . . I thought about it in a different way. We actually got to see it and experience what it would have been like. I did know quite a lot but *I wasn't able to picture it.*

Handling objects enabled her to imagine the experience of slavery in a new way; history became picturable. For Lucy, a black British girl of Afro-Caribbean origin, imagining slavery increased her determination to prove herself:

If I wasn't gonna try before, I would try now, because the sort of people who didn't believe in black people, I would try just to show them, wherever they are. . . . I'd try at schoolwork; just *try a little bit harder.* . . . It makes you think more openly, it gives *you more determination* . . . because they didn't believe that black people could do things as well as white people, or that they weren't worth having, so they used them as slaves. So, [I'd try] to do things for myself, to push myself harder and *prove that I can do something.* [The experience] inspired me in a different way that I haven't been inspired before. It makes you feel that learning, pushing yourself is actually *worth something.* Sometimes you think, what's the point, but if you went to the museum, you think well it is actually worth something, that pride and dignity that they took away from the slaves, it's worth giving it back to them.[28]

Through identifying with the experience of enslaved people, this young woman developed an increased sense of purpose. The museum project adopted a specific approach to the legacies of the slave trade, emphasizing resistance and resilience where possible.

Both of these individuals were involved with the museum over a period of some weeks and months.[29] Both have been moved and changed by the engagement with collections, having been able to make them meaningful in ways that related to their own senses of identity. Both found that it was working with and analyzing the objects that enabled them to think in new and productive ways.

THE POWER OF MUSEUM PEDAGOGY

Learning in museums is multidimensional. One of the reasons for the power of this learning is that, in museums, learning is based on experience; it is performative. Through acting, doing, performing, the deepest learning occurs.

It is generally agreed that there are various levels of knowing. The strongest form of knowing comes about when we have had a suitable experience of something. That kind of knowing is coded inside us in a felt, compacted, living, tacit form and is part of our total mental structure. With some effort, we can sometimes make this kind of knowledge conscious and think about it verbally. That can help us to do things like rehearse it, modify it, extend it, plan ahead or communicate it. We can do these things because, through language, we are able to link events, or objects, that may be far apart in space and time.[30]

Through experience, feelings become engaged and response is direct, apprehending the experience and the related knowledge in an immediate and sensory way. "Experiential learning is the process of creating and transforming experience into knowledge, skills, attitudes, values, emotions, beliefs and senses. It is the process through which individuals become themselves."[31]

While the construction of meaning by individuals is constrained by the interpretive communities to which they belong and the systems of intelligibility that, as a result, can be deployed,[32] identities and subjectivities are not fixed and may be modified. As the research cited in this chapter into the outcomes of museum experiences shows, museums can provide opportunities for productive learning, for empowerment, and for reshaping of identities.

Learning in museums arises from collections and sites, but the content of what is learned is not limited to the disciplines into which these collections or sites may be placed. Learning is not always intentional or purposeful, but may occur in an unpredictable way as a by-product of a range of interpretive processes. Learning in museums is performative, based on experience, tacit, not always fully articulated. It is powerful, culturing identities. In museums, bodies and senses as well as the mind are used to engage with and explore new things; to deepen or challenge what is already known; and to lay down tacit knowledge that can be called upon in the future.

However, learning in museums is learning through and about culture— and the character of that culture must be taken into account. Where museum narratives are tightly framed, presented in a highly didactic manner, appear nonnegotiable, and are built around a high level of knowledge of scholarly disciplines, some may feel uncomfortable, or simply not visit. Where the narratives are more loosely bounded, acknowledge alternative perspectives, are more closely linked to the everyday, use multiple communication channels, and invite individual response from visitors, then there is greater possibility of engagement for more people. The visual narratives of museums will present specific perspectives, which may be inclusive or exclusive. The politics of recognition suggest that questions need to be asked about both the narratives that are produced or silenced in respect of specific social groups, and also about the social relations, and relations of access, between the museum and different social groups. Both sets of questions are framed by an understanding of social justice as parity of participation.[33]

Museums have tremendous pedagogic power and, because of this, have opportunities to act across society for the purpose of social justice in a way open to few other institutions. This is not to deny the capacity of museums to inspire and to carry their visitors above and beyond their everyday lives; on the contrary, it is a strong endorsement of these powers and capacities, and a plea to use them in a more open, collaborative, and inclusive manner. However, it is clear that, while museums have the power to act in democratic and socially inclusive ways, they do not always choose to do so. Strong forces within museums act to maintain existing cultures and practices.[34]

There are many different ways of being a museum, but there are few museums that have fully embraced their pedagogic potential. Recent research shows clearly how museums and their collections can open up the joy of interpretation and learning through engagement with collections, performativity, and the opportunity to reframe personal narratives. Those who find formal educational environments challenging, because of learning difficulties, poor learning or language skills, illness, or cultural difference, have found museums to be sympathetic learning environments. While using museum artifacts, children in hospital schools have been able to look beyond their medical conditions for a short while,[35] refugees and asylum seekers have found museums enabled them to begin to engage with British history and culture,[36] and, equally, activity-based workshops have inspired those on formal school visits[37] and also adult visitors who do not always use museums for specifically "educational" purposes.[38] Research demonstrates the potential and the power of museum-based learning; this power opens up new routes to follow as museums redefine and reinvent themselves in the twenty-first century.

NOTES

1. Brian Fay, *Contemporary Philosophy of Social Science: A Multicultural Approach* (Oxford: Blackwell, 1996), 5, makes this point in a general way about the philosophy of the social sciences.

2. See, for example, Lisa C. Roberts, *From Knowledge to Narrative: Educators and the Changing Museum* (Washington, D.C.: Smithsonian Institution Press, 1997); George E. Hein, *Learning in the Museum* (London: Routledge, 1998); Eilean Hooper-Greenhill, *The Educational Role of the Museum*, 2nd ed. (London: Routledge, 1999); John H. Falk and Lynn D. Dierking, *Learning from Museums: Visitor Experiences and the Making of Meaning* (Walnut Creek, Calif.: AltaMira Press, 2000); Scott G. Paris, ed., *Perspectives on Object-centred Learning in Museums* (London: Lawrence Erlbaum Associates, 2002); Gaea Leinhardt, Kevin Crowley, and Karen Knutson, *Learning Conversations in Museums* (London: Lawrence Erlbaum Associates, 2002); Gaea Leinhardt and Karen Knutson, *Listening in on Museum Conversations* (Walnut Creek, Calif.: AltaMira Press, 2004).

3. See, for example, Tony Bennett, *The Birth of the Museum* (London: Routledge, 1995); Steven Conn, *Museums and American Intellectual Life, 1876–1926* (Chicago: University of Chicago Press, 1998); Carol Duncan, *Civilizing Rituals; Inside Public Art Museums* (London: Routledge, 1995); Eilean Hooper-Greenhill, *Museums and the Shaping of Knowledge* (London: Routledge, 1992).

4. There are some notable exceptions. Sharon Macdonald, *Behind the Scenes at the Science Museum* (Oxford: Berg, 2002), for example, analyzes both the production of an exhibition and the responses of visitors.

5. E. Doyle McCarthy, *Knowledge as Culture: The New Sociology of Knowledge* (London: Routledge, 1996).

6. Stuart Hall, "Unsettling 'The Heritage': Re-Imagining the Post-Nation," in *Whose Heritage: The Impact of Cultural Diversity on Britain's Living Heritage*, 13–22 (London: Arts Council of England, 1999).

7. Jennifer L. Eichstedt and Stephen Small, *Representations of Slavery: Race and*

Ideology in Southern Plantation Museums (Washington, D.C.: Smithsonian Institution Press, 2002).

8. See, for example, Donald Preziosi and Claire J. Farago, *Grasping the World: The Idea of the Museum* (Hampshire, UK: Ashgate, 2004), 364, and my review of this book, in the *Journal of Design History* 18, no. 3 (2005): 299–301.

9. Danielle Rice, "Museums: Theory, Practice and Illusions," in *Art and Its Publics: Museum Studies at the Millennium*, ed. Andrew McClellan, 77–95 (Oxford: Blackwell, 2003).

10. These concepts are explored in detail in Eilean Hooper-Greenhill, *Museums and the Interpretation of Visual Culture* (London: Routledge, 2000).

11. See Ranginui Walker, *Ka whawhai tonu matou: Struggle without End* (Auckland: Penguin, 1990), for the historical and cultural background.

12. Eric Sotto, *When Teaching Becomes Learning: A Theory and Practice of Teaching* (London: Cassell, 1994).

13. Sotto, *When Teaching Becomes Learning*; Stanley Fish, *Is There a Text in This Class? The Authority of Interpretive Communities* (Cambridge, Mass.: Harvard University Press, 1980); and Etienne Wenger, *Communities of Practice: Learning, Meaning, and Identity* (Cambridge, UK: Cambridge University Press, 1998).

14. Fay, *Contemporary Philosophy of Social Science*, chapter 4, page 88, offers a clear discussion of how all cognitive activity "occurs within and through a conceptual framework," but that this does not mean that all knowledge is relative. As he puts it: "people may be living differently in the same world."

15. Eilean Hooper-Greenhill and Theano Moussouri, *Making Meaning in Art Museums 1: Visitors' Interpretive Strategies at Wolverhampton Art Gallery* (Leicester, UK: RCMG, 2001), 20.

16. Hooper-Greenhill and Moussouri, *Making Meaning in Art Museums 1*, 24.

17. Fish, *Is There a Text in This Class?*

18. Fish, *Is There a Text in This Class?* 355.

19. Jean Lave and Etienne Wenger, *Situated Learning: Legitimate Peripheral Participation* (Cambridge, UK: Cambridge University Press, 1991), 33.

20. For example, Will Alsop, museum architect, equates learning with "academic connotations" and sees museums as very different—"the stuff of dreams" and concerned with "extraordinary things." See Eilean Hooper-Greenhill, "Measuring Learning Outcomes in Museums, Archives and Libraries: The Learning Impact Research Project (LIRP)," *International Journal of Heritage Studies* 10, no. 2 (2004): 151–74.

21. See, for example, Hein, *Learning in the Museum*; and Falk and Dierking, *Learning from Museums*.

22. Sotto, *When Teaching Becomes Learning*.

23. I have found Shaun Gallagher, *Hermeneutics and Education* (Albany: State University of New York Press, 1992), very useful in the linking of hermeneutics (interpretive theory) with educational theory.

24. Guy Claxton, *Wise Up: The Challenge of Life-long Learning* (London: Bloomsbury, 1999), 7–8.

25. Jocelyn Dodd, Helen O'Riain, Eilean Hooper-Greenhill, and Richard Sandell, *A Catalyst for Change: The Social Impact of the Open Museum* (Leicester, UK: RCMG, and London: The Heritage Lottery Fund, 2002).

26. These and the other quotations are from Dodd et al., *A Catalyst for Change*, 18–20 and 29. The italics have been added for emphasis in this chapter.

27. Eilean Hooper-Greenhill, Jocelyn Dodd, Martin Philips, Ceri Jones, Jenny Woodward, and Helen O'Riain, *Inspiration, Identity, Learning—The Value of Museums: The Evaluation of DCMS/DfES Strategic Commissioning 2003–2004: National/Regional Museum Partnerships* (London: Department for Culture, Media and Sport, and Leicester: RCMG, 2004a), 385–95. www.le.ac.uk/museumstudies/rcmg and www.culture.gov.uk/global/publications/archive_2004/valueofmuseums.

28. Eilean Hooper-Greenhill, Jocelyn Dodd, Martin Philips, Ceri Jones, Jenny Woodward, and Helen O'Riain, *Inspiration, Identity, Learning—The Value of Museums: The Evaluation of DCMS/DfES Strategic Commissioning 2003–2004: National/Regional Museum Partnerships* (London: Department for Culture, Media and Sport, 2004b), 29. The italics in these quotations have been added for emphasis.

29. Three recent national evaluation research programs have shown the potential of museums to enthuse and inspire the vast majority of the school children involved in both short and long events and workshops. See Hooper-Greenhill et al., *Inspiration, Identity, Learning* (2004a); Hooper-Greenhill et al., *Inspiration, Identity, Learning* (2004b); and Eilean Hooper-Greenhill, Jocelyn Dodd, Martin Phillips, Helen O'Riain, Ceri Jones, and Jenny Woodward, *What Did You Learn at the Museum Today? The Evaluation of the Impact of the Renaissance in the Regions Education Programme in the Three Phase 1 Hubs (August, September, and October 2003)* (London: Museums, Libraries and Archives Council, and Leicester: RCMG, 2004). www.le.ac.uk/museumstudies/rcmg and www.mla.gov.uk/information/publications/00pubs.asp; and Julian Stanley, Prue Huddleston, Craig Grewcock, Faith Muir, Sheila Galloway, Andrew Newman, and Sue Clive, *Final Report on the Impact of Phase 2 of the Museums and Galleries Education Programme* (London: Department for Education and Skills, 2004).

30. Sotto, *When Teaching Becomes Learning*, 99–100.

31. Peter Jarvis, John Holford, and Colin Griffin, *The Theory and Practice of Learning* (London: Kogan Page, 1998), 46.

32. Fish, *Is There a Text in This Class?* 311.

33. Hall, "Unsettling 'The Heritage,'" 17; and Nancy Fraser, "Social Justice in the Age of Identity Politics: Redistribution, Recognition, and Participation," in *Culture and Economy after the Cultural Turn*, ed. Larry Ray and Andrew Sayer, 34 (London: Sage, 1999).

34. Hooper-Greenhill et al., *Inspiration, Identity, Learning* (2004b), 38.

35. Hooper-Greenhill et al., *Inspiration, Identity, Learning* (2004b), 27.

36. Hooper-Greenhill et al., *Inspiration, Identity, Learning* (2004b), 26.

37. The two examples given in this chapter are of learners who spent some period of time engaged in museum workshops; research studies of national museum education programs show how one-off school visits are found to be inspirational by the vast majority of participants. See Hooper-Greenhill et al., *Inspiration, Identity, Learning* (2004a); Hooper-Greenhill et al., *Inspiration, Identity, Learning* (2004b); and Hooper-Greenhill et al., *What Did You Learn at the Museum Today*; and Stanley et al., *Final Report on the Impact of Phase 2 of the Museums and Galleries Education Programme*.

38. See Hooper-Greenhill and T. Moussouri, *Making Meaning in Art Museums 1*.

21

Defining Our Museum Audience: An Extraordinary Opportunity

Jeffrey H. Patchen

The intention of this chapter is to make the case for a more purposeful and substantive inclusion of children and their families into the mission, vision, core values, and strategic and operating plans implemented by museums today and in the future. Museums face extraordinary challenges and opportunities as they face the middle of the first decade of the twenty-first century. How will museums attract audiences in the future? Will societal factors result in more discretionary time for museum-going, or less? Will our future visitors be willing to pay for museum visits? What opportunities exist to compel the next generation of donors to support the work of museums? Many of the challenges confronting children and their families in 2006— decreased family time, compressed childhood, and limited social and cultural context for learning in K–12 education—are linked directly to philosophical, educational, and economic challenges facing museums and educational institutions.

A pessimist might refute this link and deduce that the health of the American family is not the core business of museums and cultural institutions. Besides, museums have their hands full with business at hand, and formal K–12 schooling has never fully embraced arts and humanities education in a comprehensive way.

An optimist, however, might recognize the extraordinary opportunity for museums to further expand their mission, vision, and programs to fulfill the educational, social, and developmental needs of children and their families. When museums and cultural institutions augment the efforts of formal schooling by embracing American families with children, the result may be a significantly larger museum-going public and an improved financial bottom line both short-term and for generations to come. Let's explore a few of the challenges and opportunities!

THE CASE FOR AN EXTRAORDINARY MOMENT IN TIME

This extraordinary moment in time can be characterized in part as a confluence of two sets of factors—one negative (families in stress, shrinking family time, compressed childhood, struggling K–12 schools), and one positive (perception of museums by the American public as trustworthy centers of learning, with a large percentage of museums offering K–12 programming). Jointly, this convergence can present a set of opportunities and challenges for the world of museums and cultural institutions.

Shrinking family time and compressed childhood. Let's face it—today's American family has less time together than ever before. Parents struggle to share quality time with their children and families amid unstable jobs in a slow economic recovery. Although they overwhelmingly believe the family is responsible for instilling values in their children, parents recognize that the entertainment industry—TV, film, music videos, and the celebrities it creates—has more influence over their children than they do.[1] David Elkind notes that these new expectations of childhood competence and adolescent sophistication may be further reinforced by the additional responsibilities placed on children due to divorce, single-parent households, and dual-income families. When parents place their children in day care or leave adolescents at home alone, they assume their children are mature enough to cope with these experiences. K–12 schools have accommodated these new family configurations by offering full-day kindergarten classes as well as before- and after-school programs in both elementary and secondary schools.[2]

Formal learning without context. In our K–12 schools, teachers are challenged to meet state education standards with available textbook content and classroom learning experiences. Field trips to museums and cultural institutions continue to dwindle due to limited funds for transportation and a reigning commitment to "time on task" tied to standards and testing.[3] While a growing number of states are expanding their statewide testing initiatives beyond reading and mathematics to include writing and science, the arts and humanities continue to be minimized. There are few statewide tests to assess a student's ability to create works of art, music, theatre, or dance. And while the humanities bring to the arts and sciences a meaningful sociocultural context, state tests to assess knowledge of historical and sociocultural context are relegated to multiple choice and an occasional short essay.

Museums as trusted institutions with authentic content. In contrast to these discouraging observations, one finds the American public positively receptive to the important role of museums in American society. Recent surveys suggest the adult public views museums as respected centers of learning, trustworthy sources of objective information, and valuable connections to K–12 schools through educational programming. In fact, the American Association of Museums (AAM) reports that Americans rank the more than 750 million artifacts and living specimens cared for in our nation's museums as significant connections to the past, second only to their own family history.[4]

Family-friendly museums connect to travel and tourism and have real economic impact. In at least one mid-sized American city, a children's museum reports an annual economic impact of more than $58 million, surpassing that of professional football and professional basketball in that city.[5] The multiplier fact that families bring to cultural tourism is significant. Lodging, meals, and visits to more than one cultural destination in a single city account for a sizeable share of this effect. AAM reports that tourists who visit museums spend nearly twice as much on their travel as those who do not.[6]

There are many serious challenges facing families today, and yet these challenges, along with the public's positive perception of museums, have created an extraordinary moment in time for museums to embrace families and family learning. Doing so in a positive way will have a mutual benefit for museums and the families who visit them.

WHAT IS FAMILY LEARNING?

Family learning occurs when two or more people who have an ongoing relationship visit a museum and interact as they engage in activities together. Of course, "families" can be defined in many different ways. Used here, "family" does not necessarily mean there is a blood relationship between/among the group or that they live in the same household. Rather, it simply means they have an ongoing relationship. At The Children's Museum of Indianapolis, family learning is defined as a special type of "free-choice learning." Coined by Drs. John Falk and Lynn Dierking of the Institute for Learning Innovation, free-choice learning is a type of learning where people choose what, where, how, and with whom they will learn.[7] Indeed, this learning represents the bulk of all the learning that takes place in a lifetime. A visit to a museum, zoo, church, library, amusement park, or mall, as well as a classroom that allows children some choice in their learning, are all examples of free-choice learning environments.

Creating Exhibits, Programs, and Spaces That Are Family-Learning

Friendly. There are at least four guiding ideas that are important to consider when designing exhibits, programs, and spaces for families.[8]

First, family learning is a playful, fun, and social experience. Another way to describe this is that family learning is a pleasurable research activity, motivated by a child's—and, hopefully, an adult's—curiosity and desire to discover something of interest. Just as "play is a child's work," adults value the opportunity to choose and determine for themselves how long to engage in an activity—an important element of play. It is the museum's goal to create environments where aspects of play are present.

Second, family learning is influenced by the ages of the children and adults in a group. Just as the field of child development refers to activities or ideas as being "developmentally appropriate," this idea is also applicable to adults. For example, most children visit museums with adults. Purposefully providing rich content for adults in exhibit spaces that focus on young children and relating the content to adult time periods can be especially effective. Further, grandparents may have physical, hearing, or visual challenges. Striving to provide physical accessibility for adults and children, offering amplified listening devices for the hearing-impaired, and selecting the right font size for printed materials are as important developmentally for older adults as children.

Third, families learn in different ways. Just as different children learn in different ways, so, too, do families. Whether a museum uses the 4-MAT System, Howard Gardner's theory of multiple intelligences, or a combination of approaches, museum settings can and should support a variety of different learning approaches and styles. In creating exhibits and programs, museums should strive to share information through diverse methods. However, successfully achieving a diversity of delivery methods requires a purposeful commitment to planning, creativity, and allocation of space.

Fourth, and most important, families find value and meaning in their own personal observations and experiences. This idea refers to the notion that each person creates his/her own knowledge and experience as he/she ages and develops in unique ways that relate to his/her previous knowledge and background. Such an approach to personal meaning making is powerful and transforming, but poses the greatest challenge in the case of a family group in which there may be many different starting points, depending on each family member's age, interests, experiences, and background. However, experienced learners—often, but not always, adults—ask appropriate questions or provide the needed materials to help the novice learners construct their understanding of a concept and build their knowledge of a subject. Families do this all the time as the adult in the family (or sometimes the child!) assists other family members in understanding how to complete a task and derive meaning from that task.

How Do We Know Family Learning When We See It? Family learning is a special type of free-choice learning, and free-choice learning takes place throughout a lifetime. Therefore, family learning in a museum setting is just part of what might be described as a much larger continuum of learning that ebbs and flows from formal (schooling) to informal (library, Internet, television, and museum). In other words, learning doesn't stop when family members leave the museum. Longitudinal research conducted by Falk and Dierking indicates that visitors are not only able to articulate their thoughts about learning many months after a museum visit, but are also able to connect the experience to other media and learning environments.[9]

A few contextual examples may help museum professionals better recognize what family learning can look like in a museum:

- Family members engaging in conversations directed toward or in response to an exhibit, particularly if the family is connecting that experience to their own family history.
- Family members engaging in modeling or learning by watching. When a more knowledgeable learner—often the adult, but not always—engages in an activity, and then the less knowledgeable learner—often the child, but not always—attempts the activity in the way the other person has already demonstrated it.
- Family members collaborating to complete an activity and/or learn together.
- Family members watching or attending an interpretation activity that may provide opportunities for conversations at a later time.

Family Learning Away From The Museum. Although learning does happen at a museum, much family learning also takes place after the family leaves. Museum and assessment/evaluation professionals are not privy to the conversations and other activities that may take place in the car on the way home, during the next trip to the library, or while in school the next week. Assessment/evaluation studies by museums that examine the impact of museum learning away from the museum can uncover much about how their exhibits and programs impact visitors long after their visit. Families who use museums on a regular basis are more aware of how those experiences are further explored and developed within daily life. These are the families who view the museum as a resource and understand the value of making repeat visits throughout their child's life and the life of their family.

By purposefully serving families, museums grow their educational outreach, ensure lifelong learning for visitors and their families, and increase economic impact. If the goal is to more purposefully serve children and their families, what are some characteristics of family-friendly museums?

SOME CHARACTERISTICS OF FAMILY FRIENDLY MUSEUMS

Of course, there are museums that focus on subject matter that is arguably inappropriate for children. Yet, I would argue that one of the unique responsibilities of nonprofit museums in America is to give back to their communities and this country something unique that, in part, justifies their nonprofit status. Children's museums and science centers are not the only models of "family friendly" cultural institutions, though vast majorities are fully dedicated to reaching and serving children and their families. A summary of my observations and experiences of many museums over three decades has revealed a number of characteristics that reflect purposeful attention to the learning needs of children and their families:

- *Serving children and families is stated as a core value or principle.* Board and staff members build the museum's public programs around the core value/principle of serving children and families.
- *The museum's mission recognizes children and families as important audiences.* At the core of institutions dedicated to meeting the needs of children and families is a mission statement that refers to their audience, which includes children and/or families.
- *Purposeful physical design that drives the creation of dedicated space and physical environments that meet the needs of children and families.* In the best institutions serving children and families there is evidence of design that not only promotes shared learning among children and their families, but also encourages individual learning.
- *Incentives for family participation/membership.* Family-friendly institutions offer incentives for families to participate in the life of the museum. These may include, but are not limited to, family memberships, family discounts, take-home museum kits for families, family-themed events, and activity guides for parents and/or children.
- *Children and their families are seen as the beginning of the member-donor continuum.* Family-focused institutions create member- and donor-focused activities that stress the importance of meeting the needs of all families, including underserved families. In these institutions "membership" may become a first step toward donorship.
- *Families are embraced.* In the best institutions, families are embraced by museum staff and volunteers—they are made to feel welcome! Special accommodations are made to include children and families for opening/special events.
- *Museum learning experiences are enjoyable for participating families.* If children and their families view their museum learning experience as

fun, they will be more likely to extend their stay, return for a repeat visit, and tell others about their experience.

IMPLICATIONS FOR THE FUTURE OF MUSEUMS

Museums, including their leaders and boards, that do not embrace children, families, and family learning in a substantive way will confront the same extraordinary challenges faced by all museums. How will the museum attract future audiences? Will the pressures of daily life result in more time for visiting museums, or less? Will there be an adult public willing to embrace and pay for the museum's mission? How will the museum attract the next generation of community-builders and philanthropists willing to support its enterprise?

Museums that are committed to a more purposeful and substantive inclusion of children and their families into their mission, vision, core values, exhibits, and programs may well embrace a larger continuum of museum-goers. This larger continuum, and thus larger audience, represents for many museums an untapped public hungry for more time spent together with family in a safe, trusted, content-rich environment unlike any other in society. Extraordinary times and extraordinary challenges call for extraordinary measures—embracing America's children and their families in America's museums will create a legacy of family learning and museum-going for generations.

NOTES

1. Staff of *Psychology Today*, "Value Shift: Life with Father (and without Madonna)," *Psychology Today* (March/April 1992): 18–19.

2. David Elkind, "The Social Determination of Childhood and Adolescence," *Education Week* 18 (1999): 48–50.

3. Leslie Power, "Survey of K–12 School Field Trip Attendance Trends At Selected Museums" (working paper, School Services Department, The Children's Museum of Indianapolis, Indiana, 2004).

4. American Association of Museums, "Museums Working in the Public Interest," American Association of Museums, www.aam-us.org/resources/general/publicinterest.cfm (accessed May 18, 2004).

5. Mark Rosentraub, "The Economic Impact of The Children's Museum of Indianapolis" (commissioned study, The Children's Museum of Indianapolis, Indiana, 2006).

6. American Association of Museums, "Museums Working in the Public Interest," American Association of Museums, www.aam-us.org/resources/general/publicinterest.cfm (accessed May 18, 2004).

7. John Falk and Lynn Dierking, *Learning from Museums: Visitor Experiences and the Making of Meaning* (Walnut Creek, Calif.: AltaMira Press, 2000).

8. Kay Cunningham and Jeffrey Patchen, "Family Learning at The Children's Museum" (working paper, Education and Experience Development Division, The Children's Museum of Indianapolis, 2004).

9. Cunningham and Patchen, "Family Learning at The Children's Museum."

22

How Can Museums Attract Visitors in the Twenty-first Century?

Scott G. Paris

Museums today face a crisis of attendance because visitors of all ages have more competitive choices for their leisure activities than ever before. Perhaps museums have always endured crises of attendance, and perhaps they always will because they are cultural institutions serving a fickle public. A recent newspaper cartoon depicted a young child asking his older sister if the family was going to Themeland that day and the sister replied, "No, Mom is making us go to the museum." In the next panel, the boy asks, "Why is she punishing us?" Although the cartoon is not very amusing, the child's perception of a museum visit is downright grim to a museum professional. What can be done to counteract a view of museums as boring family excursions? In this chapter, I examine several ways that museums in the future can be more appealing to visitors, especially children and families. My perspective is based on psychological experiences of visitors, rather than on a curator's view of the collections and the intellectual disciplines of the museum, so it is an "outsider's" view rooted in psychology and education. Thus, it affords liberty from the practical constraints of budgets, benefactors, and buildings, and I take the opportunity to explore why people find museums appealing.

IS THAT A REAL DINOSAUR?

To the chagrin of museum professionals, visitors frequently ask questions to verify that they are looking at the "real" things. Being in the presence of original and famous objects has always been a vicarious thrill for people. Whether it is the British Crown jewels or a moon rock, rare objects attract attention. Displays of genuine objects used to be the raison d'être for museums. Collections of exotic, unique, and exemplary artifacts and specimens were the bases for the early "cabinets of curiosities,"[1] and they became the foundations for public visits as well as academic studies of objects. Throughout the nineteenth and twentieth centuries, museums fortified the public appetite for discoveries and informal learning about unknown worlds as much as they gave sustenance to scientific, artistic, and historical investigations. However, the appetites were sated in the past twenty to thirty years as museums proliferated, exposure of unfamiliar objects increased, and novelty diminished. At the same time, new generations grew up in interactive, media-rich worlds where viewing static objects in solemn silence was more boring than inspirational. In my opinion, the demise of the appeal of viewing objects in museums, especially traditional strolling and viewing of staid collections, is the main reason visitors do not attend museums today as they did in 1900 or 1950.

Museum professionals understand the need to respond to more sophisticated and more demanding audiences. Every museum staff has annual discussions about redefining its mission, reinventing its programs, and reconnecting to local communities, and all are worthwhile reflections. In addition, I think there are psychological and educational principles of visitor learning that can guide new approaches. The principles need to reflect more than collective intuitions of what works and popular "infotainment"; they need to embody psychological principles of learning and motivation that are supported by empirical evidence. Psychology can provide more than a lens for evaluation research; it can provide a foundation for understanding what motivates visitors of various ages and backgrounds to become recurring visitors. The cross-fertilization of ideas between museum staff members and both academic psychologists and educators can be enormously important because museum educators can apply relevant principles to practical problems, whereas psychologists and educators can study the principles in free-choice learning environments.[2] In this brief chapter, I'll describe four fundamental psychological principles that are heuristic for the future of museums because they integrate typical visitors' activities such as searching, viewing, and discussing objects in museums. They include (1) transactions with objects, (2) narrative knowing, (3) communities of practice, and (4) identity development.

DYNAMIC INTERACTIONS WITH OBJECTS

Many museums have developed clever ways to embellish objects and to create object-based interactive experiences.[3] One popular method is to provide hands-on experiences with objects. Touch pools in aquaria and petting zoos allow first-hand interactions with animals. Children's zoos and discovery centers are prime places for children to have first-hand, multisensory experiences. Docent-led tours in gardens and historical settings often permit visitors to smell, touch, and feel plants and artifacts. David Michener and Inger Schultz[4] describe activities in arboreta, such as directing children to find secret places where animals might hide, as ways of exploring the environment and learning about plants. Even art museums can support hands-on activities. For example, after viewing a special exhibition of art by Eric Carle, children were encouraged to paint pictures and create books in the same style.[5]

A second method for allowing visitors to interact with objects is based on inquiries such as "What is it, and how does it work?" Visitors try to understand objects and the concepts they represent by handling and using them, such as Bernoulli balls and soap films. The proliferation of children's museums in the past twenty years is based mainly on interactive experiences with objects, and most museum-savvy ten-year-olds have many experiences with familiar exhibits including the sand pendulum, whisper dishes, musical instruments, gyroscopes, and gears. Whether they learn much about the scientific concepts and whether families actually provide accurate information are important questions for both researchers and museum educators,[6] but exhibits can be created to entice physical interactions with objects. A third general method is to provide virtual docents, often in the form of wands, tape recorders, or computer kiosks, so that visitors can access additional information about objects they view. Visitors have information on demand at their fingertips, but the timing and amount are under their control. A fourth method is to juxtapose objects in an exhibit with unlike objects or contexts to provoke visitors to create new responses to objects and new connections among objects.

The shared goal of these exhibit techniques is to prod visitors to experience more varied and less familiar sensory and conceptual features of objects. Consider how sterile exhibitions seem when they are viewed passively, alone, and with hushed silence. Visitors want to be active; they want to get closer to objects. Touching the cold bronze of a Rodin sculpture, listening to the guttural calls of an emu, and dancing on a huge light-activated keyboard are interactive, awe-inspiring sensations. Museums can design exhibits to allow more sensory interactions, and not just for children, but for all visitors. Facsimiles of painted landscapes, sculpture, or fabrics can be placed near original art objects so that visitors can touch them. The Hope diamond and gold bars cannot be passed around, but facsimiles could be handled so that visitors can feel their weight and texture. Exhibits can provide animal sounds, plant scents, microscopic views of ancient maps, replicas of decorative arts, time-lapse photography, and other multisensory avenues to experience objects. In a parallel fashion, creative exhibits can foster new concepts about objects by establishing new contexts. A rose, a crown of thorns, and a crucifix create a tableau that is just as meaningful as photos of a baby alligator and slaughtering poachers next to an alligator purse. The challenge is to create exhibits that allow visitors to *transact* with objects in novel, motivating ways that encourage new understandings. Visitors need to experience objects so that the objects "speak" to visitors; the two-way transaction is more than just holding and manipulating objects. A transactional model reflects an object-based epistemology that transcends the actual object by virtue of the cognitive constructions and the social experiences engendered by the object.[7]

Research provides some helpful guidelines about how to promote transactions with objects. One method emphasizes different "entry points" to engage objects in diverse ways. Howard Gardner[8] suggested that academic subjects and objects provide multiple "windows" for understanding and a person can enter into a transaction with objects through any or all of the dimensions. The aesthetic window refers to the formal and sensory qualities of an object. The narrative window refers to the human stories surrounding an object, perhaps the artist or person affected by the object. The logical/ quantitative window refers to the deductive and measurable features of an object. The foundational window refers to philosophical issues raised by the object. The experiential window refers to the responses to the object such as singing, drawing, or talking about the object. The windows afford novel and multiple avenues for understanding through dimensions that can shed new light on the provenance, utility, beauty, value, and future of any object. Mihaly Csikszentmihalyi and Kim Hermanson[9] suggest that visitors have more intrinsic motivation and deeper conceptual engagement when they can choose personal and multiple ways of interacting with objects.

A second method for promoting transactions with objects is through careful analysis or "reading" objects as texts.[10] The parallels with text make the analogy illuminating because readers construct meanings from texts and objects, and those meanings are grounded in the biases of the author and reader, biases due to history, gender, race, and experience. This situated and relativistic approach to meaning reveals why every person's reading of objects can be unique yet personally meaningful. The analogy extends far beyond "decoding" objects and understanding the explicit or public meanings of objects. Christina van Kraayenoord and I[11] describe how objects hold stories of their own past and how they engender new stories with the transactions of the reader. When readings are shared and discussed, objects are reconsidered from new perspectives and new meanings are possible. Discovering the hidden meanings and mysteries surrounding objects provides the reader with insight and ownership over the stories of the object—a transaction that exceeds viewing and familiarity.

A third method for stimulating transactions with objects is to elicit conversations that bring different perspectives and meanings into public discussion. Gaea Leinhardt, Kevin Crowley, and Karen Knutson[12] describe learning in museums as "conversational elaboration," and they provide numerous examples to show how discourse about objects can be explanatory and conceptual rather than superficial. But even fragmented conversations have value. Maureen Callanan, Jennifer Jipson, and Monika Stampf Soennichsen[13] studied parents talking to young children about representational objects (e.g., maps and globes), and they observed few conceptual explanations of the objects. However, they concluded that parents did foster learning by mentioning, pointing to, and commenting on objects in ways that were appropriate for young children. Minda Borun[14] reported similar findings in her studies of family learning in museums. Family conversations generally have more instances of identifying and describing objects briefly than interpreting and applying the knowledge in extended conversations. However, she found that exhibits that are multisided, multiuser, accessible, multioutcome, multimodal, readable, and relevant facilitate family conversations and learning in museums.

These methods are examples of ways to elicit and provoke meaningful transactions with objects; there are many others. Viewing objects and reading labels are starting points for deeper visual, conceptual, and conversational analyses that examine multiple dimensions of objects. Each one helps visitors to engage objects actively and to construct personalized meanings in ways that are motivating and satisfying.

NARRATIVE KNOWING

Who could imagine a museum without collections of genuine objects? The answer is a growing number of museum professionals who question the centrality of objects and the necessity of authenticity. Digitized images of objects allow remote viewing, virtual tours can replace first-hand encounters, and interactive experiences are more popular than passive viewing. The allure of objects has waned because television and the Internet provide exposure to history, art, and science with vivid images and animation. It is not necessary to visit a museum to see a dinosaur skeleton or rare art. It is neither novel nor motivating to view objects under glass or hanging on the wall. Walking through a replica of a coal mine or sitting in a confined space like slaves on a nineteenth-century ship place the visitors in different worlds that evoke images and magnify the objects. Indeed, the objects need not be original or authentic to create the experience, so the uniqueness of museums is diminished. That is why the differences between theme parks and museums are minimal to some visitors.

Elaine Heumann Gurian[15] questions the importance and necessity of objects in museums. She argues that the traditional mission of museums—to collect, preserve, and display rare and unusual objects—is changing, and that museums need to address the stories they are telling, the role objects play in the stories, and why the stories are being told. She suggests that objects provoke conversations and stories that may be more impotant than viewing original artifacts.

> Not meaning to denigrate the immense importance of museum objects and their care, I am postulating that they, like props in a brilliant play, are necessary but not sufficient. This paper points out something that we have always known intuitively, that the larger issues revolve around the stories museums tell and the way they tell them. Objects, one finds, have, in their tangibility, provided a variety of stakeholders with an opportunity to fight over the meaning and control of their memories. It is the ownership of the story, rather than the object itself, that the fight has been all about.[16]

Negotiating the meaning of objects through discussions, with or without the actual objects, enhances personal involvement and ownership of the story, which for many museums is the main goal for visitors.

Narrative knowing is described by Jerome Seymour Bruner[17] as a type of constructed knowledge that is imbued with the unique experiences and perspectives of the person. It stands in contrast to paradigmatic knowing that is a scientific, logical, and objective type of knowledge. Narrative knowing in museums includes the storytelling emphasized by Gurian (1999), such as stories about the people involved with an object's history and use, but also stories about the visitor's relations to the object. For example, visitors to Henry Ford Museum and Greenfield Village talk nostalgically about the old cars and farm machinery that they remember from their childhood, and their stories are poignant and personal reflections of narrative knowing.[18] Lisa Roberts[19] provides a powerful description of the importance of narrative knowing in museums. She argues persuasively that museums should shed the old model of exhibit design that is focused on knowledge transmission. Instead, museums should foster narrative knowing among visitors by making transparent the curatorial and educational reasons for choosing certain objects and displaying them in specific contexts.

The National Museum of Australia serves as a social history museum that uses many media to show the interplay of points of view within Australia's national story. As the director of the National Museum said in her address on the museum's first anniversary, "We provide a forum for debate, by offering a reflective space in which people can consider issues in context—against their historic background. . . . We provide a venue which is 'safe' in the sense of calm and comfortable, where the rules of engagement encourage respect for multiple viewpoints."[20] This museum regards the provision of space where people can reflect and debate issues, given their personal and sociocultural contexts, to be one of its key responsibilities, and it shows how narrative knowing can become an institutional priority.

COMMUNITIES OF PRACTICE

Learning is a social as well as a cognitive process. Recent approaches to learning emphasize that learning is situated in particular activities, contexts, and social groups.[21] What people learn is shaped by the local community values and practices; how the skills and knowledge are acquired is shaped by participation with experts in informal apprenticeships. The conceptual notions of community, practices, and apprenticeships can be applied fruitfully to museum experiences. For example, visitors become part of communities in museums when they visit with friends, families, or tours. They are members of implicit communities of other museum visitors and aficionados of the specific type of museum, artists or scientists perhaps. Novice visitors learn how to view objects and read signs, how to identify exhibit boundaries and themes, and how to navigate the physical spaces as part of social groups. The "practices" of visiting museums are subtle and imparted through specific community members, such as parents and docents. Novices often participate on the edge of groups or in relatively passive ways through observation and limited participation, called "legitimate peripheral participation" (LPP) by Jean Lave and Etienne Wenger.[22] With increasing experiences and skills, visitors participate more actively and eventually move from LPP to the center of the group to lead others in viewing and discussing objects in museums. Then, like experts in the community, they share stories and inculcate others into the community.

When learning is viewed as situated activities in communities of practice, it is clear that the sense of belonging to the group is a strong motivation to learn the skills of the community. Membership in a group means that novices strive to be like experts in the community; they identify with the practices and skills of the community, strive to attain them, and take pride when they master the skills. Community members share similar goals, establish similar habits and values, and help one another accomplish tasks.[23] The analogy with museum visitors is striking. Novice museum visitors may be naïve about the skills and knowledge of experts in a museum community, especially if the zoo, garden, art, or historical site is unfamiliar and novel. If novices observe experts and value their knowledge, they emulate how they interact with objects and how they experience the museum. Participating in discussions and taking pride in expanding knowledge help to establish an emerging identity as a full-fledged member of the community and an "expert" in the group. That is why docent experiences for youth can be such powerful experiences. DeAnna Banks Beane and Myla Shanae Pope[24] describe how adolescent experiences in the *Youth Alive!* program can shape the academic identities and professional lives of young people, and the program is an excellent example of creating communities of learners within museums.

Is the analogy of "communities" heuristic for museums? Yes, I think that a focus on creating communities of learners who impart knowledge through shared practices provides a social milieu for learning that is often absent in museums. Consider some implications. Docent-led experiences create groups of visitors, but more care must be given to model effective transactions with objects, such as reading objects and conversational elaboration described earlier. Beyond modeling, group members must be allowed to practice with, and teach the transactions to, others to establish feelings of competence and confidence. A second way to create communities among visitors is to provide specific activities for families, activities that allow parents to handle, explain, demonstrate, wonder about, and discuss objects even if they have limited experience with them. Shared reading of labels is not the answer, but audible directions under bubble domes, hands-on experiments suggested by diagrams, interactive video demonstrations, and computer kiosks with inquiry-guided questions can all promote parent-child learning opportunities that transcend pointing and labeling. These methods can work well with friends as well as families. A third approach is to provide structured tours guided by searches for particular objects, themes, or answers to questions. A group can be cohesive and motivated when members work together to find information or perform skills in a museum. Activities that require joint problem solving or construction are very useful for building collaboration. A fourth method to establish community is to provide a sense of achievement and membership by recognizing the group accomplishments. Discounts at the gift shop, reduced admission fees, discounted tickets to special exhibitions, similar name badges or stickers, stamped passports and memorabilia, or special T-shirts might all signify successful exploration of the museum exhibits. All of these activities reinforce learning together, building communities, and establishing a sense of identity with the group.

IDENTITY DEVELOPMENT

The personal context provided by visitors' cumulative experiences, attitudes, and knowledge influences the ways they interact with objects in museums. This is a main tenet of theories based on contextual learning,[25] situated learning,[26] social psychology,[27] and cognitive development.[28] Museum visitors discover bits and reminders of their own lives in the objects they encounter as they browse, cruise, and examine museum spaces. Visitors understand objects that they encounter in relation to their own histories and anticipated futures, through self-referenced and socially-referenced narratives.[29] Families share stories and communities of practice share stories to solidify their identity and values. The stories provide autobiographical continuity to museum experiences, concepts, and objects, and their effects can be long-lasting, subtle, and difficult to assess. Museum educators recognize that this form of learning is more like a personal characteristic or disposition than demonstrated knowledge, but it is enduring, emotional, and powerful.

Identity provides motivation during a museum visit in many ways. For example, visitors can consider various "possible selves"[30] as they imagine how they might be artists, scientists, explorers, and so forth as they encounter new and exciting examples of different lives in museums. Children are especially likely to imagine different future roles for themselves. A sense of personal identity can influence how visitors search for objects and which exhibits have attraction and holding power for them. Melissa Mercer and I[31] describe three kinds of self-object relations that sustain interactions. One relation is an identity confirmation when the visitor senses validation of personal knowledge or experience. For example, a person might be drawn to a painting that is familiar, appreciated, and consistent with aesthetic tastes, so it elicits a prolonged period of viewing or conversation. A second type of relation is identity disconfirming because the object contradicts or calls into question the person's beliefs, knowledge, or feelings. Such encounters can be troubling and discomforting but they evoke sustained transactions with objects and potentially strong reactions. A third type of relation can extend and elaborate a person's sense of identity. For example, a visitor may encounter an object created by a member of the same ethnic group and feel pride in the achievement, or the exhibit may convey new information that augments a visitor's sense of membership in a community or group. Each of these three object-self transactions can be profound because they affect a person's sense of "I-self," which is the active agent who constructs meaning, and the "me-self," which is the sum of characteristics that define the person.[32] Visitors feel empowered when their sense of efficacy is increased (for example, the I-self), and they feel confident and proud when their sense of competence and achievement is validated (for example, the me-self). These intrinsic motives can guide visitors as they search, analyze, and transact with objects in museums.

CONCLUSION

Museums have always been responsive to changes in public appetites for education and entertainment, and they need to be attuned to social, historical, and psychological cues more than ever in the twenty-first century if they want to cultivate life-long visitors. One challenge is to use psychological principles of learning and motivation to guide the design of exhibitions and programs so that visitors are engaged, cognitively and emotionally, with the objects and experiences in museums. Deep engagement provokes conversations, stories, and collaboration; it reinforces positive self-perceptions and sense of identity in a community. These processes transcend traditional notions of learning facts and concepts, and they are crucial for cultivating life-long museum visitors.

A second challenge is to balance the goal of increasing visitor appeal with other goals such as research, scholarship, membership, community service, and fiscal soundness because museums have many agenda and diverse audiences. Part of the solution might be to infuse educational responsibilities among all museum staff, not just the overburdened museum educators, so that the entire staff works toward similar goals for visitors.[33] A third challenge is to create an institutional infrastructure that is scholarly, innovative, and practical in the design of educational programs. The staff infrastructure needs leadership from museum curators and educators, but they also need input from local K–12 teachers, parents, children, neighborhood citizens, businesses, and civic organizations so that the mission, exhibitions, and programs of the museum are responsive to changing community needs and expectations. These intellectual foundations and broad-based partnerships have enormous promise for enticing visitors into museums and engaging them with collections in compelling ways. Psychological engagement is intrinsically motivating and will enhance visitors' knowledge and satisfaction with museums so they are frequent visitors to museums around the world.

NOTES

1. Stephen E. Weil, *A Cabinet of Curiosities* (Washington, D.C.: Smithsonian Institution Press, 1995).

2. John H. Falk and Lynn D. Dierking, *Learning from Museums* (Walnut Creek, Calif.: AltaMira Press, 2000); and Scott G. Paris and D. Ash, "Reciprocal Theory Building Inside and Outside Museums," *Curator* 43, no. 3 (2000): 199–210.

3. Scott G. Paris and Susanna E. Hapgood, "Children Learning with Objects in Informal Learning Environments," in *Perspectives on Object-centered Learning in Museums*, ed. Scott G. Paris, 37–54 (Mahwah, N.J.: Lawrence Erlbaum Associates, 2001).

4. David C. Michener and Inger J. Schultz, "Through the Garden Gate: Objects and Informal Education for Environmental and Cultural Awareness in Arboreta and Botanic Gardens," in *Perspectives on Object-centered Learning in Museums*, ed. Scott G. Paris, 95–111 (Mahwah, N.J.: Lawrence Erlbaum Associates, 2001).

5. Barbara Piscitelli and Katrina Weier, "Learning With, Through, and About Art: The Role of Social Interactions," in *Perspectives on Object-centered Learning in*

Museums, ed. Scott G. Paris, 121–51 (Mahwah, N.J.: Lawrence Erlbaum Associates, 2001).

6. Minda Borun, "Object-based Learning and Family Groups," in *Perspectives on Object-centered Learning in Museums*, ed. Scott G. Paris, 245–60 (Mahwah, N.J.: Lawrence Erlbaum Associates, 2001).

7. See, for example, Steven Conn, *Museums and American Intellectual Life, 1876–1926* (Chicago: University of Chicago Press, 1998).

8. Howard Gardner, *The Unschooled Mind: How Children Think and How Schools Should Teach* (New York: Basic Books, 1991).

9. Mihaly Csikszentmihalyi and Kim Hermanson, "Intrinsic Motivation in Museums: Why Does One Want to Learn?" in *Public Institutions for Personal Learning: Establishing a Research Agenda*, ed. John L. Falk and Lynn D. Dierking, 67–77 (Washington, D.C.: American Association of Museums, 1995).

10. David Carr, "Minds in Museums and Libraries: The Cognitive Management of Cultural Institutions," *Teachers College Record* 93, no. 1 (1991): 6–27; and Christina E. van Kraayenoord and Scott G. Paris, "Reading Objects," in *Perspectives on Object-centered Learning in Museums*, ed. Scott G. Paris, 215–34 (Mahwah, N.J.: Lawrence Erlbaum Associates, 2002).

11. van Kraayenoord and Paris, "Reading Objects."

12. Gaea Leinhardt, Kevin Crowley, and Karen Knutson, *Learning Conversations in Museums* (Mahwah, N.J.: Lawrence Erlbaum Associates, 2002).

13. Maureen A. Callanan, Jennifer L. Jipson, and Monika Stampf Soennichsen, "Maps, Globes, and Videos: Parent-child Conversations about Representational Objects," in *Perspectives on Object-centered Learning in Museums*, ed. Scott G. Paris, 261–83 (Mahwah, N.J.: Lawrence Erlbaum Associates, 2001).

14. Borun, "Object-based Learning and Family Groups."

15. Elaine Heumann Gurian, "What Is the Object of this Exercise? A Meandering Exploration of the Many Meanings of Objects in Museums," *Daedalus* 128, no. 3 (1999): 163–83.

16. Gurian, "What Is the Object of this Exercise?" 165–66.

17. Jerome Seymour Bruner, *Actual Minds, Possible Worlds* (Cambridge, Mass.: Harvard University Press, 1986).

18. Scott G. Paris and Melissa J. Mercer, "Finding Self in Objects: Identity Exploration in Museums," in *Learning Conversations: Explanation and Identity in Museums*, ed. Gaea Leinhardt, Kevin Crowley, and Karen Knutson, 401–23 (Mahwah, N.J.: Lawrence Erlbaum Associates, 2002).

19. Lisa C. Roberts, *From Knowledge to Narrative* (Washington, D.C.: Smithsonian Institution Press, 1997).

20. Dawn Casey, "Museums as Agents for Social and Political Change," *Curator* 44, no. 3 (2001): 230–36.

21. For example, Jean Lave and Etienne Wenger, *Situated Learning: Legitimate Peripheral Participation* (New York: Cambridge University Press, 1991).

22. Lave and Wenger, *Situated Learning*.

23. Scott G. Paris, "Situated Motivation and Informal Learning," *Journal of Museum Education* 22, nos. 2–3 (1997): 22–26.

24. DeAnna Banks Beane and Myla Shanae Pope, "Leveling the Playing Field

Through Object-based Service Learning," in *Perspectives on Object-centered Learning in Museums*, ed. Scott G. Paris, 325–49 (Mahwah, N.J.: Lawrence Erlbaum Associates, 2001).

25. John H. Falk and Lynn D. Dierking, *The Museum Experience* (Washington, D.C.: Whalesback Books, 1992).

26. Lave and Wenger, *Situated Learning*.

27. Hazel Markus and Paula Nurius, "Possible Selves," *American Psychologist* 41 (1986): 954–69.

28. Michel Ferrari and Ramaswami Mahalingam, "Personal Cognitive Development and Its Implications for Teaching and Learning," *Educational Psychologist* 33, no. 1 (1998): 35–44.

29. Roy Rosenzweig and David Thelen, *The Presence of the Past: Popular Uses of History in American Life* (New York: Columbia University Press, 1998).

30. Markus and Nurius, "Possible Selves."

31. Paris and Mercer, "Finding Self in Objects."

32. Susan Harter, *The Construction of Self* (New York: Guilford Press, 1999).

33. Roberts, *From Knowledge to Narrative*.

23

Community Choices, Museum Concerns

Robert R. Archibald

Just a few weeks after September 11, 2001, I meandered through the classical halls of the Metropolitan Museum of Art in New York City, finding solace from the horrific tragedy still lingering beyond those walls. Here, I meditated on the beauty created by humans very much like me more than two thousand years ago. Beauty is the antidote to ugliness and evil. It always has been.

At the Missouri Historical Society, which I have headed since 1988, I can examine our regional past and thus explore the future that will be based on that past. Occasionally I visit zoos, although I am a bit uncomfortable staring at the captive animals. St. Louis has a fine zoo, recently cited in a survey as offering a better visitor experience than Disneyland. Thousands of children run through the zoo. Some ride the Zooline Railroad, whose engines are named for local historic figures, or take a spin on the new Conservation Carousel, whose fares serve the worldwide preservation mission of the zoo, or clamber through the specially designed children's zoo. It's a real-life wonderland for children, and adults, too. My own favorite spots in St. Louis may be in the corners of the Missouri Botanical Garden where, surrounded by beauty, I can witness the changing of the seasons and rejoice that my favorite places will always be recognizable but never look precisely the same.

Every major city now aspires to have an aquarium, an essential ingredient in attracting a certain tourist demographic. As a lifelong fish keeper myself, I am fascinated by the underwater world and understand its attraction. Science centers now worry that the Omnimax craze is over and that they may face dwindling revenues from these former cash cows. A few years ago the exhibit *Titanic* made the rounds of science museums. This mammoth exhibition was different because, organized by a for-profit corporation, it was intended to be a sensational blockbuster—that is, moneymaker—from its inception.

There are thousands of historic house museums in the United States. Many of them once belonged to the rich and famous of the nineteenth and early twentieth centuries. Most have small numbers of visitors but a loyal cadre of volunteers. For these dedicated individuals, maintaining the historic house or school or center is both a social activity and an opportunity to indulge interests in local history, decorative arts, vernacular architecture, or genealogy. There are at least as many local historical societies, which seek to preserve community history and a sense of community identity in the face of economic change and the almost irresistible forces of homogenization. Heritage centers have sprouted in African American, Asian, Native American, Latino, and other cultural communities as important self-generated efforts at empowerment and pride by groups too often marginalized. Some outdoor museums focus on real historic sites, and others are artificially recreated sites that never actually existed. There are museums run by corporations that are really marketing efforts and museums run by the military to instill patriotism and pride in service.

This litany has a point. No two museums are alike. Museums are endlessly, enchantingly diverse. Unlike scientists' quest for a "theory of everything," no such pursuit is desirable or possible for us in the museum field.

Despite the diversity of museums, professional organizations make ongoing efforts to standardize practice both for the specific disciplinary bases of museums and for museums as a whole. During nearly thirty years as a museum professional, I have been present at debates about the primacy of collections, preferred conservation philosophies, ethics, the qualifications of people who work in museums, and issues of diversity, obligations to community, collection policies, deaccessioning procedures, and more. Defining museum work as a profession with distinct canons is a primary issue at the core of these debates.

Another primary issue is the precise definition of the "public trust" given to museums. The cultural context within which museums operate continues to change. America is radically democratic in ways that no one imagined a hundred years ago. Previously suppressed voices now successfully demand to be heard. The concept of ultimate authority and top-down decision making is called into question and frequently disputed with considerable skill. Yet many of us who work in museums persist in the idea that we, together with academic colleagues, can unilaterally define good art, decide what constitutes historical significance, and promote science and technology without caveats. Because we are "professionals," our habit is to exercise exclusive authority over all of our subject matter. This is precisely why native people are suspicious of anthropologists. It is at the root of the objections of war veterans to interpretations of war that do not adequately account for their sacrifices. It is the much-discussed issue of authority. In this new century, we will have to find ways to share authority that far transcend the marketing surveys we currently use to gauge the public's receptivity to the choices we put before them. Processes for sharing authority vary greatly but will always require that our communities, however we define them or they define themselves, have meaningful contribution and direct involvement in establishing museum agendas. Credibility requires that museums look like their communities; there can be no more excuses for the dearth of people of color and other minorities in our ranks. We must cease using "best practices" and "professionalism" as methods that define the distinction between those who have authority and those who do not. Rigid adherence to those "best practices" developed over time is not so much an indicator of progress as it is a defense of the status quo.

Some directors and institutions are evaluated exclusively by the numbers. How many visitors and how much revenue? Pressures to balance profit-and-loss issues are real. Numbers are one important performance measurement, but they are one sided, forcing museum administrators to single-mindedly focus on admissions and sales receipts. The obligation to increase revenue impels museum administrators to evaluate exhibitions and programs on the basis of their ability to drive attendance up and contribute to the bottom line. In this rush to solvency, the lines between entertainment and the educational roles of museums become indistinct. We stray further from our missions and become more like theme parks. Often I think about the Six Flags operation near St. Louis. Six Flags really understands how to increase attendance and revenue. But a museum is not a theme park. In response to pressures to be popular, we in museums need to be abundantly clear about how we will measure success. Certainly financial performance is a factor in determining the success of a cultural institution. But cultural institutions enjoy their status because of some larger purpose than making money and keeping the doors open. At the Missouri Historical Society, we agree that our standard of success has three components, of which financial performance is one. Of equal import is the degree to which we are good stewards of our collections. The third element is evaluation by our community; in our institution we meet with community representatives and ask them very specifically how we are doing and how we might do better.

Pressure for high numbers is often the result of museum expansions that are premised on overly optimistic projections of attendance and revenue. Museums must be cautious and conservative in these projections because in the end an expansion program may undermine the very purpose for which the museum sought to expand. Likewise museums must be cautious about participation in the popular assessments that seek to justify institutions based on "economic impact." Returning to my Six Flags example, no cultural institution in the St. Louis area can match the economic impact of Six Flags. We will never survive on that basis. With a few exceptions like Colonial Williamsburg, we will always be marginal to our local economies.

However, in another sense our economic impact is impressive. Portability of work is a hallmark of the information age economy. In ways that were unimaginable just a few years ago, work is becoming detached from place. Jobs and business are no longer tied to places that provide a workforce, access to markets, and raw materials. Many corporations pride themselves on their abilities to do their business anywhere from any place. Huge numbers of our workforce have broken the old rules about where the jobs are. Jobs are anywhere. So, how will businesses choose where to locate and how will the workers in this economy choose where to live? Some people love mountains, others cannot live without an ocean, and for still others climate will be a deciding factor. People with children will be concerned about schools, and nearly everyone will consider the cost of living in their decision. But, in the end, quality of life will be the determinant. For many people in this new global information age economy, cultural amenities will be deciding factors. Not individual institutions but rather an array of amenities in a city or region will be a powerful incentive to attract people and thus induce economic prosperity.

We will need to think differently about ourselves and encourage our communities to calculate competitive assets on a new scale of priority. Prosperity of one museum or cultural organization must not be the objective but rather we must consider the health of the whole group. Our value as community assets is not enhanced if my own institution prospers but the symphony falters. Likewise, if the zoo prospers but we persist in demolishing the historic fabric of our city, which gives our community a distinctive sense of place, we have gained nothing. In this new economy, we must step outside the walls of our institutions and acknowledge that museums, zoos, botanic gardens, theater companies, musical groups, and the material culture of our cities and towns constitute an aggregation of assets that will attract businesses and people. In the new economy they will choose where to live based on their personal perceptions of quality of life; it is not the existence of any one institution that will attract them but rather the menu of available cultural choices. To the extent that we can make this argument stick with the leaders in our communities, we have a greater claim on the community's resources. If community leaders perceive culture broadly defined as an asset that creates regional competitive economic advantage, they will be inclined to see to our prosperity. There is growing evidence in our nation that this is true and that many people freed from the old constraints of place are making locational decisions based on lifestyle and quality of life as opposed to the old equation that required almost all people in all fields to "go where the jobs are." The new economy potentially places museums and other cultural amenities at the center of the economic future. It is an opportunity to rethink our value to the larger society and to claim even more significant and vital roles in the future.

It is ironic that a hallmark of the just completed century was mobility. Previously many people moved multiple times in the course of climbing the corporate ladder or seeking new opportunity. Now "virtual meetings" and instantaneous transmission of information of the twenty-first century make it possible for people to move less often and to be more committed to long-term relationships with the places where they live and with their neighbors.

One successful real estate broker in St. Louis told me that her job entailed finding homes for corporate executives transferred to St. Louis. She was instructed not to show them homes in the city but instead to confine sales work to suburbs. The rationale offered by her corporate client was that, because executives were transferred so often, the corporation did not want them to become attached to particular places. A suburb in any region in the United States is much like a suburb anywhere else, and so is a shopping mall even to the names of the stores and the brands for sale. It is hard to be attached to a suburban house in a St. Louis suburb when a suburban house in a Detroit suburb is essentially identical. In St. Louis at least, there is an explosion in demand for urban housing, not because suburbs have gone away but rather because people are seeking places to live that fit with their personal lifestyle preferences. I have lived in St. Louis for fifteen years, and I have never seen as much rehabbing, conversions of old factories and warehouses to lofts and condominiums, or new urban construction as I see now. In part this is the special quality of the housing, but much of it is because people want to live closer to urban amenities—parks, mass transit, museums, eclectic restaurants, nightspots with blues and jazz, theaters, the symphony. They want to get out of cars and know their neighbors. It is a heartening trend, and it is good for museums if we position ourselves to take full advantage of it.

This positive reemphasis upon the local does not sever us from the responsibilities imposed by the new global world. Museums and cultural organizations cannot shirk or shy away from our own responsibilities as we begin to see the issues of this new century emerge as if from shadowy glass. Here, global and local become one. While I know that museums have not seen themselves as advocacy organizations, we have always been implicitly about values. In deciding what to collect and what not to collect, we have had to decide what was important. The Missouri Historical Society has defined historical significance in our collecting decisions and in our exhibit interpretations. Art museums have made similar choices. Some but not all historic places and sites have been preserved. In choosing to preserve some but not others, we have made judgments about relative value. Zoos have focused on specific efforts to preserve some species and not others and have by their very existence assumed certain attitudes toward other living species. Botanical gardens make similar judgments about biodiversity. Science centers serve in part to advocate science and technology. Values are not new to museums. What is new is the need to be specific about the values we espouse.

Two issues will be paramount in this new century, and both pivot on the values we apply. How will we create good places for people? Places that are safe, clean, and sustainable and can provide for the needs of those who will inhabit them later. Places that pursue justice and promote equal opportunity and understanding between people. Places that are sustainable for the long term and that are good for the human spirit.

Second, but equally essential, is how we as a species will divert ourselves from our current deadly course that conflicts with the planet's ability to sustain future generations in a manner that makes life worth living. Global environmental danger is neither imaginary nor alarmist. The longer we pretend that it is, the more dire the consequences will be for humanity. Can we reimagine our relationships with the planet and with each other? Can we learn to get along locally and globally? That is what most urgently must be done.

What of museums? Can we and should we have a role in working with people to seek solutions, or are these questions better left for the remainder of society to wrestle? Individual museums may respond in various ways, but I am convinced that this is both an obligation and an opportunity to fulfill our potential and to become more crucial than ever to the world and the people around us. But to do this we must explicitly state the values upon which we act, and we will have to measure every decision based on the extent to which it conforms with the values we espouse. Those of us who work in museums must see ourselves as citizens first and museum professionals second. Despite our efforts to be objective, we are integral to the world where we live. That world cries for answers to our most perplexing problems that are not objective in any conventional sense. For example, the evidence is irrefutable that human activity is causing environmental degradation. Still we persist in our deleterious behaviors and presume that, once more, science and technology will save us from looming disaster. Yet the evidence suggests that the problems are a result of two centuries of scientific, industrial, and technical "advance." In the end the question becomes "How do we change human behavior?" Behavior is in large part based on value systems, on how we respond to queries like: what is a community, what is human happiness, what is just, what is right and good, what value do we place on relationships, on home, on unspoiled places and wild things, clean air and pure rivers and streams? These sorts of questions surely fall within the purview of museums.

Our institutions ought not to recoil from being the forums for such public discussion in the informed context that we can provide.

In 2001 the trustees and staff of the Missouri Historical Society embarked on a planning process to redefine the institution. By unanimous agreement the trustees adopted this mission statement. "The Missouri Historical Society seeks to deepen the understanding of past choices, present circumstances and future possibilities; strengthen the bonds of community; and facilitate solutions to common problems." In the same process we agreed upon a set of core values to frame our historical interpretation and direct all of our activities whether research, collecting, or dissemination of information. We adopted six core values—a civil society, empathy, inspiration, integrity, memory, good stewardship. Each has its own explication, but one example will suffice:

> The Missouri Historical Society is committed to fostering a CIVIL SOCIETY, a strong and healthy community. The age-old record of human experience documents lessons on the character of civil society. We conclude that citizenship confers both rights and responsibilities. All people enjoy rights to impartial justice, equality of opportunity, freedom from violence, and enjoyment of the results of their labor. Rights are necessarily accompanied by obligations; a civil society strives to live by the rule of law, to respect the rights of others, and to provide for the common welfare.

We linked the core values to six commitments. Again I offer just one example: "The Missouri Historical Society will pursue its work, fulfill its mission, adhere to its values, and conduct its activities in a manner that is inclusive." Common stories and shared meaning cannot evolve from exclusive practices and programs. Our institution seeks diverse public representation in program planning and implementation and is pledged as well to apply this principle consistently in its business practices.

I am convinced that our approach has embedded the museum deeply in the community and simultaneously extended and deepened its reach. The Missouri Historical Society is broadly viewed by both community leaders and the general population as one of the primary places where important debates about our common future take place and choices and agendas for our future are decided.

Despite the vast evolution of museums from their origins in this nation as "cabinets of curiosities" to community advocates, we must continue to respect the best traditions that are our foundations. Museums and our allied institutions must acknowledge that visitors bring their own meanings to our collections of artifacts, art, plants, or animals. We must not be so didactic as to obscure the intangible link between visitor and object that has always been our most important hallmark. In our halls, exhibits, and gardens, people confront what they most trust about us, the opportunity to confront real, unmediated things. In 2004 visitors to my museum could see objects that made the continental journey with the Lewis and Clark Expedition. When I visit the zoo, I see a profusion of animal life that makes me reimagine my own place on this earth. The Botanical Garden impresses me with the diversity of planetary plant life and offers beautiful quiet corners for personal contemplation. At the Art Museum I can try to see the world through the mind's eyes of others past and present. Museums are for all of these things. They remind us that we are not alone on this planet and we are not the first and certainly not the wisest generation of humans to live here. They bring solace in times of trouble because they remind us of continuity in the midst of change, beauty in the midst of ugliness, justice in the midst of inequity, equality in the midst of oppression, and hope in the midst of cynicism. In the eye of the tiger, the transcendence of art, the continuity of times past, the beauty of the lily, we find context for ourselves. These things museums have done and must continue to do for the sake of humanity.

Index

About the Contributors

Robert R. Archibald has been since 1988 president and chief executive officer of the Missouri Historical Society, the public history institution that received the first National Award for Museum Service in 1994. He has been the director of the Montana Historical Society and of the Western Heritage Center in Billings, Montana, and curator of the Albuquerque Museum in New Mexico. An active member of many professional and community organizations, he is the author of *A Place to Remember: Using History to Build Community* (AltaMira, 1999) and, most recently, *The New Town Square: Museums and Communities in Transition* published by AltaMira Press in 2004. He writes and speaks on numerous topics from history and historical practice to community building and environmental responsibility. Archibald spent his first twenty years of life in Michigan's Upper Peninsula, born in Ishpeming and educated at Northern Michigan University in Marquette, where he achieved undergraduate and graduate degrees. He earned his doctorate at the University of New Mexico, an experience he deeply values. He has received honorary doctorates of letters from the University of Missouri, St. Louis (1998), from Maryville University (2003), and from his alma mater Northern Michigan University (2004), as well as that university's 1998 Distinguished Alumni Award, honors he thoroughly appreciates.—*Missouri Historical Society, P.O. Box 11940, St. Louis, MO 63112-0040.*

Patrick J. Boylan graduated BSc. at Hull University in geography and geology in 1960. After taking the University's Postgraduate Certificate in Education in 1961, he worked as a secondary school teacher before joining the Hull Museums as head of geology and natural history. Appointed Director of Museums and Art Gallery at Exeter at the age of twenty-eight, he moved to Leicester City's Museums Director in 1972, and went on to set up the Leicestershire County Museums, Arts and Records Service in 1974.

His more than eighteen years with Leicester and Leicestershire saw many major developments within the arts and heritage services, including the development of seven new branch museums and heritage tourism facilities, and new environmental services for archaeology, geology, and ecology. From 1988–1990 he served as the Centenary President of the United Kingdom's Museums Association, including leading the highly successful Museums Year 1989, marking the centenary of the world's first national museums association. After almost thirty years in local government senior management, in 1990 he became a professor and head of the Department of Arts Policy and Management at City University, London—probably the largest interdisciplinary postgraduate education and research center of its kind in the world. He retired in December 2003, and in June 2004 the university awarded him the title of Professor Emeritus of Heritage Policy and Management.

At the international level, he has held a wide range of offices in the International Council of Museums (ICOM) from 1977 to 2004, including service as a member of the Executive Council (1989–1998), vice-president (1992–1998), president of the ICOM International Committee for the Training of Personnel (1983–1989 and 1998–2004), and of ICOM UK (1985–1991). In October 2004 he was elected an Honorary Member of ICOM.

Professor Boylan is the author of almost 200 academic and professional publications, including *Birds in Hull* (Hull Museum, 1967) and *Museums 2000: Politics, People, Professionals and Profit* (Routledge, 1992), and coauthor with Jacqueline Sarafopoulos of *Museums and Insurance* (1999). He has also undertaken a very wide range of advisory and consultancy commissions for international organizations, including UNESCO, the Council of Europe, and the British Council, and for more than twenty governments and public agencies around the world.—*City University London, 2A Compass Road, Leicester LE5 2HF, England.*

David Carr teaches at the School of Information and Library Science at the University of North Carolina at Chapel Hill, where he specializes in collections, reading, and reference work in the humanities and social sciences. As a scholar and consultant, he also addresses learning outside schools, especially in public cultural institutions such as libraries and museums. His work emphasizes self-directed inquiry and critical thinking, adult curiosity, informal learning, and independent scholarship. He is most interested in the unfinished issues of adult life and the processes that people use to become deeply informed over time. Dr. Carr holds degrees from Drew University (B.A.), Teachers College-Columbia University (M.A.), and Rutgers University (M.L.S., Ph.D.). Over time he has consulted at the Brooklyn Museum of Art, Children's Museum of Indianapolis, Cooper-Hewitt National Design Museum, Historical Society of Pennsylvania, The Jewish Museum, Museum of Fine Arts-Houston, Museum of Jewish Heritage, National Endowment for the Humanities, Rhode Island School of Design, Strong Museum, and W. K. Kellogg Foundation, among other institutions. In recent years, he has lectured and written on the passion of reading in adult life. He has published articles in *Public Library Quarterly*; *Museum News*; *Public Libraries*; *Curator*; *Library Trends*; *The Journal of Museum Education*; *The International Journal of Heritage Studies*; *RBM: A Journal of Rare Books, Manuscripts and Cultural Heritage*; and *Teachers College Record*, among other publications. He has written book chapters on nonfiction, self-directed learning in libraries and museums, thinking and learning in cultural institutions, and library collections in museums. Among his many keynote addresses, two were delivered for the Institute of Museum and Library Services, one at the White House in October 2002. Both appear in his collection of essays, *The Promise of Cultural Institutions* (AltaMira Press, 2003). A second collection and a series of journal writings are in preparation.—*School of Information and Library Science, University of North Carolina at Chapel Hill, CB #3360, 100 Manning Hall, Chapel Hill, NC 27599-3360.*

Christy S. Coleman has served as president and chief executive officer of the Charles H. Wright Museum of African American History in Detroit, Michigan, since September 1999. She previously held the positions of Director of Midtown Operations (1997–1999) and Director of African American Interpretations and Presentations (1994–1997) at the Colonial Williamsburg Foundation. It was at Colonial Williamsburg that Ms. Coleman first gained national attention for her innovative and, at times, controversial programs centered on African American life in the Revolutionary era. She has authored a number of historical dramas both for educational television and live performance for museums around the country. She has also written articles for professional journals including "The Colonial Williamsburg Revolution" (*History Dispatch*: Spring 1999) and "The Play's the Thing: The Future of Museum Theater" (*Case Studies in Museum, Zoo and Aquarium Theater*; AAM: 1999). She has lectured extensively on early African American history and culture, museum theater, and the changing role of museums. Ms. Coleman has served on the boards of the American Association of Museums, American Association for State and Local History, and the International Museum Theater Alliance. She is an active member of a number of professional and civic organizations. Ms. Coleman is a magna cum laude graduate of Hampton University with a B.A. in interdisciplinary studies. She also earned her M.A. in museum studies from Hampton University.—*Charles H. Wright Museum of African American History, 315 E. Warren Avenue, Detroit, MI 48201-1443.*

Helen Coxall has a doctorate from the University of Oxford Brookes University in museum language—a cultural investigation into the use of language in the interpretation of exhibits in museums and art galleries. For the last thirteen years, she has worked as a museum language consultant and script-writer in museums and galleries, specializing in rewriting academic prose in an inclusive, accessible way for specific audiences. She focuses on working on projects desiring to be culturally and socially inclusive. Dr. Coxall was a member of the steering committee at Resource, The Council for Museums, Archives and Libraries, London, that identified a practical guide to socially and culturally inclusive practice and a participant in the Mayors of London's Commission for African and Asian Heritage. She is a researcher at the Centre for Arts Research, Technology and Education (CARTE) at the University of Westminster, London, where she is course leader of the masters program in visual culture. Her most recent consultancies include: Sharjah Islamic Museum of Culture and Arts, Arab Emirates; Royal Ontario Museum, Toronto, *Renaissance ROM: Africa, the Americas & Asia-Pacific Gallery*; British Museum, *Living and Dying* ethnographic gallery; City Hall, London, *Local Heroes* black history project with twelve London museums; and Liverpool Museum, *World Cultures Galleries: Africa, Asia, Americas & Oceania*. Two significant earlier consultancies were Horniman Museum, London, *African Worlds* gallery and Maritime Museum, Liverpool, *Transatlantic Slavery* gallery. She has published articles on inclusive practice in: *Journal of Visual Culture*; *The Disability Directory for Museum and Galleries*; *Museum Practice*; *Journal of Museum Ethnography*; *Journal of Social History Curator's Group*; and *Primary History*. She has published chapters on textual interpretation with Routledge; Leicester University Press; I. B. Tauris; and The Stationery Office. Her research programs have been funded by CARTE and The British Academy.—*Center for Arts Research Technology and Education, University of Westminster, 70 Great Portland Street, London W1W 7NQ, England.*

Charles Dailey is now chairman of the museum studies program at the Institute of American Indian Arts in Santa Fe. He has received a public award as "Outstanding Faculty in the State of New Mexico" in 2002, and he has been recognized by students of the IAIA on thirteen occasions as "Outstanding Faculty." Being director of the IAIA Museum on three occasions for a total of more than twenty years since 1971, and growing the museum from a staff of one to over eighteen staff members, is a quiet accomplishment. Over one hundred items were given to Mr. Dailey as "faculty" and are now in the permanent collection of the museum. He received his education at the University of Colorado, working with famed museologist Hugo Rodeck. He also worked for the Museum of Northern Arizona in 1960–1961 as an exhibit specialist and the Museum of New Mexico from 1962 to 1971, finishing as the curator of exhibitions. He has invented manikin systems, hanging devices, and security systems for use in museums. Chuck Dailey has written the illustrated textbooks *Museum Administration I* (IAIA Press, 2004), *Introduction to Museology* (IAIA Press, revised yearly 2004), *Collections Care and Management* (IAIA Press, revised ed. 2004), *Exhibitions* (IAIA Press, revised ed. 2004), *Repatriation: An Introduction to Repatriation* (IAIA Press, 2003), and *Creating a Manikin* (El Palacio, Museum of New Mexico, 1970). In 1998, a survey was completed, with the results indicating that over one hundred Native American museum professionals had been inspired by Chuck's efforts. He has designed entire museums in America and abroad. The Southwest Museum in Cavona, Italy, was designed, built, and installed by Mr. Dailey and his family in 1996. He has designed and served as the guest curator for exhibits at the Smithsonian Institution, Daybreak Star Museum in Seattle, Jicarilla Museum in Dulce, NM, Maturango Museum in Ridgecrest, CA, and the Indian Pueblo Cultural Center in Albuquerque. His academic life is shared by alpine skiing, kayaking, and bicycling. He devotes himself to his museums.—*Institute of American Indian Arts, Museum Studies Department, Avan Nu Po Road, Santa Fe, NM 87508.*

Jennifer Eichstedt is an associate professor of sociology at Humboldt State University in Arcata, California, and taught previously at Mary Washington College in Fredericksburg, Virginia. She teaches in the areas of race, social movements, and popular culture. She received her Ph.D. from the University of California, Santa Cruz. Her primary areas of research have been in the areas of race, whiteness, and social justice activism. She held a National Endowment for the Humanities College Teachers Fellowship in 2000–2001 to investigate representations of slavery and whiteness in the plantation-tourism industry in the contemporary South; her book, *Representations of Slavery: Race and Ideology in Southern Plantation Museums* (2002), is on this subject and co-written with Professor Stephen Small, Department of African-American Studies at University of California, Berkeley, published October 2002 by the Smithsonian Institution Press. Additional publications are in the areas of white privilege, multiculturalism, and the pedagogy of oppression and resistance. She also is an antiracism, gay and lesbian rights, and education activist.—*Department of Sociology, Humboldt State University, 1 Harpst Street, Arcata, CA 95521.*

Hugh H. Genoways is a professor of museum studies and natural resources at the University of Nebraska, Lincoln. He received his A.B. from Hastings College in Nebraska and a Ph.D. in systematics and ecology from the University of Kansas. He served as a Fulbright Fellow at the University of Western Australia in 1964. Following his graduate studies, he held the position of Curator of Mammals at the Museum of Texas Tech University (five years) and Carnegie Museum of Natural History in Pittsburgh (ten years) before coming to the University of Nebraska in 1986 as director of the University of Nebraska State Museum. He held the latter position for eight years, during which time he oversaw a $4 million renovation of the museum's primary exhibit building and the installation of five new exhibit galleries, before taking up his current position, as well as serving as a professor in the State Museum until 2003. At Texas Tech University, he was the junior member of a team that established and taught in the Museum Science Program. At the University of Nebraska, Lincoln, he served as the chair of the planning and implementation committee for a Museum Studies Program. He served as chair of this program for thirteen of the fifteen years of its existence, graduating over 200 M.A./M.S. students during this period. His research has focused on the systematics of mammals, with an emphasis on those in Latin America and the Caribbean. He has published fourteen books and 228 articles in mammalogy and museology. His books (coauthored and coedited) have included *Systematics and Evolutionary Relationships of the Spiny Pocket Mice of the Genus Liomys* (Texas Tech University, 1973), *A Guide to the Management of Recent Mammal Collections* (Carnegie Museum, 1977), *Biological Investigations in the Guadalupe Mountains National Park, Texas* (National Park Service, 1979), *Mammalian Biology in South America* (University of Pittsburgh, 1982), *Current Mammalogy* (Plenum Publishing Corporation, 1987, 1990), *Biology of the Heteromyidae* (American Society of Mammalogists, 1993), and *Museum Administration: An Introduction* (AltaMira Press, 2003). He served as the managing editor of the *Journal of Mammalogy* and is the founding editor of *Collections: A Journal for Museum and Archives Professionals* (AltaMira Press, 2004). Dr. Genoways served as president of the American Society of Mammalogists (1984–1986) and was honored by the society with the C. Hart Merriam Award for research excellence (1987), Honorary Member (2002), and Hartley H. T. Jackson Award for service to the society (2004). He also has served as president of the Southwestern Association of Naturalists (1984–1985) and the Nebraska Museums Association (1990–1992) and received the first Achievement Award from the latter organization in 1994.—*W436 Nebraska Hall, University of Nebraska, Lincoln, Lincoln, NE 68588-0514.*

Hilde Hein is currently a visiting associate at the Brandeis University Women's Studies Research Center, and is writing a book on museums and public art. Upon retiring after more than three decades of teaching philosophy at Holy Cross College, Tufts University, and Boston University, in Massachusetts, she served a two-year term with Peace Corps, teaching English in Morocco. While there, she worked at the Casablanca Jewish Museum, the only museum of its kind in the Arab world. Her account of this experience is published in *Curator* (46/3). Her Ph.D. in philosophy is from the University of Michigan. Her books include *The Museum in Transition: A Philosophical Perspective* (Smithsonian Institution Press, 2000) and *The Exploratorium: The*

Museum as Laboratory (Smithsonian Institution Press, 1990). She is coeditor of *Aesthetics in Feminist Perspective* (University of Indiana Press, 1993). In the 1970s she began using museum exhibition design as a component of her aesthetics courses and was subsequently invited to curate an exhibition on art and science for the Worcester Art Museum, followed by another exhibition ten years later. In between, she spent a fellowship year at the Exploratorium, writing essays for the museum and gestating her own book. During other sabbaticals and academic leaves, she held internships at the Smithsonian Institution and the New England Science Center (now Ecotarium, Worcester), and has held incidental appointments with the Association of Science and Technology Centers, the Newton Arts Center, the Cambridge Art Association, Women's Caucus for the Arts, and the American Society for Aesthetics, where she edited the newsletter (1980–1990), served on the board of trustees, and was National Program Chair (1970, 1980). She has published numerous essays and reviews in the *Journal of Aesthetics and Art Criticism*, including a symposium on public art (1996). She is a longstanding member of the American Philosophical Association, where she served on the Committee on the Status of Women, and edited the newsletter on feminism and philosophy (1992–1997). She is a founding member of the Society for Women in Philosophy, an editor of *Hypatia: A Journal of Feminist Philosophy*, and serves on the editorial board of the *Journal of Value Inquiry.—Women's Studies Research Center, Brandeis University, Waltham, MA 02453.*

Eilean Hooper-Greenhill is a professor of museum studies and director of the Research Centre for Museums and Galleries at the University of Leicester. She has a degree in fine art (Sculpture) from Reading University and a doctorate in the sociology of education from the University of London, and has worked in schools, museums, and universities. Since joining the Department of Museum Studies at the University of Leicester in 1980, she has been a leading international lecturer and writer on museums and education; in 2002 *The Independent on Sunday* listed her as one of the top ten people in the museum sector in Britain, as nominated by their peers. She is the writer of *Museum and Gallery Education* (Leicester University Press, 1991); *Museums and the Shaping of Knowledge* (Routledge, 1992); *Museums and Their Visitors* (Routledge, 1994); *Writing a Museum Education Policy* (Museums & Galleries Commission, 1996); and *Museums and the Interpretation of Visual Culture* (Routledge, 2000). She is the editor of three further volumes including *The Educational Role of the Museum* (Routledge, 1994 and 1999) and *Museum, Media, Message* (Routledge, 1995). A fifth monograph, *Museums and Learning—New Dimensions*, is in preparation. She is an editor (with Flora Kaplan) for the well-known *Museum Meanings* series. Established in 1999, Research Centre for Museums and Galleries has established a reputation for high quality research and has a full-time staff of four, with consultants and research assistants joining the core team according to the needs of projects. Research has been funded by university research councils, government departments, and a range of museums and related bodies. Some twenty research reports have been published over the last five years. Further details can be found at www.le.ac.uk/museumstudies/rcmg/rcmg.htm. Professor Hooper-Greenhill was head of the Department of Museum Studies at the University of Leicester from 1996–2002; in 2001, the department was graded 24/24 by the Quality Assurance Agency for Higher Education in England, and in the 2001 Research Assessment Exercise, the department was rated 5/ 5. Between 2002 and 2005, Hooper-Greenhill was a member of the arts and humanities peer review panels for research funding in England.— *Department of Museum Studies, University of Leicester, 105 Princess Road East, Leicester LE1 7LG, England.*

Lesley Lewis became chief executive officer of the Ontario Science Centre in Toronto in 1998. Her vision includes a significant transformation of the center that will build on the expertise of the center's staff and partners, expanding visitor experiences by sparking innovation and promoting science literacy. In October 2003, Lesley became vice-president of the Association of Science-Technology Centers, the largest international organization of science centers. She is a member of the boards of the Canadian Association of Science Centre, the international Giant Screen Theater Association, and Toront03, a not-for-profit leading the international marketing of Toronto following the devastating impact of SARS on the economy. Ms. Lewis recently addressed the Austrian Academy of Sciences on innovative concepts for the public presentation of science. She spoke at the 3rd World Congress of Science Centres in Australia in 2002 on the future role of science centers and chaired two panels at the 4th World Congress in Rio de Janeiro in 2005, one an international forum on equity and diversity and the second on increasing the level of public engagement by science centers. In June 2008, the Ontario Science Centre will host the 5th World Congress, meeting for the first time in North America. Ms. Lewis has a solid grasp of the challenges faced by major cultural institutions in today's competitive economic environment. Previously, she spent two years as executive director of the Ontario Human Rights Commission and six years as executive director of the Ontario Heritage Foundation. Ms. Lewis completed a B.A. at Glendon College, York University, and an M.A. and doctoral course work at the University of Toronto. In 1970–1971, she was one of a three-person team who developed and taught the first post-graduate course in women's studies in Canada. Ms. Lewis's interest in education and innovation stems in part from her role as a parent with three children, all now in their twenties.—*Ontario Science Centre, 770 Don Mills Road, Toronto, Ontario M3C 1T3, Canada.*

Timothy W. Luke is University Distinguished Professor of Political Science at Virginia Polytechnic Institute and State University in Blacksburg, Virginia. He also is the program chair for government and international affairs in the School of Public and International Affairs, and co-coordinator of the Alliance for Social, Political, Ethical, and Social Theory in the College of Liberal Arts and Human Sciences at Virginia Tech. He holds degrees from the University of Arizona (B.A., M.A.) and Washington University (M.A., Ph.D.). During 1996, he was named Visiting Research and Teaching Scholar at the Open Polytechnic of New Zealand, and in 1995 he was the Fulbright Professor of Cultural Theory and the Politics of Information Society at Victoria University of Wellington in New Zealand. His recent books are *Capitalism, Democracy, and Ecology: Departing from Marx* (University of Illinois Press, 1999), *The Politics of Cyberspace*, edited with Chris Toulouse (Routledge, 1998), and *Ecocritique: Contesting the Politics of Nature, Economy, and Culture* (University of Minnesota Press, 1997). A cultural theorist as well as a political theorist, he is very interested in evaluating museums, memorials, and monuments as examples of cultural discourse and political rhetoric at work in the development of the economy and society. The author of over a hundred and fifty journal articles and edited book chapters, he writes extensively on the politics of museums as well as environmental politics, international affairs, and social theory. His latest book, *Museum Politics: Power Plays at the Exhibition*, was published in spring 2002 with the University of Minnesota Press.—*Department of Political Science, 531 Major Williams Hall-0130, Virginia Tech University, Blacksburg, VA 24061.*

Didier Maleuvre is an associate professor of comparative literature at the University of California, Santa Barbara. He received his Ph.D. from Yale University in 1993. He is the author of *Museum Memory: History, Technology, Art* (Stanford University, 1999), which defends the validity of art museums against their philosophic detractors. He has written articles on the philosophy of art, among which are "Hegel and the Museum," "Must Aesthetic Understanding be Interpretive?", and "Painting Mortality." His conference papers and teachings stand at the crossroads of esthetics, philosophy, and religion. He recently completed a book manuscript titled *The Religion of Reality* on art and transcendence.—*Department of French and Italian, Phelps Hall 5206, University of California, Santa Barbara, Santa Barbara, CA 93106-4140.*

Suma Mallavarapu is a third-year graduate student in the psychology department at Georgia Institute of Technology. She holds a B.S. in zoology from Southern Illinois University and a M.S. (2004) from Georgia Tech, with a thesis entitled "Post-conflict Behavior in Captive Western Lowland Gorillas." She is currently continuing her study of post-conflict behavior in western lowland gorillas at Zoo Atlanta, while being funded by a National Science Foundation Graduate Research Fellowship. Her research interests include great ape social behavior, mother-infant interactions, and infant development.—*TECHlab, Zoo Atlanta , 800 Cherokee Avenue, Atlanta, GA 30315.*

Terry L. Maple is a professor of psychology and Elizabeth Smithgall Watts Professor of Conservation & Behavior in the School of Psychology, Georgia Institute of Technology, and Director Emeritus of Zoo Atlanta. He served as president and chief executive officer for seventeen years before he retired from the zoo in 2003 to resume his full-time faculty duties at Georgia Tech and establish the new Center for Conservation & Behavior. Professor Maple is internationally known for his research on the effects of captivity on non-human primate behavior, scientific animal management, behavioral enrichment, applied behavior analysis, mammalian socialization, and post-occupancy evaluation. He is a past president of the American Zoo and Aquarium Association, and an advocate for best practices, standards, and values in the operation of zoos and aquariums within AZA and throughout the world. He studied psychology at University of the Pacific (A.B. 1968) and earned Masters (M.A. 1971) and Ph.D. (1974) degrees in psychobiology from the University of California at Davis. Between these times, he studied sociology and politics at the University of Stockholm as a Rotary International Foundation Graduate Fellow (1971–1972). Professor Maple, his students, and collaborators have published more than 150 scholarly papers in prominent journals and reference books including the *American Journal of Primatology, Behaviour, Developmental Psychobiology, Environment and Behavior, Folia Primatalogica, Journal of Comparative Psychology,* and *Zoo Biology.* He has written, edited, and coedited eight books including *Orangutan Behavior* (Van Nostrand Reinhold Co., 1980), *Zoo Atlanta Urban Redevelopment, Atlanta, GA* (Bruner Foundation, 1993), *Zoo Man: Inside the Zoo Revolution* (Longstreet Press, 1993), *Ethics on the Ark* (Smithsonian Institution Press, 1995), *Saving the Giant Panda* (Longstreet Press, 2000), and *Great Apes & Humans: The Ethics of Coexistence* (Smithsonian Institution Press, 2001). He is a frequent public speaker on the subject of leadership and activism in animal welfare and conservation. In 2003, Professor Maple received a presidential appointment to serve on the board of the Institute of Museum and Library Services. He is an elected fellow of the American Psychological Association and the American Psychological Society. He has been teaching at Georgia Tech since 1978.—*Center for Conservation & Behavior, School of Psychology, Georgia Institute of Technology, Atlanta, GA 30332.*

Michael A. Mares is Presidential Professor and Research Curator of Mammals at the Oklahoma Museum of Natural History and Department of Zoology of the University of Oklahoma. In early 2003, he completed a twenty-year tenure as director of the museum. He has held academic appointments at various universities in the United States and Argentina. He received a B.S. degree from University of New Mexico, a M.S. from Fort Hays Kansas State University, and a Ph.D. from University of Texas, Austin. He studies desert mammals, with an emphasis on South America. He has worked in international museum studies and has consulted for museums throughout the country. He has published twelve books and 180 articles, including *Heritage at Risk* (Oklahoma Museum of Natural History, 1988), *Encyclopedia of Deserts* (University of Oklahoma Press, 1999) (Outstanding Academic Book, 1999, *Choice Magazine*), and *Desert Calling: Life in a Forbidding Landscape*, (Harvard Press, 2002) (winner 2003 Oklahoma Book Award for nonfiction; *ForeWord* magazine book of the year, 2002). He has discovered fifteen mammals new to science, and three organisms are named in his honor. He produced an award-winning documentary film (with Mark Richman and Roberta Pacino), *Behind the Rain: The Story of a Museum*, which detailed the story of the development of the Sam Noble Oklahoma Museum of Natural History. Mares was a Fulbright Scholar, National Chicano Fellow, and Ford Foundation Minority Fellow. He won the first Sullivant Award for Perceptivity in 2002 and was inducted into the Oklahoma Higher Education Hall of Fame. He received the University of Oklahoma Regents Award for Superior Accomplishment in Professional and University Service and was twice awarded the University of Oklahoma Associates' Distinguished Lectureship Award. He has held office in twenty-five national and international professional organizations, including the board of directors of the Fulbright Commission and the Commission on the Future of the Smithsonian Institution. He received the Donald W. Tinkle Research Excellence Award from the Southwestern Association of Naturalists and the C. Hart Merriam Award for Research Excellence in Mammalogy from the American Society of Mammalogists. He is presently a member of the Smithsonian Council.—*Sam Noble Oklahoma Museum of Natural History, 2401 Chautauqua, University of Oklahoma, Norman, OK 73072.*

Jennifer L. Martin is Director of Visitor Experience at the Ontario Science Centre. She joined the staff in 1986 as an exhibit and program developer in environmental sciences. Prior to this position, she was employed at Science North (Sudbury, Ontario) as a member of the startup team, where she developed the "Nature Exchange" concept and led a team of researchers and scientists to recover a Fin whale skeleton, which is now permanently on display at that science center. While at the Ontario Science Centre her career has progressed through several positions. As the center's planning officer, she advised senior management on strategic planning issues, information management, and operational issues. When Ms. Martin moved to the position of project manager in the exhibits division, her responsibilities included establishing the project management program at the center, as well as the planning and management of several permanent exhibition projects. In 1992, Ms. Martin obtained the position of Associate Director of Research and Exhibit Planning. Since 1998, Ms. Martin has held the position of Director of the Visitor Experience. Her responsibilities include overseeing all facets of the development, design, fabrication, and delivery of the center's exhibition and public program activities. In 2001 the Ontario Science Centre embarked on a $40 million capital campaign to renew over 30 percent of exhibit areas by 2006. Ms. Martin led the conceptual development, and now the experience and exhibit implementation for this project. Ms. Martin has made numerous presentations and written articles in trade publications on the future of science centers, especially related to innovation. Ms. Martin holds a Bachelor of Science degree (biology) from Laurentian University (Sudbury, Ontario) and a Master of Business Administration from York University (Toronto, Ontario) with emphasis on organizational strategy and planning.—*Ontario Science Centre, 770 Don Mills Road, Toronto, Ontario M3C 1T3, Canada.*

Jean-Paul Martinon has a Ph.D. in art history from Reading University, United Kingdom. He is currently a lecturer in museum studies and curatorial theory in the Department of Visual Cultures at Goldsmiths College, London. He was the cofounder and curator of "Rear Window" (1991–1998), an independent arts trust that staged a series of exhibitions and conferences in temporary sites across London. Each project presented, outside the conventions of the gallery space (in and around different frames, themes, media, and locations), new or collaborative work by young or established contemporary artists, writers, and poets. One such project, "Care and Control" (1995), was sited in a fully functioning psychiatric hospital in East London and involved thirty psychiatric patients and eighteen contemporary artists. He has published numerous essays in exhibition catalogues, the latest of which was published for the catalogue of the exhibition *Art, Lies and Videotape* (Tate Liverpool, 2003). He is currently the chair of the board of trustees of The Showroom Gallery, an Arts Council–funded public art gallery in London for which he has recently organized a conference on art and global politics, "To Change An Opinion" (2004). He is a member of RePublicArt, a transnational research project exploring and developing progressive practices of public art (www.republicart.net), for which he is organizing a conference on artists and activists, invisible strategies. He also is an advisor for the "2005 Stop AIDS Campaign" public art project. He is currently completing his first book, *Of Times to Come* (Palgrave Macmillan, 2007), which comprises a series of essays on the notion of futurity in philosophy and modern art.—*Department of Visual Cultures, Goldsmiths College, University of London, New Cross, London, SE14 6NW, England.*

Scott Paris is a professor of psychology and education at the University of Michigan where he graduated with a B.A. in 1968. After receiving his Ph.D. from Indiana University in 1972 in psychology, he was a faculty member at George Peabody College and Purdue University until he joined the combined program in education and psychology at Michigan in 1978. He has been a visiting professor at Stanford, UCLA, the University of Hawaii, the University of Auckland (New Zealand), and the University of Queensland (Australia). Professor Paris has taught many undergraduate and graduate courses in developmental and educational psychology at Michigan and received the Dean's Award for Outstanding Undergraduate Teaching twice; in 1995 he was one of two faculty to receive the Amoco award for Distinguished Teaching. He has served on many university committees and has been chair of the graduate program in psychology since 2001. Dr. Paris's research has focused on the development of children's memory, literacy, metacognition, and self-regulated learning. His research on reading has provided practical methods for teaching and assessing reading, and he has worked extensively with teachers and publishers to design effective methods and materials. Professor Paris has written more than 120 book chapters and research articles, coauthored several psychology textbooks including *Developmental Psychology Today*, 6th ed. (McGraw Hill, 1994), and *Psychology*, 4th ed. (West, 1996), and coedited *Global Prospects for Education: Development, Culture, and Schooling* (American Psychological Association, 1998) and *Children's Reading Comprehension and Assessment* (Lawrence Erlbaum Associates, 2005). During the past ten years, Dr. Paris has examined children's learning and motivation in museums in an effort to bridge education in schools and communities. He has conducted evaluation research with museums, taught graduate courses on learning in museums, and been on the steering committee of the museum studies program at Michigan. His edited volume *Perspectives on Object-Centered Learning in Museums* (Lawrence Erlbaum Associates, 2002) summarizes new psychological and pedagogical approaches that connect learning in schools and community settings.—*Department of Psychology, University of Michigan, 525 East University Avenue, Ann Arbor, MI 49109-1043.*

Jeffrey Patchen, president and chief executive officer of The Children's Museum of Indianapolis, has directed the museum's vision and long-range strategic efforts since 1999. He holds bachelor and master's degrees in music education from Cornell University and a doctorate in music education from Indiana University in Bloomington. Prior to joining The Children's Museum, Dr. Patchen successfully led museum- and arts-related organizations at the state, regional, and national levels. From 1996 to 1999, Dr. Patchen served as senior program officer for National Programs for The Getty Education Institute for the Arts, an operating program of the J. Paul Getty Trust in Los

Angeles, California. He was responsible for creating, directing, and managing a portfolio of national programs and projects designed to improve the quality of learning and teaching in the nation's schools. Prior to his work at the J. Paul Getty Trust, Dr. Patchen was the Lyndhurst Endowed Chair of Excellence in Arts Education at the University of Tennessee at Chattanooga where he directed the Southeast Center for Education in the Arts, one of the nation's largest professional development programs for K–12 teachers and administrators. Dr. Patchen also served as a consultant and founding trustee for the Creative Discovery Museum in Chattanooga, Tennessee. From 1984–1990, Dr. Patchen served as the state arts consultant for the Indiana Department of Education where he led statewide efforts for improving arts education. A champion of the role of the arts and humanities in general education, Dr. Patchen has held leadership positions in numerous professional organizations and associations, including the Association of Children's Museums, the National Network for Educational Renewal, the National Council for State Music Consultants, Music Educators National Conference, National Art Education Association, and the Transforming Education Through the Arts challenge grant program funded by the Annenberg Foundation.—*The Children's Museum of Indianapolis, 3000 N. Meridian Street, Indianapolis, IN 46208.*

Marilyn Phelan, J.D. (with honors), University of Texas; Ph.D, Texas Tech University, is the Robert H. Bean Professor of Law at Texas Tech University School of Law and is director of the tax clinic at the law school. She has taught an interdisciplinary course on laws related to museums for over twenty-five years and is the author of several publications on the subject. She authored the first book on laws relating to museums, entitled *Museums and the Law,* which was published in 1982 by the American Association for State and Local History. She later authored two editions of another book on the subject, published by Kalos Kapp Press, in 1994 and 2001, entitled *Museum Law–A Guide for Officers, Directors, and Counsel.* She is the editor and a coauthor of *The Law of Cultural Property and Natural Heritage,* published by Kalos Kapp Press in 1998. She also is a coauthor of a casebook entitled *Art and Museum Law,* which was published by Carolina Academic Press in 2002. Dr. Phelan has authored several books, published by Thomson West, on laws relating to nonprofit organizations, and in 2003 she completed a textbook, entitled *Nonprofit Organizations Law and Policy,* which was published by Thomson West. She is the author of a three-volume treatise, *Nonprofit Enterprises: Corporations, Trusts, and Associations,* also published by Thomson West, in 1985 and 2000, and updated semiannually. Dr. Phelan has served as chair and co-chair of the International Cultural Property Committee and as chair of the International Taxation Committee of the American Bar Association Section of International Law and Practice. She currently serves as a member of the Legal Affairs and Properties Committee for the Executive Council of the International Council of Museums. She is a member of American Law Institute and is a Texas commissioner to the National Conference on Uniform State Laws. *Texas Monthly* listed her as a "Super Lawyer" in 2003 and 2004.—*School of Law, Texas Tech University, 1802 Hartford, Lubbock, TX 79409.*

Donald Preziosi is the author of eleven books on art, architecture, archaeology, and museology, the most recent being *Brain of the Earth's Body: Art, Museums, and the Phantasms of Modernity* (Minnesota, 2003) and, with Claire Farago, *Grasping the World: the Idea of the Museum* (Ashgate, 2004). His 1989 volume *Rethinking Art History: Meditations on a Coy Science* (Yale) and his 1998 volume *The Art of Art History* (Oxford) are among the most widely used critical and historiographic texts on art history in the United States and Europe. A recent book on prehistoric archaeology in Greece (*Aegean Art and Architecture*) was published in 1999 by Oxford. A collection of his essays entitled *In the Aftermath of Art: Aesthetics, Ethics, Politics*, appeared from Routledge in winter 2004. He received a doctorate in art history at Harvard University, and has lectured extensively in North America, Europe, and Australia. In 2001 he delivered the Slade Lectures in the Fine Arts at Oxford University, where he is now a member of the faculty in the Department of the History of Art and Centre for Visual Studies, after having taught at various universities in the United States, including Yale University, MIT, State University of New York, and most recently UCLA. At UCLA, in addition to developing a graduate program in art historical critical theory, he designed, developed, and codirected the UCLA museum studies program, which included an undergraduate museum studies minor, several interlinked MA programs in museum studies in several departments (art history, art, and information science), as well as MAs in archaeological and film preservation and conservation, coordinated with the Getty Institute and UCLA's Cotsen Institute of Archaeology and UCLA's cinema department.—*Department of the History of Art, Oxford University, Littlegate House, St Ebbes, Oxford OX1 1PT, England.*

Franklin W. Robinson currently is the Richard J. Schwartz Director of the Herbert F. Johnson Museum of Art at Cornell University where he has served since 1992. He received his B.A. (1961), M.A. (1963), and Ph.D. (1970) from Harvard University. He has taught at Wellesley College, Dartmouth College, Williams College, and the Rhode Island School of Design. Before assuming his current position, he was director of the Williams College Museum of Art for three years (1976–1979) and director of the Museum of Art at the Rhode Island School of Design for thirteen years (1979–1992). He held a Fulbright Fellowship to the University of Utrecht, the Netherlands, in 1961–1962. He has written numerous exhibition catalogues as well as articles in *Museum News, New Art Examiner, Drawing, Nederlands Kunsthistorisch Jaarboek, Bollettino d'Arte*, and *Oud-Holland*. He has presented invited lectures at the University of Pittsburgh, University of Rhode Island, and Vassar and Smith Colleges, to over twenty-five museums, and for numerous civic and charitable organizations. His museums have received grants from the Institute of Museum Services, National Endowment for the Arts, National Endowment for the Humanities, Andrew W. Mellon Foundation, Georges Lurcy Trust, and Getty Foundation. His research interests have centered on the Dutch and Flemish masters, leading to the publication of *Gabriel Metsu (1629–1667): A Study of his Place in Dutch Genre Painting of the Golden Age* (New York: Abner Schram, 1974). His other books include *Dutch and Flemish Paintings in the John and Mable Ringling Museum of Art* (co-author, Sarasota, Fla.: 1980), *A Handbook of the Museum of Art, Rhode Island School of Design* (editor, Providence, R.I.: 1985), and *A Handbook of the Collection, Herbert F. Johnson Museum of Art* (co-editor, Ithaca, N.Y.: 1998).—*Herbert F. Johnson Museum of Art, Cornell University, Ithaca, NY 14853-4001.*

Douglas Sharon currently is the director of the P. A. Hearst Museum of Anthropology at the University of California, Berkeley. He formerly served as the director of the San Diego Museum of Man from 1981 to 2002. In San Diego, he was a founding member of the San Diego Coalition for Arts & Culture, the Mexican Cultural Institute of San Diego, and the Balboa Park Cultural Partnership. He has been a member of the Association of Science Museum Directors since 1984. He holds a Ph.D. in anthropology from UCLA, where he worked in the 1970s as a research anthropologist at the Latin American Center. Prior to his years at UCLA, he was the executive secretary of the Andean Explorers, headquartered in Trujillo, Peru. He keeps current on research and collecting activities in Latin America, specifically in Ecuador and Peru, but also has conducted fieldwork in Mexico, Guatemala, Colombia, and Bolivia. Dr. Sharon has published extensively on Peruvian shamanism, a topic on which he produced an award-winning documentary film, *Eduardo the Healer*. The film received the 1979 Red Ribbon Award, Anthropology, American Film Festival, NY; 1979 Golden Prize Modern Language Film Festival; and 1980 Medical Anthropology Award, John Muir Medical Film Festival. In Peru, he recently established a field school for ethnobotany as part of a collaborative effort among the San Diego Museum of Man, San Diego State University, and the National University of Trujillo.—*P. A. Hearst Museum of Anthropology , University of California, Berkeley, 103 Kroeber Hall, Berkeley, CA 94720-3712.*

Sherene Suchy is in private practice, based in Australia, as a specialist in individual and organizational change. Dr. Suchy has over twenty-five years of experience in human resource development and organization change with corporate, public, and nonprofit organizations in Australia, Malaysia, Singapore, and the United States. Since 1991, she has been a full-time consultant and adjunct academic with the School of Management at the University of Technology Sydney. Dr. Suchy is particularly interested in emotional intelligence competencies and facilitates leadership development programs using museum director case studies described in her book *Leading with Passion: Change Management in the 21st-Century Museum* (AltaMira Press, 2003). Current museum consulting projects focus on emotional intelligence competencies for audience development, to create lasting emotional bonds with cultural consumers. She holds a Bachelor of Social Work (psychology) from the Royal Melbourne Institute of Technology; a Graduate Diploma in communication management (training) from the University of Technology Sydney where she won the Australian Institute of Training and Development Award for Academic Excellence; a Master of Art Administration from the University of New South Wales where she won a contract to manage an exhibition of Australian artists in the Singapore Festival of Arts; and a Ph.D. (philosophy) from the University of Western Sydney where she won a scholarship to complete international research on change and museum leadership in Australia, the United States, the United Kingdom, and Canada. Dr. Suchy is an advocate for museums as sites for cultural orientation and intelligent play. Since 1996, she has presented and written about change and leadership and creating bridges between organizational psychology, management, and the cultural industry sector. She has articles published in *Museum International* (UNESCO) and *Museum Management and Curatorship* and conference papers published with Museums Australia, the Canadian Museum Association, the World Federation of Friends of Museums, the Museums and Gallery Foundation of New South Wales, and the Oregon Museum Association.—*DUO PLUS PTY LTD, Individual and Organisation Change, PO Box 758, North Sydney NSW 2060, Australia.*